D1572324

W. SOMERSET MAUGHAM: THE CRITICAL HERITAGE

THE CRITICAL HERITAGE SERIES

GENERAL EDITOR: B. C. SOUTHAM, M.A., B. LITT. (OXON.)
Formerly Department of English, Westfield College, University of London

For a list of books in the series see the back end paper

W. SOMERSET MAUGHAM

THE CRITICAL HERITAGE

Edited by
ANTHONY CURTIS
and
JOHN WHITEHEAD

ROUTLEDGE & KEGAN PAUL
LONDON AND NEW YORK

First published in 1987 by
Routledge & Kegan Paul Ltd
11 New Fetter Lane, London EC4P 4EE

Published in the USA by
Routledge & Kegan Paul Inc.
in association with Methuen Inc.
29 West 35th Street, New York, NY 10001

Phototypesetting by Thomson Press (India) Limited, New Delhi
and printed in Great Britain
by T J Press (Padstow) Ltd
Padstow, Conwall
Compilation, introduction, notes, bibliography and index
© Anthony Curtis and John Whitehead 1987

Library of Congress Cataloging in Publication Data

W. Somerset Maugham: the critical heritage.

(The Critical heritage series)
Bibliography: p.
Includes index.
1. Maugham, W. Somerset (William Somerset), 1874–1965—
Criticism and interpretation. I. Curtis, Anthony.
II. Whitehead, John, 1924– III. Series.
PR6025.A86Z894   1987   823'.912   86–17299

British Library CIP Data also available
ISBN 0–7100–9640–2

General Editor's Preface

The reception given to a writer by his contemporaries and near-contemporaries is evidence of considerable value to the student of literature. On one side we learn a great deal about the state of criticism at large and in particular about the development of critical attitudes towards a single writer; at the same time, through private comments in letters, journals or marginalia, we gain an insight upon the tastes and literary thought of individual readers of the period. Evidence of this kind helps us to understand the writer's historical situation, the nature of his immediate reading-public, and his response to these pressures.

The separate volumes in the *Critical Heritage Series* present a record of this early criticism. Clearly, for many of the highly productive and lengthily reviewed nineteenth- and twentieth-century writers, there exists an enormous body of material; and in these cases the volume editors have made a selection of the most important views, significant for their intrinsic critical worth or for their representative quality—perhaps even registering incomprehension!

For earlier writers, notably pre-eighteenth century, the materials are much scarcer and the historical period has been extended, sometimes far beyond the writer's lifetime, in order to show the inception and growth of critical views which were initially slow to appear.

In each volume the documents are headed by an Introduction, discussing the material assembled and relating the early stages of the author's reception to what we have come to identify as the critical tradition. The volumes will make available much material which would otherwise be difficult of access and it is hoped that the modern reader will be thereby helped towards an informed understanding of the ways in which literature has been read and judged.

B.C.S.

Contents

CONTENTS

The Bishop's Apron (February 1906)

II PLAYS
(1903–1914)

A Man of Honour (February 1903)

Lady Frederick (October 1907)

Jack Straw (March 1908)

Mrs Dot (April 1908)

The Explorer (June 1908)

Penelope (January 1909)

The Trembling of a Leaf
(September 1921; October 1921)

On a Chinese Screen
(October 1922; November 1922)

The Painted Veil (March 1925; April 1925)

The Casuarina Tree (September 1926)

Ashenden (March 1928)

The Gentleman in the Parlour (February 1930; April 1930)

IV PLAYS
(1916–1933)

CONTENTS

Home and Beauty (Too Many Husbands)
(August 1919; October 1919)

The Unknown (August 1920)

The Circle (March 1921)

East of Suez (September 1922)

The Constant Wife
(November 1926; April 1927)

The Letter (February 1927)

The Sacred Flame (November 1928; February 1929)

CONTENTS

CONTENTS

Cosmopolitans (February 1936; March 1936)

Theatre (March 1937)

The Summing Up (January 1938; March 1938)

Christmas Holiday (February 1939; October 1939)

Books and You (March 1940)

The Mixture as Before (June 1940; July 1940)

Up at the Villa (April 1941; May 1941)

The Hour Before the Dawn (June 1942)

The Razor's Edge (April 1944; July 1944)

Then and Now (May 1946)

Creatures of Circumstance (July 1947)

Catalina (August 1948; October 1948)

Great Novelists and Their Novels
(September 1948)
(*Ten Novels and Their Authors* (October 1954))

A Writer's Notebook (October 1949)

VI GENERAL STUDIES
(1919–1965)

Acknowledgments

We are grateful to the following for permission to reprint material within their copyright or control: Brandt & Brandt Literary Agents Inc. for No. 136, 'The Notes of a Popular Pessimist' by S.N. Behrman, originally published in the *New Yorker* (Copyright, 1949 by S.N. Behrman. Copyright renewed, 1977 by S.N. Behrman); Chatto & Windus: The Hogarth Press, Harcourt Brace Jovanovich, Inc., and the Literary Estate of Virginia Woolf for No. 13, from *The Essays of Virginia Woolf*, vol. I, ed. Andrew McNeillie; Farrar, Straus & Giroux, Inc., for No. 126, 'Somerset Maugham and an Antidote' by Edmund Wilson, from the *New Yorker*, vol. XXII, 8 June 1946; *Guardian* for Nos 129 and 139; A.N. Hartley for No. 54; David Higham Associates Ltd for No. 103; Laura Huxley for No. 77; I.H.T. Corporation for Nos 61, 69, 71, 102, 104, 114, 116 and 140 from the *New York Herald Tribune* (© I.H.T. Corporation. Reprinted by permission); *Illustrated London News* for Nos 23, 90, 94, 96 and 137; Jones Brakeley & Rockwell, Inc., for No. 85, from *Life*; Mrs Jean F. Lisle for No. 82; London Management for No. 83; *Nation* (New York) for No. 117; *New Republic* for Nos 41 and 111; *New Statesman* for Nos 39, 48, 52, 74, 81, 84, 91 and 95 from the *New Statesman*, Nos 98, 101, 107, 115, 124, 132, 134 and 146 from the *New Statesman and Nation*, Nos 28 and 80 from the *Nation*, Nos 6, 11, 12, 30, 40 and 43 from the *Athenaeum* and No. 55 from the *Nation and Athenaeum*; *New York Evening Post* for Nos 56 and 73; *New York Times* for Nos 16, 35, 42, 46, 49, 51, 59, 65, 78, 89, 97, 121, 128, 130, 135, 138, 145 and 149 (Copyright © 1909, 1913, 1925, 1921, 1923, 1925, 1928, 1930, 1919, 1928, 1934, 1944, 1947, 1948, 1949, 1953, 1954 and 1964 by The New York Times Company. Reprinted by permission); *Observer* for No. 63; A.D. Peters & Co. Ltd for Nos 86 and 88; Laurence Pollinger Ltd for Nos 99, 100 and 109; Laurence Pollinger Ltd and the Estate of H.E. Bates for No. 142, from *The Modern Short Story*, published by Thomas Nelson & Sons Ltd; Laurence Pollinger Ltd and the Estate of Mrs Frieda Lawrence Ravagli for No. 58; *Punch* for Nos 14 and 34; Mrs Eva

Reichmann for Nos 18, 22 and 26; *Saturday Review* (New York) for Nos 62, 66, 92, 106, 110, 113, 120 and 131 (© 1930, 1931, 1930, 1930, 1938, 1939, 1942 and 1940 *Saturday Review* magazine. Reprinted by permission); *Spectator* for Nos 67, 70, 93, 123, 125, 127, 133 and 147; Lindsay Stewart for No. 118; John Symonds for No. 15; *Times Literary Supplement* for Nos 38, 53, 60 and 144; Times Newspapers Ltd for Nos 33, 75, 79, 87 and 105 from *The Times* and Nos 19, 21, 24, 25, 27, 29, 31, 32, 36, 72 and 150 from the *Sunday Times*; Diana Trilling for No. 122; A.P. Watt Ltd, the Executors of the Estate of Edward Garnett and the Henry W. and Albert A. Berg Collection, The New York Public Library, Astor, Lenox and Tilden Foundations, for No. 1; Auberon Waugh for Nos 64 and 112. It has proved impossible to locate some copyright holders, to whom we offer our apologies.

We are also immensely grateful to Ella Whitehead for her care and skill in converting a mass of holograph and photocopies into immaculate copy for presentation to the publishers, and to Elaine Donaldson, our copy editor, whose professional eye has ensured that imperfections have not gone undetected.

Introduction

'I have no illusions about my literary position,' Maugham wrote in *The Summing Up* (1938), referring to his non-dramatic work. 'There are but two important critics in my own country who have troubled to take me seriously and when clever young men write essays about contemporary fiction they never think of considering me. I do not resent it. It is very natural.' But he did resent it, and what he wrote was true: clever people like Virginia Woolf and her friends had long ago reached the conclusion that there was not much to be said about Maugham. 'Class Two, Division One' was Lytton Strachey's laconic dismissal of his work. One of the two 'important critics' referred to above was Desmond MacCarthy, who did take Maugham's work seriously, especially the plays and short stories which he rated highly, tracing their roots in French naturalism. The other 'important critic' may have been Raymond Mortimer, who had written thoughtful reviews of his books in the *New Statesman and Nation*. And in this same year 1938 the cleverest young man on the critical scene, Cyril Connolly—he was thirty-five and that, after all, is still young for a critic—brought out his autobiographical-cum-critical book *Enemies of Promise*, in which, in the chapters devoted to the modern movement in literature and the development of modern English prose style, there are frequent references to Maugham. He is praised for his 'lucidity' and described as 'the last of the great professional writers'. This may have mollified Maugham's resentment but cannot entirely have eliminated it.

The fact remains that full-scale essays in the English language on Maugham's work in this pre-World War II period are hard to find, though a glance across the Channel will light upon some, notably the work of the French critic Paul Dottin, whose first essay '*Le réalisme de Somerset Maugham*' à propos the French translation of *The Painted Veil* appeared in *La Revue de France* for June 1926 and later became part of the same critic's book-length study, *Somerset*

Maugham et ses Romans. Maugham was not honoured in like fashion
in his own country; and if one works systematically through the
entries in Charles Sanders's *Somerset Maugham: An Annotated Bibliography of Writings About Him* (Northern Illinois University Press,
1970), one is struck by how little there is of substantial appraisal,
and how much 'snippety' journalism where Maugham is being
considered in the compass of a thousand-word review in conjunc-
tion with perhaps two or three other authors with whom he has
little or nothing in common.

For this situation, in which Maugham was often taken for
granted and denied lengthy evaluation, he was himself, as he
admitted, largely to blame: 'I do not resent it. It is very natural. I
have never been a propagandist.' He is thinking here of the H.G.
Wells way of writing a novel, full of topical ideas presented in a
fictional form, the interest of which lies more in the ideas than in
the novel's literary qualities. Nor was Maugham innovative in
technique. Hence, 'The intelligent critics'—we are still listening to
The Summing Up—'the more serious novel readers, have since then
given most of their attention to the writers who seemed to offer
something new in technique, and this is very comprehensible, for
the novelties they presented gave a sort of freshness to well-worn
material and were a fruitful matter of discussion.' In other words,
there is nothing new under the sun, under the literary sun anyway.
Critics may prattle on about streams of consciousness and the inner
life, but the old narrative methods retain their sovereignty.

Did Maugham really in his heart of hearts believe that? Was he
not, as an omnivorous reader and a perceptive critic of other
people's work, aware that some of the perpetrators of 'novelties'
(Proust, Joyce, Hemingway, Virginia Woolf) were changing the
face of literature? If the full answer lies outside the scope of this
introduction, what we can say is that he genuinely believed his
statement was true so far as his own work was concerned. For
Maugham as an artist there *was* nothing new under the literary sun:
the old narrative methods retained their sovereignty to the end of
his life. When the London *Times* put, as the heading to its review of
Maugham's short story collection *Cosmopolitans* (1936), 'The
Mixture As Before', he delightedly seized upon the expression as
the title for his next collection, which appeared four years later in
1940. As for innovation in literature he re-states his position, in

words reminiscent of Max Beerbohm, in the foreword to *The Mixture As Before:* 'I have seen a number of bright stars creep shyly over the horizon, travel across the sky to burn for a while in mid-heaven with dazzling effulgence, and then dwindle into an obscurity from which there is little likelihood that they will ever again emerge.' Someone who adopts this aloof pose so resolutely has to a large extent put himself *hors de combat* in the struggle for lengthy attention. (It must again be emphasised that these introductory comments relate only to Maugham's non-dramatic work: his plays never lacked substantial criticism.) He could not, however, complain that his books suffered from lack of notice; on the contrary, he was one of those authors who keep book-reviewers in full employment. The editors of the cultural pages of the more serious newspapers and magazines were for half a century bombarded by the output of Maugham's pen, and they responded to the bombardment with, in their limited terms, a generous allotment of space and considerable ingenuity in their choice of reviewers. All manner of critical soldiery, from Graham Greene and Evelyn Waugh down to dozens of anonymous hacks, were pressed into service to stem the attack. In this way, in terms of spasms of reviewing, there was a dialogue in progress between Maugham and the literary intelligentsia on both sides of the Atlantic for some fifty years, a dialogue which from Maugham's point of view alternated between peaks of approbation and troughs of censoriousness with bewildering regularity. It will be our purpose in the remainder of this introduction to try briefly to trace the course of that dialogue, to identify some of its main participants, and to see what consensus of critical opinion can be discerned.

II

It may be helpful first to give a brief description of the broad pattern in which Maugham's enormous output arranges itself. The basic division is between non-dramatic and dramatic work, the former being sub-divided into three main phases, the latter into two. The first five parts in which the articles included here have been grouped reflect those five main phases and may be summarised as follows:

I Books	(1897–1909)
II Plays	(1903–1914)
III Books	(1915–1933)
IV Plays	(1916–1933)
V Books	(1934–1959)

Part VI contains a selection of pieces concerning Maugham's work generally.

A striking fact about Maugham's work viewed as a whole is the absence of any consistent relationship between his books and his plays. On achieving spectacular success as a West End dramatist in 1907/8 he gave up novel-writing with relief, he hoped for good; and when in 1913 the burden of his memories led him to embark on his long autobiographical novel *Of Human Bondage* he laid aside play-writing for two years or so. But apart from those gaps, between 1897 and 1933 (when, realising he had lost touch with the play-going public, he abandoned the drama for good) he was writing plays and non-dramatic works in tandem, as it were. And though the techniques he learnt as a dramatist, especially as regards construction and dialogue, were put to good use in his fiction, at any given period the themes of his plays and the subjects of his books bore no relation to one another. It is therefore not inappropriate for his two careers to be treated separately in this volume.

As regards criticism of his work, there are two preliminary points to be made. In the first place, during his lifetime the best critic of his work was Maugham himself—in *The Summing Up*, the prefaces to the collected editions and elsewhere. He was under no illusions as to its quality or value, appraising it coolly and judiciously; whereas reviewers tended to be erratic, superficial or merely prejudiced. To some extent Maugham was to blame for this unsatisfactory response because he deliberately set out to be provocative, flouting convention and treating the sacred cows of the time (religion, class, sexual morality) with scant respect, especially in his plays. These often contained some scene—such as the marital rape in *The Land of Promise* (1913) and the summer-house incident in *Our Betters* (1917)—which was intended to shock.

His favourite theme was adultery. Moreover, there was something in his personality or in his sense of humour which, while appealing to some, repelled others. One reviewer's meat was another reviewer's poison.

III

Maugham's *début* with *Liza of Lambeth* in 1897 was such as no young author of twenty-three could complain about. True the story was not universally liked, for its coarse subject matter and slum setting distressed the late-Victorian sensibility. One Scots reviewer in Edinburgh, Jane H. Findlater (No. 3), waxed especially eloquent against the horrors depicted in the book and the author's attitude to them. Never mind: the book made a stir. It put Maugham on the map. His problem after that was to stay on the map; and it is interesting to see how rapidly, at this early stage in his career, the French were on to him. The French critic Augustin Filon, who kept a close watch on literature and the theatre in London, read the book and used it as the basis for a discussion of '*Le peuple de Londres et le roman naturaliste*', which he published in *Le Journal des Débats* in October 1897.

The Maugham bombardment had begun, and it was sustained for the next seven years in book after book until in 1907 the fortress of the fashionable London theatre at last crumbled under the fire of his attack. Many of the works he published in the interim he preferred later to forget, or to dismiss as apprentice stuff, which is what they were; but nonetheless he received a fair measure of review-space for them. Notices appeared in the *Athenaeum* and the *Academy*, then arbiters of taste among the intelligent reading public, whose reviewers wrote anonymously. Maugham's name began to crop up too in such American publications as the *Dial* and the *New York Times*. The tone at this time is a shade patronising but not unfriendly, and his early volume of short stories *Orientations* (1899) turned the critical tide distinctly in his favour. 'The best writing we have yet seen from Mr W.S. Maugham,' exclaimed the *Athenaeum* (No. 6) in a single-paragraph review of about 180 words, concluding: 'This little collection of stories gives rise to the hope that the author will arrive at a larger measure of success than his two previous volumes of fiction have achieved.' This controlled enthusiasm was shared by the *Academy* (No. 7). 'Mr Maugham begins to be interesting,' it told its readers in a review in which the name Maupassant was first mentioned as an influence on his work, concluding sagely: 'Mr Maugham, to our thinking, is a man who will survive many defects. He has an abundance of vitality, which is perhaps the scarcest thing in modern literature.'

The most important of these early books, *Mrs Craddock* (1902) which came next, inspired slightly longer articles, over which loomed the shadow of Mrs Grundy, still vigilant lest sex should rear its ugly head in too explicit a form, but not so as to spoil the enjoyment of the critic in *Academy and Literature* (No. 8) who wrote: 'Mr Maugham makes no attempt to disguise the fact that the basis of Bertha's regard for her vulgar husband was physical. He handles the general history of the marriage with excellent simplicity and skill.' A fellow-novelist, A. St John Adcock, put his name to the review in the *Bookman* (London) (No. 9), in which he began by telling his readers candidly: 'If, from any cause, you are afraid to look life in the face, you had better leave Mr Maugham alone. ...' And he wound up with a judgment with which most other reviewers concurred: 'The book, as a whole, is a really notable piece of work, and marks a distinct advance on what Mr Maugham had previously accomplished.'

The young Maugham was, then, welcomed into the fold and given the kind of encouragement which must have served to strengthen his resolve not to revert to medicine as his career but to stick to the literary life on which he had embarked. He soon ran into a problem which was to bedevil him more than once in later years—a sharp reaction from a reader who claimed Maugham had betrayed his confidence by putting him into his fiction. This was in a novel, partly set in Paris, entitled *The Magician* (1908), in which Maugham drew a thinly disguised portrait of Aleister Crowley, the black magic expert, whom he had first met in 1905 in a Paris restaurant called Le Chat Blanc in the Rue d'Odessa, much frequented at that time by painters and writers. Crowley took his revenge by reviewing the book himself at considerable length in *Vanity Fair* (No. 15) in an article in which he showed, quoting chapter and verse, the many instances where Maugham had lifted passages, unacknowledged, from the esoteric books on the occult which Crowley had recommended to him.

The image which reviewers had built up of Maugham as an

English disciple of the French naturalists, a stern realist who one day might be expected to produce a major novel, was blurred in 1907 when he emerged as a writer of romantic comedies in the Oscar Wilde tradition.

IV

At the beginning of the century theatre criticism as a profession had attracted some very able men. On Bernard Shaw's retirement from the *Saturday Review* in 1898 Max Beerbohm brought all his urbanity and sharpness of observation to the task of judging the current drama. There was also Shaw's friend A.B. Walkley, the drama critic of the *Times*, whose notices, written in the small hours to appear in time for breakfast the same day, were invariably anonymous. He probably knew as much about the French as the English theatre and possessed a passion for it as great as Maugham's own. Another regular London critic with a cosmopolitan view of the drama was an energetic Dutchman, J.T. Grein. 'Jack' Grein had started the Independent Theatre Club in the 1890s, where he had introduced Londoners to work by Ibsen and Shaw. In 1897 he was appointed drama critic of the *Sunday Times*, a post he held until 1918, the period during which Maugham became recognised as the outstanding dramatic craftsman of his generation. Another champion of Ibsen was the Scot, William Archer, who was drama critic on the *World* until 1898 and afterwards wrote regularly in the *Nation*.

These men, meeting night after night, formed a sodality and shared certain basic assumptions about the theatre. They saw what Maugham was trying to do, recognising the artful sense of dramatic construction he had learnt from French drama, and through their appreciative reviews gave him just the kind of encouragement he needed to release his talent as a playwright. Maugham harboured no resentment at the way he was treated by the London drama critics.

Max Beerbohm had seen Maugham's first full-length play, *A Man of Honour*, when it had been performed by the Stage Society and was in a good position to appraise it when in 1904 it achieved a commercial production at the Avenue Theatre (No. 18). 'There is no reason to suppose,' he told his readers, 'that anon Mr Maugham as playwright will not be the equal of Mr Maugham as novelist.' Unfortunately Max was away when, three years later, Maugham's comedy *Lady Frederick* was produced at the Royal Court Theatre, inaugurating his long run of successes. However, Max's colleagues were enthusiastic and Maugham the popular dramatist was launched. The success for which he had striven so hard did not catch him unprepared. He had ready several more plays which had long been rejected by theatrical managements, and soon there were four running in London at the same time. 'One has to go back to the early days of Sardou to find a popularity similar and so sudden,' commented Grein (No. 24), and noted (No. 27) the *esprit Gaulois* animating Maugham's comic gift. On another occasion he described Maugham as being 'as minute, as realistic, as brutal as Zola unrestrained' (No. 36), and later wrote: 'He is as crafty as old Scribe was and he writes ever so much better.' Meanwhile Max, who certainly made amends for missing *Lady Frederick* by writing at length about *Mrs Dot*, *Jack Straw* and *The Explorer*, ironically referred to a private conversation he had had with Maugham, when he had advised him to give up the vulgar art of drama and to restrict himself to the more refined art of the novel. How wrong he had been, he now admitted.

Part of the penalty of success in the theatre consisted in having to give interviews to newspapers, and in one such Maugham attacked the theatre of ideas: it was, he said, the playwright's business merely to entertain. This was taken up by Max in one of his discursive articles, and it was discussed again by Archer. In this rough-and-ready way a kind of dialectic on the function of the theatre, an argument never to be resolved, with Shaw on one side and Maugham on the other, was conducted, with Maugham having his right of final reply in the prefaces he wrote for his *Collected Plays* in the 1930s.

The theatre critics did not always admire his work; but for every brickbat there were some dozen bouquets. Moreover, after the Great War his plays began to find favour with a new young audience. By then the theatre critics of the 1900s had been replaced by a new generation, with Desmond MacCarthy writing in the *New Statesman* overlapping the two periods. Walkley was eventually succeeded on the *Times* by the novelist Charles Morgan, and Grein (who continued to write elsewhere) on the *Sunday Times* by James Agate.

Maugham's farce summing up the immediate post-war disillusionment, *Home and Beauty* (1919), gained plaudits on both sides of
the Atlantic. 'An evening of unalloyed amusement,' declared the
American critic Alexander Woollcott (No. 78), not the easiest man
to please. By general consent the critics considered *The Circle*
(1921) to be a watershed in Maugham's theatrical career, MacCarthy telling his readers that the work represented 'a decided step
forward on the road to the creation of his genuine cynical
masterpiece' (No. 81); while another 'highbrow' critic, Australian-
born W.J. Turner, said it was 'one of the few plays on the London
stage that persons of ordinary wit can go to without having their
intelligence insulted' (No. 82).

Even when a play did not find favour with the critics it could still
provoke a lengthy, thoughtful review. '*East of Suez* (1922) rings so
exceedingly untrue,' wrote James Agate (No. 83); then, making a
far-fetched comparison with *The Second Mrs Tanqueray*, he
continued with a perceptive discussion on how the theme of
marriage across the boundaries of caste had been dishonestly
handled by English playwrights, Maugham among them. From
what the critics wrote about Maugham's plays at the time, it
becomes clear that for all his protestations about entertainment he
was giving dramatic life to moral and social issues of some
importance. It is true that a cooler reception was accorded to the
four final plays beginning with *The Sacred Flame* (1928)—'a
well-bred bore', commented Brooks Atkinson, one of the 'butch-
ers of Broadway'; but then Maugham had not expected these plays
to find favour with the public: he wrote them because it interested
him to do so.

V

During Maugham's *années dramatiques* from 1903 to 1933 his
creative flow was at its peak, and he produced much else besides
stage-plays. At the height of his early period of success as a
playwright he had withdrawn altogether from the theatre for some
two years to work on *Of Human Bondage* (1915), part of the
point of which was to amend the impression he had created of
himself as a dandified society wit. Legend has it, fostered by
Maugham himself, that the novel was treated cavalierly by the

English reviewing fraternity, and that it was largely misunderstood until an effusive, enthusiastic article, 'As a Realist Sees It' by Theodore Dreiser (No. 41), appeared in America at the end of the year. While it is true that the Dreiser article made some difference to attitudes on both sides of the Atlantic, it is equally true that the novel had aroused much appreciative comment in the public prints in England several months before Dreiser's article came out, despite the fact that Great Britain at the time was preoccupied with fighting a war with Germany. Gerald Gould, for instance, a connoisseur of contemporary fiction, reviewed the novel in the *New Statesman* (No. 39) and, although he tended to tie himself up in knots and somewhat to hedge his bets, left his readers in no doubt that he was dealing with a major work: 'If Mr Maugham belongs to a school at all, it is to a French one. But I am not sure that he does belong to a school. I am not sure he has not written a highly original book. I am not even sure he has not written almost a great one.' While protesting at the book's excessive length and disagreeable heroine, other reviewers were impressed by the vulnerable nature of the hero and the complex of attitudes sustained in his own voice by the author. 'The view of life which the book works out,' observed the anonymous reviewer in the *Times Literary Supplement* (No. 38), 'implies certainly a profounder mind than would be expected from Mr Maugham's successful drama.' The French ancestry of the book was identified as deriving in part from Romain Rolland, then much in vogue, and Maugham was commended for not making the hero a mere looking-glass, reflecting events by which he remained unaffected. Describing the attitude to life of Maugham's hero the reviewer wrote: 'He was restless and eager; he had a great capacity for happiness and unhappiness; and like many young men he was so busy yearning for the moon that he never saw the sixpence at his feet.' It is indicative of the care with which Maugham read the reviews of his work that he picked out this phrase and adapted it as the title of his next novel, where it is really less appropriate to Charles Strickland than it had been to Philip Carey.

In retrospect it can now be seen that *The Moon and Sixpence* (1919) inaugurated the period of Maugham's greatest achievement, which lasted for some twenty years; but although his reviewers included some of the most renowned and accomplished of his fellow-writers, there was seldom much agreement between them as to the merits of his work. Not only did they tend to be erratic, superficial or merely prejudiced, but—since Maugham's reputation and standing with the general public steadily increased while reviewers continued to cavil and carp—it must be concluded that what they wrote was to a great extent irrelevant. With this in mind it is instructive to turn to certain reviews of his work by Katherine Mansfield and D.H. Lawrence.

Katherine Mansfield (No. 43) thoroughly disliked *The Moon and Sixpence*, yet was clearly disturbed by it. It happened to raise in a harsh and, to her mind, unsatisfactory form a question that deeply concerned her, the tensions between marital and family loyalties, artistic dedication and personal freedom. She found an unacceptable brutalism in the way Strickland side-steps the whole conflict by telling everyone who gets in his way to 'go to hell', and identified this attitude in a brilliant image taken from her New Zealand cultural background:

Strickland cut himself off from the body of life, clumsily, obstinately, savagely—hacking away, regardless of torn flesh and quivering nerves, like some old Maori warrior separating himself from a shattered limb with a piece of sharp shell. What proof have we that he suffered? No proof at all.

She sensed that the story must have been based on the life of some historical artist who behaved in a comparable way, but surprisingly failed to make the connection with Gauguin. She was not alone in this. The myth of Gauguin owed its early momentum to Maugham's novel.

In the case of D.H. Lawrence's review in *Vogue* (No. 58) of Maugham's spy stories, *Ashenden*—which we now know initiated an entire literary genre that has not yet spent itself—the question of total lack of sympathy arises. Whilst admitting that Maugham was 'a splendid observer' who could 'bring before us persons and places most excellently', Lawrence felt, in common with Katherine Mansfield, that his understanding of the great universal experience of human brotherhood and sisterhood was lacking; and his conclusion was damning:

But as soon as the excellently observed characters have to move, it is a fake. Mr Maugham gives them a humorous shove or two. We find they are nothing but puppets, instruments of the author's pet prejudice. The author's pet prejudice being 'humour', it would be hard to find a bunch of more ill-humoured stories, in which the humour has gone more rancid.

Such dismissive comments on a book which was to achieve the status of a classic in its genre suggest that Lawrence was taking the opportunity here of giving expression to the personal animosity he felt for Maugham, as revealed in his letters.

VI

In the same way as the profoundest influence on Kipling as a writer was his experience of India, so the principal factor which determined the course of Maugham's writing after the Great War was his discovery of the Far East. For ten years after his first journey to the South Seas in the winter of 1916/17 to gather material for *The Moon and Sixpence* he was constantly on the move, accompanied by his secretary-companion Gerald Haxton, with whom he travelled extensively in China, Malaya, Borneo, Burma and Indo-China. It was with the fruits of these peregrinations—novels, travel-books, plays and especially short stories—that critical opinion on both sides of the Atlantic shifted decisively in Maugham's favour.

The collection of short sketches *On a Chinese Screen* (1922) was hailed by Louise Maunsell Field in the *New York Times* as 'a fascinating volume' (No. 49), and Gerald Gould in the London *Saturday Review* expressed for it 'an almost unqualified admiration' (No. 50). Equally warm was the reception given to Maugham's other Oriental travel-book, *The Gentleman in the Parlour* (1930). His novel *The Painted Veil* (1925), set in Hong Kong and China—the publication of which was bedevilled by threats of libel actions—was described in a long review in the *New York Times* as 'an expert performance' (No. 51), a view echoed by P.C. Kennedy in the *New Statesman* (No. 52) except for its ending, which he considered 'the silliest ever inflicted by a brilliant writer on a brilliant story'. Maugham for all his assumed aloofness was ever sensitive to the strictures of reviewers and duly took note, and when the novel was reissued in the collected edition of his work in 1949, the effusive final paragraph had been considerably toned down. His other novel set in the East, *The Narrow Corner* (1932), elicited widely differing responses from two lady reviewers. Florence Haxton Britten's review in the *New York Herald Tribune* (No. 69) glowed with admiration:

At either extreme of handling, it might have held material for an Edgar Wallace thriller, or for something approaching a Conradian '*Lord Jim*'. Enriched as it is with shrewd characterizations and a definite philosophy of life, it comes far closer to Conrad than to the thriller prototype.

She quite failed to notice the 'defect of the book', to which Anne Armstrong, in the London *Saturday Review* (No. 68), devoted several admonitory paragraphs of her review. Noting that the novel's two heroines were 'mere types of animal lust', she roundly declared that Maugham did not understand women. With this attack on what we today call stereotypes, she even ventured to offer him her own views on the subject:

I humbly suggest to him that women, however inferior to men, are—if only because they have to deal with men—slightly more complex in their mental make-up than the evidence in *The Narrow Corner* would have us believe.

Although there may be some truth in the charge brought against these particular characters, the general accusation is refuted by the complex portraits of women Maugham drew in many of his other works. The review does, however, provide support for the proposition that in general his heroines tend to appeal rather to men than to women.

Among the leading contenders for survival out of Maugham's total literary output must be placed, on any view, the three volumes of his Eastern short stories—*The Trembling of a Leaf* (1921), *The Casuarina Tree* (1926) and *Ah King* (1933)—each containing six stories of between twelve and fifteen thousand words. As the selection of reviews reprinted in this compilation makes clear, their quality was at once and generally recognised, the reviewers only differing in the choice of their own favourites.

In the intervals between writing his exotic books Maugham published the novel, set in England, which is generally regarded as his masterpiece, *Cakes and Ale* (1930), and *Six Stories Written in the First Person Singular* (1931), a volume of short stories with European settings, influenced by Max Beerbohm's *Seven Men* (1919). Dealing first with the stories, Lee Wilson Dodd reviewing the collection in the *Saturday Review of Literature* (New York) (No. 66) qualified his praise of Maugham's craftsmanship by reference to his 'competence', a word often—to Maugham's exasperation—used disparagingly of him, as if there were some merit in an author being incompetent. Similarly, L.A.G. Strong in the *Spectator* (No. 67), after expressing admiration for his craftsmanship, belittlingly described the book's effect as 'that of music expertly played in an expensive restaurant at dinner'.

What is most surprising about the reviews of *Cakes and Ale* is that the reviewers, while finding much to praise in it, especially the portrait of Rosie—surely one of the best-loved heroines in modern fiction—without exception failed to recognise the novel's true quality. Ivor Brown in the *Observer* (No. 63) noted that, in this book at least, Maugham did not merit the charge of cynicism with which he had so often been vexed and drew attention rather to his 'brilliantly sardonic' commentary on life and letters and the 'controlled irony' of his style. Leslie A. Marchand also found something bracing about the sincerity of Maugham's style, but his review in the *New York Times* (No. 65) paid most attention to the book's autobiographical content. Evelyn Waugh's wider-ranging piece in the *Graphic* (No. 64) deplored the excitement it had caused in literary circles owing to the central character's supposed resemblance to Thomas Hardy, though he does not mention that Alroy Kear was in fact a devastating caricature of Hugh Walpole. More pertinently he identifies the novel's real interest and value as depending upon the manner and method of its construction, praising especially 'the brilliant technical dexterity' with which Maugham managed the frequent scene-changes and time-shifts. The fact that Maugham had his work so much under control he thought both a triumph and a limitation.

He is never boring or clumsy, he never gives a false impression; he is never shocking; but this very diplomatic polish makes impossible for him any of those sudden transcendent flashes of passion and beauty which less competent [that word again!] novelists occasionally attain.

VII

The period of Maugham's greatest achievement spanned the twenty years of *l'entre deux guerres*, and of the many books he then published none received greater critical acclaim than two non-fictional works, *Don Fernando* (1935) and *The Summing Up* (1938). It is of particular interest that when the former (without its original sub-title, *Variations on Some Spanish Themes*) was reissued in the collected edition in 1950 it had been substantially revised in order to take account of certain constructive criticisms made by Raymond Mortimer in his *New Statesman* review (No. 101) and by Desmond MacCarthy when he reviewed *The Summing Up* in the *Sunday Times*. MacCarthy was not the only critic to make the publication of *The Summing Up* the occasion for an appraisal of Maugham's total output, and on the whole Maugham must have read the general verdict with satisfaction. But if he entertained any idea that the hostility of his critics had been finally silenced, he was in for several rude shocks: the case for the prosecution had yet to be mounted. In its most virulent form it came from two American critics.

Perhaps it was unwise for an author of Maugham's eminence and achievement to have published, in his mid-sixties, first in an American magazine and then in book form a short novelette with no other object than to provide light entertainment. *Up at the Villa* (1941) was an elaboration of an unpublished short story entitled 'A Night in June' which he had written some twenty years earlier and which seems to have been intended as the scenario for a play. As Pamela Hansford Johnson wrote in *Books of the Month* (No. 118), although the theme of the novelette 'just borders on the footling', it is a 'fascinating and elegant' piece of writing. This view was not shared by Morton Dauwen Zabel who, in an intemperate article written for the *Nation* (New York) (No. 117), called the book 'as unmitigated a specimen of fictional drivel as has appeared under respectable authorship within living memory' and castigated its author for having turned out during the ten years since *Cakes and Ale* appeared 'a succession of luxurious pot-boilers, *Cosmopolitan* thrillers, and Hollywood slick-jobs'. So little do these three categories correspond with the books Maugham actually published during that period that it can only be surmised that Zabel's onslaught was inspired by personal animosity.

When Maugham's last major novel, *The Razor's Edge* (1944), was published in America it had the misfortune to fall among academics. Spared the intemperance of Zabel's diatribe on the subject of *Up at the Villa*, it encountered instead the cool disparagement of Joseph Warren Beach's review in the *New York Times* (No. 121), and the briefer dismissiveness of Diana Trilling in the *Nation* (New York) (No. 122). On the other side of the Atlantic it elicited a warmer response from the novelist Kate O'Brien in the *Spectator* (No. 123), but she too had a number of criticisms to make:

> But he has written it from the outside; gracefully, sympathetically, and with a sufficiency of bitterness—but using Larry too easily throughout, as a beautiful symbol, and never attempting to hack down to the bones of the man himself; spreading over all the rest of the story too, and even over Larry a bit, that gloss, that convenient, amusing *chic*, that curious *Champs Elysées décor*, which this author finds irresistible and which he does so well; indeed, excessively, sterilisingly well.

Not for the last time it was Cyril Connolly who came forward and, in a characteristically vigorous review for the *New Statesman and Nation* (No. 124), expounded clearly and definitively Maugham's many excellencies. He began with the ringing assertion 'This is Mr Maugham's best novel since *Cakes and Ale...*' and ended by expressing puzzlement that it had been so uncharitably reviewed elsewhere, ascribing the fact to prejudice of one kind or another.

Prejudice surely lay behind the case for the prosecution as presented by Edmund Wilson in his review for the *New Yorker* (No. 126) of *Then and Now* (1946), a historical novel with Machiavelli as its principal character set in sixteenth-century Italy. He begins with the admission that he had always considered Maugham second-rate, lacking both 'personal rhythm' and the ability to 'create for us a poetic world'. *Then and Now* seemed to him 'one of the most tasteless and unreadable books from which I had ever hoped to derive enjoyment'. Maugham's handling of his theme suggested to Wilson one of the less brilliant contributions to a prep-school magazine; the dim sparkles of wit that occasionally relieved the general dullness, he did not think would be beyond the competence of a schoolboy. And so on. He then broadens his attack in an attempt to demolish what Maugham had said about such writers as Henry James and Proust in an anthology he had edited a few years before, *Introduction to Modern English and American Literature* (1943). That all this was the product of prejudice, if not actual malice, is suggested by Wilson's later comment on his own review: 'You know, I think I settled that fellow's hash. And do you know, I've never read *Of Human Bondage*, *Cakes and Ale* and *The Razor's Edge*?'

VIII

As for Edward Driffield in *Cakes and Ale*, the critical climate became blander the older Maugham grew. Typical of the warm response from his fellow writers which greeted the publication of *A Writer's Notebook* (1949) was W.H. Auden's review in the *New York Times* (No. 135), which voiced the general sense of gratitude they felt for his work.

A career as long, as productive and as successful as Somerset Maugham's earns a writer his membership in that select and curious group which Jean Cocteau has aptly named *Les monstres sacrés*. When Maugham publishes a new book, therefore, it would be dishonest of the critic to pretend that he either can or wishes to read it as if it were by an unknown writer or to judge it by esthetic standards alone; in addition to any literary merit, it has inevitably and, I think, quite properly a historic interest as the act of a person in whom one has long been interested. Having for us a history, the author has become not only a novelist but also a character in our novel, and a platitude or a blind spot is scarcely less revealing (and therefore fascinating) than an insight or an area of enthusiasm.

Coinciding with his eightieth birthday there appeared a collection of critical articles on his work, *The Maugham Enigma* (1954), the question-begging title being that of a 1938 review of *The Summing Up* by Malcolm Cowley in the *New Republic* (No. 111). Instead of being reviewed in the usual way, the book, in tribute to Maugham, was made the occasion for a leading article in the *Times Literary Supplement* (No. 144), in which his contribution to literature and the drama was sympathetically appraised and, in a phrase reminiscent of Johnson's praise of Garrick, he was commended for having 'added enormously to the sum of human pleasure'. Three days later the *New York Times* (No. 145) followed with a briefer leading article in which, while the accolade of greatness was withheld from him, he was again commended for the pleasure he had given millions of readers over the years and would doubtless bring to future generations.

Of the lavish obituary notices that appeared when he died ten years later at the age of ninety-one, that of Cyril Connolly (No. 150) stands out from the ruck for its fairness and its perceptiveness. Acknowledging that it was difficult to foresee what posterity would make of Maugham's work, Connolly gave his own forecast in a memorable sentence which perhaps contains the profoundest comment so far made about Maugham as a writer:

But, if all else perish, there will remain a story-teller's world from Singapore to the Marquesas that is exclusively and for ever Maugham, a world of verandah and prahu which we enter, as we do that of Conan Doyle's Baker Street, with a sense of happy and eternal homecoming.

Note on the Selection and Its Arrangement

This selection of the first reviews of W. Somerset Maugham's books and plays, and its arrangement, have been conditioned by three basic factors. First, the sheer bulk of his literary output, published between 1897 and 1963. Section A of Stott's bibliography of his work lists seventy-eight books and pamphlets written by Maugham, and Sanders's bibliography of writings about him comprises 2,355 items. Secondly, the fact that he came to write, intentionally, for two principal markets, the British and the American. Thirdly, the broad division of his work into books written to be read and plays written for performance. The significance of this last point for our purpose is that, whilst book reviewers were addressing themselves to what was exclusively Maugham's own work, drama critics were appraising particular productions of his plays. To have mixed up together these two quite separate types of criticism would have been both confusing and misleading.

If the selection was to be kept to a reasonable size, therefore, only a mere sampling of the available material could be included—in the event, 150 reviews as compared with Sanders's 2,355 items. Obviously, our choice has had to be subjective, and we have selected those pieces which seemed to us of particular intrinsic or literary interest. As a general principle we have given preference to reviews by well-known writers, and in some cases have printed several reviews by the same critic in order to give a certain depth and continuity to the volume.

The pieces are arranged in chronological order of first publication of the books reviewed or, in the case of plays, of first production, except that, because for the reason already given drama criticism has been grouped together in separate parts, this has caused some slight overlapping. The concluding part contains a selection of general criticism of Maugham's work, the first printed in 1919, the last (an obituary essay) in 1965.

From about the time of the Great War, when Maugham's books began to be published more or less simultaneously in America and Great Britain, and many of his plays to be produced on Broadway as well as in London, the reviews printed in New York newspapers and periodicals are—from the standpoint of the history of the critical response to his work—as important as those printed in London. Accordingly, commencing with the first productions of *The Land of Promise* (1913; 1914) and the first publication of *Of Human Bondage* (1915), we have balanced our selection of British criticism with a selection of the American reviews. It is hoped that the double focus thus achieved will lend an added interest to this compilation.

In the table of contents the dates placed in brackets against the titles are those of first publication in the case of books or first production in the case of plays. Two dates against any item indicate publication or production in both London and New York.

PART I
BOOKS
(1897–1909)

LIZA OF LAMBETH
London, September 1897

Maugham's first book was published when he was twenty-three during his last year as a medical student at St Thomas's Hospital. Shortly after qualifying as a doctor he gave up medicine in order to become a full-time writer. His last, and seventy-eighth, book was published sixty-six years later.

1. Edward Garnett, reader's report on 'A Lambeth Idyll' for T. Fisher Unwin
January 1897

Edward Garnett (1868–1937), one of the earliest professional publisher's readers and editors, discerned in Maugham a talent for fiction while he was still a medical student. Garnett's recommendation that 'A Lambeth Idyll' (as *Liza of Lambeth* was originally called) be published launched Maugham on his career as a novelist. Garnett recognised at once the young writer's model in the low-life tales of Arthur Morrison (1863–1945) and predicted what the general reaction would be to his coarse and distressing subject matter. (For additional reports by Garnett on Maugham's juvenilia see *Edward Garnett: A Life in Literature* by George Jefferson (London, 1982).)

A Lambeth Idyll may be compared to *The Jago* by Arthur Morrison. *Jago* was a very clever study of the semi-criminal class, done, more or less, from life—not always artistic, but going deep in places. Mr Morrison's book has been rather well received by the intelligent section of the public. It, probably, has to be forced on the public & on the booksellers, & we understand that *Tales of Mean Streets* sold 1200 copies in response to a 300£ advertisement—but still Messrs Methuen know well that their own payment comes in reputation.

Mr Maugham has not produced so powerful a study as *The Jago*—but when all is said & done *A Lambeth Idyll* is a very clever realistic study of factory girl & coster life. The women, their roughness, intemperance, fits of violence, kindheartedness, slang—all are done truthfully. Liza & her mother Mrs Kemp are drawn with no little humour and insight. The story is a dismal one in its ending, but the temper and tone of the book is wholesome & by no means morbid. The work is objective, & both the atmosphere & the environment of the mean district are unexaggerated. The question for Fisher Unwin to decide is this—the Arthur Morrison public, a slowly growing one, will understand & appreciate the book—though of course it was through Mr Henley's backing that *Mean Streets* & *The Jago* found publisher & public, & Mr Maugham has not got Mr Henley at his back. If Fisher Unwin does not publish *A Lambeth Idyll* somebody else certainly will. Of course half the critics will call the book 'brutal'. Now it is no good trying half measures—we mean there is a definite public for & against the 'study in realism'. We should say Publish—but, of course, nobody can guarantee a very favourable reception. All we can [say] is that [the] book is a clever, a humorous, study of rather low life, & that its tone is quite wholesome & the reverse of morbid. Mr Maugham has insight & humour, & will probably be heard of again.

We suggest, if the book is taken, that one chapter—that which describes the Outing at Chingford—is too long, & has too much the effect of a piece of clever reporting. The physical details concerning the dinner & its digestion by A & B are too much insisted on. In other places some of the bad words might be softened down or Henleyized a bit—a la *Mean Streets*.

N.B. The conversation is remarkably well done.

2. Unsigned review, *Academy*

LII, 11 September 1897, 65–6

Garnett's forecast proved accurate. Maugham had succeeded, perhaps more than he intended, in shocking the anonymous Victorian reviewers who first noticed his work. The following *Academy* review is typical of others.

The successes of one season may be known by the imitations of the next, and Mr Arthur Morrison may afford to smile at the sincere flatteries of *Liza of Lambeth*. The mimicry, indeed, is deliberate and unashamed. The brutal fight between two women, the talk of plumes around a death-bed, are faithfully reproduced. Unfortunately the qualities which touch Mr Morrison's work with something akin to genius are precisely the qualities which are here omitted; the directness, the restraint, the dominance of artistic purpose. What should have been a tragedy becomes a sordid story of vulgar seduction. The realism, pursued for its own sake, sinks into incurable nastiness. I have seldom read anything more unpleasant than a chapter in which Mr Maugham borrows the old pastoral convention in order to give piquancy to his description of a Chingford bank holiday. Let me detach a jewel from this carcanet:

> 'You 'ave fust pop,' amorously remarked the lovely Phyllis, and he took a long drink and handed the pot to her.
> She, with maiden modesty, turned it so as to have a different part to drink from; but he remarked as he saw her:
> 'You are bloomin' particular.'
> Then, unwilling to grieve him, she turned it back again and applied her ruby lips to the place where his had been.
> 'Now we shan't be long!' she remarked, as she handed him back the pot.
> The faithful swain took out of his pocket a short clay pipe, blew through it, filled it, and began to smoke, while Phyllis sighed at the thought of the cool liquid gliding down her throat, and with the pleasing recollection gently stroked her stomach. Then Corydon spat, and immediately his love said—
> 'I can spit further than thet.'

'I bet yer yer can't.'

She tried, and did. He collected himself and spat again, further than before. She followed him, and in this idyllic contest they remained till the tootling horn warned them to take their places.

It is a great pity, for Mr Maugham is by no means without talent. He knows his slums, not probably as they are, but as they seem to the casual observer, and he can describe vigorously and effectively. Moreover, his principal subject, the factory girl in the clutches of a 'magerful man,' is quite capable of serious and artistic treatment. But I am afraid that Mr Maugham is less preoccupied with serious art than with the desire to out-Herod Herod in realistic audacity. And therefore I quit him with no heightened sense of the tragic pity and awe that belong to the faithful record of human life in the meanest dwelling, but with a grimy feeling, as if I had had a mud-bath in all the filth of a London street.

3. Jane H. Findlater, 'The Slum Movement in Fiction', *National Review*

XXXV, May 1900, 447–54

Jane Helen Findlater (d. 1946), Scottish novelist and critic, a daughter of the Manse, joint-author of *A Daughter of Strife* (1897), *The Ladder to the Stars* (1906) and other fiction, saw Maugham's work as part of the recently identified slum movement in fiction. She deplored both the nature of his material and his detachment from it.

The following is an extract from a longer essay.

... *Liza of Lambeth* saw the light in 1897. It is a story of brutal frankness and sickening import, and has, alas, too surely set a fashion for this sort of thing. We are spared nothing: the reek of the streets; the effluvia of unwashed humanity; but worse than all these outside things is the hopeless moral atmosphere in which the characters move. There are no wandering lights here, the moral darkness is unpierced by so much as a ray of brightness. Nor does the author seem to write in any spirit of pity, or with any love for the creatures he has made. With a stolid indifference he chronicles their hopeless sufferings; without apparent disgust he details the loathsome vices which degrade them; the whole thing is so gratuitous. Why all these horrors? Why all this filth? Such recitals cannot even be defended from the point of view of art, setting aside any question of morality—and, books being primarily supposed to be works of art, this should be the deepest condemnation that can be passed upon any work. Now this brutal—gratuitously brutal—class of book stands accused by its entire lack of light and shade, its continual overstrain. Such work is like a man who shouts at the pitch of his voice and calls the noise he produces music; or like the daubs of colour a child covers his paper with, calling it a picture. All intelligence leaves any so-called art when it is without light and shade, and where intelligence is left out art ceases to exist. It is perhaps only fair to admit that inartistic as such work may be, it has a horrid power of its own. This is the very reason, however, why it should be swept away root and branch. It is exactly the same thing in a lesser degree for us to sit down deliberately to read these books, as it was for the much-blamed crowds of sightseers to flock to the bull-fights at Boulogne. The same love of 'a new shiver' is the explanation of our interest in these horrors—or, perhaps, the aboriginal thirst for blood and violence which is said to lurk in every one of us.

I have remarked that these pictures of slum-life are inartistic—we might still consider it a painful duty to read them if they were true. For it is, no doubt, a good thing to know how half the world lives. But this is just where these books fail. Life in the slums has its joys quite as surely, if not as evidently, as life in palaces, and it is ridiculous to suppose that it has not.

THE MAKING OF A SAINT

London, June 1898

Maugham later claimed that the notion of following *Liza of Lambeth* with a historical novel came from an article by Andrew Lang, in which he expressed the view—which Maugham later realised was nonsense—that, since the young know nothing of their own time, they could only hope to write a good novel if it were set in the past. The article has not been traced. He found the bare bones of his plot in Machiavelli's *History of Florence*. His next historical novel, nearly fifty years later, was *Then and Now* (1946), which is also set in Renaissance Italy; it has Machiavelli as its protagonist.

---

4. Unsigned review, *Literature*

III, 27 August 1898, 185–6

In the constant endeavour to find something new, it is very natural that novelists should turn their attention to the only thing which is really new—namely, that which is old. But the same method will not always do for the present and for the past alike. Mr W.S. Maugham's story *The Making of a Saint* is a success, but in a limited way. It is the work of a professed realist, but to apply the method of *Liza of Lambeth* to the Italians of the end of the fifteenth century is a difficult task, and the success could not be of the same effective kind. For a really good historic novel the first requisite is sympathetic imagination, and Mr Maugham's artistic principles do not admit of his exercising that faculty in any high degree. He makes his fifteenth century Italians do the kind of things which

26

such people actually did, but he does not succeed in convincing the reader that this was the way they did them. That is the worst that can be said of *The Making of a Saint*, and it leaves us a most readable story, excellently told; exciting incidents well worked up, dialogue sufficient and not cumbrous nor flat. Furthermore, Mr Maugham's realism is not made an excuse for being disgusting; frankness and a light touch have enabled him to give an adequate indication of the manners of the time without offence to ours.

5. Unsigned review, *Academy*

LIV, 17 September 1898, 270

Liza of Lambeth, Mr Maugham's book of last year, was welcomed in certain quarters as a work of promise. A measure of fulfilment we had expected to meet with in this book, but we do not find it. The scene is no longer south-the-river, the time no longer the present century; but in Italy at the end of the fifteenth century, amid the intrigues of the town of Forli, wherein the man who afterwards became Fra Giuliano played his truculent part. We seem to discern in the persons of the play an incredible kinship to the Bills and Dicks who swear the cockney oaths and brag the easy amours of the cockney slum. It may be granted that the ladies of the age and country of which Mr Maugham writes were no models of conjugal fidelity, but we really cannot approve of Mr Maugham's treatment of the voluptuous Claudia. Giulia is more complex and more human.

'But what good can it do you to have all these people in love with you?'
'I don't know', she said; 'it is a pleasant sensation.'
'What a child you are!' I answered, laughing.
She bent forward seriously.
'But are you not in love with me?'
I shook my head. She came close up to me, so that her hair brushed lightly against my cheek; it sent a shiver through me. I looked at her pink ear; it was beautifully shaped, transparent as a pink shell. Unconsciously,

quite without intention, I kissed it. She pretended to take no notice, and I was full of confusion. I felt myself blushing furiously.

'Are you quite sure?' she asked gravely.

We do not rate Fra Giuliano's humour high. Let us hope that Mr Maugham does not either. Neither to have told a lad whose clothes had been pressed into the service of a lady that our first parents wore fig-leaves, and that in case of his being 'run in' his gaoler's daughter must find him irresistible, nor even the crowning jest of offering him Giulia's doffed raiment, seems to us to justify a man in 'leaning against a wall and laughing till his sides ache'. As to the civic tragedy with which these facetiae are interwoven we look back on it with heroic composure. No, it really is not a good book.

ORIENTATIONS

London, June 1899

None of the short stories printed in Maugham's first collection was included in any of his collected editions, but the theme of one of them, 'A Bad Example', was adapted to form the plot of his last play, *Sheppey* (1933).

---

6. Unsigned review, *Athenaeum*

3738, 17 June 1899, 751

This and the following review show the critical tide turning in Maugham's favour and mark the beginning of his acceptance by reviewers as a young writer of whom something important might be expected. When Maugham looked back from his affluent middle age to the time in his youth when he had been treated as belonging to the intelligentsia it was, perhaps, of this period he was thinking. The book's anonymous epigraph was composed by Maugham himself, since he had been unable to find an apposite passage in the French moralists and critics.

The best writing we have yet seen from Mr W.S. Maugham is contained in a volume of short stories entitled *Orientations*. They are six in number, and, with two exceptions, differ from each other widely in subject, while the matter of one of them bears some resemblance to the writer's novel *'Liza of Lambeth*. If another, entitled 'De Amicitiâ,' suggests a somewhat youthful hand, it will be found none the less interesting; while in one called 'Daisy' he boldly brings fortune and happiness to a young lady who runs away with a married man. The writer's handicraft is, however, more interesting and original than the subjects he has chosen for his stories. In an imaginative narration he is seen at his best, and it contains a good passage, which we should quote but for its length. This little collection of stories gives rise to the hope that the author will arrive at a larger measure of success than his two previous volumes of fiction have achieved.

7. Unsigned review, *Academy*

LVI, 1 July 1899, 15

The influence of Maupassant on his work, which Maugham often acknowledged, is for the first time noted in this review.

Mr Maugham begins to be interesting. This book is much better than either the shrill and hysterical *Liza of Lambeth* or the rather mediocre *Making of a Saint*. It consists of a group of short stories, and from a preliminary quotation in the French tongue we gather that these stories are the result of the author's efforts to find his '*moi littéraire.*' They do not, however, differ from each other as widely as Mr Maugham would seem to imply. There are narratives of modern life, mediaeval narratives, and narratives of Arabian fantasy; but though the subjects vary so widely, the treatment is practically identical throughout. We like that treatment, particularly of modern subjects; we think it discloses Mr Maugham's veritable *moi littéraire*—a *moi* trenchant, sincere, candid, humorous, witty, and flippant (the flippancy is happily less than it used to be; one could entirely spare it). We imagine that Mr Maugham has formed his technique upon that of De Maupassant; if so, he has gone to a good master. The best work in the book is strongly reminiscent of the author of *L'Inutile Beauté*, though it has a less severe and grave style and distinctly more humour. 'A Bad Example,' being the record of an absolutely common city clerk who, through sitting on a coroner's jury, was converted to the most advanced form of altruism, is an admirable piece of writing, full of concise observation, freshness of view, and authentic humour. The concern of the wife for her husband's sanity when the convert insists on reading the Bible instead of the *Daily Telegraph* is very funny, and very pathetic too; and the subsequent examination of the patient by a specialist in lunacy is perhaps even better:

'I mean, do you see things that other people don't see?'
'Alas! yes; I see Folly stalking abroad on a 'obby 'orse.'
'Do you really? Anything else?' said the doctor, making a note of the fact.
'I see Wickedness and Vice beating the land with their wings.'
'*Sees things beating with their wings,*' wrote down the doctor.
'I see misery and un'appiness everywhere.'
'Indeed!' said the doctor, '*Has delusions.* Do you think your wife puts things in your tea?'
'Yes.'
'Ah!' joyfully uttered the doctor, 'that's what I wanted to get at—*thinks people are trying to poison him.* What is it they put in, my man?'
'Milk and sugar,' answered Mr Clinton.
'Very dull mentally,' said the specialist.

There is nothing else equal to 'A Bad Example.' The more fantastic tales lack point, or such point as they have is unoriginal; they also suffer severely from a flippancy which can only be called inane. 'De Amicitia' has a certain vigour of presentation, and some wit, but it is a little late in the day to relate how a man and a woman tried to be platonic friends and then fell in love. Mr Maugham, to our thinking, is a man who will survive many defects. He has an abundance of vitality, which is perhaps the scarcest thing in modern literature.

MRS CRADDOCK

London, November 1902

Maugham made numerous minor textual revisions to this novel before reissuing it in the Collected Edition of his works in 1937.

---

8. Unsigned review, 'The Strong Crude Novel', *Academy and Literature*

LXIII, 29 November 1902, 577

Maugham's first full-length study of marital incompatibility was at once recognised as a great advance on his previous novels. He duly noted the reviewer's remark about flippancy and provincialism and endeavoured in future to correct these tendencies.

There are sundry things in, and aspects of, this novel which will annoy the reader of nice taste. And the first is the long 'Epistle Dedicatory' to one of the characters in the book. It is a pity that Mr Maugham cannot yet perceive the infantile absurdity of such literary freakishness. He evidently thinks the dedication rather a clever idea cleverly executed. It is nothing of the kind. It is merely tedious tomfoolery. He evidently thinks it smart to begin his story thus:

This book might be called also 'The Triumph of Love.'

And to insert (on p. 41) an italicised aside about English novelists and their heroines, in the form of a dialogue. The morning will certainly come when Mr Maugham will wake up to the provincialism of such literary smartness. He will also regret the too ripe lusciousness of a few tender passages in *Mrs Craddock*. Some pages are as crude as the crudest parts of *Liza of Lambeth* and in a more offensive way. And finally he will regret numerous pages of feeble witticism and facile satire. Speeches like the following are out of place in a novel purporting to be a serious study of life:

'That is one advantage of women,' she told herself. 'After twenty-five they gloss over their birthdays like improprieties. A man is so impressed with his cleverness in having entered the world at all that the anniversary always interests him; and the foolish creature thinks it interests other people as well.'

We are convinced that Mr Maugham will ultimately realise his faults, because we are convinced that he has in him the essentials of a thoroughly sound novelist. By far the larger part of this elaborate study of an ill-assorted marriage is very good indeed—strong, quiet and occasionally beautiful. The character of Edward Craddock, the gentleman-farmer, is drawn with absolute conviction. His lack of imagination, his impassivity, his equanimity, his good nature, his utter inability to put himself in another person's place, even the trait of obstinate vanity which leads to his too timely death—all these things combine to make a human mediocrity that is vividly alive. Bertha, his wife, that curious admixture of sensuality, sensuousness, and intellectual pride, is an extremely clever invention, but not so authentic as Craddock. Miss Leys, the aunt, suffers, as a creation, from the same defects as Bertha. But Miss Glover, the Vicar's sister, another mediocrity, is in her way as good as Craddock. When Miss Glover read a particular chapter of the Bible to Bertha, Bertha being in a delicate state of health, Mrs Craddock remarked that she didn't think the chosen chapter was quite to the point; and Miss Glover replied: 'My dear, I don't want to reprove you—that's not my duty—but all the Bible is to the point.'

Mr Maugham makes no attempt to disguise the fact that the basis of Bertha's regard for her vulgar husband was physical. He handles the general history of the marriage with excellent simplicity and skill. The revulsion of Bertha's feelings is rendered almost to perfection. Later—when he has separated the husband and wife— he is less good, as Mr Meredith was less good when he separated

33

the husband and wife in *Richard Feverel*. The passionate episode between her good-for-nothing young cousin in London is a daring piece of naturalism, and within the possibilities of Bertha's character. But it alienates the sympathies of the reader, and in so far as it does so, it is either badly invented or badly executed. In the last reconciliation between Bertha and Edward, the incident of the ball-dress, diamonds, and hashed mutton was a brilliant thought, but despite its brilliance, its raw symbolism cannot be defended. Craddock's death, too, though carefully and ingeniously approached, is unsatisfactory, and has the air of forcing the conclusion. Such marriages as Bertha's do not end with a broken neck.

In fine, the book is full of faults, but it has earned our genuine respect.

9. A. St John Adcock, 'Mr W.S. Maugham's New Novel', *Bookman* (London)

XXIII, December 1902, 108

Arthur St John Adcock (1864–1930), novelist, essayist, journalist, and editor of the *Bookman*, had at the date of this review already published stories with a slum background in collections such as *Beyond Atonement* (1896), *East End Idylls* (1897) and *The Consecration of Hetty King* (1898). He was later to publish short appraisals of his contemporaries, Maugham among them, in *Gods of Modern Grub Street* (1923) and *The Glory That Was Grub Street* (1928).

If, from any cause, you are afraid to look life in the face, you had better leave Mr Maugham alone and turn for solace to some of the thousand-and-one novels that concern themselves with the improbable romances of ideal men and women who have little or no footing at all on the earth we know; but if you prefer that your fiction should reflect the truth and, by opening magic casements on the world as it is, enlarge your knowledge of and sympathy with actual humanity—then Mr Maugham is a novelist who will count with you. Despite certain crudities, his *Liza of Lambeth* survived most of the novels of its season, and *Mrs Craddock* shows him maturer and more reticent, both in his choice of subject and his manner of handling it. There are only three or four characters of prime importance in the book, and the most important of them is Mrs Craddock herself—a subtle and even masterly study of a certain feminine temperament that is probably not so uncommon as we would like to believe. At the start, she is Bertha Ley, unmarried, on the eve of attaining her majority, and living with an indolent, worldly-wise aunt, 'whose attitude towards life was a shrug of the shoulders and a well-bred smile of contempt.' Returning from a lengthy sojourn abroad, Bertha meets Edward Craddock, a young tenant-farmer on her estate, whom she had known in earlier years. With all her birth and breeding, she is a woman in whom the primitive animal instincts are strongly developed, and Edward's manly good-looks and great physical strength, the very perfume of strong tobacco and horses and cattle that always pervades him, appeal to this sensuousness in her irresistibly. Her fierce passion fires a feebler responsive love in him, and, in defiance of their social inequality and of public opinion, she marries him. Thereafter, for a while her passion increases; she is happy only in his presence, and is constantly caressing him and wheedling him to kiss and caress her, and he being a bluff, stolid, unsentimental man, this soon palls upon him, and he is brusque and impatient with her. 'Love to her was a burning fire, a flame that absorbed the rest of life; love to him was a convenient and necessary institution of Providence, a matter about which there was as little need for excitement as about the ordering of a suit of clothes,' and, at length, when his easy stolidity hurts her, he cannot understand her tears and is unmoved by them, his view being that 'women were like chickens; give 'em a good run properly closed in with stout wire netting, so that they can't get into mischief, and when they cluck and cackle, just sit tight and take no notice.'

So, inevitably, disillusion comes to Bertha, at last; she had married her ideal of the man, and wakes by painful degrees to a recognition of the reality and finds herself 'linked to a man she did not know.' With a cunning and fine insight Mr Maugham traces the petty gradations by which she drifts away from him till, after the child she had thought to love in place of him is still-born, she leaves him to travel with her aunt, and coming back, sees him with wholly disenchanted eyes, and grows to loathe him with angry physical repulsion. She leaves him again, and having burnt through an almost fatal passion for a Byronic younger cousin, again returns, and then comes the end, which is more or less happy or unhappy, according to the standpoint from which you look at it. The minor characters and episodes are cleverly drawn, and the social life of the Kentish countryside is touched in with fidelity. The book, as a whole, is a really notable piece of work, and marks a distinct advance on what Mr Maugham had previously accomplished.

THE MERRY-GO-ROUND

London, September 1904

Of the four unrelated stories which are interwoven in this novel, one is a novelisation of Maugham's first play, *A Man of Honour*, first produced in 1903, and another provided the plot for a later play, *Grace (Landed Gentry)* (1910).

10. Unsigned review, *Academy and Literature*

LXVII, 15 October 1904, 338

'Sometimes men seem to me cripples ever seeking to hide their deformity, huddled in a stuffy room, lit by one smoky taper.' These words, taken at random from one of the speeches of the philosophic Frank Hurrell, appear to give the keynote to the author's present work. The social world, this merry-go-round, as he terms it, is to him nothing but a hospital, and the different wards are filled to choking with victims of a fantastic passion. Concerning the problems of love in its endless variety—illicit love, degenerate love, vulgar intrigue, and voluptuousness, there are many questions to be asked, but few can be answered. At any rate, the author offers no solution, but rather presents a few examples, illustrative of an idea. There is the rising young barrister, madly in love with a widow, but, in a moment of folly, he seduces a barmaid. His sense of duty makes him marry her. Result: suicide of the wife, and return of the man to his original love. There is the loveless old maid, who seeks in the love of a consumptive youth to win back the lost days of a possible happiness. Result: death of husband and tears and flowers. There is the rake, spoilt by a deluded mother, who philanders with a married woman and accepts her money. Result: suicide of an innocent third party, and more tears. And so on. The author takes these several characters—

37

delineated with no common skill—and strings them together into the semblance of a little world. He does not deliberately turn away from what is ugly in life; nor does he make great effort to exploit it. The redeeming character in the book is Miss Ley, who is at once wholesome, kind, sympathetic. Mr. Maugham understands his patients and their symptoms; he knows the wards of his hospital; he has seen the smoky taper. And there is no dull page, no prosy line, no coarseness, no offence in working out the problem which he has set himself to expound.

11. Unsigned review, *Athenaeum*

4018, 29 October 1904, 586

Three several plots, all developed with considerable power, though joined by the slightest possible thread of connexion, are contained in this very clever novel. That concerned with the love story of a middle-aged lady who marries a consumption-stricken youth twenty years younger than herself as the only means of giving him her fortune, and thus perchance saving his life, is by far the least painful of the three, for the poor doomed lad repays his wife's devotion with boyish idolatry, and their short married life, despite its sorrowfulness, is altogether lovely. Much more distressing is the history of the barrister who by honourably marrying the mother of his child, a beautiful girl of hitherto blameless character, but hopelessly beneath him socially and intellectually, only delays her death by suicide for a year—a year of utter misery for both. The third strand of narrative recounts the squalid intrigue of a society woman with a peculiarly worthless 'bounder,' who is ultimately converted into a tolerably respectable member of society by marriage with a shrewd and sharp-tongued actress, while his forsaken mistress succeeds, in the course of some powerful, but not wholly convincing scenes, in obtaining her husband's forgiveness. The characterization is remarkable for its depth and width of range. Perhaps the most successful, and certainly the most pleasing, example is the charming old lady who is theoretically committed to principles of the laxest toleration, but in practice is almost always working on the side of the angels.

THE LAND OF THE BLESSED VIRGIN

London, January 1905; New York, July 1920

Maugham was unable to persuade a publisher to accept his first travel-book, first written in 1888/89. Completely rewritten, it was eventually published in 1905 by William Heinemann, who had published his previous novel, *Mrs Craddock*. Except for his next novel, *The Bishop's Apron*, which was brought out by Chapman & Hall, Heinemann was the English publisher of all Maugham's subsequent books.

12. Unsigned review, 'Spain and the Spanish', *Athenaeum*

4039, 25 March 1905, 366

The following is extracted from a review dealing with several books on Spanish themes.

By giving to his work the charming, popular, traditional name of Andalusia, Mr W.S. Maugham raises expectations of legend and folk-lore, which are not fulfilled in *The Land of the Blessed Virgin*. The author is frankly in love with everything Spanish, except the cooking, and he writes his romantic recollections with a boyish enthusiasm that makes one forgive his gorgeous superlatives. There is too much liquid gold and emerald and sapphire in his rivers; the sun is too habitually blood-red, both at Ronda and Granada; 'all was silent' in one place, and 'all again was still and lifeless' in another; white teeth gleam and eyes flash darkly in the ordinary course of things. It is absolutely fantastic and unreal, but it is agreeable juvenile rhapsody, no more likely to impose on any reader than the description of the conventional impossible sky, where the stars 'shone in their countless millions.' It all happened at Seville when Mr Maugham was twenty-three, and his reminiscences make very pleasant reading—at all events, for the first half hour. The romanticism is relieved by such sly strokes of humour as the solemn declaration that 'as many people in proportion get drunk in Seville as in London.' The joke can only be appreciated by those who know both cities. The amateur peeps out in such expressions as 'olla podrida,' 'neve,' 'Che maravilla!' and even 'toreador' (p. 53), a barbarism which is ridiculed later in the book. Mr Maugham should revise his proofs more carefully; but he leaves an impression of knowing Spain, and even something of her popular literature, though he admires in and out of season.

13. [Virginia Woolf], unsigned review, 'Journeys in Spain', *Times Literary Supplement*

26 May 1905

(Adeline) Virginia Woolf (1882–1941), novelist and essayist, was a leading member of the Bloomsbury Group which included Lytton Strachey, David Garnett, E.M. Forster and Roger Fry.

The following is an extract from an anonymous review which also discussed *Letters from Catalonia and Other Parts of Spain* by Rowland Thirlemere.

Reprinted in *The Essays of Virginia Woolf*, vol. I, *1904–1912*, ed. Andrew McNeillie (London, 1986).

Mr Somerset Maugham's single volume, *The Land of the Blessed Virgin*, is slim and reticent. He writes of Andalusia, and, so to speak, edits the country carefully. He selects certain scenes which have remained in his mind as typical and illustrative of the country which he knows so well, and they are not necessarily those prescribed by the guide-book. In his work, too, the personal element preponderates; he is content in more than one instance to let an impression stand as a permanent record which was admittedly coloured by facts of purely personal significance. But he has his pen well under control, and strikes out pictures now and again which are true in themselves and yet could have been so seen by one person only. 'Ah, the beautiful things which I have seen which other men have not!' he exclaims, and he has a sincere desire to find the right word for the beauty which he genuinely loves and which, consequently, interests him more than any peculiarities in the individual who observes it. His book thus, even when the desire is beyond his power of satisfying it, has a value of its own, both for the traveller and for the reader who remains in his study chair.

THE BISHOP'S APRON

London, February 1906

This is one of two novels Maugham hurriedly adapted from plays, then unproduced, at a time when he needed the money. The play, entitled *Loaves and Fishes*, which was eventually produced in 1911, had itself been based on 'Cupid and the Vicar of Swale', one of two short stories commissioned by *Punch* in 1900. The novel has never been included in the Collected Edition of Maugham's work.

---

14. 'The Baron de B[ook]-W[orms]' [Sir F.C. Burnand], review, *Punch*

CXXX, 21 February 1906, 144

Sir Francis Cowley Burnand (1838–1917), playwright and journalist, was the author of a number of farces and adapted *Box and Cox* for Sullivan. Although Burnand was editor of *Punch* from 1880 to 1906, he seems to have forgotten that he had commissioned the short story in which Maugham first treated this clerical theme.

The Bishop's Apron, as exhibited to us by Mr Somerset Maugham, at Messrs Chapman and Hall's, is choke-full of good things, and is in itself a real work of art. The Baron feels himself absolutely safe from all possible contradiction in asserting that, for satirical humour and quizzical observation, this novel takes a double first. As a clerical story nothing better has been written since Anthony Trollope's delightful *Barchester Towers*, which will always hold first rank on account of the inimitable Mrs Proudie. The claimant for the episcopal apron is Theodore Spratte, Vicar of St Gregory's, South Kensington, and Canon of Tercanbury (beautifully twisted name this), an 'all things to all men,' *and* women, ecclesiastic, who yearns for the apron and the gaiters, and regards the episcopal turned-up-at-the-brim topper as a kind of halo in hats. The portrait of this character is delicious, and so true to the life that every reader will from time to time lay down the book for a while, as smilingly he confides to himself, 'I know that man, he comes from—,' whatever place his experience may suggest. There should be a sequel to this novel, to be named *The Bishop's Wife's Apron*. The basis for this suggestion will be found in the Twentieth Chapter, the last, and one of the sharpest hits in the book. But what a tribute to Anthony Trollope's popularity (in this particular line) is paid by Mr Maugham's selection of Barchester as being the Episcopal See above all others in which everyone will be at once interested! The name Barchester immediately puts middle-aged readers on familiar terms with the Canon 'in waiting.' What pluck on the part of the author and what wisdom is shown, in his selection of this title. No one would dare to speak of Barchester unless he had something exceptionally good to tell. Every sketch of character in this story is admirable, from the pompous butler up to the heavy-eyed premier; while the portraits of the rising socialist, with his objectionable family surroundings, the Canon's gentle and impressionable daughter, the various members of the Spratte family, past and present, and the captivating worldly widow, are all highly finished and thoroughly representative. The novel should have a marked success.

THE MAGICIAN

London, November 1908; New York, February 1909

This novel was reissued in the Collected Edition of Maugham's work in 1956 with a new preface, 'A Fragment of Autobiography', in which he describes the period of his residence in Paris in 1905 that provided the story's background. At that time he got to know Aleister Crowley, who had married the sister of Maugham's great friend, the painter Gerald Kelly. In the new preface Maugham admits that Crowley served as the model for Oliver Haddo, the 'magician' of the novel.

Published during Maugham's *annus mirabilis* when, having had his plays rejected by theatrical managements for ten years, he found himself the talk of London with four plays running simultaneously in West End theatres, *The Magician* marks the end of the first phase of his career as a novelist. For the next five years he was to devote himself exclusively to the writing of highly successful plays.

15. 'Oliver Haddo' [Aleister Crowley], 'How to Write a Novel! After W.S. Maugham', *Vanity Fair* (London)

LXXXI, 30 December 1908, 838–40

Edward Alexander ['Aleister'] Crowley (1875–1947), founder of his own magical order, self-styled Beast 666, and Word of Aeon, was the author of several books expounding his theories of the universe, and of works of fiction. His biographer John Symonds in *The Life and Magick of Aleister*

44

Crowley (London, 1971) quotes his reaction on first reading *The Magician*: 'I found phrase after phrase, paragraph after paragraph, page after page, bewilderingly familiar...'

Not every successful author would be generous enough to give away his method for the benefit of the rising generation. Yet in Mr W.S. Maugham this nobility of nature is found in overflowing measure—the give-away is singularly complete in *The Magician*.

Yet so dull—we regret to say—are some people that it will not seem impertinent in us to analyse and explain. The first essential is to choose a vague subject—one on which everybody is curious and almost nobody well-informed. For example, we might take 'magic' and 'art.' It will thus be rather difficult to catch us out. Anyway, we can insure correctness by making a photographically-accurate portrait of somebody great with whom we have scraped acquaintance—'the spider taketh hold with her hands and is in kings' palaces.' Thus we find on pages 29 and 30 an exact sketch of one of the five or six really great landscape painters the world has ever seen, with every finest physical and moral quality particularised with exquisite accuracy. Add the slur, 'very nearly a great painter,' and we may—so you think—get back at him for his cutting contempt of us. And so on through our book. We have hastily collected some seventy personalities of this kind.

Unfortunately this method will not carry us all the way. But if we happen to know one well-educated man, the task of writing a novel is not so difficult as it may seem to the beginner. Get invited to his house—possibly some cosy vicarage—read in his library a few of the works dealing with our subject and copy them wholesale into our book; sometimes verbatim, sometimes altering words here and there—for in the case of well-known authors it is best to make a pretence of not having copied verbatim.

We give examples of both methods, italicising only identical words and phrases.

Mather's *Kabbalah Unveiled*— Introduction:	*The Magician*, p. 72:
	'This, then, is its history. *Moses,*
'Moses, who was learned in all the	*who was learned in all the wisdom*
wisdom of Egypt, was first initiated	*of Egypt, was first initiated into the*
into the Qabalah in the land of his	*Kabbalah in the land of his birth;*

birth, but became most proficient in it during his wanderings in the wilderness, when he not only devoted to it the leisure hours of the whole forty years, but received lessons in it from one of the angels. By the aid of this mysterious science the law-giver was enabled to solve the difficulties which arose during his management of the Israelites, in spite of the pilgrimages, wars, and frequent miseries of the nation. He covertly laid down the principles of this secret doctrine in the first four books of the Pentateuch, but withheld them from Deuteronomy. Moses also initiated the seventy elders into the secrets of this doctrine, and they again transmitted them from hand to hand. Of all who formed the unbroken line of tradition, David and Solomon were the most deeply initiated into the Kabbalah. No one, however, dared to write it down, till Schimeon Ben Jochai, who lived at the time of the destruction of the second temple.... After his death, his son, Rabbi Eleazar, and his secretary, Rabbi Abba, as well as his disciples, collated Rabbi Simon Ben Jochai's Treatises, and out of these composed the celebrated work called ZHR, Zohar, splendour, which is the grand storehouse of Kabbalism.'

but became most proficient in it during his wanderings in the wilderness. Here he not only devoted the leisure hours of forty years to this mysterious science, but received lessons in it from an obliging angel. By aid of it he was able to solve the difficulties which arose during his management of the Israelites, notwithstanding the pilgrimages, wars, and miseries of that most unruly nation. He covertly laid down the principles of the doctrine in the first four books of the Pentateuch, but withheld them from Deuteronomy. Moses also initiated the Seventy Elders into these secrets, and they in turn transmitted them from hand to hand. Of all who formed the unbroken line of tradition, David and Solomon were the most deeply learned in the Kabbalah. No one, however, dared to write it down till Schimeon ben Jochai, who lived in the time of the destruction of Jerusalem; and after his death the Rabbi Eleazar, his son, and the Rabbi Abba, his secretary, collected his manuscripts and from them composed the celebrated treatise called Zohar.'

From Franz Hartmann's *The Life of Paracelsus*, p. 257:

'In a book *called* 'The *Sphinx*,' *edited by Dr Emil Besetzny*, and published at Vienna in 1873 by L. Rosner (Tuchlauben, No. 22), we find some interesting *accounts* in regard to a number of *'spirits' generated by a Joh. Ferd. Count of Kueffstein, in Tyrol, in* the year *1775. The sources from which these accounts are taken consist* in *masonic manuscripts* and prints, *but more especially* in *a diary kept by a certain Jas. Kammerer, who acted in the capacity of butler and famulus to the* said *Count. There were ten homunculi*—or, as he *calls them*, *'prophesying spirits'*—preserved *in strong bottles, such as are used to preserve fruit, and* which *were filled with water*; and these 'Spirits' were the product of the labour of the *Count J.F. of Kueffstein* (Kufstein), *and of an Italian Mystic and Rosicrucian, Abbé Geloni*. They were made in the course of *five weeks*, and consisted of a King, a queen, a knight, a monk, a nun, an architect, a miner, a seraph, and finally of a blue and a red spirit. *The bottles were closed with ox-bladders, and with a* great *magic seal* (Solomon's seal?). *The spirits* swam about in those bottles, and *were about* one *span long, and*

From *The Magician*, p. 112:

[Note Mr Maugham's accurate translations of 'the' and 'of' into 'die' and 'von.']

'It was *called* 'Die *Sphinx*,' and was *edited by* a certain *Dr. Emil Besetzny*. It contained the most extraordinary *accounts* I have ever read of certain *spirits* generated by Johann-Ferdinand, *Count* von *Kuffstein, in the Tyrol, in* 1775. *The sources from which these accounts are taken consist of masonic manuscripts, but more especially of a diary kept by a certain James Kammerer, who acted in the capacity of butler and famulus to the* count. The evidence is ten times better than any upon which men believe the articles of their religion. If it related to less wonderful subjects you would not hesitate to believe implicitly every word you read. *There were ten homunculi*—James Kammerer *calls them prophesying spirits*—kept *in strong bottles, such as are used to preserve fruit, and these were filled with water*. They were made in *five weeks*, by the *Count* Von *Kuffstein and an Italian mystic and Rosicrucian*, the *Abbé Geloni. The bottles were closed with ox-bladders and with a magic seal. The spirits were about a span long, and the Count was anxious that they should grow.*

the Count was very anxious that they should grow. They were, therefore, buried under two cart-loads of horse-manure, and the pile daily sprinkled with a certain liquor, prepared with great trouble by the two adepts, and made out of some 'very disgusting materials.' The pile of manure began after such sprinklings to ferment and to steam as if heated by a subterranean fire, and at least once every three days, when everything was quiet at the approach of the night, the two gentlemen would leave the convent and go to pray and to fumigate at that pile of manure. After the bottles were removed the 'spirits' had grown to be each one about one and a half span long, so that the bottles were almost too small to contain them, and the male homunculi had come into possession of heavy beards, and the nails of their fingers and toes had grown a great deal. By some means the Abbé Geloni provided them with appropriate clothing, each one according to his rank and dignity. In the bottle of the red and in that of the blue spirit, however, there was nothing to be seen but 'clear water'; but whenever the Abbé knocked three times at the seal upon the mouth of the bottles, speaking at the same time some Hebrew words, the

They were, therefore, buried under two cart-loads of manure, and the pile daily sprinkled with a certain liquor prepared with great trouble by the adepts. The pile after such sprinklings began to ferment and steam, as if heated by a subterranean fire. When the bottles were removed, it was found that the spirits had grown to about a span and a half each; the male homunculi were come into possession of heavy beards, and the nails of the fingers had grown. In two of the bottles there was nothing to be seen save clear water, but when the Abbé knocked thrice at the seal upon the mouth, uttering at the same time certain Hebrew words, the water turned a mysterious colour and the spirits showed their faces, very small at first, but growing in size till they attained that of a human countenance. And this countenance was horrible and fiendish.'

'Haddo spoke in a low voice that was hardly steady, and it was plain that he was much moved. It appeared as if his story affected him so that he could scarcely preserve his composure. He went on.

'These beings were fed every three days by the Count, with a rose-coloured substance which was kept in a silver box. Once a week the bottles were emptied and filled again with pure rain-water.

water in the bottles began to turn blue (respectively red), and the blue and the red *spirits* would *show their faces, first very small, but growing* in proportions until *they attained* the *size of an* ordinary *human* face. The face of the blue spirit was beautiful like an angel, but that of the red one bore a *horrible* expression.

'*These beings were fed by the Count* about once *every three* or four *days with* some *rose-coloured substance which* he *kept in a silver box*, and of which he gave to each spirit a pill of about the size of a pea. *Once* every *week* the water had to be removed, *and the bottles filled again with pure rain-water.* This *change had to be* accomplished very *rapidly because* during the few moments that the spirits *were exposed to the air they closed their eyes, and seemed to* become *weak and unconscious, as if they were about to die.* But the blue spirit was never fed, nor was the water changed; while the red one received once a week a thimbleful of fresh blood of some animal (chicken) and this *blood disappeared* in the water as soon as it was poured into it *without colouring or troubling it.*

'*By some accident the* glass containing the monk *fell one day and was broken.*

The *change had to be* made *rapidly because,* while the homunculi *were exposed to the air, they closed their eyes and seemed to* grow *weak and unconscious, as* though *they were about to die.* But with the spirits that were invisible, at certain intervals *blood* was poured into the water; and it *disappeared* at once, inexplicably, *without colouring or troubling it. By some accident* one of *the* bottles *fell one day and was broken. The* homunculus within *died after a few painful respirations in spite of all efforts to save* him, *and* the *body was buried in the garden. An attempt to generate another, made by the Count without the assistance of the Abbé, who had left,* failed: *it produced only a small thing like a leech, which had little vitality and soon died.'*

The poor monk *died after a few*
painful respirations, in spite of all
the *efforts* of the Count *to save*
his life, *and* his *body was buried in*
the garden. An attempt to generate
another one, *made by the Count*
without the assistance of the Abbé,
who had left, resulted in failure,
as *it produced only a small thing*
like a leech, which had very *little*
vitality and soon died.'

Does Mr Maugham wish us to believe that his is an independent
translation from *Die Sphinx*?

Considerations of space prevent us from quoting further parallels
of this kind. One, however, occupies no less than four and a half
pages of *The Magician*, and is taken from A.E. Waite's translation
of Eliphaz Levi, *Rituel et Dogme de la Haute Magie* (pp. 113–117).

Then, too, we can take our host's sister as the heroine, but as we
are unwilling to drag the name of any lady into a mere affair of
letters, we must beg to be excused from following Mr Maugham's
example in this one matter.

The would-be novelist should not be content with actuality
alone. There are a very large number of really striking incidents in
fiction, which we can borrow with advantage. For example, it
would be a graceful compliment to the fair sex (with whom our
gold, if not our eloquence, should make us a favourite) if we were
to borrow a scene from Mabel Collins' *Blossom and the Fruit*.

We italicise identical incidents:

From *The Blossom and the Fruit,* | *The Magician,* pp. 286–289:
by Mabel Collins, pp. 144–599: |

'He had scarcely done so when
the Duchess uttered a shrill cry.

'"*My God!*" she exclaimed, in
a voice of horror, "*who is in the*
carriage with us?"

'She flung herself across and

'"There's someone in the room."
The words were no sooner out
of her mouth than she heard
Arthur fling himself upon the in-
truder. She knew at once, with
the certainty of an intuition,
that it was Haddo. But how had

knelt upon the floor between Hilary and Fleta; her terror was so great she did not know what she was doing.

'Hilary leaned across her and instantly discovered that she was right—that there was another man in the carriage besides himself.

'"Oh, kill him! kill him!" cried the little Duchess, in an agony of fear; 'he is a thief, a murderer, a robber!'

'*Hilary rose up and precipitated himself upon this person whom he could not see.* A sense of self-defence, of defence of the women with him, seized him as we see it seize the animals. He discovered that this man had risen also. Blindly and furiously he attacked him, and *with extraordinary strength. Hilary was young and full of vigour, but slight and not built like an athlete. Now, however, he seemed to be one. He found his adversary to be much larger and stronger than himself.*

'A fearful struggle followed. The carriage drove on through unseen scenery as fast as possible; Fleta could have stopped it has she thrown the window down and cried out to the postillions. But Fleta remained motionless; she might have fainted, she was so still. The little Duchess simply cowered

he come in? What did he want? She tried to cry out, but no sound came from her throat. Dr Porhoet seemed bound to his chair. He did not move. He made no sound. She knew that an awful struggle was proceeding. It was a struggle to the death between two men who hated one another, but the most terrible part of it was that nothing was heard. They were perfectly noiseless. She tried to do something, but she could not stir. And Arthur's heart exulted, for his enemy was in his grasp, under his hands, and he would not let him go while life was in him. He clenched his teeth, and tightened his straining muscles. Susie heard his laboured breathing, but she only heard the breathing of one man. She wondered in abject terror what that could mean. *They struggled silently*, hand to hand, and Arthur knew that his strength was greater. He had made up his mind what to do and directed all his energy to a definite end. His enemy was *extraordinarily powerful, but Arthur appeared to create strength from the sheer force of his will. It seemed for hours that they struggled.* He could not bear him down.

'Suddenly he knew that the

on the ground beside her, cling-ing to her motionless figure. This terrified girl had not the presence of mind to think of stopping the carriage, and so obtaining help. She was too horror-struck to do anything. And, indeed, it was horrible, for the swaying, struggling forms sometimes were right upon the two women, some-times at the other side of the carriage; it was a deadly horri-ble, ghastly *struggle, all the more horrid for the silence.* There were no cries, no exclamations, for indeed, so far as Hilary was concerned, he had no breath to spare for them. There were only gasps and heavy breathings, and the terrible sound that came from a man's throat when he is fighting for his life. *How long this hideous battle lasted none could tell—Hilary had no idea of the passage of time. The savage in him had now come so entirely uppermost and drowned all other conscious-ness, that his one thought was he must kill—kill—kill—and at last it was done. There was a moment when his adversary was below him, when he could use his whole force upon him*—and then came a gasp and an unearthly cry—and si-lence.

'Absolute silence for a little while. No one moved, no one

other was frightened and sought to escape from him. Arthur tightened his grasp; for nothing in the world now would he ever loosen his hold. He took a deep quick breath and then put out all his strength in a tremendous effort. They swayed from side to side. Arthur felt as if his muscles were being torn from the bones, he could not con-tinue for more than a moment longer; but the agony that flashed across his mind at the thought of failure braced him to a sudden angry jerk. All at once Haddo collapsed, and they fell heavily to the ground. Arthur was breathing more quickly now. He thought that if he could keep on for one instant longer, he would be safe. *He threw all his weight on the form that rolled beneath him, and bore down furiously on the man's arm.* He twisted it sharply, with all his might, and felt it give way. He gave a low cry of triumph; the arm was broken. And now his enemy was seized with panic; he struggled madly, he wanted only to get away from those long hands that were kill-ing him. They seemed to be of iron. Arthur seized the huge bullock throat and dug his fingers into it, and they sunk in the heavy rolls of fat. He ex-

stirred. The Duchess was petrified with horror. Hilary had sunk exhausted on the seat of the carriage—not only exhausted, but bewildered, for a host of other emotions besides savage fury began to rise within him. What—who—was this being he had destroyed? At that moment the horses were urged into a gallop, for they were entering the city gates. Hilary threw down the window next him with a crash. *"Lights, lights!" he cried out, "bring lights!"* The carriage stopped, and there was a crowd immediately at the windows, and the glare of torches fell into the carriage, making it bright as day. *The little Duchess was crouched in the corner on the ground in a dead faint.* Fleta sat up, strangely white, but calm. *Nothing else was to be seen, alive or dead, save Hilary himself;* and so horror-struck was he at this discovery, that he turned and buried his face in the cushions of the carriage, *and he never knew what happened— whether he wept, or laughed,* or cursed—but some strange sound of his own voice he heard with his ears.

'There was a carriage full of servants behind Fleta's carriage; when hers stopped so suddenly they all got out and came quickly to the doors.

ulted, he knew that his enemy was in his power at last; he was strangling him, strangling the life out of him. He wanted light so that he might see the horror of that vast face, and the deadly fear, and the starting eyes. And still he pressed with those iron hands. And now the movements were strangely convulsive. His victim writhed with the agony of death. His struggles were desperate, but the avenging hands held him as in a vice. And then the movements grew utterly spasmodic, and then they grew weaker. Still the hands pressed upon the gigantic throat, and Arthur forgot everything. *He was mad with rage and fury and hate and sorrow.* He thought of Margaret's anguish and of her fiendish torture, and *he wished the man had ten lives so that he might take them one by one. And at last all was still,* and that vast mass of flesh was motionless, and he knew that his enemy was dead. He loosened his grasp and slipped one hand over the heart. It would never beat again. The man was stone dead. Arthur got up and straightened himself. The darkness was intense still and he could see nothing. Susie heard him, and at length she was able to speak:

'"The Duchess has fainted," said Fleta, rising so as to hide Hilary; "the journey has been too long. Is there a house near where she can lie still a little while, and come on later to the palace?"

'Immediately offers of help were made, and the servants and those who were glad to help them carried the poor little Duchess away.'

'"Arthur, what have you done?"

'"I've killed him," he said, hoarsely.

'"O God, what shall we do?" *Arthur began to laugh aloud, hysterically*, and in the darkness his hilarity was terrifying.

'"*For God's sake let us have some light.*" "I've found the matches," said Dr Porhoet. He seemed to awake suddenly from his long stupor. He struck one. They looked down on the floor for the man who lay there dead. Susie gave a sudden cry of horror.

'*There was no one there.*

'Arthur stepped back in terrified surprise. *There was no one in the room, living or dead, but the three friends.* The ground sank under Susie's feet, *she felt horribly ill, and she fainted.* When she awoke, seeming with difficulty to emerge from an eternal night, Arthur was holding down her head.

'"Bend down," he said; "bend down."

'All that had happened came back to her, and she burst into tears. Her self-control deserted her, and, clinging to him for protection, she sobbed as though her heart would break. She was shaken from head to foot. The strangeness of this last horror had overcome her, and she could have shrieked with fright.

For our main plot though, we are probably safer if we stick to a classic like Dumas. Thus the *Memoirs of a Physician* will furnish us with a picture of a magician marrying a girl but omitting to make her a wife, using her blood in magical ceremonies, killing her thereby, the grand climax being the burning of the laboratory and all its horrors. That burning of the laboratory, too, may remind us of Wells' *Island of Dr Moreau* and his homunculi, and the incident of the broken arm. Every little helps!

The Island of Dr Moreau, by H.G. Wells, p. 261:

'Then I saw that the dawn was upon us. The sky had grown brighter, the setting moon was growing pale and opaque in the luminous blue of the day. The sky to the eastward was rimmed with red.

'Then I heard a thud and a hissing behind me, and, looking round, sprang to my feet with a cry of horror. Against the warm dawn great tumultuous masses of black smoke were boiling up out of the enclosure, and through their stormy darkness shot flickering threads of blood-red flames. Then the thatched roof caught. I saw the curving charge of the flames across the sloping straw. A spurt of fire jetted from the window of my room. . . . I bent down to his face, put my hand through the

The Magician, p. 308:

'It was dark still, but they knew the dawn was at hand and Susie rejoiced in the approaching day. In the east the azure of the night began to thin away into pale amethyst, and the trees seemed gradually to stand out from the darkness in a ghostly beauty. . . . "Let us wait here and see the sun rise," said Susie.

'"As you will.". . . And as he spoke it seemed that the roof fell in, for suddenly vast flames sprung up, rising high into the still night air; and they saw that the house they had just left was blazing furiously. It was a magnificent sight from the distant hill on which they stood to watch the fire as it soared and sunk, as it shot scarlet tongues along like strange Titanic monsters, as it raged from room to room. Skene was burning. It

rent in his blouse. He was dead; and even as he died a line of white heat, the limb of the sun, rose eastward beyond the projection of the bay, splashing its radiance across the sky, and turning the dark sea into a weltering tumult of dazzling light.'

was beyond the reach of human help. In a little while there would be no trace of all those crimes and all those horrors. Now it was one mass of flame. It looked like some primeval furnace, where the gods might work unheard-of miracles.

'"Arthur, what have you done?" asked Susie, in a tone that was hardly audible.

'He did not answer directly. He put his arm about her shoulder again, so that she was obliged to turn round.

'"Look, the sun is rising."

'In the east a long ray of light climbed up the sky, and the sun, yellow and round, appeared upon the face of the earth.'

The whole description of the homunculi suggests Dr Moreau's 'Beast Folk' in method and treatment; but it is difficult to follow out in detail. The likeness is rather one of atmosphere than anything else.

Of course, the more ingredients you are able to find for your haggis the harder it is for anyone to identify the sheep's head basis of it! After studying the make-up of *The Magician*, we are constrained to wonder whether any of Mr Maugham's numerous plays have been composed in the same way.

16. Unsigned review, 'A Feast of Horrors', *New York Times*

13 February 1909, 88

It is a good plan, while reading W. Somerset Maugham's *The Magician*, to lift one's eyes occasionally and look around at familiar things, or even to go out of doors and listen to the clatter of the 'L' and the whirr of automobile wheels. Otherwise the feast of horrors which it affords is likely to pall upon one's mental palate. The author shows not a little skill in dealing with the uncanny and tells his tale of the weird and the horrible with a simple sincerity and a constant matching of unhallowed practices with the clean, sweet things of common life that make its effect uncommonly impressive.

'The Magician,' who is responsible for all the foul havoc that is worked in the book, is a big, corpulent, eccentric Englishman named Oliver Haddo, who has delved deep into all the occult lore of the Middle Ages, of Arabia, India, Persia. He has it all at the end of his tongue and the tip of his fingers. Early in the book he exerts his evil influence over the beautiful young fiancée of an English surgeon, and almost on the eve of their marriage fills her with evil thoughts and carries her off as his own bride. Her friends hear of them now and then, even meet them occasionally, and always they are attended by rumors of the practice of magic arts, of satanism, the Black Mass, of devilish mockeries and horrible orgies.

It is said that Haddo's ambition is to follow in the steps of those mediaeval magicians who declared that they had made homunculi and create human beings. His wife is persuaded to leave him and institute divorce proceedings, but his subtle influence over her is so strong that without seeing her he compels her to return. Finally they discover that he is preparing to sacrifice her in his efforts to create living beings by his occult arts. For these, according to the works of the mediaeval magicians, must be fed upon human blood. Her friends rally to the nearest village and find that she is already dead. Her former betrothed engages in a hand-to-hand scuffle with Haddo, who seems suddenly to appear in the inn parlor.

But after the magician falls dead they look and there is nothing there. Then they gain entrance to the magician's house, penetrate to his laboratories, and find there numbers of the awful, misshapen, obscene creatures his foul arts had called into being. And presently they discover his dead body, showing all the injuries which the surgeon had inflicted upon him in the inn parlor, where he had not been. And so the feast of horrors comes to an end, with a promise of better things for those who are still alive.

PART II
PLAYS
(1903–1914)

A MAN OF HONOUR

Imperial Theatre, London, 18 February 1903 (2 performances)
Avenue Theatre, London, 22 February 1904 (28 performances)
[Written 1898; revised 1902. Published London, December 1911]

A novelisation of this, Maugham's first full-length play to be produced, is one of the four unrelated stories interwoven in *The Merry-Go-Round* (1904).

---

17. E.K. Chambers, 'Mr Maugham's Irony', *Academy and Literature*

LXIV, 28 February 1903, 207–8

(Sir) Edmund Kerchever Chambers (1866–1954), at the time this article was written a Civil Servant at the Education Department, had already begun to make a reputation as an expert on Elizabethan and Jacobean texts. His study of the mediaeval stage was published in 1903, but it was not until after the Great War that, with *Shakespeare: A Survey* (1925), he became recognised as a foremost authority on Shakespeare and the Elizabethan theatre. His critique of Maugham represents one of his rare forays into dramatic criticism.

Mr W.S. Maugham has caught his feet in the net of irony. In *A Man of Honour*, produced by the Stage Society at the Imperial Theatre, he has presented, with considerable insight and no sentimentality, an episode in the life of an idealist. Basil Kent is a barrister and a man of letters. He is full of high purposes and heroic illusions. He has volunteered to South Africa as a trooper, and has obtained a medal for distinguished service. At the beginning of the play he is in a considerable state of moral exaltation. He has seduced a girl, Jenny Bush, a barmaid, and a child is expected. Jenny is irretrievably common, and has a brother who is a bounder of the first water. Basil does not love her—in fact he more than half loves Hilda Murray. But he has resolved to marry her. In reply to the remonstrances of his friend, John Halliwell, who urges the common-sense view of the matter, he takes lofty ground. It is his point of honour; and besides, the child must not slink into the world like a thief. Nothing can stir him from his determination. Unfortunately in marriage, it is not the first step which costs. The flush of Basil Kent's heroics fades away, and he is face to face with the daily problem of the life he has set himself. He makes but little effort to solve it. Practice at the bar and a villa at Putney do not afford many opportunities for the more picturesque virtues. To earn his living is irksome to him, and debts accumulate. The impossible brother-in-law pervades the house and borrows money. The baby dies. Jenny offends his fastidious taste in every action and every word. He takes refuge in sarcasm, a weapon which unliterary people do not understand, but do not the less resent. The brother-in-law endures the lash of Basil's tongue for the occasional pickings in the way of sovereigns and good cigars which the association yields; Jenny for the love she bears him. But she is not, on her side, able to control her temper or her speech, and the villa at Putney rings with recriminations. Meanwhile, Basil has not ceased to see, and even to philander with, Hilda Murray. Jenny, who opens his letters and follows him in the street, learns this and drives him to further distraction with her jealousy. He has given her no very serious cause for it until a day when, after a more bitter scene than usual at home, he takes refuge in Hilda's house, and declares his passion for her. Hilda is also something of a moral idealist. She repulses him, and adjures him to be faithful to his duty. Ultimately, however, she gives way. At that moment enters Jenny, who has forced her way into the house, looking more vulgar than ever, and violently upbraids the woman who has robbed her of her husband. Hilda is a little moved, leaves the room, and sends in a message to Basil announcing her intended marriage to Robert Brackley, a minor poet. Jenny has a glimpse of hope, and entreats Basil to 'give her another chance,' but he is merciless, tells her that he never loved and now has done with her, and departs without listening to her entreaties or her threats of suicide. Probably he knows well enough that a threat of suicide is a common form with women of the barmaid type when they are crossed in love. Jenny, however, as a matter of fact, does commit suicide, walking the same night into the Thames. The final act shows us the idealist in the depths of remorse, crying out somewhat hysterically, but not wholly without truth, that he is his wife's murderer. The faithful John Halliwell does his best to comfort him and to point the obvious moral that you should not enter upon a path which is not that of ordinary men, unless you are quite sure that you have the strength to walk in it. He also undertakes the duty of buying off the obnoxious brother-in-law, who loudly expresses his intention of getting his knife into Basil at the inquest. Then Mr Maugham allows his irony full swing. Before long Basil confesses that after all, instead of passing, as even the housemaid had done, a sleepless night, with his wife lying dead in the next room, he had managed to drop into a doze upon the sofa; and further that, even in the midst of his grief, he is conscious, shamefully conscious, at the back of his mind, of nothing so much as an immense sense of freedom. Somewhat Ibsenitishly, he jumps up, pulls the blind, and lets a flood of morning light stream in through the window. It also emerges that he has already telegraphed to Hilda Murray, and presently Hilda enters, dressed with extreme propriety in black, and full of condolences with her 'poor friend'. Her appearance almost precisely coincides with that of the coroner's officer.

Mr Maugham's play is certainly not impeccable. There are passages which drag. The ironical intention might perhaps have been made more manifest from the beginning; and I think that the introduction of the brother-in-law, who after all is mainly of the nature of comic relief, in the middle of the stress of the last act, was an error of judgment. But it is good honest work, well written, well constructed, and with a point of view of its own; and the Stage Society may fairly claim the production of it as a feather in their cap. Of course, as my acute colleagues of the daily press have not been slow to remark, it is very probable that, for all its merits, it would not be altogether a success upon the commercial stage. As one of them very properly points out, that unfortunate last act almost wholly destroys the respect of the audience for the hero. It must be admitted, I am afraid, that the London playgoer dislikes irony, if possible, even more than he dislikes tragedy. But a few unimportant alterations would doubtless enable Mr Maugham to recast his conception into a form which would be more acceptable to the general public. Actors of more established reputation, although they would hardly give a more competent interpretation than that which I saw on Monday, would naturally prove attractive. Stress might be laid on the comic relief, and Brackley, the minor poet, might become, as one critic suggests that he ought to have been, the leading feature of the performance. And of course a more sympathetic ending is essential. I imagine it running something like this. Jenny Kent is carried streaming from the Thames and laid on the sofa. Basil, in floods of tears, realises too late that she has been his only love and that he has lost her. Suddenly she stirs, sighs, opens her eyes. Restoratives are applied. Slowly she comes back to life. Basil is kneeling by her side. There are embraces, pardons, protestations. Jenny will not be vulgar any more, nor Basil critical. Hilda Murray may go and marry her Brackley. And so the curtain falls upon a Putney villa turned into an Earthly Paradise. Once more the British public streams out into Charing Cross Road or the Strand, with the generous tear upon the satisfied cheek. I hope that Mr Maugham will take advantage of my hints. They are not copyright. He will doubtless get his reward in royalties. But I do not feel so sure that he will himself care to witness a representation of *A Man of Honour*.

18. Max Beerbohm, 'An Uncommercial Play', *Saturday Review* (London)

XCVII, 5 March 1904, 207-8

(Sir) Henry Maximilian Beerbohm (1872–1956), author and caricaturist, succeeded George Bernard Shaw as dramatic critic of the *Saturday Review* in 1898. In spite of protesting to the latter 'in fact I don't care a damn about the theatre', Max held the post with distinction until 1910, a period largely coinciding with Maugham's successful run of plays produced before the Great War. Max's theatrical criticism may be read in *Around Theatres* (2 vols, 1924), *More Theatres* (1969) and *Last Theatres* (1970), the latter two volumes edited by Rupert Hart-Davis.

Max had seen the original Stage Society production of *A Man of Honour* and written a paragraph about it (*Saturday Review*, 28 February 1903), in which he said: 'The second act, in which husband and wife are bickering, is admirably conceived and written; and the third act is a fine piece of emotional drama. The rest of the play falls to pieces.'

A Man of Honour was produced lately at the Avenue (where it is still running). Thanks to the Stage Society! For, certainly, no manager would have dared the play on the merits of the MS. Only the impression made through the previous medium of the Stage Society could have won the benefit of commercial doubt. I hope the thing will pay its way. A little tragedy of modern life, unrelieved by taradiddles or even by titles, is a rather bitter pill for the public maw. No visual splendour of frocks or scenery can be dragged in. The manager of the Avenue does not attempt to gild the pill. He does but add a little jam, nervously. Throughout the entr'actes, the orchestra plays the newest waltzes and selections from the newest musical comedies; and, when the curtain falls on the conclusion of the whole matter, the house is played out to a tune whose words (have you been to the Adelphi?) are 'My heart's

in a whirl as I kiss each curl of my cosy-corner girl.' A very fair
house it was, on the night of my visit. And the play was very well
received—with many hearty laughs in the wrong places. There,
you perceive, is the best chance of success for a modern tragedy.
The public is so very unsuspicious.

I called Mr Maugham's play 'a little tragedy' with no loose use of
the diminutive. For here we have a tragic love-conflict not between
naked soul and naked soul, but between upper-middle-class soul
and lower-class soul. An average barrister marries an average
barmaid, and all that intervenes to make them unhappy is the
divergence of their up-bringings. Their tragedy is not the less real,
however, because it is superficial, social, little; and Mr Maugham
has made of it a more poignant play than any we have had since
Grierson's Way. Not that the play is perfect, by any means. Basil
Kent, the barrister, is not so well drawn as the barmaid, Jenny
Bush. Her commonness is real and convincing, his gentility
is—genteel, in the later sense of the word. He is, in fact, a snob. In
the first act we see him with his friend Halliwell, a brother of the
woman with whom he is really in love. Jenny Bush, whom he has
promised to marry, arrives with her brother, Harry. Harry
swaggers aggressively, and addresses his host's friend as ''Alliwell.'
'*H*alliwell,' says the friend. And Kent is like unto him. He offers
Harry a cigar. Harry is impressed by the brand. 'How much,' he
asks, 'do these run you in for?' 'They were a present to me,' replies
corrective Kent; 'I do not know what they cost....Won't you take
off the label before you light it?' I do not say that well-bred people
never behave in an ill-bred way: they very often do. But Kent's
misbehaviour is dramatically an irrelevance; and it is a damaging
irrelevance, for (dramatically) it stamps him as a snob, and so mars
the right balance of the play. In the second act again, after his
marriage with Jenny Bush, we find him engaged in lording it over
Harry with long-worded sarcasms; and for us Harry becomes the
far less insufferable of the two. All our sympathy goes to the wife.
Mr Maugham, of course, meant to hold the scales evenly. He
meant us to feel no less sympathy for the husband than for the wife.
Those are the most interesting, the most moving cases of
incompatibility—the cases in which neither person is to blame.
Kent's part ought to be revised unsparingly.

The last act has been revised since the first production, but not
unsparingly enough. Indeed, I prefer the original version. Jenny, as

you may remember, had committed suicide, and there was to be an inquest. Kent gradually confessed to Halliwell his intense relief at finding himself free; and the play ended with the entry of the widow whom he wished to marry. Well, this was too harsh, too indecent, to be real. Kent was a sentimentalist. He would not have confessed to himself—much less to anyone else—the unlovely joy that was in his heart; and he would not have sent for Mrs Murray. Nevertheless, she and he would have come together, after a decent interval, and by that time he would have become callous enough not to conceal the truth about his own sensations. In fact, the ending of the play was right in itself, but wrong in its date: for verisimilitude, that decent interval was needed. In the amended last act, we don't get the decent interval, and we don't get the logical conclusion. Except for a word or two blurted out by Kent just before the curtain falls, we know nothing of his sensations, except that he is shocked by his wife's suicide. As for the future, we are left to presume that the widow will marry a ridiculous person to whom she is engaged. The whole act has to depend for its interest on the success of Halliwell in preventing Harry Bush from making a fuss at the inquest. And who of us cares twopence whether Harry Bush makes a fuss at the inquest or not? That is neither here nor there. Why niggle over this travesty of a happy ending? Such irrelevant manoeuvring is quite unworthy of the play that Mr Maugham has written—unworthy of the simplicity with which he has carried the story forward, and of the insight and sympathy with which he has drawn all the characters—yes, all of them, for the faults in the presentment of Kent, though they are so damaging, are merely superficial. I have read two or three novels by Mr Maugham, and *A Man of Honour* seems to me inferior to any of them. But it is a blessing, and a surprise, to find a novelist trying to do his best in dramatic form and failing to do it only through lack of experience in the new medium, instead of trying to do his worst, for lucre, and doing it. There is no reason to suppose that anon Mr Maugham as playwright will not be the equal of Mr Maugham as novelist. Meanwhile, as a matter of conscience, and for sake of practice, let him re-revise the last act of *A Man of Honour*, and cleanse Kent of that deadly coating of snobbishness. Also (a smaller matter, but not unimportant) let him test the vocal quality of his dialogue, throughout. For the most part his characters talk vocally enough; but now and again they tend to become scriptive. Halliwell, for example: 'Matrimony, like hanging, is rather a desperate remedy.' I have no objection to epigrams: people do occasionally make epigrams in real life. But they don't do it like that; and the sentence I have quoted is an example of how it is not done. 'Matrimony is like hanging. It is rather a desperate remedy'—there you have the speakable form. I am hair-splitting? Well, the difference between what can be written and what can be spoken is a subtle difference, I admit; but it is a difference that matters a good deal, especially in a realistic play. Sometimes, Mr Maugham errs in the opposite way: his characters sometimes talk too naturally. Halliwell, again: 'The smiles of women are the very breath of your nostrils.' Halliwell, in real life, might be guilty of that dreadful phrase—surely the most dreadful phrase ever uttered. But the dramatist must select, must edit. Nothing that does not sound as if it could be spoken by a real person should be put into the lips of a puppet; but, gentle syllogist, not everything that sounds so should be put there.

Mr Maugham's play is performed by clever people. But it is not well performed by them. They are on the wrong tack. This is not surprising. It would be surprising to find a poetic romance acted in the right manner; for poetic romance, though we still have examples of it, is a bygone dramatic form; and always the dramatic form conditions the acting; and, when it dies, the right way to act it dies also. Prosaic realism is the form towards which we are tending; but we have not reached it yet: such plays as *A Man of Honour* are only, as it were, the outposts of the form; and consequently our mimes have not yet acquired the right method of interpreting it. Their style is conditioned by the form of drama which they, and we, know best—a form in which romanticism and realism are commingled. And thus, when the curtain rises on *A Man of Honour* and discovers Mr Ben Webster as Kent and Mr Charles Hallard as Halliwell, we very soon feel that though neither Mr Webster nor Mr Hallard is a swashbuckler talking in iambics, neither the one nor the other of them is (as Mr Maugham means him to be) an ordinary young man of today, sitting in an ordinary room in the Temple, and behaving in an ordinary manner. Both are physically so very radiant, so very gallant in bearing, in manner so very significant. Both talk sometimes slowly, sometimes quickly, but always slowlier or quicklier than is usual; and always their voices either rise higher or sink lower than is usual. Of the two, Mr Ben Webster is the further from our humdrum existence; and this is a pity, for on him falls the greater burden of the play. The best scene is in the second act, when the husband and wife quarrel. It is a wonderfully natural and well-graduated scene—vulgar suspicion from the wife, weary irony from the husband, violent taunts from the wife, long-pent outburst from the husband, and so forth. But there are no gradations in Mr Webster's acting, and no naturalness: from first to last he is the agonised troubadour, desperately facing the audience. And Miss Muriel Wylford, who plays the wife—she, too, is constantly appealing to the audience. She is a clever and sensitive actress, evidently; and she does try, conscientiously, to be quite natural. But the absence of any experience in frank realism, coupled with the presence of Mr Webster, forces her to decorate an admirably conceived performance with stage-tricks. She tries hard, moreover, not to be charming and refined and obviously sympathetic; but only now and then does she succeed. All the other performers, with one exception, are of the stage stagey. Mr George Trollope, as Harry Bush, is a very sharp exception. His performance is interesting as an example of how much a part depends on its interpreter—how creative a power for good or evil the actor can be. When the play was produced by the Stage Society, the part of Harry Bush seemed to be just that bit of threadbare convention, the stage Cockney, the shade of Sam Weller. Later, when I read the play, I found that Harry Bush was quite a possible figure. But, now that he is impersonated by Mr Trollope, he becomes something more than that: one sees in him the incarnation of a whole class—of a whole modern class that is quite new upon the stage. One has seen them, these young men, lounging outside public bars and music-halls—a little lower than the baser sort of bank-clerk, a little higher than the Hooligan; pretentious, without the vitality to rise; malevolent without the vitality for mischief; gloomily dissipated; the most sordid outcome, so far, of our urban civilisation. And here we have, as it were, a synthesis of them all. Mr Trollope is a character-actor of the first water.

LADY FREDERICK

Royal Court Theatre, London, 26 October 1907 (transferred to
Garrick Theatre, Criterion Theatre, New Theatre and Haymarket
Theatre) (422 performances)
[Written 1903. Published London, 1911]

19. J. T. Grein, review, *Sunday Times*

27 October 1907, 7

Jacob Thomas Grein (1862–1935) was born in Amsterdam.
'Jack' Grein, a naturalised British subject, was an innovative
theatrical impresario and a drama critic with a wide know-
ledge of the European theatre. In the 1890s his Independent
Theatre Club had pioneered the work of Ibsen and Shaw in
London. He was appointed drama critic of the *Sunday Times*
in 1897, a post he held until 1918 when he was most unjustly
dismissed because of a libel action involving a production of
Wilde's *Salomé* which he had sponsored. (See *The Pearl of
Days: Intimate Memoir of The Sunday Times 1822–1972* by
Hobson, Knightley and Russell, London, 1972.)

Lady Frederick is what Oliver de Jalin in the *Demi Monde* calls a
'speckled peach.' Only the speckles are English and not damaging
to the goods. She haunts Monte Carlo; she has debts; she touches
up hair and complexion; she lost her husband conveniently early;
she is a woman with whom all men between eighteen and eighty
are apt to fall in love; she has antecedents of which some chapters
are shrouded in mystery. No wonder that women—'the
Competition'—look askance at her, and that Lady Mereston is
anxious to prevent a match with her boy of twenty-two, who is

terribly smitten. But Lady Frederick is a good sort. She could disarm the mother by making use of a packet of compromising letters which would rather disturb the pious memories of the late Lord Mereston. It would cost her no trouble whatsoever to lead the boy to the altar, although ugly means are used to blacken her character. She, however, prefers to adopt the methods of David Garrick; disenchantment is a patent medicine. And so we see in the last act how Lady Frederick, before her toilet table, fights time and wrinkles, and how the boy battles with his vanishing illusions. In the end Lady Frederick marries an old love whom the impulsive Irish girl had refused in her school days, when a title was more alluring than a loving heart.

Mr W.S. Maugham, who revealed such great talent in *The Man of Honour*, made in this pleasant little play his first attempt at comedy, and, on the whole, he succeeded well enough. It is not quite a lifelike comedy, nor is it free from the artifice and calculation which was customary in the days of the 'well-made play'. There is something mechanical in the humour and in the characters which would have prompted me if I had read the manuscript to advise the author to change the time of the action. To me these delightful, well-spoken, gracefully conversational people are not of to-day. I see them in the formal surroundings and clothes of the late sixties; I see them even more forcibly in the picturesque raiment of powder and wig. Indeed, if light verse were substituted for prose Mr Maugham would have found in his story exquisite material for a poetic comedy. But I must take the work as it is presented, and undoubtedly, despite its corseted form and somewhat antiquated devices, it has charm. For all that Mr Maugham is by nature not a comedy-writer: he has the mind dramatic. Give him strong situations—things which grip—and he is the right man to handle them firmly and with originality. There is a scene in the second act which is in the true vein of the author of *The Man of Honour*. It is the moment when, in order to undo Lady Frederick, the mother of her boy lover produces a letter in which the heroine stands self-confessed of a liaison. It is an old letter; all the parties mentioned in it are dead, save Lady Frederick. Her sole weapon of defence is her word of honour—the declaration that the letter served to save a friend. Of course, her antagonists doubt her word, but so powerfully, so convincingly is the scene written, and so beautifully is it acted by Miss Ethel Irving, that the hearer is fully persuaded of her truthfulness. It is a human scene which will prove the mainstay of the play.

In many respects the cast has been chosen with great acumen. Miss Ethel Irving, all mobility, impulse, emotion as the Irish widow, has never acted so well. She made the audience love Lady Frederick at first sight, she maintained the interest to the last moment. Even the somewhat laborious episode in the dressing-room, when we were initiated into many secrets of the complex-ionist, was attractive because the actors played without the least affectation. Mr C.M. Lowne handled the elderly admirer with great discretion, and never excited the derisive smile so ready at the expense of the middle-aged lovers, and Mr Arthur Holmes-Gore actually succeeded in impersonating an Anglo-Hebrew money-lender without exaggeration. He made a semi-gentleman of him, somewhat overdressed and obtrusive, but on a footing of peace with the pronunciation of English. It was quite a novel and an excellent performance. Mr Graham Browne was rather too virile for the boy lover, and Miss Beryl Faber played the mother in an effective and severe manner. A delightful little characterisation in comedy was the French dressmaker with social aspirations by Miss Florence Wood. It was fraught with heredity. When the time comes for Miss Wood to powder her hair, she may prove herself a worthy successor to her distinguished mother, Mrs John Wood. *Lady Frederick* is an entertainment which (from impressions gathered at the dress-rehearsal) should appeal to all playgoers who know how to appreciate good acting and the graceful pleasantry of an author of distinction.

20. Reginald Turner, review, *Academy*

LXXIII, 2 November 1907, 96–7

Reginald Turner (1869–1938), journalist, wit, author of several novels, devoted friend of Oscar Wilde, was the illegitimate son of the first proprietor of the *Daily Telegraph*, Lord Burnham.

The name of one great actress—a perfect artist—was on everybody's lips on Saturday night. 'What a part for her,' we all said,
'and how marvellous she would have been in it. Why is she not?'
But, really, Miss Ethel Irving made us forget our regrets and give
ourselves up wholly to her wonderful talent and charm till, by the
end of the play, she had become for us the one and only Lady
Frederick, and Lady Frederick had become Miss Ethel Irving. It
was a delicious evening, full of delight from start to finish. The
success of a first night can generally be gauged by the *entr'actes*. On
this occasion during the intervals we were all gay and good-
humoured, at our very best, pleased to see our friends, and,
infected with the author's vitality, saying our brightest things. It
was not a perfect play from the technical point of view, there were
'scenes' which had nothing to do with the main action, there were
stage tricks which have served before. But it was a perfect piece of
work, because what the author did he did deliberately, 'of malice
afore-thought,' and he got the greatest possible effect out of his
efforts. He was completely, splendidly successful.

The story details how Lady Frederick Berolles, an Irish widow
with a personality and a brogue irresistible in force and charm, is
wooed by the young Marquis of Mereston, whose mother is
horrified at the prospect of her son marrying someone whose
escapades have given a salacious world a just cause for criticism.
Lady Mereston's brother, an old adorer who, though he had once
been made ridiculous by Lady Frederick, still admires her, joins
with his sister in trying to prevent the marriage. For this purpose
they plot to bring up her past against her. Lady Frederick is
flattered by the young man's devotion, though she does not really
intend to marry him; but she wishes to refuse him in her own way,
and resents bitterly the attempt to force her to give him up. She
prefers to show her complete mastery of the situation and then to
retire gracefully with all the honours of the victory while she
declines its fruits. It is all the more magnanimous of her in that she
is desperately in need of money to save her own and her brother's
honour, when the alternative of not getting it is ruin or marriage
with a blackmailing gentleman who holds her bills. But she is not
one to worry, and she comes through her troubles with reckless
confidence and a genius for getting her own way.

In the course of her fencing with the Mereston family we see her
delivering her deadliest thrust with the sweetest of smiles and the

71

most perfect good temper, but there comes a time when Lady
Mereston brings a charge against her in the presence of her son and
brother. It is a great moment. Lady Frederick explains the matter
with a perfection of simplicity and truth, a pathetic dignity which
convinces all of us, except the (perhaps) too harshly-drawn mother.
The insulted woman goes further: she burns the letters which
would have destroyed Lady Mereston's most sacred memories, and
then—having up to now been perfectly quiet and restrained—she
breaks out into a storm of emotional protest. The scene, which was
splendidly conceived by the author and perfectly executed by the
actress, profoundly moved the audience. Having triumphed and
brought Lord Mereston, an ardent lover, to his knees, she refuses
the great prize; but that he may not suffer over-much by her refusal
she makes the renunciation at her dressing-table, appearing first in
the strong sunlight, bare of the charms her art of making-up added
to her. It is exquisite comedy, this scene in which she gradually
grows more beautiful, the while she cynically and lightheartedly
explains 'how it is done,' till, at last, radiant as ever, she has crushed
the passionate illusions out of the boy for ever.

There is a delightful interlude in the second act, when two young
lovers have a dispute as to the education of their possible son, and
the father, at first shocked at overhearing so improper a discussion,
is drawn into it and becomes the most heated of them all. The
young girl in this scene was charmingly played by Miss Beatrice
Terry, who shows great promise of worthily carrying on the torch
of her illustrious family. There is another interlude which shows
Lady Frederick wheedling a dressmaker into taking back her
demand to be paid. It was highly successful as showing one side of
Lady Frederick's power, and it delighted me. The whole company
ably seconded Miss Ethel Irving in her wonderful achievement, Mr
C.M. Lowne in a very telling part being particularly satisfactory.

The only fly in the amber of appreciation seems to be that Mr
Maugham is also the author of *A Man of Honour*. Surely that he
wrote that strong and powerful piece of realism should only make
us more laudatory when he follows it with this witty, original and
exquisitely-wrought study of a fascinating personality.

JACK STRAW

Vaudeville Theatre, London, 26 March 1908 (321 performances)
[Written 1905. Published London, December 1911]

21. J.T. Grein, review, *Sunday Times*

29 March 1908, 4

In our world of letters Mr Somerset Maugham is a remarkable personality. Since the late Grant Allen we have not possessed an author so versatile—so omniscient in the application of the pen. And in one respect Mr Maugham has even outdistanced Grant Allen, for since the latter attempted, but never established, a footing on the stage, the former was from the beginning as successful on the boards as between covers. If *Liza of Lambeth* and *Mrs Craddock* were novels which rank in English literature, *The Man of Honour* was a play which revealed at once a profound observer and a dramatist born. When we have that National Theatre, for which some of us have *worked* for twenty years when those who now merely talk about it never gave it a thought, *A Man of Honour* cannot fail to figure in its repertoire. And if there be room in it for the lighter muse, I, for one, should vote for a similar distinction for *Lady Frederick*.

Now, as regards Mr Maugham's latest and deservedly undisputed success, *Jack Straw*, which is as light as a feather and as saucy as a sparrow, the principal thing to be said is that it reveals a new feature of his chameleonic talent. *Lady Frederick* was pure comedy of fantasy, *Jack Straw* is comedy of reality broadened by farcical extravagance. It is not absolutely probable that an archduke should masquerade as a waiter in a great London hotel; then masquerade as an archduke evolved from a waiter in a hypersnobbish county

73

family of *nouveaux riches*; and finally marry the daughter of the house, who, by the alliance, would become a member of a great reigning family. But, wildly absurd as it seems, the possibility is acceptable, and the United States are there to prove it. When I was in America some years ago all New York was interested in a tram-conductor who was discovered to be a German Count, and forthwith he was admitted amongst the 400 and considered a very eligible party. And even London is there to prove it, for Society asks no questions anent ancestry when a newcomer is accompanied by the passport of untold wealth. Such is the world we live in, and it was evidently that world which Mr Maugham intended to illuminate and to blister with the radium of his satire. The success of this wily design was immediate and electric. The play is likely to fascinate all London and to irritate a good many of those 'whom it may concern.' It should likewise achieve great notoriety in the States, where the situations would strike home even more forcibly than in the old country.

With all that, there is nothing bitter in Mr Maugham's humour. His gay roguishness, the quickness of his wit, the clever finish of the game which, to a certain extent, reinstates the discomfited snobs in our sympathy, will send all his listeners away content and heartily amused. For as Sarcey so cogently puts it, our author has '*la main leste.*' He is light of touch, he sounds but does not harp on his strings; he alludes to the vulgarity of parvenus but does not render it painful; with a deft hand he outlines the inwardness of a character in a single sentence; he is a born dramatist, for he tells in swiftness a volume of detail. Besides, he possesses the gift, all too rare in the average English play, of blending humour with grace of expression. There is a speech in the second act wherein the Archduke, now temporarily exposed as the ex-waiter of the London hotel, forecasts to his snobbish hostess how his exposure will hold up the family to ridicule from one end of the land to the other, from Europe across the Atlantic to America, which is a little masterpiece of vivid imagination. To describe it rightly I should have to borrow Hervieu's title and call it *La Course du Flambeau*. One literally follows the heliograph of derision flying across township, field, and waters until the whole country is ablaze.

It may be said that I make much of a play, which is but a light comedy tinged with farce, which soars not very high, which is good fun, and nothing more, and I am willing to accept the soft impeachment. For there is justification. We are always prone to discount our own capacity and to extol the exotic. We are always ready to say: 'Ah, but see how French playwrights manage it.' Well, here is an English—real English—play which is every whit as good as the Palais-Royal and Nouveauté's plays, and a good deal better, for if its satire may propel the blush of silent endorsement, it does not contain a breath of equivocal unpleasantness. And since *esprit* in comedy is what we are always yearning for, we should rejoice now that we have got it. Those rejoicings would have been even more emphatic if the acting had been worthy of the play. But, except the impersonation of the leading parts by Miss Lottie Venne and Mr Hawtrey, and three minor parts by Messrs Hignett, Robert Whyte, jun., and Percy Goodyer, there was little to boast of. It is irksome to be ungallant, but really the fair sex by their acting scarcely adorned the canvas; often the young ladies were quite inaudible. As for the two artists named they were wholly admirable, they carried the action with unflagging spirit, and carried it to victory. Mr Charles Hawtrey as a bearded waiter and Mr Hawtrey as the princely gentleman was a study in itself to behold. He never over-acted the character, but he always let us feel that he was laughing up his sleeve; that this was comedy and destined to make us happy. As for Miss Lottie Venne, whoever knows the quaint manner of this gifted actress can imagine what she would make of a little aitchless burgess who through a windfall imagines herself better than all the world. Her portraiture cannot be described; it can only be indicated by inference. If only the whole of the cast had been selected with the same discrimination as the principals! But since it was otherwise the author of *Jack Straw* has every reason to be satisfied with his great success, and with the quality of his work.

22. Max Beerbohm, review, *Saturday Review* (London)

CV, 4 April 1908, 431–2

The opening paragraph of this article probably refers to a meeting between Maugham and Max at Merton Abbey as the guests of Mrs George Steevens (the model for Lady Frederick). See Maugham's Preface to *What a Life!* by Doris Arthur-Jones (London, 1932; reprinted in *A Traveller in Romance,* London, 1984).

One sunny afternoon, when the twentieth century was younger than it is now, a novelist and a dramatic critic might have been observed pacing up and down a lawn, in deep conversation. It was of the drama that they were talking. The novelist had not long ago written a play, which had been produced by some society and so much admired that some manager had presently put it into the evening bill. There the critics had admired it as much as ever, repeating their praises of its truthfulness, its humanity, and all that. The public, however, had not taken the advice to go and see it. It was, indeed, a play foredoomed by the melancholy grimness of its subject. The author had extenuated nothing. There was no gilding of the pill; and the pill, accordingly, was not swallowed. Disappointed, but unbowed, the author was now declaring to the critic his resolution to write more plays. The critic, who had always admired greatly the author's novels, urged him to leave the theatre alone. He pointed out that, good as the play had been, it had not been so good as the novels. Drama, he insisted, was a damnable business, at best. The outlines had to be so arbitrary, the colours so thickly laid on. The most subtle of characters on the stage was far more obvious than the simplest and most straightforward of one's fellow creatures. In writing a novel, one did not have to make these wholesale surrenders. One could be as subtle as life itself, said the critic. And, since the talent of the novelist to whom he was talking 'like a father' was essentially a subtle talent, the less traffic it had

76

with the theatre the better it would thrive. The theatre could gain little by it, whereas, insidiously, the theatre would mar it for its proper use. Commercially, of course, the theatre was a tempting thing. There were pots of money to be made out of the theatre, by some people. 'But,' said the critic, pausing in his walk and tapping the novelist on the breast, rather impressively, 'you, my boy, are not one of those people.' The novelist seemed to acquiesce, not without a certain gloom. And the critic, sorry for him, yet conscious of having done a good afternoon's work, briskly changed the subject.

I will not give the name of either the novelist or the critic. Enough that the scene recurred to me, and made me smile not a little, several times in the course of the performance of *Jack Straw* at the Vaudeville Theatre. It is seldom that the public and the critics are found at unison about a play. *Jack Straw* is one of the rare instances. The public acclaims it as loudly as it has been acclaimed by the public's guides. Personally, I cannot be quite so enthusiastic as my colleagues. *Jack Straw* does not seem to me so good an example of Mr Somerset Maugham's talent as was *Lady Frederick* (which was produced when I was away, and of which it is too late to write now). It is altogether on a lower level—the level of farce; and there is little of sheer invention in the farcical figures and situations. The Parker-Jennings family is one which we have seen—on the stage—more times than we could count. In real life they would, of course, be quite new to us. A humble family, resident in Brixton, suddenly inheriting two millions of money, and thereby launched into the great world, would become the more humble in its new environment. It would certainly not assume blatant airs. It would provide a case for sympathy, not for ridicule. By immemorial tradition of the stage, however, nouveaux riches are always blatant, always ridiculous; and Mr Somerset Maugham lays the colours on with a trowel. As Mrs Parker-Jennings, Miss Lottie Venne, in whom are no fine shades, and in whom is an incomparable command of the primary colours of farce, has the best part she has had for years. I need hardly say that Miss Parker-Jennings is very different from the rest of her family. Tradition demands a serious 'love interest' in even the wildest farces; and the public will not take seriously the heart of a maiden who is not wholly refined. In *A Man of Honour* Mr Maugham displayed to the public the golden heart of a barmaid. The public would none of it. Even were people tolerant of tragedy in modern life, *A Man of Honour* would have failed because the heroine was not a lady. Miss Parker-Jennings (like so many other daughters of nouveaux riches on the stage) leaves nothing to be desired in the matter of lady-likeness. Otherwise, how could the play be rounded off by her betrothal to the hero? Mr Hawtrey, as that hero, has a part that skilfully gives him all his usual chances, with a few new ones thrown in. The effect of him in an auburn and bifurcated beard is in itself so startling as to ensure the success of the first act. And at the end of the second act, before making a silent exit, he has occasion to turn and wink at the other persons of the play. Some twelve years ago, the United States of America were profoundly stirred by 'the Cissie Fitzgerald wink'. I shall not be surprised if the Hawtrey wink creates an equally deep impression here. In its slowness, its solemnity, its richness, it is as memorable as it is indescribable, and can be likened only to an eclipse of the sun. To deceive is (I need hardly say) the hero's business throughout the play; but the character is differentiated from the regular 'Hawtrey part' by the fact that it is a deception within a deception. Jack Straw, a waiter in the Grand Babylon Hotel, is palmed off by Lady Wanley on the Parker-Jenningses as an Archduke of Pomerania, in order that she may avenge a slight. But an Archduke of Pomerania he actually is. And hereby Mr Maugham avoids what would otherwise be a distinctly jarring note in the farce. It was all very well for Congreve, Molière, and other playwrights of the past, to show a lacquey palmed off as a great gentleman on pretentious persons. That, according to the standards of the time, was a quite legitimate joke; and we, switching ourselves back into that time, are not offended by it. But we should flinch from it in a contemporary play. We are too tender for such barbarities. We should be pitying the victims of the joke, and condemning the player of it. Lady Wanley, indeed, does not know that the waiter is what she pretends him to be; but our own knowledge is enough to soothe us, to keep us in the mood of laughter. Mr Maugham keeps us laughing loudly throughout his play. Such as it is, the thing could not have been better done. But it is far from being the best kind of thing that Mr. Maugham can do.

MRS DOT

Comedy Theatre, London, 27 April 1908 (272 performances)
[Written 1904. Published London, November 1921]

23. Unsigned review, *Illustrated London News*

CXXXII, 2 May 1908, 658

Obviously Mr Maugham has given himself over to the business of amusing the public, and has left the drama of ideas to others. Thanks to this change of policy, success has so crowned his efforts that he can just now boast of having no less than three plays running simultaneously at West-End theatres. But we have so few authors who can provide us with the champagne kind of drama, who can keep an audience in peals of laughter without resorting to illegitimate means, that it would be the height of folly not to accept thankfully what Mr Maugham is disposed to give. Of course, such 'light comedy' as *Mrs Dot* goes only skin-deep in its studies of character, though in his new piece's first act the playwright hits off very happily the main traits of his heroine—a rich widow who finds that the man she wishes to marry is already engaged and cannot, he thinks, because he has become suddenly a Peer, break his promise. That act may fairly be called comedy. The whole development of the situation therein set out is farcical, though it is wonderfully bright and inspiriting farce. Miss Marie Tempest has had many good parts, but none that has fitted her comedy gifts quite so perfectly as this of Mrs Dot; her tantrums are delicious fun. Mr Kerr, too, as the lawyer, backs her up admirably.

24. J.T. Grein, review, *Sunday Times*

3 May 1908, 4

'Have you seen Somerset Maugham's trilogy?' will probably be one of the topical questions of the season. For to-day the author who but a little while ago dispatched play after play to London managers in vain quest of recognition is the proud commander of three London theatres. His position is unique, not only in our metropolis, but in the universal sense, and one has to go back to the early days of Sardou to find a popularity similar and so sudden. And as Sardou deserved his success when he wrote *Nos Intimes* and the delightful comedies of the same kinship, so Somerset Maugham has well earned the favourable turn of the tide. One may spend three evenings with his work—with *Lady Frederick, Jack Straw*, and *Mrs Dot*, and never will there be the slightest suspicion of sameness—indeed, I venture to say that, labelled with another name, the plays might claim three different fathers instead of one. This great diversity of imagination, coupled with his keen sense of humour and human introspection (derived no doubt from his qualifications as a doctor), are the main secrets of Maugham's success. His stagecraft is perfect; he commands it by intuition and by careful observation of French methods, but it is not so much the workmanship of his plays which pleases and fascinates us so mightily, but the delicacy of style and the thousand and one little traits of humour which, in words of lightning quickness, sketch a situation, a phase of life, a characteristic of a coterie. The story of *Mrs Dot*, charming as it is, may well be termed to be of no consequence. If somebody were to characterise it as *Man and Superman*, that is, man's subjugation into marriage by woman's perseverance and stratagem, narrated by an agreeable and witty conversationalist, instead of a trenchant and cynical controversialist, he would be about right. Mrs Dot is the delightful widow of untold wealth (extracted from beer), who has made up her mind to disentangle the man she loves from a premature and temperamentally unsuitable engagement and carries the day by using infinite resource and that peculiar capacity of anticipating events which is the gift of every woman (and of so few men). How Mrs Dot renders the impossible possible; how she plots and coaxes and inveigles and gently coerces all her surroundings into the conspiracy which will end in her own happiness and everybody else's, I must leave to Mr Somerset Maugham to tell you; I can only whet your appetite, but I cannot convey by second-hand narrative the real charm of the play. For charm is the predominant quality of this little work as far as the average spectator is concerned; he feels that the world is not quite as Mr Maugham farcically imagines it; he feels that Mr Maugham bends the order of things to his *esprit;* he—outside the playhouse—would smile at Mr Maugham's all too fanciful dealings with special licenses of marriage (see *Whitaker's Almanack*); he would, if the author were not so witty, complain of the protraction of the second and third acts, but—he has no inclination nor the will to worry about details. He is under the gentle narcotic of charm, and the dramatist can sway and tickle him and manoeuvre him as he chooses; he is the master of the situation. And, after all, the mental condition of pleasure in which we find ourselves is not only due to fascination, there is in this as in all Mr Maugham's work, albeit novel or play, something which, despite seeming superficiality, prompts us to afterthoughts. He is not merely a student of human nature in detail; he is a connoisseur of society in its general constitution. His characters are types, and every one of them, besides being a capital figure of the stage, contains a spark of real vitality.

With this delightful play, delightfully acted as it is by Mr Fred Kerr, Mr Graham Browne, Mr Kenneth Douglas, Mr Herbert Ross, all suited to perfection in accordance with their personality and stage tradition; by Miss Lydia Bilbrooke, a beautiful newcomer who plays sweet eighteen in unaffected innocence, yet with intelligence; by Miss Marie Illington, who, clever as she always is, clings too much to 'suburban distinction'; with such talent, histrionic and dramatic, *Mrs Dot* is likely to bring great prosperity to the Comedy and all concerned. But next to the playwright, the greatest credit of the success is due to Miss Marie Tempest, whose Mrs Dot will rank with her famous 'Kitty.' Miss Marie Tempest has, we all know, a record to be proud of, but not for a long time has she had a part so much after her own heart as Mrs Dot. Now once again she impresses us forcibly with the fact that she is a great comedienne, that—and it is the greatest compliment of all—she equals the foremost artists of the French stage. Aye, more than that; Miss Tempest has a quality which we even seek in vain on the French comedy stage. She is (apparently) wholly unconscious of her public; she never appeals to it, addresses it, or shoots a knowing wink across the footlights. Whether Mrs Dot plots, or pouts, or worries, or casts the spell of seduction and sends forth the fervour of her love for the man she means to conquer, she never allows us to believe that this is all acting and not life. She is sincere to the core, she revels in her part, she does a hundred little things which are not in the text, yet add to its effectiveness, and, living the character as she does, she causes us to live with her through all her emotions. If Somerset Maugham, as a dramatist, is a charmer, Miss Marie Tempest is a charmeuse; between the pair of them, the critic, along with the general public, capitulates in unconditional surrender.

THE EXPLORER

Lyric Theatre, London, 13 June 1908 (48 performances)
[Written 1899. Published London, November 1912]

A novelisation of this play under the same title had already
been published in London in 1907.

---

25. J.T. Grein, review, *Sunday Times*

14 June 1908, 19

Of the four plays which Mr Maugham, after his sudden leap to
fame, is presenting simultaneously in London, *The Explorer* is the
least coruscating. But it is because of that by no means the least
considerable of the quartette. There is something in *The Explorer*
which appeals forcibly to me. It is the simplicity of the story; the
straightforwardness of the narrative; the consistency of characterisation of every man and woman in the play, be he (or she) a
principal factor or a mere collateral figure sketched in rapid lines.
There is also a sprinkling of graceful comedy—a little *vieux jeu*,
perhaps, between the charming widow and the recalcitrant
bachelor of forty or so—which at times tends to relieve and at
others to encumber the action. It is a question of individual feeling:
personally, I can do without the convention of indispensable
comedy scenes, but the public like it, and hence it has remained in
most English plays a time-honoured element. But of greater
importance with regard to the vitality of this work is whether the
axis will be considered sufficiently strong to bear the strain of four
acts. In other words, will the simple story evolved from a
somewhat debatable proposition grip, as the author intends it to
do? Perhaps it will, for the Explorer is a strong man—a typical Scot

endowed with all the qualities of his race, and such faults as in life often become virtues—and the temporary trouble to which he is exposed is due to loyalty toward the woman whom he loves. He asked Lucy to marry him on the day when her father was sentenced to seven years for misfeasance, and she, much touched by his proposal, had declined, yet given him hope in the future on condition that he would take her brother with him to Africa and prepare him for an honourable life which would redeem the family's name. Yonder in the African wilderness the boy proved a failure, a drunkard and a sensuous tyrant in his conduct to native women. Yet there was some sense of honour left in the youth, and when the Explorer's camp was beset by overwhelming numbers of tribesmen, he accepted a post of defence which would mean death on condition that the Explorer pledged his word of honour to give a good report of him to his sister. This pledge, given to a 'moriturus' to nerve his courage, would prove a scourge to the Explorer. The boy fell, and when the Explorer came back to England and glory he shared the lot of so many great pioneers—a letter in the Press by a discharged servant accused him of having driven Lucy's brother to his doom, and the majority—even his own circle—believed the reviler. Only Lucy stood by him, and, in defiance of the world as well as in defence of her lover, she proclaimed her betrothal to him. But in her mind, too, constantly influenced by her friends, there lingered doubt, and although she repressed it with all her might, circumstances forced her to examine the Explorer as to the truth of the charge.

In the third act we reach this fine scene, wherein the lips of the strong man, partly sealed by the pledge of his word, can only reveal one side of the circumstances—the part which incriminates him—whereas he must withhold his justification. Deluded by the shock of the revelation, Lucy breaks for the time being the engagement, and the Explorer once more seeks Africa and such climate as will mean no return. That Lucy repents and the play ends with a note of hope and happiness is a detail. The question is, was the Explorer justified in sacrificing, albeit temporarily, Lucy's future and his own because under stress of circumstances he had undertaken to give a false report of the brother's behaviour in Africa? It is a moot point and it all depends on the ethical view taken by the audience. There are circumstances, especially when the honour and fair fame of woman are concerned, where the pledged word is sacred beyond all dispute and where a falsehood may cease to be heinous. There are others when the self-chosen cancellation of the compact is a better action than its maintenance. Especially in the case of man and woman destined to share their lives there should be no prevarication merely because under *force majeure* a promise, as given by the Explorer, had been rashly (as he himself puts it) made. However, as I said before, that is a point of view, and it will be interesting to watch the trend of public opinion. For the rest, Mr Maugham, in this play, as in his former works, displays an astounding mastery of stage-craft as well as a fine sense of proportion—so fine indeed, that, whereas some may dispute the basis of the play, the attention of assenters and dissentients alike is riveted without intermission.

In selecting the part of the Explorer Mr Lewis Waller has been most happily inspired, it suits him to perfection, and he makes it a splendid picture of virility, restrained power, and domination by strength of character. From the first the audience was wholly in sympathy with him, and time after time he was (deservedly) cheered to the echo. The Lucy of Miss Evelyn Millard, who was warmly received—partly, no doubt, in order to give her a token of goodwill towards her prospective career as an actress-manageress—had the charm of dignity which is characteristic of the racial (and rational) Englishwoman. The weak brother was played by Mr Shiel Barry in the right key. There was no effort to render the unpleasant figure theatrically sympathetic. Mr Barry played the part just as he felt it—and we felt it with him—the surface repellent, as through an angle [*sic*] revealed the pathos of youth desirous to redeem a misspent life by an honourable exit. The comic lovers were delightfully played by Miss Eva Moore and Mr A.E. George, the latter of whom proved that he commands comedy as well as drama more austere. Minor parts were well filled by Miss Mary Rorke, Mr Chas. Rock, and Mr Owen Roughwood—in fact, there was not a flaw in the cast, although, especially at the beginning and towards the end, the atmosphere of the stage was pregnant with nervousness.

To account for the future of the play would mean to venture beyond the critic's sphere, but the first night verdict was unanimous and it proclaimed: Success!

26. Max Beerbohm, 'How Dare He?'
Saturday Review (London)

CV, 20 June 1908, 782–3

The Explorer is great fun. Quite apart from its intrinsic quality, the fact that its author is Mr Somerset Maugham is a very strong recommendation indeed. This fact is in itself enough to endear the production to us through what may be called our cumulative sense. If a horse win two important races, we are all anxious that it shall win a third, and a fourth. We want it to win a greater number of important races than any other horse ever won before. When we hear that Mr Pierpont Morgan has acquired Lord So-and-So's priceless collection of this or that, we experience a thrill of delight. We want Mr Morgan to possess *all* that is worth possessing in every kind of artistic product. Statesmen—even the imperialistic ones, nowadays—declare that the British Empire is large enough. Do they think so? Not they. Even the strictest Little Englander would inwardly rejoice if another strip of territory were added to our accumulation. So, for that matter, would the keenest Anglophobe abroad. There is nothing rational, nothing selfish, in the workings of the cumulative sense. It is a sense that defies reason, transcends self. Our colonies are of no use to the foreigner. We do not intrude on Mr Morgan's store-house in Grosvenor Gate. We do not back the sensational colt or filly that we hope will win the record sum in stakes. We may disapprove of the theatre, or be bored by it, and so have no intention of going to see any of the four plays that Mr Maugham has running in the metropolis at this moment. Nevertheless, he is for all of us the hero of the year, even as Signorinetta is like to be the heroine. We rejoice in the news that yet another play of his will be produced in July. Five plays running simultaneously! Stupendous! Even without counting provincial and American rights, he must be 'making at the rate of' whatever vast annual sum it please us to mouth. Colossal! Yet, after all, what are five theatres among so many? Why shouldn't *all* the theatres in London be Maughamised? Say that in the past five years he wrote only three plays annually. That would make fifteen rejected plays. Deduct five. That leaves ten plays now accepted for production. Come, let room be found for all of them forthwith! In such dreams do we fondly revel. We are only human.

Other playwrights than Mr Maugham have been, and are, revered by some playgoers. The privilege of being revered by the whole community has been given to him alone. His name is a household word even in households where the theatre is held unclean. They pencil it honourably in the margins of *Smiles on Self-Help*. It is lisped by children in their nurseries, and rolled over the tongue of the aged and infirm. Other playwrights complain that the majority of playgoers is bent not on seeing this or that play, but on seeing this or that mime, and leaves the theatre without having glanced at the author's name on the programme. Presently we shall have Mr Maugham complaining that the majority of playgoers is bent on seeing his plays because they are his, rather than on seeing this or that mime whom he has so exactly fitted with a part. In *Mrs Dot* have not we the quintessence of Miss Marie Tempest, and of Mr Hawtrey in *Jack Straw*? And now, what could be so quintessential of Mr Waller as *The Explorer*? Mr Maugham, sated with our enthusiasm for himself, will coldly bid us give precedence in our hearts to the leading lady or gentleman for whose genius his art is a vehicle. It is, he will remind us, the King that we cheer when he drives past, not the King's coach-builder.

I doubt whether this rebuke will be really deserved—at any rate in connexion with Mr Waller. How *could* precedence be taken of Mr Waller? The thing's impossible. As I have said, we are only human. And Mr Waller himself, perhaps, is only human. But it needs a stretch of scepticism, greater than we may compass, to imagine him other than divine, when he has a part that properly shows him off. In him we see an amalgam of the sterner deities familiar to our childhood. The voice, I admit, is the voice of Apollo; but the eyes are the eyes of Mars, and the jaw-bone is exactly the jaw-bone that Jove had beneath his beard; while the air of grimly concentrated force is Vulcan's own. As the Explorer, Mr Waller has a superb opportunity for the use of these divine assets. 'Alexander Mackenzie', the hero's name, is hardly a name well-chosen, conjuring up for us, as it does, the mildness of our native and academic music. But the misnomer does not matter after Mr Waller has been on the stage for a few seconds. 'Alexander Mackenzie' is thenceforth a synonym for all that is quietly strong and grim and fearless and overwhelming. All the more terrific is the effect of the Explorer by reason of the milieu in which he appears. If he is like this in a London drawing-room, what, we rapturously wonder, must he be like in the heart of Central Africa? If this is the figure he cuts among the dear home-birds, what *can* he be like when he is facing starvation and suppressing the slave-trade, out there? See him standing in the centre of the drawing-room, his heels joined, his shoulders squared, his fists clenched, his lips compressed as by a vice of steel, his eyes flashing luminous shafts as he turns his profile this way or that with the abruptness of a ventriloquist's puppet! See him as he paces the drawing-room carpet, and admit how inadequate is the inevitable simile of the caged lion! In the second act Mr Maugham shows us the lion at large. Night is falling on the plain, the food-supplies are all but exhausted, the native tribes are menacing, hostile Arabs are in the offing, Alexander is in his element. Vibrating as we are under his personal magnetism, we wonder that his followers, with no footlights between him and them, have not long ago been shaken to death. Some of them have indeed perished; but Alexander, with the modesty of your true hero, ascribes their decease to tribal bullets, climate, &c. Among the survivors is a young man named George Allerton, supposed to be a weakling, but in reality the toughest person in the whole retinue: he can resist Alexander's magnetism. Alexander has warned him not to drink; yet he went and drank deeply. Alexander has warned him not to outrage the sensibilities of the tribes; yet he made advances to a native woman, and finally shot her. Alexander accuses him of the crime; yet he is able to look Alexander in the face and tell a lie; nay! when Alexander bids him submit his revolver to examination, he pulls the trigger on Alexander. Of course, even if he aimed straight, the bullet could have no effect: gods are invulnerable. Nevertheless a thrill of horror passes through the entire audience. And, on the night of my visit, a young lady sitting in the front row of the pit cried out in a hollow voice, 'How DARE HE?' Her outburst was a concise expression of what we all were feeling.

I suspect Mr Maugham of not being so perfectly satisfied as we are with the part that he has written for Mr Waller. It is evident he conceived Alexander Mackenzie as a type of 'the strong, silent man', and as a man whose whole soul was devoted to the glorious hazards of exploration; one to whom woman could be no more than 'a toy'. Yet Alexander Mackenzie is loquacious, and a lover. Mr Waller, had he only his art to think about, might have accepted a play in which he had not to open his firm lips once in the whole course of the evening. There are chemical experiments in which an ingredient is said to 'act by its presence'. I can imagine Mr Waller acting by his. But there is the public to be considered. The public would be aggrieved if Mr Waller's voice, that noble organ, were not continuously exploited. Also they would be puzzled and made angry by a play in which Mr Waller's actions were not swayed by love. Such heroes as Alexander Mackenzie do not necessarily, in real life, regard woman as a toy. Mostly they do; but there are exceptions—Nelson, for example. He, however, was not so exceptional an exception as Alexander. Suppose Lady Hamilton had had a brother who was wholly unfitted for the navy, it is not likely that Nelson would have accepted him as one of his right-hand men in a naval campaign; nor is it likely that he would thereafter have chosen to alienate Lady Hamilton by letting her suppose that he had lightly sent this young man out on a forlorn hope which he himself was afraid to lead. He would not have said of her, as Alexander says of Lucy Allerton, 'I think she can live better without love than without self-respect'. What Alexander's speech really means is 'I think I am more theatrically effective without a few simple words of explanation than without an idiotic act of self-sacrifice'. And thus... but here am I indulging in my tedious old habit of testing a play by reference to reality! I catch the echo of the feminine heart-cry 'How DARE HE?' and I desist.

PENELOPE

Comedy Theatre, London, 9 January 1909 (246 performances)
[Written 1908. Published London, November 1912]

The situation expounded at the beginning of this play was developed more sardonically in Maugham's later play *The Constant Wife* (1926/27), a re-working of the same theme.

---

27. J. T. Grein, review, *Sunday Times*

10 January 1909, 9

The old Penelope sat at home unravelling at night the shirt which she wove in the daytime in expectation of her wayward Ulysses. The modern Penelope takes things less tragically. She, too, awaits her Ulysses, but she is militant. She walks straight into the enemy's camp in *casu quo* the fascinating Mrs Fergusson, an acquaintance of hers and a patient of her husband's, who is a doctor. Having struck this keynote there is hardly any need to destroy the illusion of Mr Maugham's play by extensive narrative of plot. We feel what will happen, what must happen, for this is comedy, and in a good comedy things should in the last act fall like a cat on all fours. The question is how will it happen, and that is Mr Maugham's secret and his charm. He is a worldwise man. He knows men and women physiologically as well as psychologically. He is familiar with the touch feminine as well as with the touch masculine. He makes women say and do things which elicit a nod of wonderment and assent from the fair sex, and as regards the men, well, that all depends upon their company. Alone, they laugh aloud; with other people's womenfolk they exchange a smile and a wink, and if they happen to be blessed with a somewhat exacting better half they play at bland innocence.

For what does Mr Maugham try to prove in a playful way of Parisian grace and English good-nature? The old axiom, that a normal woman is content with one man, that to her a little flirtation is all the variety she requires, and that the average man is polygamous without necessarily meaning any harm. So curious are the ethics of man, according to Mr Maugham—and I for one shall not say him nay—that when Penelope, who is as sharp as a needle and bent on the reconquest of her straying lord, pretends to look upon his peccadillo rather callously, he breaks out in sainted ire and trounces her soundly for the levity of her principles. How Penelope, in the game of mice and men, proves victorious; how, by subtle devices and exquisite *calinerie*, she brings the sinner to his knees, I must leave you to judge for yourselves, since all London, married London especially, will rush to see itself in the mirror.

Of course, there are faults; there is at times too much talk; there is an introduction of superfluous characters, amusing enough in themselves but retarding the action, but such shortcomings as there are vanish in the bright sunshine of a sparking dialogue, a human undercurrent in the action and numberless little episodes and interludes which betray the man of the world as well as the man who knows. And this I would say whilst passing from the charming play on to the charm of the acting that when we have an English author who has all the lightness and the verve of a Parisian-born we should not be churlish and thank the Muses for at least one author who knows how to graft the *esprit gaulois* upon true English comedy.

There was in an admirable cast but one error of judgment, and that was the impersonation of the fair charmer who threatened Penelope's happiness. To render such a part acceptable to people who know life, the grass-widow of hazy antecedents who is received in society should have distinction. If she be a '*chevalière d'indústrie*' she should have the impress of the *grande dame*, and this aristocracy of the doubtful was entirely wanting. It almost undid the effect of the second act. But for the rest there is nothing but praise. Admirable, one and all; the delightful old father of Mr Alfred Bishop, the sweet saintly mother of Miss Kate Bishop, the sere and yellow good uncle of Mr Eric Lewis, the fussy doctor's widow, who pesters the Profession for no remuneration, of Mrs

Calvert, even the stoic and impeccable maid of Miss Ethelwyn Arthur-Jones, who 'buttled' as well as the most time-honoured butler.

And what am I to say of Mr Graham Browne, whose touch of Irish blood made the naughty doctor the most lovable of sinners, and of Miss Marie Tempest, younger, more arch, more insinuating, more vivacious than ever? Again I must draw a comparison with Paris, and if I say that neither yonder nor anywhere else in the world there is a comedienne to cast her into the shade, I am not merely writing in the stress of enthusiasm after a delightful evening, but I pay a tribute to an artist who in the truest sense of the word is an adornment to her profession. It comes, in fact, to this, that the success of *Penelope* is the success of a triumvirate: of the ingenious author, Mr W. Somerset Maugham, and his chief exponents, Miss Marie Tempest and Mr Graham Browne.

28. William Archer, '*Penelope* and Popularity', *Nation* (London)

IV, 16 January 1909, 606–7

William Archer (1856–1924), Scottish-born drama critic and translator of Ibsen, had come to prominence as the critic of the *World* from 1894–1898 and was at this time writing regularly on the theatre in the *Nation*. The stir made by Maugham's pluralism as a West End playwright is echoed in his article. Though a friend of Shaw and a dedicated champion of the theatre of ideas, Archer nonetheless sees the point of Maugham's attack on such a theatre in favour of the theatre of entertainment, while questioning the soundness of the antithesis.

Mr Somerset Maugham—who, by the way, assures me that he is an individual, and not a syndicate or corporation—has a remarkable genius for writing characters to fit Miss Marie Tempest. So nicely did he suit her in *Mrs Dot* that the play, though a singularly empty one, and quite the poorest of his productions, has apparently been a great success. In *Penelope* he has produced a much better play, and a character equally congenial to the brilliant little actress. As is Miss Hilda Trevelyan to Mr Barrie, so is Miss Marie Tempest to Mr Maugham: that simple proportion sum gives you a pretty fair appraisement of Mr Maugham's talent; at any rate, in its present phase. For Miss Tempest is the type and incarnation of a certain aspect of modern social life, and perfection in the art of 'fitting' her is not a perfection to which everyone would aspire. I fancy, for instance, that it scarcely comes within the scope of Mr Barrie's ambition. Nevertheless, it presupposes a very distinct sort of cleverness, and we cannot afford to quarrel with cleverness of any sort or size. Where there are brains there is hope: it is pretentious stupidity that is the real enemy.

I laughed a good deal at *Penelope*, and I do not blush to own it. The second half of the play is much better than the first half, and contains some passages of irresistible humour. There is even a real touch of satiric originality in the idea of the husband who, on learning that his wife has long known of his infidelity, and has (apparently) made light of it, feels his moral sentiments outraged, and finds himself, quite sincerely, playing the part of the indignant accuser. The complications arising from the lamented decease of 'Mrs Mack' are extremely amusing, and there are touches throughout which betoken the genuine humorist. Taking the play simply on its own level, the worst one finds to say of it is that it is carelessly and unconscientiously written. It is not a well-finished piece of work. There are loose ends and rough edges that an assiduous workman would have removed. For example, Penelope is suffered, in a score of speeches, to betray her knowledge of her husband's divagations long before she ultimately confesses it. Mr Maugham has not taken the pains to render in the least plausible O'Farrell's blind belief in her blindness. Over and over again he sacrifices plausibility to a momentary comic effect, and thus discounts the one really excellent passage in the play, where Penelope's pretence of ignorance breaks down. It is this slovenliness of workmanship which makes it impossible to class *Penelope* as a first-rate play, even of its kind. Mr Maugham may, if he pleases, abjure 'taking himself seriously' as an artist; but he might at least take himself seriously as an amuser.

In the one excellent passage above alluded to, Miss Tempest's acting rose to the pitch of genius. For the rest, she was her own inimitable self throughout—an actress whom the French may well envy us, and who ought to be eulogised in French. Why does not Mr Walkley rise to the occasion? The cast, for the rest, is excellent—how could it fail to be, since it includes three such comedians as Mr Alfred Bishop, Mr Eric Lewis, and Mrs Calvert?—the pick of the basket, if one may put it vulgarly. I heard stern critics, in the theatre, objecting to the episodic nature of Mrs Calvert's part. That did not trouble me in the least. The scene was delightful, and if it did not actually advance the plot, it contributed to one element in the comic effect of the whole act—the extremely unprofitable nature of Dr O'Farrell's business on that fateful afternoon. Mr Graham Browne was good as the Doctor, and Miss Norma Whalley, whose rendering of Mrs Fergusson seemed at first a little extravagant, proved in the end to be entirely justified. To have made the character in the least serious, not to say sympathetic, would entirely have upset the balance of the play. As it was, we felt more than once that Mr Maugham was skating pretty near the edge of the intolerably cynical. To keep the play in the key of irresponsible comedy, it was necessary that it should have the unreality of the old-fashioned adaptations from the French, in which the real nature of the facts concerned was studiously dissembled, and, so far as actual words went, it seemed that much ado was being made about little or nothing. I do not say that this is either an edifying or an artistic convention; but it is the almost inevitable condition of Maugham-Tempest comedy on the English stage.

As nothing more occurs to me that can profitably be said about *Penelope*, I may perhaps eke out this article with a brief considera-tion of the confession of faith which her creator, it would seem, has recently made public. I take the confession at second-hand, as reproduced in a thoughtful article by "Max"; but there is little doubt, I fancy, that the following summary is accurate enough:

To Mr Maugham apparently, the 'serious' drama is a thing very ridiculous, very negligible. He has been telling an interviewer that it is 'most unwise' of dramatists to 'take themselves seriously.' He has no patience with 'great central ideas'; and 'to entertain' he declares... 'should be the first—perhaps the only—aim of the playwright.'

This utterance, coming from the author of *A Man of Honour*, seems to have scandalised a good many people; and certainly it carries to an extreme that tendency to make a general law of our own particular qualities and limitations from which none of us, probably, is altogether free. But I think there is a substratum of sound sense beneath Mr Maugham's exaggerations. He fails to make allowance for the wide divergency of tastes, and for the fact that many people—not mere scattered individuals or aesthetic cliques, but people who are quite capable of making a fair show on the booking-sheets—are at least as willing to be entertained by plays with 'a great central idea' as by empty trivialities. If he has a 'great central idea' lying around in his brain or in his notebooks, I think he makes a mistake, even from the merely financial point of view, in leaving it undeveloped. He is quite clever enough—for he is born with the gift of the stage—to make it a marketable commodity. To do so would cost him more pains, no doubt, than to throw off an ephemeral triviality like *Mrs Dot*; but the reward, if not larger at the outset, would be more permanent. If I am wrong in my estimate, and he really has not the power of writing thoughtful plays as well as thoughtless sketches, the inability is not a commercial asset, but the reverse. It will lessen, and not increase, the amount of the succession duty which he is so laudably desirous—though probably not impatient—to contribute to the national Exchequer.

Stripped of its exaggerations, however, Mr Maugham's pronouncement contains an element of sound sense. The playwright who despises the public, and writes simply to please himself and his little circle, makes as great a mistake as he who sacrifices everything to instant popularity. I know this is a damnable heresy in the eyes of many excellent people and my very good friends. 'What other motive is possible to a self-respecting artist,' they ask, 'if it be not to please himself? Certainly that ought to be his primary motive; but if he cannot please himself while pleasing, or at any rate keenly interesting, a very considerable public, he is the lesser, not the greater, dramatist. The strength of drama lies in its strict conditions and narrow limits, its glory in its wide appeal. So far as I know, history records no instance of a playwright failing to gain the ear of his contemporaries and then being recognised and appreciated by posterity. Alfred de Musset might, perhaps, be cited as a case in point; but he did not write with a view to the stage, and did not try for contemporary popularity. As soon as it occurred to people to put his plays on the stage, they were found to be delightful. Let no playwright, then, think it a merit that he cannot disburden his soul within the three hours' limit, and cannot produce plays intelligible or endurable to any but a specially selected audience. Of course, I do not include among the conditions which make for the strength of drama the necessity for conciliating an arbitrary censorship and providing a showy part for an actor-manager or a star actress. In the English theatre, as at present constituted, many fine plays seem to appeal only to a clique, because, for one reason or another, they cannot get at the public that would appreciate them. They are out-advertised by the star plays and the musical frivolities. But the worst mischief of this state of affairs lies in the fact that our ablest writers are so apt to abandon all hope of popularity and become intransigeant self-pleasers. They deserve our respect, perhaps, rather more than Mr Maugham, who chooses to go to the opposite extreme; but not more than the writers who make a sincere effort to do the best work of which the conditions of the popular stage admit. It is not a merit, but a defect, in a play that it should set at defiance all reasonable limits, either of human endurance or of human intelligence. The haughtiest self-pleaser must write with an ideal audience in view; and his play will not be better, but worse, if that ideal be in the nature of things unrealisable.

SMITH

Comedy Theatre, London, 30 September 1909 (168 performances)
[Written 1909. Published London, December 1913]

Although not mentioned by any of the reviewers, *Smith* is Maugham's modern version of *Cinderella*; the equivalents of Cinderella, Prince Charming, the Ugly Sisters and even Buttons can be clearly identified.

---

29. J.T. Grein, review, *Sunday Times*

3 October 1909, 4

It is curious that J.M. Barrie's *The Admirable Crichton* (1902) had not apparently prepared audiences for a play in which a domestic servant is shown to be worthier than her betters, a theme which clearly caused J.T. Grein uneasiness.

The author of *Liza of Lambeth* and other works that matter is a thinker of such depth that it would be easy to seek a hidden meaning under the pleasant surface of his latest play. On the other hand, Mr Maugham is a cynic, and as such it would no doubt amuse him vastly if I were to take him seriously and begin by questioning whether a domestic servant's love affair with the brother of the mistress of the house is, as the world goes, a decorous subject wherewith to entertain us. For, rightly or wrongly, the domestic servant occupies, in my consideration of men and women, a peculiar place in a somewhat sacred shrine. They have my entire sympathy, and often it galls me to find that the one who serves and is of a refined nature should become the

97

butt of the petty tyranny of a coarser person who is served by him or her. For this reason I dislike it when on the stage servants are pictured as submitted to facile jest or undue familiarity, and particularly to the unwelcome attentions of their superiors. Having said this, I make it clear from the first that to me personally the subject-matter of a comedy like *Smith* does not appeal. But I would be quite wrong in letting this prejudice blind me against the merits of the play or the fact that the audience in general enjoyed it hugely. Indeed, I think that a neighbour of mine, who has, like Mr Maugham, the gift of being very much in earnest and rather cynical, exactly established the standard by which *Smith* must be judged, when he said that it makes an excellent evening's entertainment.

In *Smith* we find the man who has roughed it after a life of pleasure in London, and comes back to the old country with a chastened mind and devotion to work. When he comes to his sister's house, ostensibly for a mere visit, but with the intention to seek a wife to help him on his farm in Rhodesia, he finds what one commonly calls 'a rotten lot'—women addicted to Bridge, frivolity, domestic neglect, the veneration of the 'tame cat,' in fact all those occupations which destroy home and its traditional happiness. There is a girl in that set to whom he was once engaged and who besides being a Bridge-fiend has become what I would term 'a spotted virgin.' That woman is ready to do anything to get away from debt and to obtain a permanent roof over her head. She entraps him into a second engagement and lies that she had always been true in thought. *Au fond*, that woman is not bad, but she is a victim of circumstances, and when the young man pays a debt for her she experiences such a revulsion of feeling that she is abashed at her former conduct, gives him back his word, and prepares for a new life in Australia. After a magnificent scene between the two, there arises a feeling whether after all this woman has not the qualities which would make a good wife. But Mr Maugham has other intentions.

There is the servant of the house, a farmer's daughter, Nature's child, young, pretty, a trifle masterful, and as far as character is concerned as pure as snow. Besides, like a true, strong girl of the soil, she is not over sentimental, she has practical sense, she adores male strength. In comparison with the tainted ladies around her, the young man finds that she is the ideal woman and, as he says later on, he from the first made up his mind to marry her. For he had been sickened by his surroundings, he had fulminated in the true vein of the *raisonneur* against the deterioration of modern society, and especially woman, and had reached the climax of dismay when he beheld how the sudden death of the baby of one of his sister's friends affects no one except the young servant who heard the dread message at the telephone. In that scene, which is exceedingly poignant, Mr Maugham drives cynicism to the highest pitch. I do not remember anything so distressing as the heartlessness of all these more or less unsexed women, nothing so brutal as the whole conceit whereby in the middle of a bridge party the death of a child is introduced as a dramatic element. Another thing which strikes a discordant note in this comedy is the repeated reference to Jews in terms of ungraciousness. True, the author tries to gloss it over by showing that in the Jew there is the genuine feeling of family and paternity, in contrast to the callousness of the Christian wife, but the impression remains that the Jews are considered, not as ordinary members of the community, but as something exotic, akin to freakishness. Considering that in England, as elsewhere, the Jew is the main support of all that is great and good in art, I think that unless the theme be treated seriously he should be left alone and the caricature to melodrama. I have said at the beginning that the basis of the play, which is the love affair of the man of gentle birth with the servant, does not appeal to me, but that does not do away with the fact that Mr Maugham has conducted the courtship, after a preliminary canter of conversation in somewhat questionable taste, with great acumen and a sense of humour, so intense that it vies with the best comedy of the French. And it is a great merit of the play, which scintillates with witticism like a city in illumination, that every character has a distinct individuality, albeit that save the *raisonneur* they all lack heart and several decency. But as types, not of the community but culled here and there from life, they are drawn with a masterly hand, and in this respect the play is superior to Mr Maugham's works of lighter textures. There remains one question and that is, whether in order to hit a certain woman of modern society it was necessary to descend to the servant as representative of all that is sound and normal in the nation. That point I am not going to discuss, for the cynic, Mr Maugham, would probably deride me and say, 'See how I caught him.' At the same time, it must not be forgotten that the basis of all satire must be truth, and the truth is that we need not go to the area to find a survival of domestic virtues.

The acting was admirable, and I will place in the foreground the consistent and powerful impersonation of the man from Rhodesia of Mr Robert Loraine; he looked the man, he was the man, he never flagged in energy nor in sincerity of conviction. He struck one as the incarnation of health and strength in a world of artifice. Next to him I would extend my compliment to Miss Edyth Latimer, who portrayed the girl who so tardily awoke to be a decent woman. It was a fine performance because it had all the flavour of modernity, something tired, something insinuating, above all, something fascinating, like a *fleur du mal* of Charles Baudelaire. Miss Kate Cutler, in the somewhat passive part of a flighty wife, had one scene in which to show her power. It was the scene in which everybody left the poor little wife, including the tame cat (played in his usual free and easy natural way by Mr A.E. Matthews) and she, *faute de mieux*, asked her burly husband to take her to lunch, not without dropping a tear over her loneliness. Miss Kate Cutler did this admirably and shed pathos on the comedy. Miss Lydia Bilbrooke, as the Christian wife of the 'fat old German Jew' (who does not appear), marks progress, and Mr Frederick Volpé conveys more the idea of a major domo than a K.C., although he played cosily in the right accent. There remains, then, Miss Marie Löhr, who, by her youth and her charm, appealed to her many admirers. As an idealised servant she was no doubt prepossessing to the highest degree, but in her diction there was such strange affectation, engendered by immaturity, that I for one did not feel the touch of nature. Miss Löhr speaks with all the preciseness of the student of elocution, that is to say, she pronounces every word so deliberately that one seems to hear a *précieuse* instead of a parlour maid, and this becomes all the more significant when in the midst of this refinement of pronunciation, there are little lapses into the grammar of Cockayne.

The first two acts of the play were received with lukewarm applause, the last two with signal favour, and at the close of the performance there was a peculiarly insistent demand for the author which set one wondering what the gods really meant. At any rate, Mr Maugham elected to remain in the background, which was somewhat cynical towards all those well-wishers, but perhaps an excess of modesty.

30. Unsigned review, *Athenaeum*

4276, 9 October 1909, 435–6

It is a pleasure to see Mr Maugham taking his art seriously again. Artificial *jeux d'esprit* such as *Jack Straw* are all very well in their way. With their bright wit and fancy they make a merry evening's entertainment, and they are nicely calculated to suit the tastes of the many playgoers who desire to get away from reality in the theatre, and take it as an affront if they are reminded there of the more unpleasant or tragic facts of life. But it is no business of the playwright who respects himself to pander perpetually to their wilful blindness, and there are times when, at the risk of rousing these self-deceivers from their Fools' Paradise, he feels bound to speak his mind about the follies and vices of certain sections of the society of his day. Mr Maugham must have been stirred to some such state of feeling when he wrote *Smith*, which, its title notwithstanding, is far and away the most thoughtful stage work he has given us since *A Man of Honour*. Like Sir Arthur Pinero in *Mid-Channel* and Mr Sutro in *Making a Gentleman*, he seems to have been moved to wrath over the spectacle of the modern woman of wealth and fashion, who shirks all the duties of marriage and maternity, and wastes her life in a feverish hunt after pleasure. But with that worldly wisdom which has helped him to a unique success on our stage, he has altered his methods gradually. If theatregoers are to be made to think, he would appear to have decided, they must also be allowed to laugh, they must even be permitted their happy ending. So his new play is half satire, half fairy-tale. It scarifies two or three examples of the society woman and the sort of human lapdog or tame cat who hangs on to her skirts; but it presents by way of contrast a breezy, outspoken man from the Colonies (by this time quite a conventional type, though here varied by being represented as a former man about town who has roughed it abroad) and a servant-girl, of the farmer's daughter kind, wholesome, modest, sensible, abounding in warm blood and right feeling. The scenes between the young Rhodesian who has come home to seek a wife and the housemaid who wants strength and muscle, and not gentle manners, in a husband, amused Mr Maugham's first-night audience just because of the fantastic improbability of their humour. But it was curious to note the quiver of half-indignant surprise which ran over the house when it found its Somerset Maugham abandoning now and then his jester's garb, and daring to shock his public with a sense of the actual, as in having news brought of her baby's death to a mother busy over 'bridge.' The spasm of irritation was obvious to an onlooker.

It is not for thus relating his play with life that we shall think of blaming the author of *Smith*. There is, however, one objection which may be urged against his treatment of his theme. Surely it is rather questionable taste to show a servant-girl made love to in her mistress's house by her mistress's brother. This courtship has its pretty and its laughable features; but was it quite fair to get either fun or sentiment in this particular way? Then, again, was it necessary to choose a domestic servant so conspicuously to be the foil of the sinners she serves? Mr Maugham depicts with singular cleverness the heartless sexless wife who is 'Smith's' employer; and even more striking is his study of a girl, 'bridge'-mad and tarnished in reputation, who entraps the hero into an engagement that he may pay her debts, and adds the final stroke to his disgust with his sister's set. But is there not something cheaply romantic in the contrast drawn between the servant's good heart and the fine ladies' viciousness? Perhaps, however, to ask these questions is to regard the play more solemnly than its author intended. For his is only a half-attempt at satire; even here it has been his aim to afford amusement and provoke laughter, slipping in his indictment of 'smart' folk as if it were a pill between layers of sweetmeats. Anyhow, the audience seemed to swallow the combination readily enough, and to welcome the rhetorical vigour with which Mr Robert Loraine gave the hero's denunciation of fashionable women no less heartily than Miss Marie Löhr's pretty, if rather too refined humour in the character of the housemaid. Miss Kate Cutler and Miss Edyth Latimer did good service in the less agreeable feminine parts, and the ultimate repentance of both, and a love-scene in which the housemaid accepted her gentleman-lover, sent the spectators away cheerful and enthusiastic.

THE TENTH MAN

Globe Theatre, London, 24 February 1910 (65 performances)
[Written 1909. Published London, December 1913]

For this play Maugham interwove the plots of two of his
magazine stories, 'Pro Patria' (1903) and 'The Making of a
Millionaire' (1906).

31. J.T. Grein, review, *Sunday Times*

27 February 1910, 4

Mr Maugham has the gift of the *homme du monde*. He enters, he
opens fire, he interests us. He tells his story with discretion. Men of
the world have a habit of restraining their brilliancy. Mr Maugham
knows his public, its wants, its artistic digestion. Hence he, the
craftsman, husbands his forces. He imagines a scene, he forges
ahead to a certain point, then all of a sudden stops short, drops into
banter. *Ça suffit*. I can keep my climaxes, he says, for another
occasion. I must not forget the economics of a commercial stage.

This was the train of thought, then came the hiatus and the
question surged—is this play of unhappy marriage, unscrupulous
finance, parliamentary tripotage with the end à *La Rafole* of
Bernstein, Mr Maugham's own? Is it not inspired by the said
Bernstein, by *Les Ventres Dorés* of Ferdinand Fabre, by other plays
of which the titles do not occur to me, but which I could find in my
files of years, is it not inspired above all by a French masterpiece, so
great that it is still unknown in England, which I have treasured up
for years for one of the leading lights of our stage? If I am wrong I
apologise in humility. If I am right, I appeal to Mr Maugham, both

man and friend, to remember his escutcheon and to give Caesar Caesar's due. There is no abasement in the fact that one acknowledges inspiration, but a successful man should show his cards.

For the rest the play suffers from the incongruity of its origin, as it suffered from old fashioned acting. Mr Edmund Maurice, for instance, excellent actor in his way, believes in driving home his points to a forced degree. Miss Frances Dillon, whose beauty is as bewitching as her dress in the last act was disturbing to the peace of men, has intense moments of melodrama, but a part of length and finesse is as yet beyond her experience. Mr Michael Sherbrooke, too, should abandon his ecstatic method. It passed muster in *John Glayde's Honour*, it becomes fatiguing by repetition.

The play is dull. It is transcription of *Business is Business* with slight variations, with the influence of *John Glayde's Honour* hovering in the distance; it is not good, nor inherently interesting—in fact, it is Mr Maugham's first blunder. It is time for him to reverse the arms of his semaphore. He has been on the crest of the wave and now there seems to be danger ahead! But there was a redeeming point. And that was—after due tribute to Messrs. Holmes Gore, A.E. George, and Miss Kate Sergeantson for good work in small causes—the impersonation of the 'Tenth Man' by Mr Bourchier. He will penetrate yet deeper into the part when the tense excitement of the first night renders him more self-possessed. Yet, as it was, his performance will rank in his record. It reminded us often, not by imitation, but in spontaneity of the renowned impersonation of Lechat by Feraudy. It was strong, it was powerful, it was convincing. If Mr Maugham has not added to his laurels, Mr Arthur Bourchier has.

GRACE (LANDED GENTRY)

Duke of York's Theatre, London, 15 October 1910
(72 performances)
[Written 1910. Published London, November 1913]

The plot of this play provides one of the four unrelated stories interwoven in Maugham's novel *The Merry-Go-Round*. It is not clear which was written first.

32. J.T. Grein, review, *Sunday Times*

16 October 1910, 9

A tale of two women, their fault and their atonement. The one, the wife of a rich landowner, takes a lover. The other, the daughter of an old gamekeeper on the estate, 'whose roots are in the soil,' is betrayed, and about to become a mother. According to a law of ancient date of the estate the girl must go. Her father refuses to sanction her exile, so he, too, will be turned away. The girl, in her distress, implores the wife of the owner to prevent her father's discharge. The wife pleads her cause with her husband, but duty forbids his breaking the stern rule.

To save her father, the girl commits suicide. When the wife hears of it she is rent by sorrow and remorse, and in her mental misery she decides to make a clean breast of her breach of faith to her husband. A friend—a girl who had loved her husband in silence for years—prevailed on her to keep her secret, for the truth instead of healing would create new misery. Without his wife the husband's life would be empty—she is his ideal. Thus the wife's atonement is the life-long burden of her error and her determination to make amends to her husband by her unceasing devotion.

Read in its simplicity there is a touch of tragedy in this tale, and whenever the author forgets that there is *entente cordiale* in the English Theatre between business and art (business being senior partner) the touch hits home. There are many scenes theatrically effective. I have tried to indicate them in the brief survey of the story. There are scenes of severe conflict between the girl and the lady lover and mistress, above all between the wife, her girl-friend, and her brother-in-law, a parson. If they had been allowed to stand alone on an artistic plane, the play would have attained something of the distinction of Dumas *fils' pièces-à-thèse*. But the *entente* is in the way. If an English play is expected to do well, it may not, like a picture, be purely impressionist. It must have—in subservience to convention, which carries material reward—what I would term utility-qualities. It must appeal to the gallery as well as to the stalls. Interludes are required—interludes of comedy, of linguistic pyrotechnics, of collateral characterisations which amuse, interest, touch, as the case may be. Mr Maugham provides all that, and his play is gay with window-dressing (there is an old dame in it—acted with great distinction by Lady Tree—whose portraiture by the author recalls *imitation* Chippendale and Delft), but for the sake of the show without the quality within has been sacrificed. Mr Maugham, the successful playwright, has had the better of Maugham the artist. Of course, Mr Maugham writes with his usual facility and gentle cynicism, and, from the public's point of view, that is like a delusive *mouche* of plaster on fair shoulders. But does the play strike home, does it touch, create vibration in the hearer?—that is the question, and I must leave it open. The pathetic note is there right enough, but it is mostly muffled—or I should rather say, out-voiced—by the theatricality of the structure. Even in the fourth act, the best of all, with two powerful scenes, in which Grace confesses to her brother-in-law and her girl-friend, it mars the force of the argument. The play was cast with acumen, and in one respect the selection was most auspicious. It afforded Mr Edmund Gwenn an opportunity to make the hit of his career. His old gamekeeper was intensely tragic; it justified a scene as strong as it was intensely melodramatic. Almost equally touching in her short part was Miss Gertrude Lang as the unhappy daughter: she was absolutely natural, and that implies everything. Mr Dennis Eadie played the landowner somewhat rigidly, as was perhaps demanded by the part, which was neither sympathetic nor grateful.

Miss Lillah McCarthy, as the wife's friend, gave an interesting portrayal of the woman of thirty-five, whose apparent austerity hides a vainly longing heart; and Mr Leslie Faber drew a particularly narrow-minded clergyman in vital colours.

There remains Miss Irene Vanbrugh, and of her I can only say that she lived up to the title of the play. She acted with grace, with feeling, with restraint, which only once forsook her, at the end of the third act; I contend that there is no necessity for vociferation in the truly tragic moments of life. Even the liveliest nation on earth—the French—feel that off the stage and on. But that is a detail. Miss Irene Vanbrugh deserves great praise because she succeeded in rendering Grace lovable in spite of her fault.

At the end there was much cheering, but the lion-share fell to the actors—especially Miss Vanbrugh and Mr Gwenn.

LOAVES AND FISHES

Duke of York's Theatre, London, 24 February 1911
(48 performances)
[Written 1903. Published London, November 1924]

The germ of this play was the short story 'Cupid and the Vicar of Swale', one of two commissioned from Maugham by *Punch* in 1900. In 1906 a novelisation of the play was published under the title *The Bishop's Apron*.

---

33. Unsigned review, 'Mr Maugham's New Play', *Times*

25 February 1911, 8

Mr Maugham heads his programme with a line from *Tartuffe*. But his clerical humbug does not come from Molière; he comes from Barchester. We all know him intimately—in the pages of Trollope. And that is not altogether a good thing for Mr Maugham, because it is not very easy to come after Trollope in the matter of satirizing clergymen. Trollope's satire—if satire it was—was always genial; nor did he single out one clergyman. He painted a whole clerical set, the good as well as the bad, the saintly as well as the wordly, and he set them in a clerical atmosphere, living clerical lives, showing the 'professional bias' of the clergyman. In a word, he showed clergymen *being* clergymen. Now it is hardly paradoxical to say that Mr Maugham's clergyman, though he wears clerical dress and is in time made a Bishop, is never seen actually being a clergyman. Take away his black coat and his all-round collar and he is merely the worldling, the typical 'pusher', who may be of any profession you please, or of none. Instead of the Hon. and Rev. Canon Theodore Spratte, make him Theodore Spratte, M.D., a fashionable Harley-street physician manoeuvring for a baronetcy, and the play would be in all essentials the same play as before. You cannot say of any of the foibles of this parson, 'Ah! that is a true clerical weakness; *there* is your parson, to the life!' The secret is that Mr Maugham has had to leave Barchester out. He cannot give you the clerical atmosphere. That being so, it strikes us as not quite 'cricket' that Mr Maugham should make his worldling a parson. If he had brought in other parsons, decent fellows, to redress the balance, as Trollope did, *à la bonne heure*! But he does not. He presents a single exception. Further, he presents this single exception without subtlety—the man is just the typical worldling doing worldly things continuously and unblushingly; a transparent humbug. The result is that you laugh at him, but don't for a moment believe in him. For you know that in the actual world of to-day this is not the stuff out of which our Bishops are made.

As the worldling is just like other worldlings, he must of course begin by being a snob. He brags of his noble family (forgetting the bill-broking grandfather and the greengrocer great-grandfather), and is proud of his sham coat of arms. Snobbery, he frankly declares (for he has no objection to repeating what has often been said before), is the secret of England's greatness. Of course he worships money as well as rank. He wishes his daughter to marry a rich young peer. And when his daughter has fallen in love, or thinks she has fallen in love, with a young Socialist from Peckham Rye, he cunningly invites the Socialist's h-dropping, gin-drinking mother and bumptious, vulgar sister to tea, in order that his daughter may be disgusted by their bad manners. (Evidently the worldling is also a playgoer, and had noted how this trick had made a good scene in one or two plays, notably in one of the late Mr St John Hankin's). But the worldling is also a great squire of dames, especially of wealthy dames. He proposes marriage to a rich widow, who fools him by pretending that her income under her husband's will ceases with her re-marriage. Then he makes desperate efforts to extricate himself from the entanglement. The lady, however, sees through him—as well she may, for this humbug is as transparent as an innocent child—and when she has had her fun out of him leaves him with a laugh. Thereupon he turns to the next 'fortune' handy; this time the lady is really and truly *éprise*, and the humbug triumphs. For a touch of cynicism, the triumph is made at the expense of his own son, who had himself been wooing the lady. As a crowning triumph, he gets his Bishopric. Apparently he gets it by simply talking about it in his own drawing-room. Stay! there is just a hint that he has been 'working' the Press in his own favour. But there is no picture of a real struggle, of any real capacity for intrigue. Remembering Trollope's handling of this theme, when there was an episcopal vacancy in Barchester, you feel a little disappointed. If we are to be shown a Bishopric got by scheming, at any rate let us have some scheming!

There you have Mr Maugham's characteristic, easy, happy-go-lucky way. He draws a humbug, but so simple a humbug that a baby could detect him. He makes him a clergyman, and is at no pains to give any really distinguishing marks of his profession. But you laugh at the humbug all the same, because it is just the virtue of this easy, happy-go-lucky way of Mr Maugham's to make you laugh. His people won't bear thinking about—but that is not Mr Maugham's affair. You laugh, then, at the pleasant, gentlemanly, plausible rogue, and perhaps in the end rather like him, as you rather like any thoroughly persistent rogue who, somehow or other, always 'gets there.' If you don't like him it is assuredly not the fault of Mr Loraine, who plays him genially, joyously almost, and with the lightest possible touch. You like, too, the 'merry widow' of Miss Ellis Jeffreys, who in these highly sophisticated, elegantly dressed parts is without a rival. You like, again, the bluff gentleman, brother to the humbug and honest contrast to him, played by Mr Lowne. Miss Florence Hydon and Miss Mary Barton are both excellent as the vulgar mother and daughter from Peckham, and Miss Nina Sevening plays prettily as the humbug's daughter. There was a continuous ripple of laughter through the whole house last night, which sometimes became a roar. That is the best of Mr Maugham; you can always be sure that he will make you laugh. But the moment you begin to look into his clerical humbug, and ask yourself whether he has been well and truly drawn—why, then, you think it time to go back to Barchester.

34. [A. A.] M[ilne], review, *Punch*

CXL, 8 March 1911, 177–8

Alan Alexander Milne (1882–1956), the creator of Winnie-the-Pooh, was at the period this article was written undergoing his apprenticeship on the staff of *Punch* as a writer of humorous articles, light verse and drama criticism. He was also to master the craft of playwriting, with considerable success in the West End, after the Great War.

The *Punch* reviewer wrongly, but understandably, assumed that the play was a dramatisation of the novel *The Bishop's Apron*, which was published before the play was first produced. Nor was he apparently aware that 'Cupid and the Vicar of Swale', the short story which foreshadowed the play, had appeared in *Punch* in 1908.

Mr Somerset Maugham calls his new play at The Duke of York's 'a satire in four Acts'; he may be supposed therefore to imply a moral. It is not difficult to discover what the moral is.

Theodore Spratte was a worldly man. He never tired of referring to his 'father, the late Lord Chancellor,' or to his family's supposed descent from the Montmorency stock; he admitted he was a snob and recommended snobbishness as a virtue to his children. He spared no pains or self-advertisement (within gentlemanly limits) to advance himself in his profession, and as a widower of fifty took care to marry again for money rather than for love. When his daughter fancied (quite mistakenly) that she was devoted to a bounder who wore detachable and reversible cuffs and owned unpresentable relations, he hurried on her engagement to Lord Wroxham by methods which may have seemed unscrupulous, but very certainly made for Winifred's happiness. He practised, perhaps more whole-heartedly than some, the usual insincerities of speech and manner which a civilised society demands, and accepted with considerable calm the extremely pleasant and luxurious state of life into which it had pleased Heaven to call him.

Who will rise and curse Theodore Spratte? Who will denounce vanity and egoism and pushfulness and good living? There are a few fine souls who may do so, but it is not for us to range ourselves ostentatiously among them. Theodore Spratte, as I have described him, may pass for an average man. Wait a moment, though; I find I have left out something rather important. Theodore Spratte was Vicar of St Gregory's!

This, I take it, is the meaning of the play. A clergyman, inasmuch as he is not judged by the same standards as other men, must be different from other men. The Church is not the same as other professions, to be entered light-heartedly by the younger sons. By all means let it be denied indignantly that Canon Spratte is typical of the Church; it will scarcely be denied that the Church is too frequently regarded as a means merely of worldly advancement. It is possible (and legitimate) to satirize all the reverend Sprattes without satirizing all the reverend Canons.

This is much the best of Mr Maugham's later and successful plays; I don't know if it is because he has adapted it from a book, *The Bishop's Apron,* written some years ago. Recently his literary conscience has not always been as wakeful as one could wish; he has shown an ingenuous confidence in the powers of the Maugham varnish to give newness to any situation. *Loaves and Fishes* has old moments, but it is for the most part truly funny, and—thanks to a great performance by Mr Robert Loraine—makes a delightful evening's entertainment.

THE LAND OF PROMISE

Lyceum Theatre, New York, 25 December 1913
(76 performances)
Duke of York's Theatre, London
26 February 1914 (185 performances)
[Written 1913. Published London, June 1922]

This is a modern version of *The Taming of the Shrew*. Having
launched it on its successful runs in New York and London,
Maugham temporarily abandoned the drama in order to
devote two years to the writing of his autobiographical novel,
Of Human Bondage. By the time the novel was published, in
1915, the Great War had broken out, in which Maugham
engaged in war service of various kinds.

---

35. Unsigned review, 'Maugham's Play Pleases at the Lyceum', *New York Times*

26 December 1913, 11

At the end of the third act, Miss Billie Burke paused long enough to
hope that 'they' had made our Christmas as happy as we had made
'theirs.' The pronouns stood for audience and actors. Probably
Miss Burke wasn't thinking about critics. Else why speak of being
happy?

However, the combined efforts of Miss Burke, Mr Shelley Hull,
and, last but by no means least, Mr W. Somerset Maugham, did
produce about as good an effect of Christmas feeling as was to be
had away from home on that 'dark and stormy night.' And one
assumes, naturally, that the people who were there didn't have

homes, or else why spend Christmas night in the theatre? Again omitting the reviewers.

Enough, then, to admit that Mr Maugham's play was the right sort for the night. He has a happy faculty of taking old dolls and dressing them up so that they seem almost as good as new. And here, with an English 'lady,' forced to migrate to Canada because she has been disappointed of a legacy, and then married to a 'hired man' (which, by the way, suggests that the play was written for London and not for New York), though not unfamiliar, it is mostly very pleasant.

Mr Maugham's first act does little more than establish a character—that of Norah Marsh, who after ten years as companion to a peculiarly unpleasant old lady, is thrown on her own resources. Her brother in Canada has married a 'waitress'—how these mesalliances do seem to run in families—and so Norah goes to him.

With the second act the plot begins to thicken. Norah is not of much use 'in the wilds.' Moreover, she seems a bit stuck up. Furthermore, before brother Ed married she wrote a peculiarly unpleasant letter about the 'waitress.' Not surprising, then, that the two women are at loggerheads, and that pretty soon there is a flare-up. Result, Norah must apologize to sister-in-law or out she goes. What's more, having offended sister-in-law in front of the hired help Norah's got to make her apology equally public or—well, well, sister-in-law will know the reason why. Unlike M. Berstein's latest heroine, this one doesn't make any bones about letting you know that she is jealous.

Then, you must know that one of the hired men, Frank Taylor, has been expressing himself rather freely about women, but, being tired of 'baching,' he thinks he'll run up to Winnipeg and have a look in at the domestic agencies, with a view of getting himself a wife who can cook, sew, wash and iron, and make herself generally useful about the shack. Comes now the moment when sister-in-law drives Norah a bit too hard, whereupon she offers to go with Frank. She has been particularly scornful of him before; now she'll marry him for the sake of finding a home. And Frank agrees to take her.

It will not be difficult to figure out pretty much what happens after this with Norah rebellious and Frank determined to be master in his own house. Norah smashes the dishes rather than wash them, but eats humble pie presently. And the progress of events through the third act is interesting even to people with memories of *The Great Divide, The Taming of the Shrew, Ingomar,* and other plays. For Mr Maugham writes tersely, happily, and with occasional twists of fun that add human touches to the romance. In the end, of course, Norah finds it possible to go back to England, but discovers that she is in love with Frank. And as a belated check has come she can be of material assistance since a blight is on Frank's crop.

Not much depth or breadth to *The Land of Promise*, but, we repeat, a wholly pleasant thing. The same word describes Miss Burke's share in it. Repose of any sort she utterly lacked last night, and of real pliancy or variety there was little enough in her acting. But the charm and prettiness and show of fire which endear her to the great majority of playgoers were abundantly manifest, and in truth the role does not require more to produce the right effect. It is gratifying to observe the splendid development of Shelley Hull, who provided a really splendid example of good virile acting, sounding a real note of character, and lightening his role with a delightful suggestion of dry humor.

Admirable, too, were Lillian Kingsbury and Marion Abbott, while Lumsden Hare, Norman Tharp, Thomas Reynolds, and Barnett Parker each added a share of the amusement. In fact, the entire cast is entirely equal to all of the demands, and the play, as has been said, is breezy, bright, and entertaining. That, on 'such a Christmas night,' was something to be thankful for.

36. J.T. Grein, review, *Sunday Times*

1 March 1914, 6

There are two aspects to Mr Maugham's latest play. It endeavours to give us a picture of the Dominion in the making; it analyses the characters of a man and a woman cast together by circumstance in the solitude of a land in reclamation.

We may take it for granted that the first picture is substantially correct. Mr Maugham has been in Canada and the keen observer he is, he makes it clear to us that the El Dorado of finance and rising cities is not a land of milk and honey. It is rugged with climate and toil—and rugged are the people in the plains whether they have come from the Mother Country to unlearn formality and luxury, or whether they are children of the soil. What buoys them up in their struggle with nature, and for the wherewithal, is the boundless horizon of acres cheap and free, and the hope to do well before age stiffens limbs and energies. We scent the earth in the farm of the master and the shack of the man. We witness the life of these folk, we understand their solitude yet their happiness, their preference for the freedom of the unconventional to the narrow groove of Europe and civilisation. We also perceive keenly how the strange girl, the ex-lady's companion—one of those women in whom the rank of a lady, the wages of a servant, the slavery to the whims of age, have bred rebellion—felt, when she came to her brother's house. She brought culture, and she found nature unveneered; she was a 'lady' and in her brother's wife, wedded from an inn, she felt the instinctive antagonism of the woman of all work. She had hoped for a legacy for her ten years' subservience, but when the will was opened there was nothing for her—all her visions of Italy and sunshine and well-being were dashed to pieces. So she set out for the land of promise and on the farm she was even more forlorn than in the perpetual sameness of the drawing-room in Tunbridge Wells. She did her best to fit in, but it would not work; her sister-in-law was jealous of her, bickerings matured to words, she let fall something which hurt the ex-waitress and the ransom was an apology in front of the men—master and hired men alike. She tried, she tried hard, but her suppressed pride had the better of her—rather than make amends to that common woman she would accept the offer to be the wife and housekeeper of the handsome rough Canadian on her brother's farm. And so they wedded and came to the shack so far untrodden by woman's feet, unadorned by woman's hand. It was a sad wedding-night. No romance but all work—menial work exacted by a commanding voice. She remained the lady and defied the man. She gave him tit-for-tat. When he shook her she struck him, bit him, pointed the unloaded gun at him and pulled the trigger in hope of effect. Yet he cowed her, he claimed obedience—in every sense of the word. It sickened her

soul, it infuriated her to vixenism; but there was no escape, no
house within miles and dread frost upon the plain, there was only
one way—to accept the yoke of matrimony with all it implied. She
passed to the adjoining chamber as one going to doom. The act, a
duologue from first to last, is one of great power and pain. It held
the audience, but it chilled it. In a sense it was a revelation. Is it thus
that the man by his strength still rules woman in civilised British
dominions? It recalled the days of Shakespeare's *Taming of the
Shrew*. But that was jest; this was grim earnest; as minute, as
realistic, as brutal as Zola unrestrained. True it rang, but it repelled
by its veracity. A masterpiece of technique, charged with insight,
but so crude, so full of obvious intent to impress by causing hurt.
A little less of the slice of life, a slightly subtler touch of artistic
restraint, and the scene would have stirred our emotions. Now the
feelings were mingled. We admired the dramatist, but we found
fault with his discretion. Physical subjugation of a woman is the
most painful of all domination. And in this case there was not even
the excuse of latent attraction on her part. There was physical
repugnance. She, the poor little soul, so neat and so narrow,
shuddered at his kiss.

The next episode showed how these two became really mated,
how material misfortune brought them nearer to one another. But
we could hardly believe the happy issue. What we did believe was
that the wife, having tasted the freedom of the plains, would not
accept once more the crabbed life of a lady's companion, and would
remain in Canada—or—and on this 'or' I pause. Mr Maugham has
shirked the real issue, but this is certain, however true it may be
that some women accept the mailed fist and feel content under its
sway, this woman—with her decorous soul of a lady's
companion—a soul apart modelled by life—could not have
forgiven the outrage of the wedding night. The fourth act is a
sacrifice to convention, as the third is exuberance of realism.

For all that a play that matters, a play to be seen, a play that
reveals the undiminished power of the Maugham who wrote *Liza
of Lambeth* and *A Man of Honour*. A play, too, that will be ardently
discussed—especially by women.

The burden of the two principal interpreters was heavy. The
third act demands great dramatic powers and both Miss Irene
Vanbrugh and Mr Godfrey Tearle were equal to it. He was the
incarnation of male vigour; she the woman rebelling against

suppression. In him the will and consciousness of force dominated; in her the stubbornness born of inherent weakness. It was wonderfully portrayed. We felt deeply moved and intensely repelled. That must have been the author's aim, and his actors reached it in unswerving triumphant directness. There were others who deserved well of the cause. Mr C.V. France and Miss Marion Ashworth as the Canadian couple, Miss Mary Rorke in her short scene of a farmer's wife's woe and joy concerning the harvest, and the ensemble was flawless. The play and the acting created a lasting impression.

37. S.O., 'Pygmalion (at Home and Abroad)', *English Review*

XVII, May 1914, 276–8

This review places Maugham's last pre-Great War play in its Edwardian context by comparing it with the first London production of Shaw's contemporary *Pygmalion*. 'S.O.' has not been identified.

In these feminist times it is interesting to see two playwrights such as Mr Somerset Maugham and Mr Bernard Shaw handling the eternal theme of fashioning womanhood; and though they see woman at acutely different angles and cast characteristically different projections upon the Boards, the conclusion in both cases is the same, and in neither is the vote a contributory instrument. Put them together, and they form a two-nights' philosophy and entertainment, the one male, a little brutal, sexual, catastrophic, that of Mr Shaw epicene, bloodless, intellectual, and neuter: two kinds of Pygmalions, in short, yet both culminating prettily enough in the lap of Venus. If Mr Shaw's object was to be funny, evidently it was Mr Maugham's to be serious, and woman remains the Sphynx, not because she really is enigmatic any more than the Egyptian blocks of stone are enigmatic, but because she is extrinsically so malleable and intrinsically so static, whereas man is so strange a contortionist.

The Pygmalion of Mr Maugham is muscular; with Mr Shaw he is intellectual; in other words, abroad the process is a matter of sex domination, at home it is a mollentrave* for the mind. Mr Maugham's male has the harder task of the two, because, in the first place, he is a rough-hewn settler on the prairie in Canada, with no Latin and not much else in the way of education beyond the vigour of his own natural schooling, and, in the second, because the woman he takes into his house is of that superior, eminently respectable middle-class type of femininity which, profoundly ignorant of every truth and profundity of life, makes such admirable ladies' helps and maiden aunts. But this one is pretty, moreover she has a temper and considerable grit, and it never occurred to her when she accepted the man's invitation to live with him as housekeeper, and actually went to church to solemnise the righteousness of her position, that a share in the bed was as integral a part of the matrimonial bond as a share in the board, still more so in the primitive conditions of prairie life alone with a man and— nature. The situation—at once, and not a bad one either. She never thought the man meant union, and he a common fellow, whereas she is a 'lady.' True, she married him, but what is man? No doubt she had read some recent feminist pamphlets. Nothing physical had ever entered into her existence. 'Fie, sir. Touch your wife,' and she puts up a pair of fists, like Mr Mitchell engaging Carpentier. Unfortunately the Church had licensed the union. Life 'out there' is physical; Pygmalion is dreadfully obstinate too, and besides very strong. It is a ninety seconds' round, and on the stage the sparring being handled with consummate delicacy, we have a big scene which leaves us all wanting to talk about it. And physical wins. Her chance comes months later. She has a position at home, she can go back. But she has not been her man's mate for nothing. Gradually she has learnt to love. Now she will stay, and Pygmalion in his new troth looks so radiant when the curtain falls upon their first common love-embrace that we feel they will be happy ever afterwards.

* *Mollentrave on Women*, a play by Alfred Sutro, 1907 (eds).

At His Majesty's, Sir Herbert has a more subtle task, which provides him with great opportunities for silent by-play, and the art of 'making presence' on the stage in which accomplishments he obviously revels. He, however, is an oddity—a professor of phonetics, an asexual intellectualist. He has to repickle Smollett, dramatically, and so, of all people, he chooses Mrs Patrick Campbell and, for the fun of the thing, makes her a flower-girl. She, of course, is physical, deliciously so on the stage, but here Pygmalion is modern. He will make a Duchess of her in six months, teach her to clip her words, drawl, emphasise, use the right slang, instruct her in deportment and the social niceties of the big 'family' which calls one another by their Christian names only. Incidentally there is a philosopher dustman, essentially an entertainment projection as old-fashioned in contrivance as the Greek chorus, who helps things along 'considerable'; and he, having some telling things to say and being excellently acted, is a delight, though quite as artificial and quite as irrelevant to the movement as the tenor who comes in and sings a sentimental lyric in middle-class musical comedy. The thing resembles a cinema. Good films are the dustman's soliloquies, epigrams, and plaint of the 'undeserving poor'; Mrs Patrick Campbell's imperturbability of mien and throat modulations in the scene where she justifies her master's teaching, her gowns and the whole look of her generally; some of the curtains, especially the cab scene, a number of the talks; some of Sir Herbert's elliptic smiles, and the end which presumably means that the professor has fallen in love with his creation and means to keep her. All these sallies and situations are amusing and unnatural enough to appear natural. The professor is a lovable type, unusually objective a figure for Mr Shaw, a new Svengali, and if only the flower-girl had been provided with a *clou* or *cliché* such as Du Maurier got hold of with the 'foot' of his Trilby, this *Pygmalion* might well catch the fancy of the town. Perhaps she hasn't been worked up yet, as they say of our lighter drama. Certain it is she lacks animation. (The truth is that only one side of her is represented; characteristically, Mr Shaw has only drawn a torso of a flower-girl.) Mr Shaw seems afraid of her. We don't seem to get the perspective of this girl. The fun hangs on the interpolated dustman, on the professorial solicitude, the frolic is implied rather than attested, which is a pity, for there are certainly stage possibilities in a flower-girl crystallising into a lady—opportunities, at any rate, for a second version when the time comes for the 'new' dresses and outrig.

Comparing the two plays technically, it is significant to observe how boldly Mr Maugham has freed himself from the entertainment label, what a fresh and strong note he rings, as with what conservative insistency Mr Shaw sticks to the old formula of artifical type designed primarily for the laugh. Though Mr Maugham's situation is theatrical, and it is difficult to believe in the enormity of his lady-help's prudery, the theme makes a good play, and he must be congratulated on having recaptured his true art and made the public swallow it.

The acting in both Houses is notable. Miss Irene Vanbrugh excels in the difficult *rôle* of the ferocious virgin, plays all through with a fine understanding. In the other place the most physical actress on our stage has a part as invertebrate as a marionette, but contrives to have an epic moment with the jubilation of a full-mouthed 'bloody.'

PART III
BOOKS
(1915–1933)

OF HUMAN BONDAGE

New York, London, August 1915

If Maugham had been able to arrange for the first version of this autobiographical novel, written in 1899, to be published on terms acceptable to him, it would have followed *Liza of Lambeth*. It was then entitled 'The Artistic Temperament of Stephen Carey', and when in 1950 Maugham presented the manuscript to the Library of Congress in Washington he stipulated that it was never to be published. He had intended to call the later version 'Beauty from Ashes', but had to think up a new title when he learned that name had recently been used by another author. When he corrected the proofs he was serving with a Red Cross ambulance unit with the British Expeditionary Force in France.

38. Unsigned review, *Times Literary Supplement*

12 August 1915, 269

The reference in this review to the hero being 'so busy yearning for the moon that he never saw the sixpence at his feet' was to suggest to Maugham the title of his next novel, published in 1919.

No lover of Fielding is likely to complain of the long, biographical form of novel which time (helped, perhaps, a little by M. Romain Rolland) has brought into favour again with the novelists. If the hero or subject of the biography is worth knowing at all, it is a good thing to know him in childhood. And it is not only the hero whom the biographical novel is to elucidate. With Fielding in mind, the reader expects that the writer shall give him also a view of life—not the suggestion that comes from a 'slice,' but some kind of general answer, whether the author present it 'dramatically' or didactically, to the problem set by the whole cake.

Some recent experiments suggest that a capital difficulty in this form of fiction is to maintain the balance between life and the man. Life is very various and very interesting: the temptation is to keep the man too strictly to the function of a looking-glass, in which life, hurrying by, is reflected without being affected; as if personality, which means in some degree limitation and in some sense choice, went for nothing, and a man were equally susceptible to everything that crossed his field of reflection. Mr Maugham has avoided that mistake. His Philip Carey is often pretty helpless, as man is wont to be; but he has flavour and individuality. He reacts, as chemists say, to this or that, and not equally to everything. As the book goes on Mr Maugham wins the reader's confidence, and at the close has his full agreement. Just that, and no other, was Philip Carey—a good fellow, a fool, much to be pitied, much to be envied, worth knowing and worth learning from. Mr Maugham takes him from a dismal childhood to a minor public school; to Heidelberg instead of to Oxford; to an office in the City; to the art schools in Paris; to a London hospital; to a draper's shop; back to the hospital, and finally to a country practice. The setting of each phase in his career is elaborated in vivid, and doubtless accurate, detail, but in each case it remains a setting for this particular man.

Philip Carey was a cripple and an orphan. He was exceptionally sensitive, and he had the kind of pride which leads sensitive people to self-torture. He was restless and eager; he had a great capacity for happiness and unhappiness; and like many young men he was so busy yearning for the moon that he never saw the sixpence at his feet. His story is the pilgrim's progress from illusion into reality, from dreaming into knowing, from gaping after the future into making the most of the present. It is the common experience, though in no two lives does it ever take the same form or the same time; and one point in Mr Maugham's favour is that this is obviously Philip Carey's particular experience. But the effect is not gained without a little straining. We believe that to be less Mr Maugham's fault than the fault of his day. He is not, that is, untainted with the prevailing notion that only the miserable things are worth writing about. A very great injury was worked on Philip Carey's life by his low passion for a detestable woman called Mildred. Mildred is so brilliantly drawn that the reader cannot but share the author's obvious delight in his own skill. Yet, before we have done with her, we dread the sight of her name on a page as Philip dreaded seeing her in the street. It is not only that we resent being forced to spend so much time with so unpleasant a creature. We resent the twist that is given to the figure of life. Another of Philip's love affairs was carried on with a woman called Norah. Norah was charming, and she gave Philip some happiness; therefore Norah must be kept as much as possible out of sight. There was more of true 'life' in one of Philip's evenings with Norah than in all his expense of spirit in a waste of shame with Mildred; and when Norah is tucked away into a grudged chapter or two we feel that the life account is being made up unfairly, with a big sum left out on the credit side. Perhaps Mr Maugham will adjust it by telling us in some future novel about Philip's life with the adorable Sally who becomes his wife. For love and happiness are no less 'life' than lust and misery—and quite as good material for fiction, if only our novelists would see it.

The view of life which the book works out implies certainly a profounder mind than would be expected from Mr Maugham's successful drama. He does not, like Fielding, talk to us in intimate prefaces; nor does he, like some novelists, throw the mass of facts before us and bid us make what we can of it. It is all Philip Carey's story, and Philip Carey's thoughts; but Mr Maugham has no objection to telling us quite clearly what he is at—what Philip Carey made of it. Philip was no seer. He referred everything to his own experience. He had no faith in God and very little in man. His morals were a matter of so much of 'good form' as was left over from his public school life, and of what Christian ethic survived his loss of Christian belief. On the road from illusion to reality he is robbed, one by one, of the comforts which he had not tasted by his own experience. The last to go was the desire for happiness. Life is the pattern in a Persian rug; joy and pain make up the colours. That

is all. There is no meaning to the design (and there Mr Maugham
and Philip Carey and the drunken poet Cronshaw, who suggested
the idea, are all a little hard on Persian rugs, in which every figure
has a symbolical meaning). But a man may at least make the design
beautiful, and may accept bravely and gladly what colours come.
Poets and seers see something more, or something other, in life
than that. Mr Maugham has presented, very clearly and very ably,
the view of human bondage to circumstance which was conceived
by the keen intelligence and eager spirit of one who was no poet.

39. Gerald Gould, review,
New Statesman

V, 25 September 1915, 594

Gerald Gould (1885–1936) was a poet, critic and journalist.
After the Great War he became chief fiction reviewer on the
Observer and also a reader for Victor Gollancz, thus having
considerable influence over the fortunes of contemporary
British fiction.

The following review dealt also with a novel by Mrs Henry
Dudeney.

Mr Maugham has produced a very big book in every sense of the
word. It has six hundred and forty-eight pages and as many merits.
Only—and the effect is odd—the merits are not precisely those
which one would expect from Mr Maugham. He has shown
himself in the past capable of finished construction and sparkling
verbal wit: here he gives us neither the one nor the other. The
succession of incidents is almost wantonly casual (so, he might say,
is the succession of incidents in life). The conversations and
descriptions are often amazingly vivid, but seldom amusing:
several characters are introduced who, we are given to understand,
talk brilliantly, but Mr Maugham does not allow them to talk in the
least brilliantly. There is minuteness without realism, passion

without romance, variation without variety: one might say that Mr Maugham's line is length without breadth. There is a fury of concentration in every detail of what is by superficial tests so diffuse. The limitations are clearly not due to any defect of power: they are deliberate. They are an essay in the admirable artistic thesis that the part is greater than the whole. Life is constrained by them to suit a point of view. This method, of disguising selectiveness by profusion, of making life conceal art, is not new, but it has not often been practised in England. If Mr Maugham belongs to a school at all, it is to a French one. But I am not sure that he does belong to a school. I am not sure he has not written a highly original book. I am not even sure he has not written almost a great one.

Philip Carey has a club foot, and a profound sensitiveness about it. His whole character is modified by it; but, even apart from that, he looks at facts from a peculiar angle. His childhood and school days make one conscious of his queerness, his intensity—of the extent to which his friendships, his decisions, his mode of life, are affected by resentment and the passion of self-pitying pride. After school, he has a career of exceptional diversity. It takes one to Germany, to a London office, to Paris (the Quarter, the art students' life), and back to a London hospital. Philip is everything by starts and nothing (until he finally qualifies as a medical man) long. Even the hospital period contains a break during which, having lost all his money, he is reduced to earning his living as a shop assistant: more variation, more local colour! The amount of difference and detail in the book is incredible—it would furnish the settings for a dozen or so ordinary novels. It is obvious that we can give no idea of it by quotation. But, perhaps, this picture of the Bal Bullier is as typical as anything:

It was a sordid scene.... They danced furiously. They danced round the room, slowly, talking very little, with all their attention given to the dance. The room was hot, and their faces shone with sweat. It seemed to Philip that they had thrown off the guard which people wear on their expression, the homage to convention, and he saw them now as they really were. In that moment of abandon they were strangely animal: some were foxy and some were wolflike; and others had the long, foolish face of sheep. Their skins were sallow from the unhealthy life they led, and the poor food they ate. Their features were blunted by mean interests, and their little eyes were shifty and cunning. There was nothing of nobility in their bearing, and you felt that for all of them life was a long succession of petty concerns and sordid thoughts. The air was heavy with the musty smell of humanity. But they danced furiously as though impelled by some strange power within them, and it seemed to Philip that they were driven forward by a rage for enjoyment.... They were hurried on by a great wind, helplessly, they knew not why and they knew not whither. Fate seemed to tower above them, and they danced as though everlasting darkness were beneath their feet. Their silence was vaguely alarming. It was as if life terrified them and robbed them of power of speech so that the shriek which was in their hearts died at their throats. Their eyes were haggard and grim; and notwithstanding the beastly lust that disfigured them, and the meanness of their faces, and the cruelty, notwithstanding the stupidness which was worst of all, the anguish of those fixed eyes made all that crowd terrible and pathetic.

Now I venture to say flatly that anyone who knows the Bullier will deny the truth of this picture. There is much true gaiety there, and a love of pleasure which, so far from being terrible, is quite simple and natural—the ordinary excitement of youth. Nevertheless, the picture is true as seen through Philip's eyes: it has the truth of the angle. And that brings me to the main point. The interest of the story is chiefly sexual. You cannot have love without sex, but when he is scarcely more than a boy Philip has an 'experience' with a pitiful and unpleasant woman much older than himself: when he is in Paris he is loved, unreciprocally, by a far more pitiful and unpleasant woman—a queer, passionate, ugly, vengeful, disagreeable creature, absolutely unforgettable, whom it wrings one's heart to read of. The best years of his life are wasted on an abnormal physical craving for a vulgar, empty-headed girl, alternately cold and lustful and always treacherous, whose physical defects—her greenish complexion, her anaemic lips, her flat chest—are dwelt upon insistently. For this girl he makes the extremest sacrifices, undergoes the most horrible humiliations, and with it all succeeds neither in satisfying himself nor in keeping her off the streets. He has, in an interval, an affair with a really charming, if ugly, woman: but even there there is none of the fine quality of permanence. He finds peace and the prospect of a simple, homely, satisfactory life—a rest from his morbidities—in marrying a child of nature, a girl of clear visions and calm moods, magnificently healthy; but even with her he approaches marriage only by what is, after all, the unusual road of seduction. Of this whole view of sex, the romantic (who is the best realist) will say, as of the view of the Bullier quoted above—'It simply isn't like that.' And yet it is so far-fetched that from that very fact it draws a certain convincingness. It *may* be true—*from the angle*. But what an angle! And still I am misrepresenting Mr Maugham. I have made his book sound revolting, and it is not. Many things in it are painful, but the philosophy informing it has so much tenderness, patience, endurance, that the total effect is not revolting and not hopeless: the whole is exceedingly strange, but it is on the grand scale, and in some ways beautiful....

40. Unsigned review, *Athenaeum*

4582, 21 August 1915

To-day, when so many are teaching us tersely enough how to live and to die, it requires some little patience to wade through over five hundred pages describing the process as leisurely and none too adequately carried out by a member of the male sex in the Victorian era. The hero of Mr Maugham's novel was hampered by a concatenation of disadvantages. Many have suffered from the early loss of parents and guardianship assumed by a person who ought not to have had the upbringing of a dog, far less a human being, but the added defect of a club foot from birth is happily unusual. In other words, the author has so handicapped his hero as to remove him out of the category of the average. This, however, is largely a record of sordid realism.

Until he reached manhood the hero had never experienced anything which could be designated by the name of love except from the wife of his guardian, and she was really nothing but a shrivelled old maid. None the less we regret her death before the middle of the book as she is the most sympathetically drawn of all the characters. As a matter of fact the author's women are all in our opinion better drawn than his men. Even the selfish A.B.C. girl, whom the hero could not succeed in making one of his mistresses, has many redeeming qualities, but we find none in the man himself. The other subjects of his amours are very real, not least in their inconsistency in caring for him.

We learn a good deal concerning the three careers which he tried—accountancy, painting , and doctoring—but none of these was adopted from anything approaching a real motive. The picture of the kindly humanity of the one family that gave him a welcome in his medical student days affords a welcome relief. We would gladly have dispensed with much else to hear more of the head of it. The discussions concerning art and morality which take place in the Latin quarter are somewhat discounted by the principal talker, who, after holding his audience entranced by verbal fireworks, declares himself to be very drunk. The values accorded by the hero to love, realism, and religion are so distorted as to have no interest beyond that which belongs to an essentially morbid personality. In such a long novel reiteration is peculiarly tiresome and apt to reduce the gratitude which should be felt for the detailed portraiture and varied aspects of life the author presents to us.

41. Theodore Dreiser, 'As a Realist Sees It', *New Republic*

V, 25 December 1915, 202–4

Theodore Herman Albert Dreiser (1871–1945) was an American novelist who began his career as a journalist. One of the pioneers of realism in the American novel, influenced by Balzac, his novels include *The Financier* (1912), *Sister Carrie* (1900) and *An American Tragedy* (1925).

From the publication of this effusive, emphatic review Maugham dated the start of the novel's journey towards becoming a modern classic.

Sometimes in retrospect of a great book the mind falters, confused by the multitude and yet the harmony of the detail, the strangeness of the frettings, the brooding, musing, intelligence that has foreseen, loved, created, elaborated, perfected, until, in this middle ground, which we call life, somewhere between nothing and nothing, hangs the perfect thing which we love and cannot understand, but which we are compelled to confess a work of art. It is at once something and nothing, a dream, a happy memory, a song, a benediction. In viewing it, one finds nothing to criticize or to regret. The thing sings, it has colour. It has rapture. You wonder at the loving, patient care which has evolved it.

Only recently I finished reading Mr W. Somerset Maugham's *Of Human Bondage*. It was with some such feeling as this that I laid it down. In recent years, and quite definitely, we have been getting on in a literary way. Despite our complaints as to the intolerance of a philistine age, many interesting things are being done. In England, particularly in the last few years (though France has produced *Jean Christophe*), we have had George Moore, all of him; *The New Machiavelli* of Wells, *Fortitude* by Hugh Walpole; *The Old Wives' Tale* by Arnold Bennett, *Sinister Street* by Compton Mackenzie, *The New Grub Street* by Gissing, *Joseph Stahl* by J.D. Beresford, and also such minor volumes as *The Rat Pit* by Patrick MacGill, and *Mushroom Town* by Oliver Onions. (What a name!)

In America, on the other hand, we have lagged. There have been *Predestined* by Stephen French Whitman, *Quicksand* by Hervey White, *The Story of Eva* by Will Payne, *The Turn of the Balance* by Brand Whitlock, *With the Procession* by H.B. Fuller and *McTeague* by Frank Norris, but all of these, transcendent as are their narrative merits, are lacking somehow in the vast undercurrent of which these newer and more forceful writers seem cognizant.

Here is a novel or biography or autobiography or social transcript of the utmost importance. To begin with, it is unmoral, as a novel of this kind must necessarily be.

[There follows an outline of the novel's plot.]

Curiously, the story rises to no spired climax. To some it has apparently appealed as a drab, unrelieved narrative. To me at least it is a gorgeous weave, as interesting and valuable at the beginning as at the end. There is material in its three hundred thousand and more words for many novels and, indeed, several philosophies, and even a religion or stoic hope. There are a series of women, of course—drab, pathetic, enticing, as the case may be—who lead him through the mazes of sentiment, sex, love, pity, passion, a wonderful series of portraits and of incidents. There are a series of men friends of a peculiarly inclusive range of intellectuality and taste, who lead him, or whom he leads, through all the intricacies of art, philosophy, criticism, humour. And lastly comes life itself, the great land and sea of people, England, Germany, France, battering, corroding, illuminating, a Goyaesque world.

Naturally I asked myself how such a book would be received in America, in England. In the latter country, I was sure, with its traditions of the *Athenaeum* and the *Saturday Review*, it would be adequately appreciated. Imagine my surprise to find that the English reviews were almost uniformly contemptuous and critical on moral and social grounds. The hero was a weakling, not for a moment to be tolerated by sound, right-thinking men. On the other hand, in America the reviewers for the most part have seen its true merits and stated them. Need I say, however, that the New York *World* finds it 'the sentimental servitude of a poor fool'; or that the Philadelphia *Press* sees fit to dub it 'futile Philip', or that the *Outlook* feels that 'the author might have made his book true without making it so frequently distasteful'; or that the *Dial* cries, 'a most depressing impression of the futility of life'? 'No brilliancy of style', mourns the Detroit *Times*. 'Young folks are warned off', urges the Portland *Oregonian*. (As if that young person could be induced to examine so profound and philosophic a book!) 'Certainly the story cannot be said to be in any sense a wholesome one, and it would require a distinctly morbid taste for one to enjoy it thoroughly'. (Note the 'thoroughly'.) This from the New Orleans *Time-Picayune*. 'One longs after reading these novels where spineless men and women yield without a struggle to the forces of evil'—but I cannot go on. It is too trite. You must judge for yourself how the reviewer on the *Saturday Evening Post* of Burlington, Ia., felt about it.

Despite these dissonant voices, it is still a book of the utmost import, and has so been received. Compact of the experiences, the dreams, the hopes, the fears, the disillusionments, the ruptures, and the philosophisings of a strangely starved soul, it is a beacon light by which the wanderer may be guided. Nothing is left out; the author writes as though it were a labour of love. It bears the imprint of an eager, almost consuming desire to say truly what is in his heart.

Personally I found myself aching with pain when, yearning for sympathy, Philip begs the wretched Mildred, never his mistress but on his level, to no more than tolerate him. He finally humiliates himself to the extent of exclaiming: 'You don't know what it means to be a cripple!' The pathos of it plumbs the depths. The death of Fanny Price, of the sixteen-year-old mother in the slum, of Cronshaw, and the rambling agonies of old Ducroz and of Philip himself, are perfect in their appeal.

There are many other and all equally brilliant pictures. No one short of a genius could rout the philosophers from their lairs and label them as individuals 'tempering life with rules agreeable to themselves', or could follow Mildred Rogers, waitress of the London ABC restaurant, through all the shabby windings of her tawdry soul. No other than a genius endowed with an immense capacity for understanding and pity could have sympathized with Fanny Price, with her futile and self-destructive art dreams; or old Cronshaw, the wastrel of poetry and philosophy; or Mons. Ducroz, the worn-out revolutionary; or Thorne Athelny, the caged grandee of Spain; or Leonard Upjohn, airy master of the art of self-advancement; or Dr South, the vicar of Blackstable, and his wife—these are masterpieces. They are marvellous portraits; they are as smooth as a Vermeer, as definite as a Hals, as brooding and moving as a Rembrandt. The study of Carey himself, while one sees him more as a medium through which the others express themselves, still registers photographically at times. He is by no means a brooding voice but a definite, active, vigorous character.

If the book can be said to have a fault, it will lie for some in its length, 300,000 words, or for others in the peculiar reticence with which the last love affair in the story is handled. Until the coming of Sally Athelny all has been described with the utmost frankness. No situation, however crude or embarrassing, has been shirked. In the matter of the process by which he arrived at the intimacy which resulted in her becoming pregnant not a word is said. All at once, by a slight frown, which she subsequently explains, the truth is forced upon you that there has been a series of intimacies which have not been accounted for. After Mildred Rogers and his relationship with Norah Nesbit, it strikes one as strange.

I feel about this book, as I look back on it now, much as old Cronshaw in the story felt about the rug which was to clarify for Carey the meaning of life:

As the weaver elaborated his pattern for no end but the pleasure of his aesthetic sense, so might a man live his life, or, if he was forced to believe that his actions were outside his choosing, so might a man look at his life, that it made a pattern. There was little need to do this or there was little need to do that. It was merely something that he did for his own pleasure. Out of the manifold events of his life, his deeds, his feelings, his thoughts, he might make a design, regular, elaborated, complicated or beautiful; and though it might be no more than an illusion that he had the power of selection, that did not matter; it seemed and so to him it was. In the vast warp of life, with the background to his fancies that there was no meaning and that nothing was important, a man might get a personal satisfaction in selecting the various strands that worked out the pattern. ... What happened to him now would be one more motive to add to the complexity of the pattern, and when the end approached he would rejoice in its completion. It would be a work of art and it would be none the less beautiful because he alone knew of its existence, and with his death it would at once cease to be.

And so it is, Mr Maugham, this life of Philip Carey as you have woven it. One feels as though one were sitting before a splendid Shiraz or Daghestan of priceless texture and intricate weave, admiring, feeling, responding sensually to its colours and tones. Or better yet, it is as though a symphony of great beauty by a master, Strauss and Beethoven, has just been completed, and the bud notes and flower tones were filling the air with their elusive message, fluttering and dying. Mr Maugham, as I understand it, has written eleven conventional books and as many plays. It may be that for years, as the paragraph quoted suggests, he has lived willing that the large knowledge which this book reveals should remain unseen and even perish with him. For all of that he is none the less a great artist. Vicariously, it seems to me, he has suffered for the joy of the many who are to read after him. By no willing of his own he has been compelled to take life by the hand and go down where there has been little save sorrow and degradation. The cup of gall and wormwood has obviously been lifted to his lips and to the last drop he has been compelled to drink it. Because of this we are enabled to see the rug, woven of the tortures and the delights of a life. We may actually walk and talk with one whose hands and feet have been pierced with nails.

42. Marcus Aurelius Goodrich, 'After Ten Years of *Of Human Bondage*', *New York Times*

25 January 1925, 2

Marcus Aurelius Goodrich (b. 1897) was a journalist, screen-writer and novelist. His novel *Delilah* (1941) was based on his experience of naval warfare in the Great War.

During the last decade, the vast, passive jury, in whose hands rests the fate of all writing aspiring to a berth among the classics, have been attending in ever increasing numbers to the steady, unacclaimed arcing [*sic*] over the turmoil of William Somerset Maugham's *Of Human Bondage*. Among New York's literary guild the quite long book, no doubt, has been forgotten. Experiment has shown that when it is possible for a moment to shunt the attention of most of that eminent crew from the uproarious business of literature to the name Maugham, the inevitable response is an exhibitionistic shout referring to a play that he did not write, or to another novel about a tired English business man who retreated to life among the blue skies and corals with a leprosy ridden negress.

But in the less spectacular realms of those who read books merely because they like to read, or those whose culture shelters a vibrant attraction towards authentic performances in English prose, or those who are thrilled to find the universal aspects of life on a printed page, *Of Human Bondage* has, after ten years of steadily increasing activity, risen in England almost to a place beside *The Way of All Flesh*, and in the United States is on the way to becoming an uncanonical sensation. When the book was first published in the United States, it managed to live through three anaemic editions, despite the general critical preoccupation with other matters. Then four years went by and the publishers suddenly discovered that there was a quiet, unheralded demand for more copies of *Of Human Bondage*. They issued another small edition. Two years later, without a single pat on the back from the literators, the supply was again exhausted. The publishers prepared another edition. In 1923 the steady demand for the novel assumed such proportions that it was introduced into a special edition of works that seem to be in permanent demand. In this last edition, which is a fixture of its publishing house, it has gone through three printings. The universities just seem to have discovered the novel, libraries report an increasing call for it, second-hand book dealers number it among the old novels that still sell easily, and the price in London of a first edition of it has multiplied itself by three in the past five years. In New York's clubs and drawing rooms and at exoteric dinner tables, one is a bit surprised to find so old a book talked of as if it had been written yesterday, surprised that any volume could have resisted for so long the gigantic flood rushing every second from the printing presses. The explanation, perhaps, is that *Of Human Bondage* has become a classic.

A short time after Heinemann in England and Doran in the United States simultaneously published *Of Human Bondage* in 1915, the perfunctory, unenergetic ripple that it had caused in the critical puddle had smoothed out. The book was allowed to go unpublicized on its quiet way down the trail to oblivion, while the critics turned to raddle themselves in more spectacular rouge pots. In England the critics evidently had felt that something was expected of them, but most of them just did not seem to be very much interested. They admitted generally that it was a realistic character study. Richard King in the *Tatler*, as was to be expected, dismissed it facetiously in a short commentary that ended with the information that *Of Human Bondage* is scarcely a story. The *Westminster Gazette* decorously passed on the word that it had 'excellence'; the *Saturday Review* admitted that it was 'arresting'; the *Nation*, in a flabby article, pronounced it to be an experimental attempt to follow in the steps of Compton Mackenzie; and *Punch* inquired plaintively, 'Why have so many of our novelists taken to producing enormous volumes marked by a pre-Raphaelite fidelity to detail?'

In the United States the case was pretty much the same. The *New York World* in four careless little unsigned paragraphs intimated that the novel was not worth all the space it took up and complained of the title. *Harper's Weekly* printed: '*Of Human Bondage* is a fat, comfortable volume that will hold the attention of all those who read fiction seriously.' The *Dial* commented sententiously on its length and said that 'the book is far from being compellingly great.' The *Outlook* devoted a few lines to the opinion that the book 'shows marked ability in its own way.' Most of the papers throughout the States contented themselves with minor, routine observations that the book was 'startlingly realistic,' and with excerpted paragraphs let it go at that. In several journals appeared the same, mild, stereotyped review that had probably emanated from some syndicate; but what might be held up as the symbol of the whole critical attitude, both here and in England, leaked off the pen of the critic on the *Pittsburgh Chronicle-Telegraph*:

> The reviewer has looked at this book time and again, and just as often has refrained from looking into it. The reason is that there are 648 pages of the story—300 pages too many for careful reading and candid review. But this much can be said: It opens with a funeral and ends with a wedding. As the author is one of the most successful of the younger dramatists, and is said to have made several fortunes from his plays, it may be taken for granted that his novel will repay the reading of it by those who have the time to do so.

Both abroad and in the United States, however, there were some who were fired into eloquent approval of Mr Maugham's novel. The journals in Dublin, Ireland; Los Angeles, Cal., and Chicago, Ill., the *Boston Evening Transcript* and Theodore Dreiser in the *New Republic* came out flatly with the news that a great and thrilling masterpiece had been born into the world.

When Mr Maugham, after fashioning a monument of such stoical brilliance as *Of Human Bondage* unmolested by overmuch critical booming, went down among the critics and burst out in their midst with *The Moon and Sixpence*, his fleshy, vivid gesture was not, perhaps, so much a normal literary development, as it was a comment on the middlemen who stood between him and promptly rewarded literary achievement.

After coming face to face with the universal, simple beauty and verity that rears itself symmetrically through the 648 pages of Maugham's book, one realizes that he confronts a tremendous emotional, not merely sensual, upheaval. He has seen life, if not defined, at least epically epitomized.

That *Of Human Bondage* suffered tardy intellectual approval, may be due to the gaudy critical methods that began to come into vogue about the time Mr Maugham started writing. The chief impetus behind these methods seems to be, as somebody has pointed out, an intent on the part of the critic to call attention to himself rather than to the work he is criticizing. A book received the spotlight if it were capable of reflecting sensational and startling colors back upon him who directed the light. There are in Maugham's novel no color splashing areas nor purpureal periods that could be used to decorate the sort of spectacular critiques inspired, for instance, by the efforts of Messrs. Huxley, Hergesheimer and Firbank. But *Of Human Bondage* is built with pure, meagre-syllabled phrases that twist and cling thrillingly in their unsensational contexts. It is only when the simple, almost primitive, words sum up into the whole absorbing performance that they partake of the nature of sensation. Without once relapsing into dullness, Maugham has consistently passed by the opportunity to indulge in poster effects, so that in the end he might attain to a vital sweep of living, effulgent, integral color. He has succeeded. Even in those passages wherein he depicts events and situations than which there are no more spectacular in man's existence, he maintains his Homeric restraint to an extent that almost makes them seem flat when extracted from their contexts....

THE MOON AND SIXPENCE

London, April 1919; New York, July 1919

For the title of this novel, see the headnote to the previous section on *Of Human Bondage* (page 123).

The Moon and Sixpence, written in a sanatorium whilst Maugham was recuperating from tuberculosis contracted during his arduous years as an intelligence agent during the Great War, marks the commencement of the second phase of his career as a novelist and differs entirely in style and intention from his pre-war fiction. The last part of the novel, set in Tahiti, forms part of the harvest of themes he brought back from the first of the several journeys to the East he made between 1916 and 1926, which gave such a distinctive flavour to the fiction of his middle period.

---

43. K[atherine] M[ansfield], 'Inarticulations', *Athenaeum*

4645, 9 May 1919, 302

Katherine Mansfield (1888–1923), short-story writer, author of *In a German Pension* (1911), *The Garden Party* (1922), etc., was born in Wellington, New Zealand, as Katherine Mansfield Beauchamp. In 1923 she married the critic John Middleton Murry, who was editor of the *Athenaeum* from 1919 to 1921.

Katherine Mansfield, unlike several other reviewers, failed to connect the character of Strickland with the painter Paul Gauguin.

Had Mr Maugham confessed to his hero Charles Strickland, a painter of genius, his great desire to present him, to explain him to the public, with all his eccentricities, violences and odious ways included, we imagine the genius would have retorted in his sardonic way: 'Go to hell. Let them look at my pictures or not look at them—damn them. My painting is all there is to me.' This discouraging reply is not without a large grain of truth. Strickland cut himself off from the body of life, clumsily, obstinately, savagely—hacking away, regardless of torn flesh and quivering nerves, like some old Maori warrior separating himself from a shattered limb with a piece of sharp shell. What proof have we that he suffered? No proof at all. On the contrary, each fresh ugly blow wrung a grin or a chuckle from him, but never the slightest sign that he would have had it otherwise if he could.

If we had his pictures before us, or the memory of them in our mind's eye, this his state of mind might be extremely illuminating, but without them, with nothing to reinforce our knowledge of him but a description of two or three which might apply equally well to a very large number of modern works, we are left strangely unsatisfied. The more so in that Mr Maugham takes extraordinary pains in explaining to us that Strickland is no imaginary character. His paintings are known everywhere, everywhere acclaimed. Books have been written about him in English and French and German. He even goes so far as to give us the authors' and the publishers' names—well-known live publishers who would surely never allow their names to be taken in vain. So it comes to this. If Strickland is a real man and this book a sort of guide to his works, it has its value; but if Mr Maugham is merely pulling our critical leg it will not do. Then, we are not told enough. We must be shown something of the workings of his mind; we must have some comment of his upon what he feels, fuller and more exhaustive than his perpetual: 'Go to hell.' It is simply essential that there should be some quality in him revealed to us that we may love, something that will stop us for ever from crying: 'If you have to be so odious before you can paint bananas—pray leave them unpainted.'

Here are the facts. Charles Strickland, a middle-aged stockbroker, the husband of a charming cultured woman and the father of two typically nice English children, suddenly, on a day, without a hint of warning, leaves his home and business and goes off to

Paris to paint. The reason is unthinkable. A sturdy, ruddy middle-aged man cannot so utterly change his nature. He can; he does. Living in poverty, great untidiness and discomfort, he renounces his old life and seemingly never gives it another thought. For the moment he sheds that respectable envelope and is away, it is no longer part of his new self. He is grown out of its roundness and firmness and is become a lean pale creature with a great red beard, a hooked nose and thick sensual lips, possessed with one passion, ravaged by one desire—to paint great pictures. Paris he accepts as though he had always known it. He lives the life of its disreputable quarters as though he had been brought up in them and adopts its ugly ways with a kind of fiendish glee. Then he is discovered, half dead of a fever, by a stupid kind-hearted little Dutchman who takes him into his flat and nurses him. The adored gentle wife of the Dutchman falls under Strickland's spell and ruins her life for him. When he is sick of her (for his contempt for women is fathomless) she takes poison and dies. And Strickland, his sexual appetite satisfied, 'smiles dryly and pulls his beard.'

Finally, he leaves Paris and makes his home in Tahiti. Here he goes native, living in a remote hut with a black woman and her relatives, and painting masterpieces until his body takes its great and final revenge upon his spirit and he becomes a leper. He lives for years, painting the walls of his house. When he is dying he makes his black wife promise to burn the house down so that the pictures may be destroyed. 'His life was complete. He had made a world and saw that it was good. Then, in pride and contempt, he destroyed it.'

This strange story is related by a friend of Mrs Strickland's, a young, rather priggish author, who is sent over to Paris after the first tragedy to discover with whom Strickland has eloped and whether he can be induced to return.

'You won't go back to your wife?' I said at last.
  'Never'.
  '...She'll never make you a single reproach.'
  'She can go to hell.'
  'You don't care if people think you an utter blackguard? You don't care if she and her children have to beg their bread?'
  'Not a damn'.

That is very typical of their conversations together. Indeed, the young man confesses that if Strickland is a great deal more [sic] articulate than that, he has put the words into his mouth—divined them from his gestures. 'From his own conversation I was able to glean nothing.' And 'his real life consisted of dreams and of tremendously hard work.' But where are the dreams? Strickland gives no hint of them; the young man makes no attempt to divine them. 'He asked nothing from his fellows except that they should leave him alone. He was single-hearted in his aim, and to pursue it he was willing to sacrifice not only himself—many can do that—but others....' But what does the sacrifice matter if you do not care a rap whether the creature on the altar is a little horned ram or your only beloved son?

The one outstanding quality in Strickland's nature seems to have been his contempt for life and the ways of life. But contempt for life is not to be confused with liberty, nor can the man whose weapon it is fight a tragic battle or die a tragic death. If to be a great artist were to push over everything that comes in one's way, topple over the table, lunge out right and left like a drunken man in a café and send the pots flying, then Strickland was a great artist. But great artists are not drunken men; they are men who are divinely sober. They know that the moon can never be bought for sixpence, and that liberty is only a profound realization of the greatness of the dangers in their midst.

44. Unsigned review, 'The Primitive Man', *Saturday Review* (London)

CXXVII, 17 May 1919, 481–2

This book is so purely a study in psychology that we doubt whether it deserves to be classed as a novel. Of plot, incident, or love, there is none, and the psychological problem is not new; it is the analysis of the naked soul of the barbarous or natural man. The question which Mr Maugham asks and answers in these pages is how would the primitive man, who acknowledges no obligation to

God or man or woman, who accepts no creed or code of ethics, bear himself to his fellows in his passage through life? The subject, as we said, is familiar, but Mr Maugham handles it in a novel way, because as a rule the savage in fiction is afraid of his fellow men's opinion or the police; he requires the invisible cap to do himself justice. The perfect ruffian in polite society we have long known under the names of Barry Lyndon, Lord Monmouth and Lord Steyne, and there were Jekyll and Hyde. But Charles Strickland, the artist, does really not care what other people say or think of him. By the way, Mr Maugham must have written this book before the war, when the words 'go to hell' were capable of thrilling suburbia, and were not, as to-day, what lawyers call 'common form,' as commonplace and jejune as 'rotten' or 'ripping.' When you asked Charles Strickland to dine with you, he answered, 'Go to hell'; when you offered him medicine on the sick-bed he replied, 'Go to hell'; when you inquired his opinion of a picture or whether he would like a game of chess, his monotonous formula was, 'Go to hell.' Mr Maugham admits that his genius was deficient in the art of expression in words: he was rather wearisomely so. Charles Strickland lived till the age of forty in a flat off Victoria Street, as a stockbroker, with a wife and son and daughter, secretly going out at night, as he approached the *cap de quarantaine*, to attend classes in drawing and painting. Suddenly he decamped to Paris and took to the life of the poor genius artist. When Mr Maugham, a callow youth and the friend of the wife (we mean, of course, the 'I' of the book), followed him to Paris and asked him why he had deserted wife and children, his answer, after many 'Go to hells,' was that he had supported them in comfort for seventeen years, and it was time they supported themselves, or if they couldn't do it, they had relations who could. For himself, London bored him and he *must* paint, and paint he does, without selling, pictures which after his death are fought for as masterpieces by dealers and collectors. We must here observe that if Mr Maugham is bent on analysing the genius whose art forces him to break with society, it is unlikely, if not impossible, that he could have suppressed himself until forty. Painting like poetry breaks out early, and though we do not say (not knowing) that all painters do their best work before forty, as all poets certainly do, we are sceptical about the crypto-Monet living the stockbroker's life till that age.

Artistically, Mr Maugham exaggerates his effects. His primitive man is too much of a brute to be true to nature. Strickland is rescued dying from his garret by a Dutch painter and his wife, who instal him in their studio and nurse him to health. The dirty diseased genius inspires the wife with a horrible animal passion, which he catches, and the two turn the husband out of his studio. When Strickland has satisfied his lust, he deserts the woman, who commits suicide. This is *Sadisme* with a vengeance. The life of a beach-comber in the purlieus of Marseilles is very well described, but the best part of the book, to our taste, is the life in the South Sea Island, a subject which it seems impossible for travellers and novelists to stale. Strickland drifts out to Tahiti, and paints, and retires with a native girl to a bungalow in the woods, where he dies of leprosy, a death described with all the knowledge of St Thomas's. Clever Mr Maugham has not written popular plays without learning the trick of a good curtain. We suppose the meaning of the title to be that they who try to realise impossible ideals get sixpence for their trouble. The artist tried to live for his brush and canvas alone, and to leave the world an image of the truth. Mr Maugham tells us the price he had to pay: but he might have tried for the moon, surely, without being a beastly lunatic.

45. Maxwell Anderson, 'In Vishnu-Land What Avatar?' *Dial*

LXVII, 29 November 1919, 477–8

Maxwell Anderson (1888–1959) was a prolific American verse playwright whose most famous play, *Winterset* (1935), was suggested by the Sacco-Vanzetti case.

The title of *The Moon and Sixpence* is an admission and a defense—an admission by Somerset Maugham that explaining genius is as impossible as expressing moonlight in terms of the decimal system, and a defense of his method against such critics as will assuredly accuse him of failing in a task he never attempted. He has no illusions about cutting his green cheese to a super-mundane thinness. He gives us, flatly and baldly, the external aspect of the evolution of genius, not bothered in the least by the fact that what happens in his narrative is neither explicable nor probable. He merely sees to it that it happens and that we are convinced. His task was to present an extraordinary phenomenon as it appeared to the ordinary folk of the social vicinity in which it occurred. It is his theory that this is what we can understand, and truly this is what most concerns us. When a whirlwind sweeps the dozing harbor, we take no interest in the scientific explanations of the weather bureau, but pick our way down to the littered beach to view the wreckage and gossip about the losses. It was a whirlwind of overmastering creative desire that caught up Charles Strickland, tore him from his wife, ruined the lives of Stroeve and Blanche, and upset innumerable tidy schemes. Society saw nothing but a most deplorable confusion; Strickland was aware of nothing save an essential freedom.

At the age of forty, Strickland was a heavy-featured monosyllabic stock-broker with an intellectual wife who went in for literary lions. Mrs Strickland remembered vaguely that he had dabbled a bit with paints when they were first married, but he had painted very badly and the family seemed to have laughed him out of it. The facts of his life were dull and usual. As a boy fresh from school he 'went into a broker's office without any feeling of distaste. Until he married, he led the ordinary life of his fellows, gambling mildly on the Exchange, interested to the extent of a sovereign or two on the result of the Derby or the Oxford and Cambridge Race. I think he boxed a little in his spare time. On his chimney-piece he had photographs of Mrs Langtry and Mary Anderson. He read *Punch* and the *Sporting Times*. He went to dances in Hampstead.' He was equally usual as a husband—kindly, affable, undemonstrative, no doubt, but also thoroughly sane and respectable. Then unexpectedly he departed for Paris, leaving no word save a brief note to his wife, stating that he would never come back. His wife and her relatives assumed a woman in the case. In the words of Maugham, 'whenever a man does anything unexpected, his fellows ascribe it to the most discreditable motives.' But the friend who looks him up to reason with him finds no woman, but a bearded, shabby, sardonic Strickland alone in one room of a dilapidated hotel—learning to paint.

Told in synopsis, the fable would seem too wildly unreasonable to be taken seriously. It is Somerset Maugham's achievement to have made it real by the accuracy of his circumstance and his finesse in the handling of ricocheted ideas. Nothing is presented to the reader first-hand. Rumors at the second and third and fourth remove crowd upon him, casual impressions sway him, until the fame of Strickland is built up in his mind out of accumulated fragments, as the fame of Shakespeare is forced upon those who have never read a play. The result is attained despite difficulties that an author less sure of his power would have avoided or skirted gingerly. There was no necessity for making Strickland so brutal, sensual, and tongue-tied as he is shown.

I wondered what a stranger would have taken him to be, sitting there in his old Norfolk jacket and his unbrushed bowler; his trousers were baggy and his hands were not clean; and his face, with the red stubble of an unshaved chin, the little eyes, and the large, aggressive nose, was uncouth and coarse. His mouth was large, his lips were heavy and sensual.

One feels instinctively that genius does not take this guise, and that mastery is gained through understanding rather than through demonic impulse. Maugham consciously discards the modern theories of genius, and returns to the romantic notion of revelation and the hidden flame. He denies the potency of the desire for fame, at least in this instance. Strickland cares nothing for his pictures once they are finished. His greatest work is destroyed by his own order. He prefers to live in an out-of-the-way corner. It is a question worth asking whether any man would have been quite content with the joy of fashioning beauty and with that alone.

But whatever objection may be raised to the philosophy of art involved in the tale, there is likely to be little but praise for its workmanship and its criticism of life. The author sees things squarely. If he errs at all, it is on the side of disbelief. Mrs Strickland and Blanche Stroeve and Ata, the native girl, make up a trio from which we can derive a whole conception of womanhood. Perhaps it is old-fashioned. It is at least as much so as Shaw's artist man and mother woman. '"In the end they get you," says Strickland, "and you are helpless in their hands. White or brown, they are all the same."'

When one closes the book and looks back over the varied scenes, civilized and barbaric, one has a memory of powerful and inevitable movement and the light and shadow of life itself. The English dinner table, the underworld of Marseilles, the village of Papeete are drawn in strong lines and bold colors that suggest the last paintings of Strickland on Tahiti. The book might have gained in epic quality had Mr Maugham placed the island scenes first as he originally planned, but as it is, the dramatic effect is heightened. We begin with absolute disbelief in this 'dull stock-broker.' He seems a meager personality to follow through three hundred pages. The plot of the narrative is the revelation, one by one, of reasons why he is worth following. When we have put the novel by, we may disbelieve in him again if we will, for he is improbable enough, but it is none too easy to shake off the conviction that, for all the agnosticism we can muster, he did exist, all the way from Westminster to the leper's hut, concrete in flesh and blood.

Somewhere it is reported that certain persons came upon Mr Maugham in New York and charged him with 'denuding human nature of its fundamental goodness' in *The Moon and Sixpence*, and, further, that Mr Maugham replied by saying that he took his model for Strickland from Gauguin. The charge is silly enough. Human nature is, at bottom, never any better than Strickland, and frequently far worse, from a moralist's point of view. But Strickland chose to demolish for himself the pretty temple of niceties and restraints which we are taught to build up from childhood over the black and fuming pit of the subconscious, and the revelation is naturally a shock to the self-worshiping. It is well, no doubt, that few of us care to disrobe mentally, especially in public. But Maugham's defense was quite unsound. Gauguin, the burnt-out Parisian, is no parallel for Strickland. Gauguin fled from a sickly civilization to a healthy barbarism. Strickland was neither burnt-out nor Parisian. He was English, a Philistine, and a barbarian in his own right. There is no explanation of his craving for Tahiti, as he is shown us in *The Moon and Sixpence*, save another form of the impulse that sent out the twelve apostles or drove the swine into the sea. He was inspired or mad or possessed of a devil—as you please. And Gauguin was merely sated.

THE TREMBLING OF A LEAF

New York, September 1921; London, October 1921

These six stories form the remainder of the material Maugham brought back from his journey to the South Seas in 1916/17. The collection was the first of five, each containing six stories of between twelve and fifteen thousand words, published between 1921 and 1933, on which his reputation as a major short story writer rests.

46. Louise Maunsell Field, review, *New York Times*

20 November 1921, 16

Louise Maunsell Field was a novelist, the author of *Katherine Trevalyan* (1908), *A Woman of Feeling* (1916), *Love and Life* (1923).

The siren song of the South Sea Islands has never been more alluring than at the present time, when it sounds with musical softness through the harsh discords of a disordered world. They seem a refuge for romance, those islands with their lagoons and flowers and palm trees and splendid tropical skies. There life, we feel, must be simpler and easier; there the struggle for existence is abated, and men have time to dream. But now comes Somerset Maugham, the brilliant and sophisticated, to show us how the dreams may end, to show us that life and love lose none of their ironies when their dramas are played beside a forest pool or in the cabin of a schooner sailing the Pacific 'under the immensity of the

148

starry sky, remote from all the world.' People do not react from emotional experiences according to formulas. Some men lose their souls out there amid the soft airs of the Pacific, others find them.

There are six long short stories in the volume, and not one which is ordinary, not one which fails to give the reader a sense of reality. Ending as they do on a note of sadness, or irony, or of a blending of both, always there comes the feeling that the ending is the true one. Thus and not otherwise was it with all these different men and women. With 'Mackintosh,' for instance, whose justifiable anger, whose very virtues indeed, dragged him down to tacit crime. In this, the opening tale, there is a vivid picture of the administration of an island populated principally by natives, and of the gross, selfish, domineering white man who strangely loved the island he ruled with startling efficiency. 'The Fall of Edward Barnard' tells of one who put aside his old ambitions and chose to live on an island, where he believed that he might have 'a happy, simple, peaceful life...lived in beauty,' far away from the motor cars and thés dansants of his previous existence. The note of satire sounds loudly in this story, but the picture of the lotus eater's paradise is an enchanting one—until Mr Maugham shows us its reverse side, in the story called 'The Pool,' the story of yet another white man who married a lovely half-caste. Nothing could be more exquisite, more charming and idyllic, than the beginning of Lawson's romance: 'There was a little river that bubbled over the rocks in a swift stream, and then, after forming the deep pool, ran on, shallow and crystalline, past a ford made by great stones.' It was at 'The Pool' that Lawson first saw Ethel, the girl who seemed to him the very spirit of the silent water. And it was there that the end of it all came at last, after the idyl had become tattered and soiled and sordid, a thing of horror and of loathing.

'The tragedy of love is not death or separation...the tragedy of love is indifference,' declared Neilson, the trader, and those who know The Circle will remember that the same thing was said by Lady Kitty. No irony of civilization could be more poignant than the irony of this South Seas episode ['Red'], when after long and weary years that happened which the lover had always dreaded—and when it came, meant nothing. Time had done its work, there where the coconut trees grew down to the water's edge, as thoroughly as ever it did anywhere else. Not a story in the book but probes far down into the secrets of character. Men's courage

and their weakness, meanness and generosity, fidelity and fickle-
ness, are all pictured, not divided and embodied in different
individuals, but mingled with one another in that strangest of
composites which is human nature. And though all this is pictured
upon the colorful South Seas background, only once, in the tale
called 'Honolulu,' does the author insist especially on the contrast
between action and background. Then it is because Honolulu is so
civilized in comparison with the tale of primitive superstition he
has to tell, a tale with a characteristic Somerset Maugham twist at
the end. For Honolulu is 'a typical Western city,' where motors line
the pavements and 'dilapidated frame houses stand next door to
smart stores with plateglass windows,' and there is an air of
respectability. Yet 'you cannot but feel that it is a respectability
only of the surface; a little below there is darkness and mystery,' the
darkness and mystery which seem to pervade every place where
East meets West.

But it is the last story in the book, the one entitled 'Rain,' which
is the most forceful, the most unusual of them all. It is not a
pleasant story, this tale of a soul's tragedy. Told with less artistry,
and by any other method, it might be almost unendurably horrible.
It is only because we see it all through the eyes of Dr Macphail, the
disinterested, tolerant third person, and never come too close to it,
that we can bear to watch the drama which was enacted there in
Pago-Pago during the rainy season. The courageous, sincere,
intolerant missionary, who in what he believed to be a righteous
cause did not scruple to use a power in which there was something
sinister, inexorably pursuing his ends, while 'outside, the pitiless
rain fell, fell steadily, with a fierce malignity that was all too
human,' is drawn with a wonderful vividness, but so, too, is every
character in this short masterpiece—the wife who spoke of the
depravity of the natives 'with a vehemently unctuous horror,' yet
had a fine courage of her own, the half-caste Horn and the outcast
woman, Miss Thompson. It is a story which shows what an artist
like Mr Maugham can do with a situation which a writer less
skillful, less rich in understanding, would have made merely
tawdry and offensive.

There is no space here in which to speak of the beauty of Mr
Maugham's descriptive passages. It is his people who matter most,
not their surroundings, definitely and greatly as those surroundings
often affect them. And in his presentation of them, these captains

and traders and half-castes and gentlemen, there is a broader sympathy, a deeper, clearer comprehension, a finer tolerance than any shown in his earlier work. Brilliant as always, keen in its discernment of life's ironies and inconsistencies, his power has strengthened and matured. There have been many books telling of the wonders of the South Seas, but little South Sea fiction as well worth reading as Mr Maugham's *The Trembling of a Leaf.*

47. Unsigned review, *Saturday Review* (London)

CXXXII, 5 November 1921, 540

There may be only the trembling a leaf between extreme joy and extreme despair, but there is the whole crashing of a tree between mediocre short stories scraped together from magazine publication, and a volume, like that before us, in which each separate tale is begun by inspiration and completed by artistic perfection. Mr Somerset Maugham has chosen the South Sea Islands for his setting because he obviously enjoys heightening the contrast between the wonderful serene backcloth of lagoon, hibiscus blossom, cocoànut tree and scented romantic dusk, and the bitter futile tragedies thrown up against it in strong black. To keep intact our youthful illusions about magical coral islands where the bread-fruit grows, we should firmly refuse to read accounts of them by any author who has voyaged further than Southend. Gross wheezing men, with bald shiny heads, and their necks roll upon roll of pink flabbiness, appear to populate Honolulu, Tahiti and Samoa in enormous quantities; and only one story out of the six, 'The Fall of Edward Barnard', could possibly be used as even a mild advertisement for these places by any enterprising steamship or hotel company. Edward Barnard must have been conceived in a rare moment of softness, for he does actually find peace and magic upon Tahiti, and a semi-humorous shrug-of-the-shoulders contentment; but all the other depraved white men who have drifted to these fairy-tale islands live mainly upon one another's screaming nerves; they drink, and dope, and marry half-caste wives, and lose their self-respect, and are flouted and jeered at, and commit suicide, and the rain drums malignantly on the corrugated iron roofs, and they all live happy ever after.

In the story which should be placed second on the list of excellence, 'Mackintosh,' the author has undoubtedly sacrificed subtlety to his preference for a sudden brutal push as a final effect. Mackintosh is assistant to the Governor of one of the Samoan group, Walker, a coarse, genial, thick-skinned old ruffian who wins our respect in his poignant death-bed scene, surrounded by the natives whom he has bullied, threatened and underpaid, but who are nevertheless 'his children.' One of them has shot him with the revolver which Mackintosh, his patience flayed by his chief's chaffing treatment of him, had left lying about on his desk. But Walker gasps out, 'Don't make a fuss about this... They're damned fools at Apia. If they make a fuss they'll only punish the wrong people. I don't want anyone punished.' He dies—and Mackintosh walks out to sea and shoots himself. But a man of his type is much more likely to have passed through the successive stages of utter misery—less misery—slight uneasiness—and, succeeding Walker at his job, pleased consciousness of being the better Governor of the two.

'Rain' is a sheer masterpiece of sardonic horror, beyond criticism.

48. Rebecca West, review, *New Statesman*

XVIII, 5 November 1921, 140, 142

(Dame) Rebecca West (1892–1983), journalist, critic and novelist, was born Cicily Fairfield and took her *nom de plume* from Ibsen's heroine in *Rosmersholm*. From the start of her career in 1911 she became known as a brilliant book-reviewer as well as a writer on topical issues, especially those concerning women. In addition to her fiction (*The Return of the Soldier* (1918), *Harriet Hume* (1929), *The Birds Fall Down* (1966)), her contemporary reportage (*The Meaning of Treason* (1949)) and her travel-writing (*Black Lamb and Grey Falcon* (1942)), she contributed book-reviews to magazines and newspapers until the end of her career when she was under contract to the *Sunday Telegraph*. Rebecca West tended to avoid reviewing Maugham's books in later life; while not rating him very highly as an artist, she admired his wit and tenacity.

The following is an extract from a review which also dealt with a novel by Francis Brett Young.

Mr Somerset Maugham is the very antithesis of Mr Brett Young, for (as the Americans put it) certainty is his middle name; he has an indomitable character which enables him to make the best and most remunerative use of every grain of talent that he possesses. He creates a prejudice against the six stories about the South Sea Islands by putting on the flyleaf a remark of Sainte-Beuve's to the effect that '*L'extrême felicité à peine séparée par une feuille tremblante de l' extrême désespoir, n'est ce pas la vie?*' This is one of the generalisations which make one hate and despise French literature. It would be a nice winter game for the children to try and find substantives which could not be substituted for '*l'extrême felicité*' and '*l'extrême désespoir*'; 'love' and 'hate' would do, also 'good' and 'bad,' also 'a pain in one's sash' and 'appendicitis.' Mr Maugham's choice of this whiff of sententiousness as a motto is unfortunately indicative of a certain cheap and tiresome attitude towards life, which nearly mars these technically admirable stories. They are charged with a cynicism which one feels Mr Maugham has stuffed into them to conceal his lack of any real philosophy. That it is not a real attitude is proven by its inconsistency. In one story, 'The Fall of Edward Barnard', Mr Maugham is cynical at the expense of an earnest young American who goes out in search of a friend who has gone to Tahiti, and is shocked when he finds him settling down to those pleasures which are symbolised by a hibiscus and upbraids him for not coming home and leading a respectable life as a Chicago business man. But in 'Red' he tells the story of a bloated old man with a paunch and purple veins on his hanging cheeks, who visits a beautiful spot on an island and is told the romantic tale of how a native girl and a beautiful red-haired stripling of an American sailor lived together there in love, and how the girl spent her life grieving after her lover was shanghaied; and then laughs, and divulges the horrid truth that he is that stripling grown old. Mr Maugham is, in fact, just as cynical at the expense of the hibiscus ideal; and the philosophy of the two stories cancels out and leaves an impression of nothingness. But there are two more than admirable stories in this volume. One is 'Mackintosh', which is the story of a weak man who makes the discovery that the gross man may be saintlier than himself though demonstrably less delicate. The other is 'Rain,' which describes how a missionary and his wife hunt down a prostitute in an island hotel, and how the missionary prays with the woman and wrestles with her spirit till she repents of her evil life and consents to go back to the United States and face imprisonment for a crime she has committed. When you get to the end you find, what you had expected, that these prayerful orgies culminate at last in a physical orgy, and what you had half-expected, that the missionary then cuts his throat. But you also find, what you had not expected, that the missionary's wife, on hearing the news of his death, instantly knows what has happened. 'Her voice was hard and steady. Dr Macphail could not understand the look in her eyes. Her pale face was very stern.' And from that one knows what a foul den of lust and suspicion of lust these people's hearts had been, before what corroding consciousness of their own squalor they had retreated into this religion. That story is a notable achievement.

ON A CHINESE SCREEN
New York, October 1922; London, November 1922

A journey to China undertaken by Maugham in 1919/20 provided him with material for these travel sketches as well as for his novel *The Painted* Veil (1925) and his play *East of Suez* (1922).

49. Louise Maunsell Field, 'Maugham's Chinese Sketches', *New York Times*
4 February 1923, 11

A traveler's notebook, filled with thumbnail sketches of persons and places and points of view, *On a Chinese Screen* has a distinctly tantalizing quality. So many of these jottings might be expanded into fascinating stories—stories of the kind Mr W. Somerset Maugham does so particularly well. What could not the man who wrote 'Rain' do with, for instance, the material suggested by the brief sketch entitled 'Fear'? That short sketch—short though it is one of the longest in the book—gives a glimpse into the tormented soul of the missionary who for days and months and years had forced himself to maintain a benevolent, sympathetic attitude toward what he hated, martyring himself 'with a passionate exasperation.' Inevitably the time must have come when the strain proved too great, when something snapped; and then—what then? Mr Maugham could tell us completely, so admirably, if he only would! And then there is that other suggested story, of Doctor Macalister, what he had been, and how he came to be what he was, which Mr Maugham admits he would 'like to write,' while the reader ardently hopes that he will eventually yield to his desire.

Of the fifty-eight short papers contained in the book there are many which suggest stories, while others are concerned with moods and impressions. Vividly we see the long line of blue-clad coolies, human beasts of burden, picturesque and terribly pitiable. For, 'beating heart or angry sore, bitter rain or burning sun notwithstanding, they go on eternally, from dawn till dusk, year in and year out, from childhood to the extreme of old age,' hopeless, enduring. But the coolies are only one among the many sights of 'The Road' along which we accompany Mr Maugham, pausing now and then to rest at 'The Inn,' to listen to 'The Song of the River,' to see 'The Sights of the Town' or to discuss the close relationship between 'Democracy' and smells. For, declares Mr Maugham, 'the matutinal tub divides the classes more effectually than birth, wealth or education.... The invention of the "sanitary convenience" has destroyed the sense of equality in men' of the West, which still exists among the Chinese, whose nostrils are not sensitive. But for the most part he is interested more in people than in places or theories, and this notebook contains impressions of men and women of all sorts and kinds, from the Chinese philosopher whose verses, when translated, proved to be of such a totally unexpected type, to the missionary and reformer who was cruel as only reformers can be. Mrs Fanning, 'that little grotesque ugly woman' who by means of 'the passion of love' which was in her had accomplished what might well have been regarded as an almost impossible task, and the 'Missionary Lady' whose conversation was truly 'devastating' bear small relation to each other.

Yet there is a link which joins together the many men and women who appear in these pages, since they are all shown as they seem in their connection with China. Semi-occasionally, that relation is sympathetic; far more often it is one of gross ignorance and self-satisfaction. The good-natured, well-meaning 'Seventh Day Adventist' who was so completely 'ignorant of the history, art and letters of China' had plenty of company in his belief that the Chinese must be abysmally ignorant 'because they did not know the same things he did.' The commercial men who have spent the better part of their lives in China without ever learning more than half a dozen words of Chinese are no more narrow than the groups of important persons gathered at dinner parties in the 'Legation Quarter' or 'At a Treaty Port.' The impression of hardness, narrowness, self-satisfied lack of understanding among the whites—an impression occasionally relieved by a gleam of such spiritual beauty as that of 'The Nun' or courage like that of 'Her Britannic Majesty's Representative' who unhesitatingly 'stepped forward between the leveled rifles and the three miserable men and told the soldiers to shoot and be damned'—becomes more and more pronounced with almost each page one turns; yet Mr Maugham holds no brief for the Chinese.

It is a fascinating volume, this new book of Mr Maugham's, vivid, thoughtful, full of color, picturesque, stimulating to the imagination. By means of it one feels that one is coming into contact with an unusually interesting mind, keenly intelligent, sensitive and sympathetic, quick to perceive and to understand. There is so much in it upon which one would like to comment choice is all but impossible.

50. Gerald Gould, review, *Saturday Review* (London)

CXXXV, 13 January 1923, 54

Curiously, the review of which the following is an extract purports to discuss 'New Fiction'.

...Mr Maugham provides something exceptionally good, with a gesture almost of carelessness. His technical competence—which may have come easily to him from the first, or have been acquired by long and loathly labour: one cannot tell, and it does not matter—has presumably passed into his subconsciousness, and become as effortless as breathing or walking. He is amusing, and illuminating, in the account he gives of a Chinese 'student of the drama.'

He sent in a neat card of the correct shape and size, deeply bordered in black, upon which, under his name, was printed *Professor of Comparative Modern Literature*.

... I resigned myself to discuss the drama. My professor was interested in its technique, and indeed was preparing a course of lectures on the subject, which he seemed to think both complicated and abstruse. He flattered me by asking me what were the secrets of the craft.

'I know only two,' I answered. 'One is to have common sense and the other is to stick to the point.'

'Does it require no more than that to write a play?' He inquired with a shade of dismay in his tone.

'You want a certain knack,' I allowed, 'but no more than to play billiards.... If you can't write a play, no one can teach you, and if you can it's as easy as falling off a log.'

And easier, no doubt, than rolling one. That 'knack,' that miraculous certainty, that facility which is felicity, is not to be put in opposition to technique: it is technique that justifies itself by success: for the work that is 'only technically' successful is technically a failure.

Mr Maugham's ease and assurance are so complete that they are in danger of destroying themselves by becoming self-assertive and therefore self-conscious (the process is not an unfamiliar one among contemporary men of letters). But from this book of his it is impossible to withhold an almost unqualified admiration. He has attempted a difficult feat, and not merely achieved it, but made it look simple. He has recorded his impressions of a visit to China, in about sixty little sketches, some of them views, some of them points of view. I confess to being quickly distressed by most descriptions of natural scenery: my spirits ebb at the bare prospect of a solid page full of adjectives: I detest a catalogue. But Mr Maugham always stops soon enough, and never insults us with catalogues. He picks out vivid points, and the rest is implied. His descriptions are not so much natural as psychological: he reproduces states of mind. And he intersperses his pictures with little stories, doubtless suggested to him by what he actually saw and divined of the effect exercised on westerners by an eastern environment. Probably this is the best method he could have adopted of conveying atmosphere. Instead of going straight to the Chinese mind, which has such different preconceptions from ours that we cannot arrive at it however straight we try to go, he shows the actual effect of China on minds with preconceptions similar to ours; and thus we learn the 'feel' of that ancient and alien civilization.

The power of some of these brief narrative sketches is heavy and cruel. Mr Maugham has an expert's knowledge of mental fever and aberration, and he does not, like so many modern authors, misuse it in the service of a theory. Moreover, if the cold violence of his method suggests cruelty, the philosophy underlying it is kind; for, as he himself says in one of the grimmest and most ironical of his studies, 'the normal is the rarest thing in the world,' and that implies that we should be tolerant of one another's idiosyncrasies. He is quoting his old anatomy-teacher: he might, to the same effect, have quoted Mr Bernard Shaw. So we return to familiar quotations, and recognize that we cannot interpret anything at all except in the light of what we know already. I hesitate to confess it in these days, when every other week produces a new 'scientific' philosophy, but the maxims I have just been laying down come some of them from Plato and some of them from Aristotle. The ancients are a short cut to the moderns.

THE PAINTED VEIL

New York, March 1925; London, April 1925

The material for this novel was gathered during Maugham's journey to China in 1919/20. Because of a libel action brought when the novel was being serialised in *Nash's Magazine* and a second threatened libel action, the name of the protagonist was changed from Lane to Fane, and Hong Kong to Tching Yen. Some time after the novel had been re-issued in the Collected Edition of Maugham's work, the name of Hong Kong was restored, and as a result of adverse criticism—in particular in the *New Statesman* (No. 52)—the final paragraph was revised.

51. Unsigned review, 'Mr Maugham Excels as a Craftsman', *New York Times*

22 March 1925, 7

In the book reviewer's arid vocabulary is an arid cliché about 'the art which conceals art,' borrowed from some bigwig of the past and now thrown in for journeyman duty; but even this ghastly platitude freshens up a bit when applied to Somerset Maugham. Maugham's art does truly conceal art. The unpretentious style and form of his *Of Human Bondage* set off his chief character in that book brilliantly against a colorless background. Mr Maugham did not rival the heat of *The Moon and Sixpence* with verbal pyrotechnics; nor did he soften the blazing color of 'Rain' behind a mist of purple style. If Stevenson could have learned his trade in Maugham's shop! And now in *The Painted Veil* he reveals himself again as expert craftsman, knowing what many novelists never learn—the simple art of telling a story.

In his previous books and plays (if *Of Human Bondage* be alone excepted) Mr Maugham has relied too completely upon intelligence. They are cerebral performances, molded deliberately, shaped, fashioned and polished. In them the reader brushes against a cold, imperturbable intellect. Indeed, Mr Maugham has learned his trade so completely and has become so perfect a master of his instrument that his appeal has been too much limited to the mind. What of the sensibilities ? Are they not to be touched also? And it is in this new story, *The Painted Veil*, that one feels Mr Maugham does begin to let himself go a little and does lose himself in the tale of his own creating. Intellect, if one may postulate timidly, is a story teller's weakness; but the matter of *The Painted Veil* has put the mind where it belongs.

In the first pages we are prepared for the usual objective performance, for pitiless characterization and motivation and the thump of doom beating ominously in the offing like an overtone, like that maddening, savage drum in *Emperor Jones*. Here again are vulgar English folk, cruel, selfish, grasping, thorough villains, careful never to break the law, faithful only to arbitrary concepts self-created and self-obeyed. Here again is the sinister heroine, Kitty by name, weak and unemotional, pushed on by a managing mother, ignored by a pliant, wretched father who gives his name but nothing more constructive to an upper middle-class English family.

In twenty-five years Mrs Garstin never invited any one to dine at her house because she liked him. She gave large dinner parties at regular intervals. But parsimony was as strong in her as ambition. She hated to spend money. She flattered herself that she could make as much show as any one else at half the price. Her dinners were long and elaborate, but thrifty, and she could never persuade herself that people when they were eating and talking knew what they drank. She wrapped sparkling Moselle in a napkin and thought her guests took it for champagne.

Of such unlovely quality was Mrs Garstin's character. That portraiture is the more damning because it is faithful to a respected social group. Kitty was weaker than her mother, but of similar mettle nevertheless; and she married Walter Fane, an obscure bacteriologist in Government employ in Hong Kong, because at the age 25 she knew she was 'missing her market.' Moreover, a younger and less attractive sister was on the point of marrying a title.

These are the people, and this is the treatment of them, to which we are accustomed in a Somerset Maugham novel. And the course of their married life in the Orient does not smudge his technique. For the official society of Hong Kong, by reason of its small size, was merely a trifle more obvious than London society, though governed by similar motives. After the preliminary bustle of her introduction there Kitty had found that bacteriologists were very small beer indeed; their wives had conspicuously dull partners at dinner. Walter now retired within himself and his profession, except for brief moments of passion, which struck Kitty as being somewhat ridiculous: she was bored, chagrined, humiliated. But she looked outside for amusement. Quite unexpectedly she found it in Charles Townsend, Assistant Colonial Secretary; he became her lover. 'He was tall, six foot two at least, she thought, and he had a beautiful figure; he was evidently in very good condition and he had not a spare ounce of fat on him. He was well dressed, the best dressed man in the room, and he wore his clothes well.' Indeed, after their little intrigue had been running on smoothly for a few weeks the situation between Kitty and her husband seemed to her 'exquisitely absurd.' He most certainly knew himself to be cuckold, she reasoned—but what could he do? After all, bacteriologists were very small fry, and Charles would be the next Colonial Secretary. Kitty made up her mind just what her husband must do when the tension broke: he must divorce her; Mrs Townsend must divorce Charles; this gay fellow must, of course, marry Kitty, and of course he would want to.

Things did not turn out just that way, however, for when Walter came to grips Kitty found that Charles Townsend had no intention of ruining his Colonial career by private scandal. In fact, when Walter proposed to carry Kitty off to Mei-tan-fu, where he had volunteered to risk his life in the cholera epidemic, Townsend was glad enough to have her go. That was the easiest way out, for him at least. He assured her warmly that she would probably not die; every one does not die in a plague. So this young married couple set out grimly on a grim expedition to the cholera region. For days they traveled in chairs; they scarcely spoke; and in Mei-tan-fu Walter went doggedly about his business by day and by night with a sort of desperate pertinacity, while Kitty sat bored at home and made vague overtures at reconciliation.

She was beginning to feel a trifle impatient with him. Why could he not realize what suddenly had become so clear to her that beside all the terror of death, under whose shadow they lay, and beside the awe of the beauty which she had caught a glimpse of that day their own affairs were trivial? What did it matter if a silly woman had committed adultery and why should her husband, face to face with the sublime, give it a thought? It was strange that Walter, with all his cleverness, should have so little sense of proportion. Because he had dressed a doll in gorgeous robes and set her in a sanctuary to worship her and then discovered that the doll was filled with sawdust he could neither forgive himself nor her. His soul was lacerated. It was all make-believe that he had lived on, and when the truth shattered it he thought reality itself was shattered. It was true enough, he would not forgive her because he could not forgive himself.

At just about this point *The Painted Veil* begins to glow with a warmth and sympathy that Mr Maugham does not ordinarily blow up in his novels. It would be too much to say that Kitty changed; Mr Maugham knows that such people do not; that human nature in general remains thoroughly constant. But by virtue of her confined situation in a ghastly township, the quarrel with her husband depressing her spirits, Kitty began to develop and find new resources within herself. A convent in the town, where Chinese children were cared for by a group of nuns, was overcrowded and also shorthanded. Almost before she knew it Kitty was assisting the nuns with these little Oriental charges, and she began to look upon life with fresher eyes. When Walter died quite suddenly from the plague she found herself too much attached to this sweet life of the convent to consider returning to Hong Kong, despite the prospect within a few months of bearing a child. But especially on this account the Mother Superior insisted on packing her off to Hong Kong.

There she found herself a heroine. Word had come of her daring, her charity and her tragedy. Mrs Townsend, blind to her husband's amours, took Kitty into her house, despite some very serious objections. But Charlie, toward whom Kitty's feelings were now a little mixed, pressed her again under his own roof; she felt degraded; the situation was not only distasteful but intolerable, and she knew that beneath it all she was not the sort of woman she had let herself become.

Her shoulders shook with her sobs. Everything was gone now. She had thought herself changed; she had thought herself strong; she thought she had returned to Hong Kong a woman who possessed herself; new ideas flitted about her heart like little yellow butterflies in the sunshine and she had hoped to be so much better in the future; freedom like a spirit of light had beckoned her on, and the world was like a spacious plain through which she could walk light of foot and with head erect. She had thought herself free from lust and vile passions, free to live the clean and healthy life of the spirit; she had likened herself to the white egrets that fly with leisurely flight across the rice fields at dusk, and they are like the soaring thoughts of a mind at rest with itself: and she was a slave. Weak! weak! It was hopeless, it was no good to try; she was a slut.

If she could not live up to her principles, however, she could flee; and she did flee forthwith, back to England and her unaffectionate family. Before she arrived there her tyrannical mother died suddenly in a hospital. No one mourned with much fervor. Her father now looked for release from an unhappy life by accepting a colonial post in the Bahamas, where he might be free of all the old burdensome ties. When Kitty asked if she might not come, too—

He closed his eyes for a moment and she thought he was going to cry. His face bore an expression of utter misery. It wrung her heart. She had been right: the death of his wife had filled him with relief, and now this chance to break entirely with the past had offered him freedom. He had seen a new life spread before him and at last after all these years rest and the mirage of happiness. She saw dimly all the suffering that had preyed on his heart for thirty years.

In three brief pages after this incident Mr Maugham brings *The Painted Veil* to a close on a new note, a rounder, fuller note; but for all that a note in the general harmony of the story. After all the malevolence of their stupid past Kitty and her father face a new life together and weigh its possibilities. So Kitty utters these last words in the volume:

I have hope and courage. The past is finished: let the dead bury their dead. It's all uncertain—life and whatever is to come to me, but I enter upon it with a light and buoyant heart. There's so much I want to know; I want to read and I want to learn. I see in front of me the glorious fun of the world, people and music and dancing, and I see its beauty, the sea and the palm trees, the sunrise and the sunset and the starry night. It's all confused, but vaguely I discern a pattern. And I see before me an inexhaustible richness—the charity, the Way and the Wayfarer, and perhaps in the end—God.

Well, that is a good deal to expect, especially for the heroine of a Somerset Maugham novel. It is of a piece with Kitty's character, nevertheless, once her complacency has been rudely upset by her own incompetency. The reader is never in doubt as to her character. Mr Maugham weaves it all in by dialogue and action, as integral parts of the story; and he paints Walter and Charles at full length also. And, although Kitty's father remains in the shadowy background of the novel, somehow the reader knows him through and through. *The Painted Veil* is an expert performance. Mr Maugham is no stylist in the usual literary sense; he is no Pater or Meredith, choosing every word deliberately, arranging for rhythm as well as color. His style is sharp, quick, subdued, casual. It never heaps his story with efflorescences: it is neither rank nor cultivated. It tells a story. And, after all, is that not style?

52. P.C. Kennedy, review, *New Statesman*

XXV, 9 May 1925

The following is an extract from a review dealing with several works of fiction.

The end of *The Painted Veil* is the silliest ever inflicted by a brilliant writer on a brilliant story. But, up to the last few pages, the book is so good that I should doubt whether the whole year will show more than two or three novels fit to be mentioned beside it.

Kitty, a beautiful but vulgar and empty-headed girl, marries Walter, a queer, cruel, uneasy, passionate man, who is abjectly devoted to her. He takes her to China with him, and she immediately, behind his back, has a love-affair with Charlie, the shallow and handsome. Walter finds out, and insists on her coming with him up-country to a district smitten with cholera. Kitty discovers the cowardice and worthlessness of Charlie, and, though she never in the least loves her husband, begins to admire him. But—and here comes the veridical touch of the true creator—her admiration is soon superseded, or at any rate modified, by impatience: he is making himself miserable, in the midst of realities like plague and death, because a worthless woman has committed adultery with a worthless man! Walter dies of cholera; his last remark is: 'The dog it was that died.' Kitty feels free—free of a loveless marriage, but free also of her old fleshly weakness: yet, when she gets back to within reach of the fatuous Charlie, she melts, loathing herself, into his arms. The author's really tremendous irony—not of comment, but of fundamental idea—is at its best in this scene. But another scene remains. Kitty comes home to England. She is pregnant, and lonely. She finds that her father, whom she has always ignored, has been made Chief Justice of the Bahamas. She asks to go with him, and he shows plainly that he doesn't want her: the irony holds. But she weeps and pleads, and softens him: and this is what, at the very end, she says to the poor old man:

There's so much I want to know; I want read and I want to learn. I see in front of me the glorious fun of the world, people and music and dancing, and I see its beauty, the sea and the palm-trees, the sunrise and the sunset and the starry night. It's all confused, but vaguely I discern a pattern, and I see before me an inexhaustible richness, the mystery and the strangeness of everything, compassion and charity, the Way and the Wayfarer, and perhaps in the end—God.

Her poor father! Fancy taking that to the Bahamas!

53. Unsigned review, *Times Literary Supplement*

14 May 1925, 332

Mr Somerset Maugham continues, by his studies of sexual frailty, to exploit the perennial interest in that subject. Without questioning the morality of his intention, and while applauding his talent for satire, one may doubt whether it is strictly necessary to the indictment of lust that purely lustful episodes should be described so conscientiously. An adult intelligence, unless it happens to be devoted to the study of animal psychology, cannot interest itself in the spectacle of mere appetite. But in *The Painted Veil* Mr Maugham is, perhaps, not addressing himself to adult intelligences, but rather to those for whom a story of illicit love and salutary disillusionment may still possess some freshness and piquancy.

Kitty Fane is the wife of a Government bacteriologist stationed at Tching-Yen. She is first discovered to us cowering with her lover, Charlie Townsend, in a darkened bedroom. Someone has just tried to open the door, and she believes it to be her husband. Fane, next day, offers her the alternative of being divorced or accompanying him to Mei-tan-fu, a cholera-infested area. In this extremity her lover miserably fails her, and so provides Mr Maugham with the occasion for his cleverest chapter. The Fanes, fatally estranged, go to Mei-tan-fu, where, after much heart-searching, Kitty finds temporary relief in working with the convent sisters. Her husband dies of cholera, and she is forced to return to Tching-Yen, to be sheltered by Mrs Townsend and seduced again by Townsend. Then, full of self-disgust, she flees to England, embraces her father, and, in a series of unnatural speeches that belong to the cruder convention of the theatre, announces her change of heart. Mr Maugham's irony is not all-pervading.

THE CASUARINA TREE

London, New York, September 1926

The material for these stories was gathered during a journey Maugham made to Malaya and Borneo in 1921. He later rewrote 'The Letter' as a play which had a successful run in London in 1927.

---

54. L.P. Hartley, review, *Saturday Review* (London)

CXLII, 18 September 1926, 317

Leslie Poles Hartley (1895–1973), novelist and critic, best-known for *The Go-Between* (1953), also wrote *The Shrimp and the Anemone* (1944), *The Sixth Heaven* (1946) and *Eustace and Hilda* (1947), a trilogy, and many other novels and volumes of short stories.

The following is an extract from a review dealing with several works of fiction.

For the Englishman residence in the Far East seems to be a tedious ticklish business, eked out by murders and mixed morganatic marriages. At least this is the conclusion arrived at by most novelists, and Mr Somerset Maugham is no exception. One woman cuts her drunken husband's throat. Another empties the contents of her revolver into the body of her lover who had been cohabiting with a Chinese woman. ('I fired and fired till the revolver went click, click, and I knew there were no more cartridges.') Mr Warburton's assistant is stabbed by a native servant, whose pay had been withheld pending good behaviour. ('Cooper was lying in bed, with his mouth open, and a kriss sticking in his heart.') On board ship, bound for the Emerald Isle, Mr Gallagher looks like reaching a ripe old age; but no. The Malay woman whom he had abandoned (and pensioned) casts a spell on him, and he dies of hiccups, at once chronic and acute, to the dismay of the ship's doctor who did not like to appear inexperienced, and the disgust of the passengers who longed to have a dance. Involved in a tidal wave Mr Izzart hears a companion's cry of distress, and decides not to notice it. *Propter vitam vivendi perdidit causas*: all is saved except honour. Lastly, when Doris, a delighted and delighting bride, observes with what persistence three dusky children and their darker mother haunt her husband's gates, and laments the rough handling the woman receives from his servants—but we must stop. This tale, though no less painful than the rest, is quite unsensational and reveals the Malay Peninsula and Mr Maugham at their most merciful.

Great narrative power, an unfailing eye for dramatic effect (most of the stories could be put on the stage with very little alteration) and a ruthless insight into and insistence upon the ignobler motives distinguish these 'Plain Tales of the Ills.' Not that finer instincts are wanting, but they are secondary and passive, mere material for selfishness to mould what shape she please. The dominion of fact and event lies heavy upon Mr Maugham's world, and these facts and events are like crimes reported in the newspaper—sensational rather than strange. 'A work of fiction,' he says in a postscript... 'is an arrangement which the author makes of the facts of his experience with the idiosyncrasies of his own personality.' We can hardly believe that the facts of Mr Maugham's experience have included so many deeds of violence; but even if they have we do not think the author's business is finished when he has assimilated them into his private system. Even at the expense of mistiness and ambiguity he should surely aim at some larger, more impersonal correlation. Within its limits Mr Maugham's work is nearly perfect, but its horizon is bounded by a cynicism into which, as into a cul-de-sac, it continually retires. In concluding his work the artist has to provide emotion with a direction or a point of rest. A dead-end is neither; it is a substitute for completion. Art longs to cease; but the artist who in his conclusion ignores the determination of life to go on weakens the effect of his work.

55. Edwin Muir, review, *Nation and Athenaeum*

XL, 9 October 1926, 30

Edwin Muir (1887–1959) was a Scottish poet, critic and translator (with his wife Willa) of Kafka into English. Muir's *Collected Poems, 1921–1958* appeared in 1960 and his *The Structure of the Novel* in 1928.

The following is an extract from a review dealing with several works of fiction.

Almost all the six stories in *The Casuarina Tree* are well constructed and sincerely wrought. Mr Maugham has not Mr Kipling's brilliant and delightful powers of characterization, but he gives us, what Mr Kipling never gives, an intelligent criticism of life. We feel that he is dealing with his themes seriously, and with a permanent sense of the nature and ends of human existence. This endows his stories with the dignity of good writing; we have the sense that we are contemplating and judging a section of experience as well as feeling it. Sometimes, indeed, Mr Maugham's judgment over-balances his sensibility; the theme is too rigidly worked out, so that the tragic note does not sound spontaneously; the author does not merely let things happen inevitably, he wishes to demonstrate that they must happen inevitably, and this is unnecessary. Certain of the stories do not move us quite so intensely as they should; for instance, 'Before the Party' and 'The Letter,' both of them, curiously enough, concerned with murder by violence. But there is one remarkably fine story in the book, 'The Outstation,' and two others only less admirable, 'The Force of Circumstance' and 'The Yellow Streak.' The first of these is surely one of the best short stories written in our time; the action is simple and moves inevitably to the catastrophe, which we feel must come just when it does come. This is an exceptionally good collection of stories.

56. Henry Albert Phillips, 'In the Shadow of the Casuarina Tree', *New York Evening Post*

VII, 2 October 1926, 7

Henry Albert Phillips (1880–1951) was the author of *Other People's Lives, White Elephants in the Caribbean,* etc.

In a preface, Mr Maugham enlightens and illumines us upon the nature of the Casuarina tree:

> Of the Casuarina tree they say that if you take in a boat with you a piece of it, be it ever so small, contrary winds will arise to impede your journey or storms to imperil your life. They say also that if you stand in its shadow by the light of the full moon you will hear, whispered mysteriously in its dark ravage, the secrets of your future....

The author could not have chosen a more appropriate symbol, for the principal characters in each of the six tales told must have stood in the shadow of the Casuarina tree by the light of the full moon.

Mr Maugham's literary manner is so casual throughout all six of these stories that he is in danger of so exasperating an impatient reader that he or she might be taunted into casting the book aside after reading a dozen pages in the beginning. Here is one case, however, wherein that *bête noire* of the plotting author, she who turns to the last page of a story before she finishes the first, would be justified. We can almost say—although not quite—that Mr Maugham's ends justify his means.

Sooner or later, one becomes conscious that Mr Maugham has deliberately suited his manner of narration to his purposes, his tempo to the droning symphony of fatalism that beats on the emotions like a tomtom long after the climacteric finale has ceased in print. In their very drabness lies their strength. Here is 'art' without the usual whirring of dynamic machinery.

The locale of all the stories is really Malayan, although they may be narrated, as in the case of 'P. & O.,' on board a liner, or, taking 'Before the Party' as an example, in a middle-class English home. In every case the character occupying the center of the stage stands grimly in the shade of the Casuarina tree with a Malay kris or curse, climate or custom, lurking in the background. There is something sinister in the air that seems to 'get' them down around Singapore and Borneo like the sting of a strange insect that changes their very identity and poisons their lives.

The first story, 'Before the Party,' opens and closes in England as the family is getting ready to go to a garden party. The daughter, Millicent, has recently returned from Borneo after the mysterious death of her husband. Millicent's mother is more concerned over just how much mourning weeds she should wear than about poor Harold, the deceased son-in-law. Millicent has acted strangely reticent about the whole affair. They have a few spare minutes before the party. She resolves to employ this fragment of time in getting the truth out of Millicent. Millicent's father and sister join her, and they corner the widow. The bereaved wife tries to beg off in vain; then she lets them have it. Harold had been a drunkard, it seems. She tried to reform him and in doing so fell deeply in love with him. He promised to stop drinking, and did—for a while. Then he became beastly. He promised and reformed again and again. The loneliness, the shame, the humiliation and something in the Malayan atmosphere, day in and day out, month in and month out, maddened her. There was a Malayan kris hanging on the wall... 'I ought never to have been told!' said her father, who was an upright barrister. 'I think it was most selfish of you.' Then they all entered the waiting motor car and drove off to the Canon's garden party.

'P. & O.,' the next story, strikes the reviewer as a piece of needless homicide on the part of the author. Why create poor Mr Gallagher, if only to have him 'hiccup' (Mr Maugham's spelling) himself to death? There seems no point to it all. We do not know what we are led to expect, and if we were expected to expect anything, it does not come off. It all takes place aboard a P. & O. liner. Mrs Hamlyn's husband has run off with another woman; she is running away from it all. A most uninteresting man, a Mr Gallagher, gets aboard the boat. He had left a Malay concubine, who had pronounced a curse upon him, prophesying that he would never step foot on land. He gets hiccups—of all things—and is buried at sea. From this, Mrs Hamlyn sees the futility of bucking against fate and writes her husband a nice letter. Mr Maugham always has a big idea behind his stories, but this time he did not put it across.

'The Outstation' is a splendid piece of characterization that will rank with his portrait of Sadie Thompson. Mr Warburton, the resident, is a Piccadilly snob. An assistant is sent to him, who is his antithesis in all things—a boor of a colonial he-man, who loathes the conventional English 'gentleman.' Neither can change—will change. Thrown together day after day, in the feverish heat and imprisoning downpours, they develop a hate that becomes the obsession of their narrow lives. The resident cannot get rid of his assistant. The brutal assistant sows his own doom by maltreating the natives. The resident tries to save him and is insulted by him. The boor goes to his self-made destruction and the resident dresses faultlessly for dinner—the first happy one in months.

'Force of Circumstance' is a dull title for a brilliant story. It opens with an idyl of conjugal happiness. An Englishman has just brought his wife out from home. It is all so wonderful. But that very night a Malay woman bursts in and reveals a strange relationship with the new husband. He is forced to confess that when he was sent out as a boy of eighteen he had taken up with her. They had had three children! From this on it is the superb study of a woman's soul as she fights against the thing that has come into her life, and her decision is a finished piece of drama. It is told with breathless suspense. She does not blame him, but can never live with him again. Alone again in that wilderness, his life wrecked, he sends for his Malay woman.

'The Yellow Streak' is again not in Maugham's best vein. A man with an English father and a Malay mother tries in vain to conceal his 'yellow streak.' But fate brings about an episode that reveals it for him. It is not a bad story, but too long drawn out.

The last shall be first. 'The Letter' is Maugham of *The Circle* and 'Rain' at his dramatic best. He builds up a fine situation with the meticulous care shown in a Greek tragedy. A matter of fact, commonplace, good wife Englishwoman, shoots a man. The coroner's inquest shows that she did it to defend herself from rape. Then a letter, in the hands of the murdered man's Chinese concubine, written by the woman who shot the man, discloses that she lured him to her on the fatal night! The Chinese woman asks $10,000 for the letter. The husband is ruined in buying his first knowledge of his wife's shame.

Throughout the telling of these stories the author never interposes his presence, yet his presence is a subtle potentiality, just like the mysterious fatalistic personality of the Malay people with whom in each case the fate of the character is enmeshed as though in the almost invisible web of a spider. Taken as a whole, *The Casuarina Tree* is like a fine Oriental tapestry. The longer one contemplates it, the better one understands and likes it.

ASHENDEN

London, New York, March 1928

The six stories in this collection are based on Maugham's experiences as an intelligence agent and envoy extraordinary during the Great War. In retrospect they can be seen to have been the forerunners of an entire new genre of spy fiction.

---

57. Edward Shanks, review, *London Mercury*

XVIII, May 1928, 98

Edward Shanks (1892–1953) was a poet, novelist and critic. One of the leading members of the Georgian school of poets, Shanks's *Collected Poems* appeared in 1933; he was also the author of *The Old Indispensables* (1918), *Queer Street* (1932) and several other novels. Shanks had been Assistant Editor of the *London Mercury* from 1919 to 1922.

This is extracted from a review dealing with several other books.

Mr Somerset Maugham makes me think of the old division between jokes that are funny only because they are true and jokes which would be funny anyway. Much of his book would not be interesting if it had been invented. Much of it is inconclusively enigmatic, which is something no story ever should be. But there is about the whole surprising work an atmosphere of truth and it is not hard to see that it was necessary, as well as convenient, to present it in the guise of fiction. For my part, I prefer those parts of it which would have been interesting anyway. Mr Maugham has never done anything better in this particular style than his final episode which takes the British Agent by way of Vladivostok to revolutionary Russia. In this there are two characters, a Russian woman and an American man, of whom any novelist might be proud. The woman drives away her lover by insisting that he shall eat scrambled eggs for breakfast every day for a week. The man spends the whole long journey from Vladivostok to Petrograd in obedience to his principle that 'man is a social animal and he exercises the highest part of his nature when he takes part in social intercourse.' The two are united at the end in that sort of ironic and pathetic tragedy of which Mr Maugham is a master.

58. D.H. Lawrence, 'Four Contemporary Books', *Vogue*

20 July 1928

David Herbert Lawrence (1885–1930) was a novelist, poet and travel writer: *Sons and Lovers* (1913); *The Rainbow* (1915); *Lady Chatterley's Lover* (1928); *Pansies* (1929); *Last Poems* (1932), etc. Lawrence's powers as a literary critic, of which this extract is a cogent example, have tended to be overshadowed by his other achievements.

Ashenden is the last of the four books reviewed in the same article, the other books being by Robert Byron, Clough Williams-Ellis and Maurice Baring. That Lawrence's strictures on Maugham were not entirely dispassionate is suggested by his dismissal of him, in a letter from Mexico of 29 October 1924, as a 'narrow-gutted "artist" with a stutter' and his further sneer, in a letter from Bandol written two months before he died, about 'Maugham and Wells and Co. rolling their incomes round Nice for Xmas, rich as pigs'.

Mr Somerset Maugham is even more depressing. His Mr Ashenden is also an elderly author, who becomes an agent in the British Secret Service during the War. An agent in the Secret Service is a sort of spy. Spying is a dirty business, and Secret Service altogether is a world of under-dogs, a world in which the meanest passions are given play.

And this is Mr Maugham's, or at least Mr Ashenden's world. Mr Ashenden is an elderly author, so he takes life seriously, and takes his fellow-men seriously, with a seriousness already a little out of date. He has a sense of responsibility towards humanity. It would be much better if he hadn't. For Mr Ashenden's sense of responsibility oddly enough is inverted. He is almost passionately concerned with proving that all men and all women are either dirty dogs or imbeciles. If they are clever men or women, they are crooks, spies, police-agents, and tricksters 'making good', living in the best hotels because they know that in a humble hotel they'll be utterly *déclassé*, and showing off their base cleverness, and being dirty dogs, from Ashenden himself, and his mighty clever colonel, and the distinguished diplomat, down to the mean French porters.

If, on the other hand, you get a decent, straight individual, especially an individual capable of feeling love for another, then you are made to see that such a person is a despicable fool, encompassing his own destruction. So the American dies for his dirty washing, the Hindu dies for a blowsy woman who wants her wrist-watch back, the Greek merchant is murdered by mistake, and so on. It is better to be a live dirty dog than a dead lion, says Mr Ashenden. Perhaps it is, to Mr Ashenden.

But these stories, being 'serious', are faked. Mr Maugham is a splendid observer. He can bring before us persons and places most excellently. But as soon as the excellently observed characters have to move, it is a fake. Mr Maugham gives them a humorous shove or two. We find they are nothing but puppets, instruments of the author's pet prejudice. The author's pet prejudice being 'humour', it would be hard to find a bunch of more ill-humoured stories, in which the humour has gone more rancid.

59. Unsigned review, 'Mr Maugham's Latest', *New York Times*

15 April 1928, 14

Since Somerset Maugham is incapable of writing anything dull, *Ashenden* is an entertaining book. But since his material in this case is neither new nor important, it is quite forgettable. Only Mr Maugham's urbanity and wit prevents it from being just another story of sleuths and plots. On the whole, it is a specimen of Somerset Maugham writing in second gear. In the course of the Spring and Summer you are apt to see it prevalent in steamer chairs and at holiday resorts. But a year from now it is not apt to stand on the library shelves that hold *Of Human Bondage*.

When Ashenden, who is by way of being an author and playwright with a point of view remarkably like Somerset Maugham's, was offered a post in the British secret service at the beginning of the war, he was told that the work ought to give him a lot of interesting material. In fact, the official who told him that gave him an incident which had actually occurred. It told of a French Minister who had gone down to Nice carrying some important documents, and there lost them while under the influence of a beautiful and unscrupulous adventuress. Ashenden listened to the official's 'damned good story' and then, from the point of view of a writer, remarked:

Why, we've been putting that incident on the stage for sixty years; we've written it in a thousand novels. Do you mean to say that life has only just caught up with us?... Well, sir, if you can't do better than that in the secret service, I'm afraid that as a source of inspiration to the writer of fiction, it's a washout. We really can't write that story much longer.

The official was a trifle disconcerted at that. But Somerset Maugham wasn't. For he proceeded to write 'that story' and half a dozen of its allied variants down once more, and when he had finished he had produced this book.

The narrative is strung together by the participation of Ashenden in every episode, but each one is a complete entity in itself. Having been given his final instructions, which were 'if you do well you'll get no thanks and if you get into trouble you'll get no help,' Ashenden started for Geneva to take up his work of gentlemanly espionage and director of several minor spies in the service of England. It was there that he met the inevitable lady of the snares and wiles he had scorned as material for fiction. He met Prince Ali, and a Pasha, too, but he outwitted them all. And presently he was engaged in the adventure with the Hairless Mexican, who became progressively Hawkshaw by changing wigs as he went about the business of assassination. There is, of course, a story involving a dancer, and another one about a traitor. Mr Maugham tells them all with ease and distinction.

THE GENTLEMAN IN THE PARLOUR

London, February 1930; New York, April 1930

The journey from Rangoon to Haiphong described in this travel-book was undertaken in the winter of 1922/23, seven years before the book was published.

---

60. Unsigned review, *Times Literary Supplement*

20 March 1930, 230

Mr Somerset Maugham would probably admit that, like Lord Essex and Dr Johnson, he would rather 'go a hundred miles to speak with one wise man, than five miles to see a fair town.' For him sight-seeing has few charms; he prefers impressions to facts; nor would he require wisdom in the man he had gone a hundred miles to see, so long as he brought away from the meeting some curiosity of human behaviour.

> I travel [he tells us] because I like to move from place to place, I enjoy the sense of freedom it gives me, it pleases me to be rid of ties, responsibilities, duties, I like the unknown; I meet odd people who amuse me for a moment and sometimes suggest a theme for a composition; I am often tired of myself and I have a notion that by travel I can add to my personality and so change myself a little. I do not bring back from a journey quite the same self that I took.

He warns his readers, therefore, that they will find little information in this record of a journey from Rangoon to Haiphong. In a sense that warning is justified, and with precision Mr Maugham deliberately has little concern. He does not tell us the year of his journey; he does not trouble even to spell Burma consistently; on one occasion at least he is definitely misleading, when he speaks of the 'immense difficulty' of reaching Angkor from Phnom-Penh, as though that difficulty still existed; for while at the time of his visit, doubtless, the traveller could reach Angkor only by water, now he may motor all the way from Saigon. These things matter little, because Mr Maugham gives us something more than facts, for he can recreate a scene in a sentence, so that it comes as vividly before the eye as the day he saw it: in this book there are many such pictures, and they are as unusual as they are delightful, for Mr Maugham did not travel merely by train and steamer, but spent six weeks in making slow stages from the railhead in Upper Burma, through the Shan States, to the railhead in Siam. And while he can recreate the atmosphere of those lonely jungle paths and faraway villages in the hills, he has no less skill in reconstructing those personal encounters that to him are one of the greatest pleasures of travel. There is the story of George, who became engaged to Mabel on leave, lost his nerve the day she came out, and fled in panic from Burma to China, until Mabel finally came up with him and married him; there is the story of Masterson, who sacrificed his happiness with a Burmese girl because the dream of his life was to settle down when he retired in an English country town; there are the Buddhist monks who watched Mr Maugham playing patience, and, picking up the measure of the game, crowded round and snatched at his arm to point out a card that he should move. These are real people. One comes upon them unexpectedly, as one might in life. Indeed, its unexpectedness is one of the chief charms of this book; for Mr Maugham is the best of travelling companions and he has something fresh to show at every turn.

61. Bellamy Partridge, 'Rare Traveler', *New York Herald Tribune*

20 April 1930, 5

Bellamy Partridge (1878–1960) was an author, editor and critic. He wrote *Country Lawyer* (1939) based on his father's life, which was later made into a film, and *January Thaw* (1945), which became a Broadway play.

When European authors have reached a certain point in their careers they turn from whatever they are doing to write a book of travel. From Gide we get a volume on Africa. From Ludwig a biographer's transcript of the Mediterranean country. From Aldous Huxley a sophisticate's reaction to a tour de luxe around the world. And now in *The Gentleman in the Parlour* Mr Maugham is telling us some of the things he saw and most of the things he thought while rambling through Burmah, the Shan States, Siam and Indo-China. He says the book was written for his own diversion and in the hope that it may also divert some others as well as earn him a 'certain amount of money and perhaps a little praise.'

We find the author in a rare mood. This is not the ironic Maugham who with such fiendish glee made an utter monkey of a despicable though well meaning missionary in 'Rain.' Nor is it the cynical Maugham who in *The Circle* raised such hob with love and marriage, and after showing the futility and inconvenience of a union without marriage, brought down his final curtain on the elopement of a guest with the host's beautiful young wife. Nor have we here the savage Maugham who in *The Moon and Sixpence* turned a man into a brute in order that he might make a great artist of him.

As a traveler Maugham is genial and tolerant. He never bores one with useless description or fills up his pages with facts cannily gleaned from Baedecker. He seldom bothers with scenery or points of interest, but he never overlooks a muleteer or a priest or a boatman if the fellow has a story in him. There is nothing de luxe about travel in this part of the world. The author makes little of setting out on a six-hundred mile journey on a Shan pony with a long mule-train to carry his food and his effects. But Maugham is getting along in years and is thinking a little more of metaphysics and the idea of future rewards and future punishments, if any. And he is thinking keenly though not unkindly, and while travelling in Asia he has put his finger very neatly through some of the tissue-paper arguments on which the West has based its claims to some very considerable mansions in the skies. This is by no means a Maugham novel or a Maugham play, but never was Mr Maugham more readable or so wholly delightful as in this, his latest work.

62. Arthur Colton, 'Travelling with Composure', *Saturday Review of Literature* (New York)

VI, 28 June 1930, 1159

Mr Maugham went up the Irrawaddy by boat, across to Siam by trail and caravan, to Bangkok by motor and train, and up the coast by steamer. He was not looking for adventure and surprise, but for the pleasant amusements of motion, freedom, and chance meeting with odd people. It is the effortless ease of his style, its quiet efficiency, which reminds one that the traveller is a famous novelist and a practised writer. The anecdotes are choice and perfectly told. He calls himself a bad traveller because he has not 'the gift of surprise. I take things for granted so quickly that I cease to see anything unusual in my surroundings.' That, however, is one kind of a good traveller, though it defines a limitation. He travelled as an English gentleman, whose composure is valuable to him, habitual, intelligent, independent; an Englishman of distinction, in fact, whose coming was announced and provided for even in jungle villages. All this makes very agreeable reading. It was probably an easy book for Mr Maugham to write, but it would not have been easy for everyone. He notes, and notes without excitement, that the British Empire is tottering because the ruling Briton has become a sentimentalist, 'a master whose conscience is troubled because he is a master. What had happened to the race that had produced Clive, Warren Hastings, and Stamford Raffles that it must send out to govern its colonies men who were afraid of the authority entrusted to them—officials who held their position by the force of the guns behind them, trying to persuade the races they ruled that they were there only on sufferance? They offered efficiency to people to whom a hundred other things were of more consequence and sought to justify themselves by the benefits conferred on people who did not want them.' When the historian of The Decline and Fall of the British Empire, however, comes to write his great work, 'I venture to express the wish that he will write with sympathy, justice, and magnanimity. I would have him eschew rhetoric, but I do not think a restrained emotion will ill become him. The British Empire will have been in the world's history a moment not without grandeur.'

It has perhaps some connection with this that Mr Maugham's selection of stories of the Englishmen in the East are usually touched with tragedy, whereas those of Frenchmen and Americans there are equally vivid but amusing. And so he ends neatly with the American Jew, Elfenbein, who was odious and yet not wholly so, and who remarked: 'I'll give you my opinion of the human race in a nutshell, brother: their heart's in the right place, but their head's a thoroughly inefficient organ.' He ends as neatly as he had begun, gracefully with reflections on Lamb and Hazlitt and the latter's exclamation: 'Oh! it is great to shake off the trammels of the world and of public opinion—to lose our importunate, tormenting, everlasting personal identity—to owe nothing but the score of the evening—to be known by no other title than The Gentleman in the Parlor.'

CAKES AND ALE

London, September 1930; New York, October 1930

Although the connection between the book's nominal hero Edward Driffield and Thomas Hardy is tenuous, other characters have a closer relation to real persons. Having originally denied it, Maugham afterwards admitted that Alroy Kear was based on Hugh Walpole; and other literary figures feature in the novel in thin disguise, for example Edmund Gosse. The original of the warm-hearted heroine Rosie has also been identified as Ethelwyn ('Sue') Sylvia Jones, the actress daughter of the playwright Henry Arthur Jones.

J.B. Priestley's comments on the novel will be found in his review of Maugham's play *The Breadwinner* (No. 92, p. 264).

63. Ivor Brown, 'Private Lives', *Observer*

5 October 1930, 6

Ivor Brown (1891–1974) was a critic, essayist and journalist. He was made drama critic of the *Observer* before World War II and continued as such while taking over as editor during the war on the retirement of J.L. Garvin in 1942. He returned to being drama critic without other duties at the end of the war. A prodigiously hard worker, Brown published many books on words, and on Shakespeare, aimed at the common reader, in addition to his journalism.

The title of this article refers to Noël Coward's play of that name, which had opened at the Phoenix Theatre, London, on 24 September 1930.

Mr Maugham dislikes shams, and what he dislikes he lacerates. His punishing stroke is precise; there is no flourish, no rhetoric, just cut upon cut until the dismissive 'You may go now.' *Cakes and Ale* is the tale of a literary sham and the castigation falls justly on the people who make it and not on its victim, Edward Driffield, who had been a shabby nonentity of fiction, and at last acquired immense fame as the unrolling stone gathers its moss, simply by going on being there. He was discovered and adopted by the passionate few; living beyond eighty and with his collected works running to thirty-seven volumes, he was bound to be accepted by the obedient many. After his death the life is to be written by Alroy Kear, the prosperous, the ubiquitous, the safe and serene novelist, whose genius is an infinite capacity for rolling logs. Kear approaches Ashenden, who tells the story. Ashenden, as a boy, saw much of Driffield in his middle, and still unhonoured, period. He knew the first Mrs Driffield, an ex-barmaid, plump and rosy and unvirtuous, and, of course, a considerable skeleton in the cupboard for those who are to put the finishing touches on the Driffield legend and turn the gentle, squalid, companionable old man into the National Hero and Grand Old English Gentleman whom the myth requires.

So Ashenden narrates his boyhood's acquaintance with the couple in a Kentish harbour-town. They were kind to him, took him bicycling, gave him tea, and taught him how to rub brasses. Driffield had had a rough and wandering boyhood, liked to tipple in the pub, was a trifle shy of soap, and did a bolt from his creditors. His wife was an amiable wanton. But, when his name as a novelist was rising, she left him; the lion-hunters sprang and boxed him up with fame, and hot water and a trim, managing wife. He had only to survive and renown would come with the relentless march of age itself. Ashenden has little opinion of Driffield's novels, save one; but his description of the man is rich in quiet charity. His genius was only his longevity, but he was kind, unobtrusive, and happy in the rough habits formed in vagrancy and need. His first wife was kind, too; unchaste, but comforting, not a nuisance in the world.

Mr Maugham's ears must be vexed beyond endurance with the word 'cynical,' which here he hardly merits. There is much that is brilliantly sardonic in his commentary on life and letters, but even Kear, whom he submits to searching analysis, gets his due. Log-rolling needs stamina and perseverance; the man is industrious and benign. The study of the affable Kear and of the whole process whereby Driffield is canonised is exquisite in its justice. The style is a model of irony controlled. Mr Maugham never raises his voice too high, nor brandishes his arms too widely. It is true that he stops too soon. We never know how Kear finally composed the embarrassing muddle of Driffield's life. We are left suddenly in the air; but the air is Alpine in its power to sting and quicken and enchant.

64. Evelyn Waugh, 'The Books You Read', *Graphic*

CXXVII, 15 October 1930, 426

Evelyn Waugh (1903–66) was a novelist, biographer, travel-writer, critic, diarist and wit. This review was written shortly after Waugh was received into the Roman Catholic Church (September 1930) and two years after his satirical first novel, *Decline and Fall* (1928), had appeared.

The other novels reviewed in the article, of which the following is an extract, were written by John Dos Passos and Margaret Kennedy.

Considerable excitement has been caused lately in what are called 'literary circles' by Mr Somerset Maugham's new book. The central figure, Edward Driffield, is presented as the Grand Old Man of English Letters, the last of the great Victorian novelists. He occupies, in fact, a position very much like that of Thomas Hardy in the years immediately preceding his death.

A scare was promptly started in certain newspapers that this character was intended as his portrait. If that had been so the book would have been a highly improper one; but to anyone who knows the details of Hardy's life it will be immediately apparent that the dissimilarities tend to outweigh any apparent similarities. Mr Maugham has published an emphatic denial that any part of his book was derived from or suggested by Hardy's life. There, for any intelligent person, the matter ends.

If only the public could be dissuaded from these recurrent, impertinent attributions! They are an intolerable nuisance and, occasionally, even a danger to authors. No one, not even the novelist himself, can follow the processes by which personal experience is transformed into impersonal, artistic creation. People should realise that the eager 'Oh, Mr Maugham, it is so exciting to meet you; now you will be able to tell me who all your characters *really* are,' is not only embarrassing but insulting.

The real interest and value of *Cakes and Ale* depend upon the manner and method of its construction, rather than upon its subject. Mr Maugham works with supreme adroitness and ease; he has in literature that quality which Americans, in social life, describe as 'poise.' I do not know of any living writer who seems to have his work so much *under control*.

This is, of course, both a triumph and a limitation. He is never boring or clumsy, he never gives a false impression; he is never shocking; but this very diplomatic polish makes impossible for him any of those sudden transcendent flashes of passion and beauty which less competent novelists occasionally attain. Indeed, he does not attempt or desire anything of the kind. 'Let us face it,' he remarks in the course of this book, 'beauty is a bit of a bore.'

The theme of *Cakes and Ale* is the life of Edward Driffield. He was a writer who attained recognition late in life. Until middle age his career was slightly disreputable. He married a barmaid, Rosie, and came to live in his native village; he left suddenly with heavy debts.

Rosie was unfaithful to him, with most of his male friends. The most important of these were Ashenden, who tells the story, and George Kemp, a builder; this jolly man was her first lover; he always maintained supremacy in her affections because he was 'such a perfect gentleman.' Eventually she eloped with him to

America. After that Driffield fell into the hands of a lion-hunting hostess; he escaped from her by marrying a hospital nurse. With her he settled down to a period of eminence and respectability, enlivened by occasional, rather furtive visits to the village 'pub.'

After his death, his widow conspires with Mr Alroy Kear, a writer to whose deficiencies Mr Maugham gives unbalanced prominence, to suppress the less presentable features of his career. They solicit the help of Ashenden, Rosie's lover, more with the intention of securing his silence than his information. Ashenden is silent for his own reasons. Among other facts he keeps to himself the knowledge that Rosie is still alive, happy and prosperous in America.

This simple story is transformed into a novel by Mr Maugham's brilliant technical dexterity. He is a master for creating the appetite for information, of withholding it until the right moment, and then providing it surprisingly. One knows that an incident is imminent and does not know in what direction to watch for it. He flits from past to present, now giving a merciless analysis of literary humbug, now recounting the upbringing of Ashenden in provincial refinement, now racing on with an exciting love scene, now pausing to moralise.

65. Leslie A. Marchand, 'Maugham Paints a Sardonic Portrait', *New York Times*

12 October 1930, 7

Leslie Alexis Marchand (b. 1900) is a critic, biographer and Byron scholar. His edition of Byron's letters is an outstanding work of editing.

No English writer is more transparently, more unblushingly autobiographic than Somerset Maugham. His frank introspective studies in *Of Human Bondage* laid the foundation for a literary formula which has been the constant guide to all that he has written since. That formula was so successful in gaining the attention of both the sober critical world and a public that had first been inattentive to his serious work and then tickled by what he admittedly wrote with his tongue in his cheek, that he consciously developed and extended it to objective studies. It consisted in a disconcerting and sometimes even devastating unmasking—dispassionate and unemotionalized even when opening the way for pity—of the secret and irrational motives that trouble the currents of our lives.

It is this disparity between the surface picture and the truth of inner fact, motive and desire which continues to occupy his interest as a writer. In *Cakes and Ale* he has exposed the skeleton in the cupboard of a famous literary man, the Grand Old Man of English Letters, the last of the Victorians, Edward Driffield. And the skeleton turns out to be the living and all too flesh and blood Rosie, the barmaid who was the first wife of the great novelist. The author has pictured this woman with a reminiscent care which makes her nakedly and embarrassingly real, both in her prime, when as a guileless child of nature 'apt for love' she offered her beauty to men with innocence and a clear conscience and gave pleasure to those she liked with the ingenuousness of a happy animal, and in her seventieth year, when her beauty has turned to a double chin. This last portrait is one that shows Maugham at his sardonic best. With a few bold strokes as masterfully economized as those of Maupassant, he limns a terrifying sketch of the aged beauty with her blood-colored nails, her plucked eyebrows and powdered bosom.

Driffield really stands for the most part as a vague figure in the background, gaining what reality he may have from the subtle plausibility of a tantalizing, synthetic personality. Every other character is so transparently drawn from the life that the reader feels baffled when he is confronted with this well-camouflaged composite novelist. Driffield is only the peg upon which the author hangs his cloak of mordant irony while depicting the rise of a literary personality. Mr Maugham's mellowed cynicism has almost allied itself with humor in his daring exposure of the manner in which mediocrity becomes crowned as genius. There is, for instance, an amusing paragraph on the reverence that the English pay to longevity.

One who is acquainted with the earlier work of Maugham will see an interesting conflict of interests in this last novel. Just after the war he felt that he had written himself out in *Of Human Bondage* so far as the English scene was concerned. In the hope of leavening his artistic stock he traveled in the Orient and the South Seas. He tried for a time to get out of the autobiographic strain, to picture an objective life in which he was not an actor. But, egocentric and introspective as he was, he never completely identified his point of view with that of his characters. His persons were 'cases' whom he analyzed in the impersonal laboratory manner. In *Cakes and Ale* he has returned to England and to his youth once more, but brought with him much of the zest for exploring strange personalities.

There is something bracing about the sincerity of his style. His simplicity is neither affected nor self-consciously mannered. It is the plain speaking of the man from the laboratory. It is a style that serves his general purpose of stripping life to the bone with a thin, sharp knife that lays open to view the normal flesh and the healthy flow of blood as well as the cancerous sore beneath.

SIX STORIES WRITTEN IN THE FIRST PERSON SINGULAR

New York, London, September 1931

---

66. Lee Wilson Dodd, 'Set of Six', *Saturday Review of Literature* (New York)

VIII, 17 October 1931, 206

Mr Maugham is the most competent, the most professional of authors. Indeed, he is perhaps a little too publicly aware of his almost ruthless competence, his slightly hard-boiled professionalism. In his introduction to the present 'set of six' there is a tone of uneasy truculence. 'I have been accused of bad taste,' he says:

I have at one time or another been charged with portraying certain persons so exactly that it was impossible not to know them. This has disturbed me, not so much for my own sake (since I am used to the slings and arrows of outrageous fortune) as for the sake of criticism in general. We authors, of course, try to be gentlemen, but we often fail and we must console ourselves by reflecting that few writers of any consequence have been devoid of a certain streak of vulgarity. Life is vulgar. I have long known that journalists, in private free in their speech and fond enough of bawdry, are in print great sticklers for purity, and I have no doubt that this is as it should be; but I fear that if they become *too* refined there will be so few points of contact between them and the writers whom it is their pleasant duty to appraise that criticism will become almost impossible.

This passage is irony at its worst—that is, at its least convincing. Something is troubling Mr Maugham, and he is trying to curl his

192

lip contemptuously and shrug it away. 'I have been accused of bad taste,' he says....

Nevertheless, as novelist, as playwright, as teller of tales, Mr Maugham is always professionally competent, and from time to time he is a great deal better than that. From time to time he ceases to be merely slick, hard, and brilliant; he forgets himself in his material, his characters come alive, he illuminates the mind and touches the heart. There are two superb stories in the present volume—one a masterpiece of comedy, the other a tragedy of character and circumstance that is uncompromisingly seen and yet deeply and truly felt. The comedy, 'Jane,' may be left to speak for itself; every line of it is right, and Jane herself is the sort of woman who would never insist upon being remembered, but whom discriminating readers will find it very difficult (and unnecessary) to forget. The tragedy, 'The Alien Corn,' is a different and more difficult accomplishment. In this story Mr Maugham seems to me to pass far beyond the usual range of his distinguished talent.

'The Alien Corn' is a study of a Jewish family of great wealth who are trying to escape from all the tremendous implications of their racial inheritance and turn themselves into the perfect, the complete, English county family. All the passionate pride and hope of Sir Adolphus Bland (the name was originally Bleikogel) and of his wife, Lady Muriel, are centered in their eldest son, George.

George was a scratch at golf, and though tennis was not his game he played much better than the average; the Blands had had him taught to shoot as soon as he was old enough to hold a gun, and he was a fine shot; they had put him on a pony when he was two, etc.—George was so tall and slim, his curly hair, of a palish brown, was so fine, his eyes were so blue, he was the perfect type of the young Englishman.

Harry, the second son, was

stocky, broad-shouldered, and strong for his age, but his black eyes, shining with cleverness, his coarse dark hair, and his big nose revealed his race. Freddy (Sir Adolphus) was severe with him...but with George he was all indulgence. Harry would go into the business, he had brains and push, but George was the heir. George would be an English gentleman.

But, unhappily, George had other needs, another ambition. He wished to become a great concert pianist. He fled to Munich on five pounds a week, and the resulting tragedy is a deeper sounding of those strange, compelling mid-sea currents of race than you might easily suppose. The story takes on passion, heartbreak, and a certain grandeur—only marred, alas, by a touch of cynical smartness in its concluding sentence. 'One reads of such accidents in the paper often.' But the blemish, if it be a blemish, is slight.

The other four stories are well enough in their way. Mr Maugham knows how to plan a story and carry it through. Competence is the word. His style is without a trace of imaginative beauty; one feels that like Stendhal he has been studying the *Code Civil*. 'There entered a youth in a very well-cut dinner jacket.' That is the tone of his writing, clear, cold, charmless, efficient; an occasional glitter of wit, or the salt taste of irony. No nonsense about him; he knows perfectly how to do what he desires to do. And then, from time to time, unexpectedly, as in 'Rain' or 'The Alien Corn,' he feels something, as if in spite of himself, intensely—and knows surprisingly more.

67. L.A.G. Strong, 'The Test That Failed', *Spectator*

CXLVII, 10 October 1931, 468

Leonard Alfred George Strong (1869–1958) was a British novelist and poet, of Irish extraction on his mother's side. His publications include the novel *The Brothers* (1932), collected poems under the title *The Body's Imperfections* (1957), and studies of James Joyce and John McCormack.

This review of four widely differing works of fiction is so integrated as to deserve reprinting in its entirety, and it is interesting to note that a contemporary 'middle-brow' reviewer was more at home with these Maugham stories than with Virginia Woolf's *The Waves*. The other two novels reviewed were *Nixey's Harlequin* by A.E. Coppard and *The Wild Orchid* by Sigrid Undset.

'...Few writers of any consequence' says Mr Maugham, in a foreword to *First Person Singular*, 'have been devoid of a certain streak of vulgarity.' When I read that, I exulted, for it has long been a pet theory of mine that much high-class modern writing was devitalized by the authors' inability to be vulgar. If vulgarity means coarse rather than false values: a thickening of fibre: ability to get inside the skin of lout, cad, snob, and profiteer: then the possession of a streak of it would seem essential to any writer who aimed at more than a partial rendering of life.

Yet—salutary fact, or malicious exception—to the other books here listed Mr Maugham's acid test seems hardly to apply. *The Waves* looked a certain victim. Apart from *To the Lighthouse*, a most beautiful and moving book to which I utterly surrender, I have always felt that Mrs Woolf's work suffered precisely from the lack of this saving streak of vulgarity. Its importance had to be acknowledged, but it irritated me with its almost antiseptic refinement: and when, in part of *Orlando*, she essayed an Elizabethan breadth, her failure confirmed my feeling that here was an artist incapable of sharing with the humanity that relishes its food and feels the heat. I would have said, in short, that whereas the literary personalities of Mr Maugham and Mr Coppard and Sigrid Undset would sit down delightedly to table with Falstaff, Mrs Woolf's would plead a headache and lie down with a handkerchief soaked in eau-de-cologne.

But the matter turns out to be less simple. We shall see why when we examine the books. Mr Maugham, at any rate, thrives by his own admission. He is beautifully detached, and can be vulgar when he wishes. I have the greatest admiration for his professional craftsmanship, and with all that he says in these pages about amateur and professional I am in complete accord. He knows his craft from A to Z; but there are disquieting signs that he is tending to despise it. The perfect cut and finish of these stories cannot hide the fact that they are not all of the best material. He sets himself the technical poser of the first person singular: contemptuously cuts a resulting knot (the interview between Mrs Tower and Jane, at which his narrator was not present): and dispenses, in four stories at least, with the element of surprise. Writing far better than nine highbrow writers out of ten, he yet seems to have them on his nerves, and the book resounds to the grinding of the axe with which he neatly beheads their effigies. 'The Round Dozen' is an

excellent story: 'The Human Element' and 'The Alien Corn' are
very good: but the effect of the whole book is that of music
expertly played in an expensive restaurant at dinner. Mr Maugham
surely cannot believe that anything of his is to last only 'ninety
days,' as he says in his foreword? If he does, then something is
badly wrong with one of the most subtle craftsmen of our time.

Mr Coppard has no axe to grind. He sees life through the leaded
panes of a country pub, a little oddly, with a strange innocence, and
with a naked understanding. The test of vulgarity, when applied to
his work, loses all meaning. He writes of vulgar characters with
complete knowledge: but there is no vulgarity in his stories. I leave
readers to deal with this paradox as best they may. Mr Coppard
was born to elude rules and definitions. He is a master of his
medium. He does not accent his irony—see 'The Green Drake.'
His descriptions seem casual and uncontrived.

In time, I came to a dark lake lying in a collar of rocks...

As for the title story, in which a girl's twenty-two lovers are
taken by a detective in a charabanc to attend her inquest, he
convinces us with a skill which even Mr Maugham could not
surpass. Mr Coppard is a great artist, and his work seems destined
for long life.

The Waves is an elusive, beautiful, and baffling book. The
characters, starting as children, express their complex thoughts in a
language of equal complexity, which makes no pretence to realism.
'The fact is,' says one of them, 'that I have little aptitude for
reflection.' He need not worry: Mrs Woolf will make good his
deficiency. Her powers of observation are little short of marvellous, and often an exact phrase sends a thrill of joy through the
reader.

I sit snug in my own corner going North...in this roaring express
which is yet so smooth that it flattens hedges, lengthens hills....The
distance closes for ever in a point; and we for ever open the distance wide
again. The telegraph poles bob up incessantly; one is felled, another rises.

On the other hand,

'The man lay livid with his throat cut in the gutter,' said Neville. 'And
going upstairs I could not raise my foot against the immitigable apple tree
with its silver leaves held stiff.'

This sort of thing is over my head. I can appreciate the design of Mrs Woolf's book, and many of its felicities, but I prefer something which is easier to read.

For instance, *The Wild Orchid*. Sigrid Undset can get the broadest and subtlest effects. The word vulgar will not exist in her neighbourhood, but one never feels that her intellect is a filter which excludes everything of coarser grain. She has told, with grandeur, tenderness, and beauty, in the most straightforward language, the boyhood, young manhood, love story and marriage of Paul Selmer, child of divorced parents, who sided with his mother but could not dislike his father. So faithful is the portraiture, so accurately realized the world, that one sheds one's nationality and becomes one of these sensitive, warm-hearted Norwegians. There is a large, austere beauty about the work of Sigrid Undset which is impossible to describe. Mrs Woolf's book engages one's mind, one's separate faculties and sensations, with stimuli exquisitely apprehended and conveyed. In Sigrid Undset's, one simply lives.

Yet, after all, comparisons take us nowhere. Is not Mrs Woolf perfectly justified in selecting what she wishes or what she must? Of course she is. To have written *To the Lighthouse* is justification for any manner, or excuse for any limitation; and, though I still believe Mr Maugham's dictum to be broadly true, it must be confessed that here are three books to which it has little application.

THE NARROW CORNER

London, New York, November 1932

68. Anne Armstrong, review, *Saturday Review* (London)

CLIV, 26 November 1932, 564–5

The other three novels reviewed in the article, of which the following is an extract, were written by Eric Linklater, R.H. Mottram and Nathaniel Gubbins. It contains the most explicit statement of the occasional complaint that Maugham did not understand women; a more discriminating reviewer might have modified this to criticism of *The Narrow Corner* and the sort of women Maugham chose to portray in that novel. Anne Armstrong did, however, stoke a controversy that still burns.

Mr Somerset Maugham recently announced that he had done with the theatre. For good or evil he was sick of the business of writing plays, and whatever stars or managers or producers or public liked to say, Mayfair and Manchester had seen their last Somerset Maugham first night. I forget the reason he gave—it was certainly not lack of success—but in future, one understood, he was going to cultivate the novel.

Actually he has written about as many novels as plays in the last thirty years, and if the world knows him better as playwright than novelist it must be because the world has made up its mind that his plays are better worth seeing than his novels worth reading. That's as it may be; the world is often wrong, and anyway it is no concern of mine. An author, like a criminal, is tried on his latest performance, and previous successes or convictions ought not to weigh with the jury at all.

Let me say at once that *The Narrow Corner* is beautifully written. (Why is it that almost all doctors—the world has forgotten that Mr Maugham is a physician by profession—from Sir Thomas Browne downwards, write better English than, say, lawyers or parsons?) There is nothing whatever in the easy, flowing, but never rhetorical style to suggest the short, staccato stage direction; rather does one think of the pure man of letters playing with words, pleasurably conscious of the wealth of the English vocabulary but careful never to abuse it by ostentation or extravagance. Not exactly 'No Flowers' as Leslie Stephen once said, but at any rate only the proper decorations.

Nor, though I looked for it carefully, could I find anything theatrical in the dialogue. There are occasional soliloquies, such as nobody would speak in real life, but neither literature nor drama, apparently, can quite do away with this convention. Eric the Dane on poetry and the Planter on religion were sometimes lengthy and tedious, but the conversation, like the descriptions, is as a whole easy and natural.

The plot, however, and some of the characters are another matter. It is no legitimate ground for criticism that the love affair, or rather the seduction of a boy of twenty by a woman in the fifties, is unpleasant as a theme; after all these things do sometimes happen. But the murder of the awkward husband, on which the story hangs, is not merely theatrical—it reeks of melodrama. Such things may happen, do happen, but not quite like that.

Again, it is no legitimate ground of criticism that the boy of twenty next seduces a girl of eighteen *pour passer le temps*; after all these things do happen and they happen rather more often that way than the other. But it is almost unbelievably crude in the way it is told, and once again the subsequent suicide of the futile and jilted lover reeks of melodrama. Especially when a little later the young seducer also commits suicide. Such things certainly happen but not quite like that.

The defect of the book, in short, is its women. The men, or at least the two chief men—the detached and philosophical doctor and the crooked but pluckily entertaining sea captain—are quite excellent. And the first and greater part of the book, when these two have the stage to themselves, is wholly admirable, whilst their sea journey down to Kanda, a beautiful island, and the description of the island itself, is quite beautifully done. But the two women are no more than 'types'—mere types of animal lust, exactly the same except for differences in age and beauty—mere types that had not the slightest inkling of the glory and beauty that was their heritage.

And as there are, after all, other types of women in the world it was hard indeed on the boy, who is alternately seduced and seducer, that these are the only two women he met.

The truth is, on the evidence before us—and we agreed that he must stand on this his latest performance—that Somerset Maugham does not understand women. He realises that man is a complex animal, part good and part bad; but women to him are all of a piece—100 per cent. uninteresting angels (off stage) or passionate and consuming vamps in the spot light. I humbly suggest to him that women, however inferior to men, are—if only because they have to deal with men—slightly more complex in their mental make-up than the evidence in *The Narrow Corner* would have us believe.

Oddly enough, Mr Maugham tacitly admits his lack of understanding in this direction. For the first woman in the book does not appear directly in person at all—what she has done (and there was not much she left undone) is told by a male character. And the second woman, although she does actually appear on the stage, hardly speaks—and what she does is again told *by a man*.

I cannot but think that this method of indirect presentation spoils an otherwise admirable book. It is no disgrace to Mr Maugham that he is so obviously a man's man; but as a novelist his art is bound to be incomplete if he does not at least attempt to draw credible women.

But the scenery descriptions of the islands (and the setting is in the East Indies) and the trip down the coast—these are unforgettable.

69. Florence Haxton Britten,
'A Cynical, Gifted Story Teller',
New York Herald Tribune

13 November 1932, 3

'Nothing,' says Marcus Aurelius, in the very *Meditations* from which Mr Somerset Maugham draws the title for his latest novel, *The Narrow Corner*, 'has such power to broaden the mind as the ability to investigate systematically and truly all that comes under thy observation of life.'

Yet the progress of Mr Maugham's whole career as a novelist seems, oddly enough, to give these words of Marcus Aurelius the lie. For Maugham, looking on life with acute and undiminished interest, studying it, weighing it, recreating it tirelessly in novels of extraordinary brilliance and fascination, has grown from year to year more restricted in his version of it—measurably more narrow minded and disillusioned. A world once rich in possibilities has become for him a mean place, in which trivial things happen to trivial people. The horizon of man's dreams has been narrowed and battened down. Man himself is a pretty bad lot. In the course of the passing years Mr Maugham has grown callous to that intricate internecine strife which goes on inside even the most obvious natures.

Yet what a first-rate story teller Maugham is. One approaches his pages with confidence. Here, invariably, will be wit and skill and the fruits of an imagination ranging afar. From his varied settings one could construct a vivid colored fictional atlas which would nearly cover the globe. And the personalities and human situations which have piqued his roving fancy long enough to supply him with the gist of novels are legion. And, more than all this, he possesses that indefinable quality of writing personality which makes what he has to say inevitably of interest.

The Narrow Corner is a neat, vigorously written story of psychological adventure at sea and among the Malaysian islands well-nigh forgot by God and man. Dr Saunders, one of those

201

derelict doctors once favorably known in Harley Street, but anchored now, for reasons best known to himself, in the tolerant Orient, offers his keen if distorted intelligence and his indifferent patience as the scroll on which the events of the story are written. It is he to whom Captain Nichols, that complete rascal of the sea, who 'needed a spice of crookedness to counteract the depression his dyspepsia caused him,' confides all that he knows and something of what he suspects of the reason why young Fred Blake, of Sydney, is cruising the islands without destination or cargo save a ballast of stones. Blake, too, in due course confides in Dr Saunders; as does Louise, the pale-haired island girl who, as events move forward, brings disaster on the men who love her. And months after Saunders has left the island, his chance meeting with Captain Nichols on the dusty little terrace of a hotel in Singapore gives him the epilogue and brings the tale to the full stop.

In its mere outline, *The Narrow Corner* is a slick, swift story of mystery and crime. At either extreme of handling, it might have held material for an Edgar Wallace thriller, or for something approaching a Conradian *Lord Jim*. Enriched as it is with shrewd characterizations and a definite philosophy of life, it comes far closer to Conrad than to the thriller prototype. And for sheer entertainment, and the spell of narrative, it is to my mind better than either. Maugham is like a not too scrupulous acquaintance who claims that he knows the world well and vows that he has found it without exception helpless or vicious. You can derive amusement and considerable knowledge from his vivacious reports of it, without being required to subscribe to the scepticism which has colored his findings.

AH KING

London, September 1933; New York, November 1933

The Malayan journey which furnished material for these six stories was undertaken in the winter of 1925/26. Maugham only visited the East once more, in extreme old age, and *Ah King* marks the close of the Far Eastern phase of his writing.

70. William Plomer, review, *Spectator*

CLI, 29 September 1933, 420

William Plomer (1903–73) was a novelist and poet born in South Africa. His novels include *Turbott Wolfe* (1925) and *Museum Pieces* (1952), and his *Collected Poems* appeared in 1960. He edited the diary of Francis Kilvert, acted for many years as literary adviser to Jonathan Cape, and wrote reviews for various journals.

Mr Maugham's short stories are among the best now being written. To be a man of the world, to be acquainted with all sorts of different people, to be tolerant, to be curious, to have a capacity for enjoyment, to be the master of a clear and unaffected prose style—these are great advantages, and Mr Maugham knows how to make use of them. If he seldom explores the depths and intricacies of human nature, he certainly has little to learn about human behaviour in general or the principal forces by which many people are actuated. He has that 'stern sense of the practical' which he has noted in the *Sailing Directions* published by the Admiralty, but he has also the power of discovering what strange and remarkable lives are often led by those 'ordinary' people whom a superficial observer would be little able to distinguish from their fellows. These stories are mostly about English people in the Malay States:

What was one to do with these people? The men had come out to the colony as lads from second-rate schools, and life had taught them nothing. At fifty they had the outlook of hobbledehoys. Most of them drank a great deal too much. They read nothing worth reading. Their ambition was to be like everybody else. Their highest praise was to say that a man was a damned good sort. If you were interested in the things of the spirit you were a prig. They were eaten up with envy of one another and devoured by petty jealousies. And the women, poor things, were obsessed by petty rivalries. They made a circle that was more provincial than any in the smallest town in England. They were prudish and spiteful.

Certainly it is the exceptions who are interesting—Alban Torel, the conceited highbrow who was no administrator; Mr Gruyter, the Dutch *contrôleur*; Olive Hardy, whose unlawful passion was her undoing. The best of these stories, 'Neil MacAdam,' seems to me as good as Maupassant: the conflict between a chaste and handsome young Scotchman and a lustful Russian woman in the jungle is beautifully told and terrible in its implications.

71. Florence Haxton Britten, 'Maugham's Tragic Tales', *New York Herald Tribune*

12 November 1933, 4

The quaint title *Ah King*, attached to these six short stories whose setting is 'out from Singapore,' is delightfully accounted for by Mr Maugham. In Singapore he hired a self-possessed and singularly aloof young Chinese servant to travel with him—Ah King by name. For six months Ah King attended excellently all his wants. When they parted Mr Maugham gave him a testimonial, his wages and a present. The lad burst into tears, to Mr Maugham's considerable embarrassment. 'I had never thought of him as a human being,' he says. 'He wept because he was leaving me. It is for these tears that I now give his name to this collection of stories that I invented while he was travelling with me.'

The stories which follow are fascinatingly characteristic of Mr Maugham. Quintessentially a spiritual world-traveler and sightseer among the emotions, he looks on the vagaries of his fellow beings from Lambeth to Singapore and the South Sea Islands with that same aloof yet penetrating and interested gaze which the experienced tourist turns on strange lands and diverse customs. Mr Maugham makes his little journeys coolly, carefully into the lives of many kinds of people whom he finds, most often, pursuing their ways in remote, exotic corners of the world. But the impulses which dictate their conduct and provide Mr Maugham with his invariably dramatic stories are deeply human and universal. Mrs Bronson, playing a somewhat nervous game of bridge in the English club at Tanah Merah, than which 'there is no place in Malaya that has more charm,' while her lover shoots her husband's head off as he rides his bicycle quietly homeward along a shortcut through the jungle, had no more—and no less—aplomb than our own Ruth Snyder. And was moved by precisely the same motives, translated from economic into social terms.

The shy and idealist young Scotsman in 'Neil MacAdam,' who permits a flamboyantly erotic woman to perish horribly in the jungle so that her husband may never discover what depths of abandon she is capable of, would conduct himself somewhat differently at home in the tight little isle. But his motives would be the same.

And so it is with the rest of the stories. 'Back of Beyond' and 'The Book Bag' are both of them compellingly tragic tales of love in which one can believe utterly. 'The Vessel of Wrath,' which amounts almost to a tirade against the narrow bad taste of the missionaries who ply their, to Mr Maugham, loathsome trade in the Orient, is a cumbrously humorous extravaganza rather than a serious effort to build a credible short story. But its next-door neighbor, 'The Door of Opportunity,' a study of an arrant, yet nonchalant, coward and his devoted wife who suddenly comprehends in a blinding flash that her husband deserves his nickname 'Powder-puff,' is a beautifully turned piece of character and scene building.

It seems to me that Mr Maugham's extraordinary felicity as a writer inheres not only in this capacity of his to make a coldly scientific appraisal of human nature and so proceed with utter certainty to the building up of credible and compelling narrative. He has another gift which fully matches this: an intense interest in what goes on before his eyes. Persons—their physical appearance, their carriage, their character—places, with all the circumstance and infinite, rich detail which builds a recreated, romantic reality out of observed facts, are at his finger tips, intense and vivid.

When one gets aboard a Maugham story one is committed to stay on till the end of the journey. One has no impulse whatsoever to walk out of any of the dull, stodgy little English clubs or forsake Mr Gruyter in the middle of his stengah while Mr Maugham is telling you about them. Yet toward these painfully human paper characters and scenes of his Mr Maugham seems always to carry an aloof, even a derisive, attitude. His own shadow as a novelist appears to hover over the thoughts which he attributes to one George Moon, Resident in charge of Timbang Belud, in the Federated Malay States, in 'Back of Beyond.' Moon, having given some sage advice to one of his subordinates, who is in the throes of marital trouble, is left alone to reflect on human nature. A wintry smile touches his thin lips, and he recalls with interest that quaint animal, the Jumping Johnnie, with which the mud of their dry creeks teemed. 'They were the color of the mud they lived in. They sat and looked at you with large round eyes and then with a sudden dash buried themselves in their holes. It was extraordinary to see them scudding on their flappers over the surface mud. ... There was something uncanny about them, but something amusing, too. They reminded you very much of human beings. It was quite entertaining to stand there for half an hour and observe their gambols.' ...

Thus also, I believe, Mr Maugham.

PART IV
PLAYS
(1916–1933)

CAROLINE (THE UNATTAINABLE)

New Theatre, London, 8 February 1916 (141 performances)
[Written 1915. Published London, December 1923]

This play was written in Switzerland during the Great War, at a time when Maugham was using his profession of dramatist as a cover for intelligence activities. The situation is described in 'Miss King', the first of the *Ashenden* stories (1928).

72. J.T. Grein, review, *Sunday Times*
13 February 1916, 4

Some Old Egyptian some 8,000 years B.C. has said 'the ideal realised means suicide.' He was a sage and what he said in a more civilised age still holds good to-day. Mr Somerset Maugham, a witty man and one who has lately breathed French air in fulfilling patriotic duties, has bethought himself that there would be an excellent comedy in the grim saying of old. And the result is *Caroline*.

For ten years Caroline has been wooed in honourable grass-widowhood by the eminent K.C. Then her husband obliged by dying in Nairobi and, when the announcement appeared in *The*

Times, the two lovers discussed their marriage as such a matter of course, that they both decided not to risk the permanency. There was also another swain, the inevitable twenty 'mothing' around the riper thirties. This youth doted on Caroline married or Caroline prospectively belonging to the K.C., but when he heard that Caroline was free, and when she told him that he might enter the gates of Paradise, he sought, deeply crestfallen, solace with another grass-widow, more unattainable, while maintaining his illusions. There are such Werthers who revel in hopelessness.

Meanwhile Caroline became *désoeuvrée*, worried, restless. She sent for the doctor who diagnosed what I could call 'quarantophobia'—fear of middle-age, when one studies the glass, finds the new policeman on the beat so young, finds young people in the ballroom too noisy, etc. She was swayed by her boring friends, the pretty chatterbox and the lying minx; both always scheming some matrimonial idea for Caroline which would not interfere with their own. She reopened the matrimonial question again with the K.C. and they quarrelled over house and bath room decorations. Once more the doctor was called in, as a guest this time, and, for want of a handier victim, Caroline made it plain to him that he would be a very desirable husband. But the doctor—old practitioner (admirably done by Mr Dion Boucicault as to the manner born)—fought shy of *that* nostrum, and, incidentally, to save his skin and his patient, he mooted 'Why not revive the dead husband *pour le besoin de la cause*.' That did the trick. The K.C. and the young swain were in the field again with a vengeance, and this time the elder engineered the love scene so romantically that Caroline was quite convinced that he was the right man and that the climax of their love was yet planing in delightfully unattainable heights.

You see that it is as light as a feather and as bright as a diamond of Gophir—nothing real, but something very whimsical, seasoned with vivid dots and crosses of acute observation. To those who love *badinage* and *bavardage* that might go on till doomsday—a treat; to those less fond of the ephemeral and the preciousness of playful insincerity—an ambiguous entertainment divided between the laugh that comes from within and that obbligato laugh which some people have always in readiness when a reputed witty man says something or other. But apart from these possible diversions of opinion, there is no gainsaying that there must be general admiration of Mr Maugham's dexterity and verve to fill two hours with an idea woven into a mantilla of colour and gossamer. He is as crafty as old Scribe was and he writes ever so much better. So his play was a success, and half of it was due to Miss Irene Vanbrugh and to Mr Leonard Boyne.

Miss Vanbrugh frivolled delightfully as the unsettled Caroline; she was quite the Irene Vanbrugh we love best—the gay, *insouciante*, birdlike young woman, who, as it were, seesaws on the branches of life. Mr Boyne's manner as the K.C. was at first very halting, but anon he developed the character into a man whom women must love for his upgrown boyishness, his old bachelor caprices, his kindness of heart, and his chivalry towards woman— all that was finely portrayed by Mr Boyne. The Werther-like young lover of Mr Martin Lewis had the merit of restraint, and a doleful sincerity all the more comic because it seemed real. Miss Nina Sevening and Miss Lillah McCarthy made what they could of the two boring friends of Caroline, and as the maid, Miss Florence Lloyd had just one little chance of making a point, when explaining to her mistress how in her world walking out ripens into engagement.

OUR BETTERS

Hudson Theatre, New York, 12 March 1917 (112 performances)
Globe Theatre, London, 12 September 1923 (548 performances)
[Written 1915. Published London, September 1923]

The play was written in Rome during the Great War, when Maugham was an intelligence agent. The contrasting reactions of the reviewers of the American and London productions respectively highlight the two factors that need to be discounted when a play is being assessed by reference to reviews of its first productions in London and New York. The first is national prejudice, the second the quality of the productions themselves.

The play contains many echoes of—even borrowings from—the stories of Henry James.

---

73. Unsigned review, *New York Evening Post*

13 March 1917, 9

There is a little of the best and much of the very worst work of W.S. Maugham in his latest comedy, *Our Betters*, which was presented before a very large audience in the Hudson Theatre last evening. The former included pleasant samples of the vivacious, apt, humorous, or incisive dialogue which he writes with uncommon facility, and the latter interludes of cheap and unworthy sensationalism and contemptible coal-heaverish vulgarity. As a whole the piece is shambling, invertebrate, verbose, trite, and, because of its exaggerations and manifest insincerity, utterly insignificant. For its professed satirical motive it has a theme which, although it has been worn somewhat threadbare, is perfectly legitimate and, unhappily, by no means destitute of solid foundation in present fact. In one guise or another it has furnished plots to most of the principal English and American playwrights for more than a century. Disgraceful bargains in the fashionable marriage mart—wherein budding poverty has been sold to satyr-like age, or bankrupt and besmirched titles proved a fatal bait for golden beauty—have often inspired contemptuous, wrathful, and righteous denunciation, which doubtless has had its effect in the past, and is neither superfluous nor futile now. In this case the stage has often done good service. But not much public benefit is likely to accrue from pieces in which the possible underlying satire, or moral, is subordinated to the devices of a purely commercial and money-grubbing theatricalism. And in this category *Our Betters*, which bears all the outward marks of the 'pot-boiler,' only too clearly belongs. In spite of its occasional references to affairs of the moment, it might well be an early and neglected invention rescued from a pigeonhole, and touched up here and there, to find a sale, now that the repute of the author has given it a fictitious value. In many ways it suggests inexperience, in the looseness of its construction, its remoteness from actuality, its awkward mechanism, and its oscillation between farcical comedy and the crudest of melodrama. Unquestionably it offers a variety of entertainment—good, bad, or indifferent—and therefore it may fulfil its purpose of attracting tolerant spectators, but its heterogeneous character exempts it from detailed description or serious consideration.

Briefly, it deals with the experiences, amorous and financial, of an American adventuress—of an exceedingly ancient and popular but always incredible type—who, having, as a comparatively innocent girl, bestowed herself upon a penniless and complacent baronet, thrusts him into the background, and endeavors to break into the upper circles of society by means of her title and her private fortune of eight thousand pounds a year. Finding her funds unequal to her ambitions, she puts herself under the secret protection of a coarse American capitalist, who finds the money for the establishment and the feasts, which other degenerate compatriots and Englishmen, pertinaceous tuft-hunters like herself, are only too willing to share with her. Her intimates are a French Duchess, unattached—a former Chicago girl who spends her father's millions in paying the bills of her English lover—and an Italian Princess, formerly a Boston girl, who, having drained the matrimonial cup of bitterness to the dregs, is now devoting herself and her money to good works. Her cherished plan is to marry her innocent young sister, betrothed to a fine young American, to a penniless lordling, and she is only defeated in this object through the girl's discovery of an abominable intrigue which she was carrying on with the man who was the private property of her friend the Duchess.

No more of the story need be told. Obviously it is sordid and abominable, but it is also, as a pretended representation of any imaginable phase of society, almost ridiculously unlifelike and untrue. Mr Maugham, in attempting to write an international drama, has only succeeded in basely libelling both countries. A burlesque, which might have been a wholesome satire, has been robbed of all excuse by the grossness of its exaggeration and the vulgarity of its illustrations. These are only compensated for partly by the amusement provided by the lighter passages, which abound in sparkling dialogue. If they contain little that is fresh in the way of incident or character, Miss Chrystal Herne deserves credit for the earnestness and intelligence with which she labored to give plausibility as well as vitality to the repulsive part of the impossible heroine. She was hopelessly out of her proper element, but she proved herself a clever and conscientious actress. The part could scarcely have been congenial to a performer hitherto associated with refined and sympathetic methods. Nor was it altogether pleasant to see the fine ability of Rose Coghlan wasted upon a part so completely unworthy of it as that of the vulgar, selfish, jealous duchess. But she vivified it with amazing skill, spirit, and resourcefulness. Her acting was the one sheer delight of the evening. One of her jealous love scenes—poor as the thing was in itself—was a splendid bit of artistry. Even she could not save the great melodramatic scene from ridicule, although she did for it all that an actress could. Mr Fritz Williams is almost as amusing now as he was thirty or forty years ago and in exactly the same way. Ronald Squire, as the Duchess's lapdog, acted humorously and neatly, and John Flood, Joseph McManus, Leonore Harris and Cecil Fletcher are all entitled to a word of approval, but none of the cast, except Miss Coghlan, really shone.

74. Desmond MacCarthy, review, *New Statesman*

XXI, 6 October 1923, 738–9

(Sir) Desmond MacCarthy (1887–1952) was a man of letters *par excellence*. He became literary editor of the *New Statesman*, where many of his essays first appeared, and also its theatre critic; then chief reviewer on the *Sunday Times* from 1928 on the death of Gosse until his own death. He suffered from an unconquerable reluctance to write books: the only ones he published during his lifetime were a collection of his reviews of the Shaw season at the Royal Court Theatre and a small volume on *Leslie Stephen* (1937); but posthumous collections of his essays may be found, the most recent being one edited by his son-in-law Lord David Cecil, *Desmond MacCarthy: The Man and His Writings* (1984), with a biographical portrait. Mac-Carthy was an early member of the Bloomsbury group and a close friend of the Woolfs. He met Maugham when they were part of the same ambulance unit in France in the Great War, and, in spite of the mutual coolness between Maugham and Bloomsbury, remained on amicable terms with him thereafter.

I do not know if Mr Somerset Maugham, who has travelled a great deal lately, has visited M.Coué at Nancy, but certainly every day and in every way his work gets better and better. This is as it should be with successful dramatists, yet how far more usual it is to begin well and tail off! Mr Maugham, after a period of vain endeavour, I understand about as long as the briefless period of an able but unconnected young barrister, suddenly blazed into success. The first time I heard of him, though he had already written a grim, pathetic and remarkable little novel, he was being interviewed by the papers as an astoundingly fortunate young man who had actually three plays running in London at the same time. This was certainly an unusual triumph, but not one which excited my curiosity; indeed, looking back, I see I was then so convinced that a certain measure of ill-success was the concomitant of merit, that this put me off. Thenceforth, like everybody else, when a Maugham play appeared with expected frequency, I took a long run for granted; but, as a critic, that the play would not furnish me matter for discourse.

I went to one or two. They were eminently actable; they had the handy compactness, the shop-finish and alluring shininess of a new dressing-case. The dialogue was clear, but the diction, like Pinero's, was insensitive. I was not interested till *Home and Beauty* opened my eyes to the fact that Mr Maugham had, in addition to his solid stage aptitudes, a far prettier gift for comedy than I had supposed. And I discovered something else: that this gift sprang from a clear-sighted, hard-edged cynicism, rare in English writers; it was Latin, in quality. It came later to the surface, here and there, in *The Unknown*; it disappeared again in a play* so negligible that I am no longer sure of its name—Miss Marie Löhr was the heroine and there was a kind-hearted doctor in it; and, to my joy, it fairly dominated his next play, *The Circle*. There the flavour of it was a little too pungent for palates which had relished *Lady Frederick*, etc. Yet in America, oddly enough, *The Circle* was a prodigious success. They must have been too innocent to feel its devastating implications; for as a rule no people strike one as more determined than Americans to insist that life is a crescendo of happiness or more prone to regard cynicism as treason. *East of Suez*, which followed, was an obvious compromise with the raree-show traditions of His Majesty's: I took it as such. The masculine characters in it were conventional and negligible; but the woman in it was admirably portrayed. She was a creation of that attention, at once indulgent and hard, characteristic of Mr Maugham, which when directed upon certain feminine types, enables him to present them alive upon the stage, with their energies, duplicities, passions and trivialities.

Consequently, having taken *East of Suez* as a work constructed to meet rather unfortunate theatrical conditions, I went to the Globe Theatre with *The Circle* still uppermost in my mind.

Having arrived, then, at a general notion of the kind of play Mr Maugham was born to write, the critical question for me was

---

* *Love in a Cottage* (1918), unpublished (eds).

whether or not he was going to proceed along lines which, with the arrogance which is one of the drawbacks of the critical tempera- ment, I had peremptorily decided he ought to travel: and I was delighted. With the exception of a single kink—one episode in which the dramatist had seemed to wince and refrain—the play went deep and straight, directed from beginning to end by what I believe to be Mr Maugham's true instinct as an artist.

The people who are presented as 'Our Betters' are Lady George Grayson, the Duchesse de Surennes, the Principessa della Cercola, the rich, bumptiously and sentimentally possessive Arthur Fen- wick, the impecunious Tony Paxton, and Thornton Clay 'who calls more countesses by their Christian names than any other man in London'. The curtain has not been up many minutes before we grasp the irony of the title.

The play itself is a mercilessly amusing picture of a rootless, fruitless, extremely vulgar, smart set of people; a much para- graphed, photographed set, whose habits are luxurious, whose standards are common and cynical, whose love-affairs, relieved by a certain engaging candour, are canine. And who are the ladies with high-sounding names? They are American heiresses who have married for rank.

As far as experience enables me to check the verisimilitude of the general picture, the dramatist has stressed their nationality unfairly. All the characters in the set, sympathetic as well as vulgar, are American, with the exception of the fair Tony, who gets his living in it by complaisances which used to be considered unmasculine and dishonourable, and of the harmless Lord Bleane, who fails to secure in the end his scared young transatlantic heiress. This stressing of nationality has, however, two advantages from the point of view of success: in England the play in its implications will have the air of being confined to a merely alien portion of the fashionable rich—though, goodness knows, our social soil pro- duces 'Pearl's' and 'Minnie's'; while in America its satire will seem directed only against a small, and naturally unpopular group of denationalized American snobs.

Yet satire is not the right word to describe the play. It is only a 'satire' for those who attribute to the author their own moral reactions to what he shows them. Each character is allowed rope, and if, at the end of the performance, in your estimation the whole set is left dangling from the gibbet, either it was *you* who strung them up or they hanged themselves; it was not Mr Maugham who put on the black cap. *Our Betters* is rather a sardonically detached comedy; an exposure in the manner of Maupassant of one luxuriant corner of the social jungle. If it had entered Miss Margaret Bannerman's head (she gave us an extraordinarily good performance) that Pearl Grayson was a satire on the smart modern hostess, the play would have been lost. Happily she had imagination enough to play Pearl with delicious appreciation, and intelligence enough to expect us also to delight, like naturalists, in the admirable equipment of some sly, swift animal; in Pearl's witty agility, her shameless courage, her claws and caresses, her gorgeous silly snobbishness, her tight, ferocious clutch upon money and prestige. Against a background of spiritual values, or the heart, Pearl shows up as indeed graceless and ignoble; but against the background of her own world she has a certain lustre; not so the duchess Minnie, whose comical, helpless lack of dignity, whining amorousness, and sluggish, hysterical malevolence Miss Collier acted profoundly well, Pearl is a very vulgar woman, but still she has 'form'—however bad—and gay effrontery; Minnie is a shapeless jelly-fish that stings when trod upon.

When to expose it Maupassant explored the *demi-monde* in *Yvette*, he used the panic of a girl who believed her surroundings to be dazzling and enviable. Elizabeth Saunders, Pearl's sister fresh from America and an heiress herself, also at first believes her sister's *monde* to be splendid. The invisibility of Lord George, and the ill-mannered ubiquity of 'Arthur' (excellently played by Mr Drayton), who pays Pearl's bills; the cynical conversation of the set, their insensitive discussion of her private affairs (it is taken for granted she has hooked Lord Bleane) surprise but do not deeply disturb her. When the play opens she is thoroughly used to the atmosphere, and ready to believe she cannot do better than imitate her sister Pearl. The arrival, however, of a young American lover who is a fish out of water, increases her hesitation to take the worldly matrimonial plunge. She puts off Lord Bleane. She will give him an answer when they meet again at Pearl's country house. It is there ('Arthur', as usual, is a quasi-host) she gets her scare.

We have already seen Pearl handling him and heard, too, how she talks of him behind his back; her methods are the admiration of her friends. 'Tony', who finds dependence on the too exactingly amorous Minnie very trying, has a fancy for Pearl, who is herself as dependent on 'Arthur'. There is a rapid scene between them: 'Let's go down to the tea-house.' 'No I won't.' 'We shall be quite safe there.' 'I daren't, it's too risky.' 'Oh, damn the risk.' Pearl arranges poker for the rest of the party and they disappear. But the lynx-eyed Minnie has seen them go. While the cards are being dealt she exclaims that she has left her bag with her money in the garden tea-house; Lord Bleane gets up to get it. He returns saying he can't find it, and Elizabeth volunteers to hunt, for it must be there; on which Lord Bleane becomes agitated. 'No, no, don't go—besides the door is locked.' 'Oh, it can't be,' says the Duchesse, quietly, 'I saw Pearl and Tony go in just now.' Elizabeth bursts into tears; the Princess jumps up, 'Minnie, you devil!'... The game goes on; Fenwick with distorted face dealing and muttering, 'The slut, the slut!' Elizabeth sobbing, presently the absent couple stroll airily in. Here was the test of the dramatist! The quick closing dialogue is a triumph. Pearl has barely begun her bland excuse before she grasps what has happened. She turns to Tony: 'You damned fool, I told you it was too risky.' The fall of the curtain hides what we gather, in the next act, to have been a very ugly row: the Duchesse in hysterics and 'Arthur' in little better, though he would no doubt have described it as a strong man's wrath. And it is in this last act that Mr Maugham, I think, shows his remarkable power. The sardonic comedy of anti-climax is here of the first order. The kink in his treatment of his subject, which I mentioned above, is, of course, that it should have been *Elizabeth* who went for the bag, and *her* agitation which produces the disclosure; for it is her distress, her *volte face* which is the pivot of the play.

Doubtless Mr Maugham thought this, however, too excruciating a turn to give the scene, and the explosion is still most effective. It leaves Pearl with two objects: to get back Arthur and to prevent her party breaking up and her friends spreading the story. Her successful contrivances are as remorselessly comic as Minnie's reconciliation with Tony, to whom she offers marriage. The emotional squalor of these people's relations, the absence of anything approaching loyalty between them, is coolly exposed. Their lack of all standards, even of superficial elegance, is deliciously suggested by their enthusiastic reception of 'Ernest', on whose egregious vulgarity and capers the curtain descends.

I have not mentioned the Princess (Miss Marion Terry is beautifully natural in the part); she is of, but not happy in, this group of *Our Betters*, and she is the mouthpiece of the explanation: how it was that the lure of romance has decoyed these women into trashy snobbery. Her character is another test of her environment.*

---

* In the following issue of *The New Statesman* Mr Maugham wrote to say that it was the Censor who had objected to Elizabeth being the one to discover the lovers in the garden tea-house, and that he had altered the play to meet that objection: a very good example of the sort of public interference to which dramatists are subjected in this country. [Original note.]

CAESAR'S WIFE

Royalty Theatre, London, 27 March 1919 (241 performances)
[Written 1918. Published London, June 1922]

The theme of the play, virtue triumphing over passion, was
suggested to Maugham by Madame de La Fayette's novel *La
Princesse de Clèves* (1678).

75. Unsigned review, *Times*

28 March 1919, 15

There is a finish, a neatness, an air of accomplishment about every
work of Mr Maugham's, whatever its subject matter, which
ensures for the playgoer a certain quantity of pleasure. Good
workmanship may not be the supreme thing in art, but 'with such a
being as man in such a world as the present one' it will do very well
to go on with.

Even the oldest of themes Mr Maugham can furbish up for you
and relacquer and make it look as good as new. How often have
playgoers been invited to sympathize with the conjugal difficulties
of a husband twenty years older than his wife and to admire the
patient tact with which he overcomes them! Indeed, Mr Aubrey
Smith himself must have been playing tactful elderly husbands *post
hominum memoriam*. But Mr Maugham can find some new way for
him of being tactful, can help him to wear his elderliness with a
difference. Of course, when we say elderly we only mean forty-ish;
just as, according to Mr Angelo Cyrus Bantam, nobody was fat or
old in Bath, so in the theatre no elderly husband is really elderly.
Well, this (theatrically) elderly husband, when the inevitable young
spark comes along and threatens his domestic happiness, has the

tact to hold his tongue. What, you say, a *mari complaisant!* Bless you, nothing so vulgarly rococo as that. He only holds his tongue because, on general principles, silence is golden, and, further, because he thinks the thing may blow over. Even when the lady—who cannot, of course, be expected to hold her tongue— tells him she is in love with the young spark he is still smoothly tactful. These little accidents will happen, he seems to say; we elderly husbands cannot hope to escape them, so just do your best, my dear, and see if you can win through.

Nor (as the graver historians say) is that all. Even when the opportunity occurs of getting the young spark transferred to another post (our elderly husband is British Consul-General at Cairo) he resolutely keeps him on the spot, because he will be more valuable there to his country. What are the feelings of a husband weighed in the balance against the integrity of a public servant? Tact, then, and patience must be the only arm. Perhaps our elderly husband carries discretion to a point of almost inhuman detachment. He interrogates his wife from time to time about the progress of her unfortunate passion, much as a kindly physician would interrogate a patient with the measles. 'Well, and how are *we* this morning?' It is true that he shows signs of distress when alone; he is not really so confident about the outcome of the malady as he pretends to be. But in the end the patient makes a good recovery. The advent of another lady has done much to clear the air, and the wife summons up courage to dismiss the young spark, with the pretence of having only been flirting all the time. No real harm has been done. All parties, in their several degrees, have been tactful. 'Some natural tears' have been shed, but no hearts are broken.

Mr Aubrey Smith as the elderly husband, Miss Helen Haye as his acidulated (oh, agreeably acidulated) sister, and Miss Eva Moore as a lady who once loved him but never told her love, all play smoothly and tactfully. It is a triumphantly tactful evening. Indeed the young spark (Mr George Relph) is so tactful an amorist as almost to be tame. Only with the young wife is nature allowed to break through. Miss Fay Compton represents her as a child of nature—perhaps rather too petulant a child. The petulance is in the part, no doubt, but the actress seems inclined to emphasize it. It is a skilful, forceful performance; also it is a little hard.

76. William Archer, review, *Weekly Review* (New York)

I, 14 June 1919, 110

Caesar's Wife, a play by Mr Somerset Maugham, has made a great success at the Royalty Theatre. An elderly proconsul—British not Roman—has married a girl-wife, who falls deeply in love with his private secretary. But they are extremely well-brought-up young people, who would not dream of anything wrong; and the husband, who sees all that is going on, wins the day in the end by dint of sheer magnanimity. Mr Maugham's psychology is rather superficial, and the proconsul's ineffable superiority to all human weakness becomes at times just a little exasperating. But there are some very well-written scenes in the piece, and the heroine is played to perfection by Miss Fay Compton, an actress who has come much to the front of late. Miss Compton belongs to one of those old theatrical stocks in which talent is handed on from generation to generation. Her grandfather, Henry Compton, was one of the group of fine comedians of the old Haymarket Company, and played the Gravedigger to Irving's Hamlet at the Lyceum. Her father, Edward Compton, was the manager and leading actor of a famous Old Comedy company. Her mother, Virginia Bateman, was a sister of Miss 'Leah' Bateman, and acted with Irving at the Lyceum. Miss Fay Compton herself is the widow of Henry Pelissier, a much-lamented comedian, and is, if I mistake not, a sister of Mr Compton Mackenzie the novelist.

HOME AND BEAUTY (TOO MANY HUSBANDS)

Playhouse, London, 30 August 1919 (235 performances)
Booth Theatre, New York, 8 October 1919 (15 performances)
[Written 1919. Published London, December 1923]

---

77. [Aldous] H[uxley], 'A Good Farce', *Athenaeum*

4665, 26 September 1919, 956

Aldous Huxley (1894–1963) was a novelist, poet, essayist. Grandson of T.H. Huxley and brother of Julian, his work reflects the scientific strain in his background, notably in his prophetic anti-utopian satire, *Brave New World* (1932) and his pioneer popular work on hallucinogenic drugs, *The Doors of Perception* (1954). His pre-war novels such as *Crome Yellow* (1921), *Point Counter Point* (1928) and *Eyeless in Gaza* (1936) contain satirical sketches of the English literary and social worlds. Before World War II he moved to California and became attracted to oriental philosophy, an interest reflected in his novel *Time Must Have a Stop* (1943). His most influential non-fiction work was *The Devils of Loudun* (1952) which inspired a stage-play and a film.

A good farce is something so rare and precious that we are all gratitude to the dramatist who can write one for our delectation. And he has not only our gratitude, but our admiration as well. For the farce-writer must possess many talents—invention, the clockmaker's patient ingenuity in fitting together, wheel within wheel, the incidents of his plot, sufficient insight into life and character to caricature them convincingly, and finally, wit to enliven the dialogue. Most farces fail because the caricature of life which they present is too much burlesqued to be convincing, and because they are insufficiently witty, They rely for their effect solely on the plot's wealth of ingenious incident. But mistaken identities, old roués, young widows, boys fresh from school who want to see life, even lovers hiding under beds, pall in the long run.

Home and Beauty is made of more solidly comic stuff. There is no unreal complication of incident; the original fantastic premiss granted, the rest follows naturally. The pastiche of life and character is real enough to be very amusing, and the dialogue is often genuinely witty.

The story of the play is simple. Victoria did her bit in the Great War by marrying two D.S.O.'s. William perished on the field of battle, and his widow, after a due period of mourning, consoled his best friend Frederick. But William, being Mr Charles Hawtrey, is not to be got rid of so easily. One fine day after the armistice he turns up. The situation is delicate; Victoria feels herself compromised. She finally decides to divorce them both and marry Mr Leicester Paton, who has done *his* bit by building ships, and consequently finds himself in a position to buy several Rolls-Royces and a country cottage with twenty-seven bedrooms. The two heroes fall in readily with this idea; they have both tasted the delights of married life with Victoria, tasted them and drained them to the dregs. Victoria takes herself off, and the curtain descends like a benediction, a promise of 'happily ever after,' on the two new widowers.

Mr Hawtrey's acting is unaffectedly good, as it always is, and Mr Malcolm Cherry makes an excellent second hero. Between them they succeed in covering up the weaknesses of the second act, in which Mr Maugham's cleverness seems at times to fail him and the action becomes rather mechanical. Miss Gladys Cooper hardly does justice to the part of Victoria. She is too impassive, too statuesque, playing all the time as though she were Galatea, newly unpetrified and still unused to the ways of the living world. Victoria should be all that is most lively, most worldly, least statuesque. One can think of plenty of French actresses who could have played the part to perfection, enriching it with the mobility of expression, the by-play, the subtle intonations of voice, which are lacking in Miss Gladys Cooper's somewhat rigid methods of acting.

But there is one really brilliant performance. In the part of Miss Montmorency, the professional Third Party in all the best arranged divorces, Miss Jean Cadell scores a histrionic triumph. Her scene in the third act is inimitable. We could wish that all English comic acting might come up to the standard she sets.

78. Alexander Woollcott, 'A Delightful Maugham Farce', *New York Times*

9 October 1919, 16

Alexander Humphreys Woollcott (1887–1943) was a New York dramatic and literary critic and essayist, and author of *Mrs Fiske* (1917), *Mr Dickens Goes to the Play* (1923), *The Story of Irving Berlin* (1925). The play and later film *The Man Who Came to Dinner* (1939) was based on his dominant personality.

W. Somerset Maugham, a powerful novelist and an adroit craftsman of the theatre, has given us the new and delightful farce which was presented here for the first time last evening at the Booth Theatre. In England they call it *Home and Beauty,* but here we call it *Too Many Husbands.* It is a play so fragile, so light of touch, and so thoroughly and untranslatably English that it would be puzzling and dismal beyond expression if it were left to the casual interpretation of the American stage, but the American producer has put it into the hands of several of the most deft and accomplished English players to be had. The result is an evening of unalloyed amusement.

It is a curious experience to look up from the rather saturnine pages of *The Moon and Sixpence,* and find Mr Maugham's eyes twinkling in as nonsensical a vein as the most frolicsome of his contemporaries. It is a luxurious experience to go to any play in any theatre and sit at the feet of such whimsical comedians as Kenneth Douglas, Lawrence Grossmith and Estelle Winwood, to say nothing of our own Fritz Williams, who seemed to feel a certain communicable gayety in finding himself back home again, with the O.D. gone and his faultless lounge-suit once more adorning his permanently buoyant person.

Too Many Husbands is the fairly descriptive title of a farce which unfolds the really frightfully annoying predicament in which a decorative little mollusc of an Englishwoman finds herself. She certainly felt that she had done her bit when she married two D.S.O.'s—not both at once, of course, but in proper sequence, after one had been adequately killed by the War Office. But he comes back and after the true situation dawns on him he is rather glad he reconsidered his first intention of rushing in melodramatically in the middle of the night and crying: 'Home!' This particular Enoch Arden then tries to make an effectively noble departure into the night, but foiled in that he determines to get away anyway.

He is foiled in this also by the equally determined spirit of resignation shown by the present incumbent, and in the midst of their altercation the dear little woman decides to divorce them both and marry one who had stayed at home during the war. Judging by his recently expanded income, this new candidate had had a good many irons in the home fires and both the D.S.O.'s seem to think it will serve him jolly well right to marry Victoria. Not that either of them would have missed the experience of marrying her for worlds, as they confide to each other jovially over the profiteer's wine when the final curtain falls.

It is rather a pity to have given even that much outline of *Too Many Husbands*, because it tells absolutely nothing of the idle, leisurely and pleasant humor which overlays the framework of the play. Furthermore, one American can relish hugely the entertainment afforded when one quizzical Englishman chaffs his shy, ineloquent countrymen without expecting all other Americans to shake with laughter at the same spectacle. Indeed, it is natural to guess that the public which will appreciate Mr Maugham's latest is not a multitudinous one. This point is not made loftily, as who should say:

'This play is way over your head, but, dear me, how I do appreciate it.'

It is merely made in an effort to report honestly that *Too Many Husbands* lies outside the taste and interest of most of us in this neighborhood.

It requires a knowledge of, an interest in, and a sneaking fondness for the English. It will be appreciated most by those who shake with laughter over every number of *Punch*. It will be enjoyed most by those who think the page of Charivaria is much more amusing than Goldberg's cartoons, and who suspect that one, W.S. Gilbert, to whose humor Mr Maugham's is growing somewhat akin, had a prettier wit and turned rather more arousing verse than the Smith brothers' cough lyrics.

All this is reported with an uneasy feeling that some one is going to admit every word of it, but come out crushingly with the undeniable charge that *Too Many Husbands* is rather slight. It certainly is. It is almost as slight as *The Importance of Being Earnest*.

And surely nothing we grow here is any better than the artful comedy of Kenneth Douglas, who has not been with us since the days of *A Pair of Silk Stockings*, and of Lawrence Grossmith, who comes up smiling shyly from the regions of musical comedy to give a performance just as good as Mr Douglas's. Which is fulsome praise.

THE UNKNOWN

Aldwych Theatre, London, 9 August 1920 (77 performances)
[Written 1920. Published London, October 1920]

The play is virtually a dramatisation of Maugham's early
novel *The Hero*, published in 1901 before *Mrs Craddock*
though actually written after it.

79. Unsigned review, *Times*

10 August 1920, 8

The village of Stour, in Kent, had an energetic young vicar, who
was prevented from going to the war and who was also made
pathetically 'interesting' by a slightly diseased lung. The Church
Militant was, in the Reverend Norman Poole, almost the Church
Pugnacious. That the simple, hearty fellow always said 'our brave
lads at the front' when he meant soldiers we took for granted; but
he was exceptional in the fervour with which, in season and out of
season, he attacked the religious beliefs of his parishioners, should
they not happen to agree precisely with his own.

It must be admitted that the gentlefolk of Stour gave every
excuse to their vicar and to his tactless, good-hearted wife. They
seemed to like talking about their faith and their souls and the most
sacred mysteries of their religion in the drawing-room over the
tea-cups. There was old Colonel Wharton, a Christian of the true
soldierly type, 'an honest, upright, God-fearing gentleman.' There
was his wife, a lady of the fluffy, soulful kind, who maundered in
sing-song about the 'dear Vicar,' and tried to behave as if she
wasn't a thoroughly practical and useful woman. There was Miss
Sylvia Bullough, a devoted sister in the Church. With all these, of

227

course, the Rev. Norman Poole was perfectly safe. And his safety encouraged him to attack—not, indeed, wary old Dr Macfarlane, who was a deeply religious man, though he had shirked church for 25 years, but two other 'brands,' which might be plucked from the burning.

One of these brands scorched his fingers badly. Mrs Littlewood, a widow, came back from the deathbed of her last surviving son in France to tell the people of Stour how much she had enjoyed the music-halls in London, and how pleasantly she looked forward to giving parties in her great and now empty house. And when they began 'going on at her' about her heartlessness and want of faith, she said she would rather play picquet with old Colonel Wharton than discuss her love and her religion. And when still they went on at her she sprang up suddenly from the card-table with a thrilling cry: 'And who will forgive God?'

That, of course, was FitzGerald's Omar put into Mr Maugham's prose:—

> For all the sin wherewith the face of man
> Is blackened, Man's forgiveness give—and take!

But Mrs Littlewood spoke it with all the force of her being; and later, when she 'went on' a bit on her own account at the Vicar and his supporters, she gave us the most dramatic and exciting moment in the whole play.

Mrs Littlewood was acted by Miss Haidée Wright. You can imagine the shock of that sudden outcry, the intensity of passion with which her tale of misery and brave despair came hissing through her all but clenched teeth. And at the close of that act the audience would not be satisfied until they had Miss Wright before the curtain and thundered their applause at her.

The other brand was Colonel Wharton's son, young Major Wharton, home on a few days' leave from the war and on the eve of marriage to Miss Sylvia Bullough. This part of the story is less clear-cut than the episode of Mrs Wharton, less susceptible of thrilling dramatic treatment. Major Wharton is not by any means an atheist, as the vicar calls him; but after a year or two of real war he cannot any longer acquiesce in the doctrines of the Rev. Norman Poole. And though he will go to church, to please his people, he will not take the Holy Communion. The vicar talks and talks; his wife chips in with a rough hand. Mrs Wharton coos and bridles; the

Colonel blusters a little. The unhappy youth is forced to discuss in public subjects which he prefers to keep to himself. None can make him give way. Then Sylvia tries her hand. First, she declares that she will not marry him. Then, intoxicated with the luxury of woe, she plays upon him as dirty a trick as can be imagined. She cheats him into taking the Holy Communion. When he comes back from acting the lie to find that he has been meanly tricked, Sylvia hugs his cold rage and his hot shame to her bosom with glee. She has now a glut of misery. She has sacrificed everything, including her own honour and her lover's, to her ideal, and henceforth she can live in radiant and unrelieved woe.

Well, there are people like Sylvia Bullough; but they are unpleasant company. And there are people like the Rev. Norman Poole, but we are glad to get away from them in the drawing-room. To set against these worthy but tiresome people, Mr Maugham can give us no one but young Wharton; and he, good fellow though he was, did not take us very far, either in sentimental or in intellectual interest. There was no one in the play (not even old Dr Macfarlane, with his Wellsian deity) who could be said to have 'come through'—no one, though the play is strongly anti-clerical, who could give us a view of life to set against that of the clerical party. To anyone who has read and thought at all seriously about these things, most of the argument to and fro must seem a little shallow; to all who have not, it must seem more than a little dull and lacking in drama. Yet so devoid are most plays of anything like thought that Mr Maugham's new play seemed at moments extraordinarily interesting; and we would gladly have sat out a far duller play for the sake of that outburst of Miss Haidée Wright.

Lady Tree was all herself as Mrs Wharton. Miss Ellen O'Malley played Sylvia Bullough with fine conviction. Mr Hignett did wonders of tact in the part of the Vicar, and Mr Charles V. France was never so dear and so real an old fellow as when, faced with certain death from a painful disease, the brave Colonel loses his nerve and is miserably afraid to die. Mr Basil Rathbone managed to keep young Wharton a convincing and engaging young man, and Mr Clarence Blakiston sees the sly humour of old Dr Macfarlane.

80. Frank Swinnerton, review, *Nation* (London)

XXVII, 21 August 1920, 637–8

Frank Arthur Swinnerton (1884–1982) was a novelist and critic. Like Maugham, Swinnerton had begun his career as a fiction-writer depicting working-class characters, and he had become a friend and follower of Arnold Bennett. The bitterness he felt about Maugham's success has coloured his review.

I suppose that all the amusing things have been said about God, and the semi-amusing as well; and that as a consequence they have grown over-familiar. Either that, or an extraordinary lapse into solemnity, must account for the tedium of *The Unknown*, which has just been produced at the Aldwych Theatre. Mr Maugham's play is certainly not amusing. Assuming one's impressions from a single visit to be reliable, it is the over-serious effort of a dramatist who is most successful in light comedy. Being over-serious in this instance, through a wish to treat with gravity a subject which he regards as perhaps a grave one, Mr Maugham cannot move with any lightness among his characters. He seems not to have been able to detach himself from them, but to have remained bewildered—as well he might be—in the centre of their *mêlée*. It is as though the author knew no better than his dramatis personae what they were all talking about. Otherwise he could hardly have taken their desiccated controversy with such seriousness. The characters discuss God for three acts, and reach no conclusion about Him; but they reach no conclusion about God because Mr Maugham appears not to have had the intellectual energy to provide a conclusion to his feeble little love story. He has not imagined the problems of his young lovers, or taken his own large view of death and the manner in which it should be met by young and old; but has simply, as it were, plagiarized from life, with the failure in amusingness which marks all such abortive religious discussion, whether at school or in the home. That is why *The Unknown* (presumably in part owing to the exasperating delays of theatrical production) is already out of date as a topical play, and why it is without emotional importance as a study of lovers disunited upon a matter of religious belief.

Intellectually the play strikes me as superficial. The problem posed is whether faith in God can be maintained through the course of an exhausting war. The moral problem is whether a young woman of sedate character is justified by means of a pious lie in making her lover take the Sacrament unwillingly and unbelievingly. The young woman expects a miracle, and is in her own eyes justified; but Mr Maugham does not seem to believe in miracles, and so he rather sentimentally makes the lover learn the truth, and ends his play with a further discussion upon the subject of luncheon. This is a feeble cynicism, because everybody knows that we must eat to live; and it is irrelevant to the design of the play, which turns upon the death of the body and the life of the spirit. The life of the spirit (apart from all questions of doctrine) is a thing which Mr Maugham has not vividly imagined. It is treated in the play as a thing of problematic and dialectical interest only. We are never made to think of the characters as compact of spirit and flesh, but only as disputatious dealers in stereotyped controversy. Words fly, but never original and personal thoughts. Obstinacies are roused upon the stage, and typical fears also, but not sincere personal emotion. There is a complete lack of intimacy and of understanding among the individuals of the play. It is as though all had met unexpectedly for the first time. They are all narrow, hard, and trivial in their arguments; and, while those objections may all be made to most human beings, we can escape more readily from stupidity in real life than we are able to do in the theatre, and so it must be urged as a fault in *The Unknown*. Unless we can take a living interest in imaginary characters we cannot take a living interest in even their intellectual difficulties; and it is this fact which Mr Maugham has forgotten.

The God the characters talk about is arraigned simply, like a Cabinet Minister, for his conduct of the war, and equally extolled for it. He is a God of War. The utmost that is claimed for Him by His least rigid apologist is that He is not omnipotent, but is engaged in an endless struggle with Evil, a struggle in which the Boy Scouts would seem to be His principal allies. More than that. By the concentration upon this little coterie of disagreeable and uninteresting people, only one of whom (a mother who has had two sons killed) has suffered in the war, Mr Maugham makes this God a mere local Squire, newly come to the district. He has allowed two young men to be killed; He has alienated the hero, who alone of all these talkers has seen what warfare is like. We are supposed, I imagine, to regard this squabble as microcosmic; but we do not do so, because the arguments are purely local, and nothing is done to show us that Mr Maugham regards them as purely local. He takes them too seriously. They are no more representative than are the characters engaged in them. That is, neither are we shown intellectually worthy antagonists, nor (except by the epilogue about food) is any indication offered to us that Mr Maugham realises the unimportance of his whole group. Of a God not exclusively concentrating upon War and the Sacrament we hear or gather nothing. Of a world that contains real life we are given no hint. Therefore we sit in the theatre, watching with discomfort figures which unhumorously pour out little debating points with the unction of schoolboys, wondering when we can return to subjects more edifying and more important. This God Who inspires His worshippers and detractors alike to such curiously kindred sterility in argument is only a God manufactured to be the scapegoat for human muddle and the triumph of muddle-headedness. He is not worth all the pother of an evening in the theatre. One cannot patiently endure a whole play of platitudes about so small a Deity, conducted by such mediocre intelligences. We could endure it better, perhaps, if we felt that Mr Maugham was maliciously exploiting their fatuousness; but at bottom our discomfort is caused by the fear that he, too, is straining his voice and his brains to express the inexpressible profundities of the unknown. It is a task (or at least an accomplishment) outside the range of his lively talent. Far better, even though it be less portentous, is such brilliant work as the first act of *Home and Beauty*.

THE CIRCLE

Haymarket Theatre, London, 3 March 1921 (181 performances)
[Written 1919. Published London, March 1921]

81. Desmond MacCarthy, review, *New Statesman*

XVI, 19 March 1921, 704–5

It is not long since I was commenting upon another play by Mr Somerset Maugham, and not very favourably, but in the course of that discourse—it was upon *The Unknown*—I made a generalisation about Mr Somerset Maugham's mind and talent which I recall now with some gratification, for his new play at the Haymarket, *The Circle*, bears it out. The generalisation was to the effect that the essential characteristic of Mr Maugham's natural response to experience was cynicism, and that his work in drama and fiction increased in merit and interest accordingly as he wrote from that point of view. I ventured to predict that some day he would, with his sense of the stage and his deftness in dramatic preparation, produce a play which in its way would be a museum piece, a work of art which would express and sum up his sense of life.

Cynicism is, of course, a vague term. What I mean by it here is scepticism with regard to the depth and persistence of human affection, disillusionment with the excitements of passion, the conviction that men and women are competitive, ostentatious and selfish, and only superficially sympathetic, that time in the end gets the better of even those who are most intelligently selfish, and a lack of faith in any cause or traditional morality. In the aquarium of life he sees aristocratic sharks, humble greedy pike, gorgeous octopuses, fair drifting jelly-fish, and occasionally he notices a flat, good-natured sole at the bottom of the tank who is content to lie modestly in the sand. It is a slight relief to contemplate such an uncompetitive creature, but the more permanent consolations come from the amusements of luxury and the security of wealth. If you ask me from where I have drawn the impression, that this is really his *weltanschauung*, I cannot point to any one play or novel, but I feel it lurking behind his laughter, which is never really merry, his sense of values as they are exhibited in his character drawing, and, above all, behind the gaps in his picture of human relations. Of course, it is—certainly this is true of most of his plays—concealed by accommodation to the public demand to be lightly and deftly entertained.

Now, *The Circle* is one of the best plays he has yet written, and—this is where I find myself corroborated—it is one of the most cynical. It is even perhaps too cynical to have a good run. At the end of it the audience has a feeling of insecurity. Are they to sympathise with the eloping young wife and virile young tea-planter, has the world indeed been well lost for love? Or was the cynical silky old father-in-law, who thought he had 'downily' circumvented their absurd passion for each other, the character who was right in the main? He was certainly wrong in his calculation that the sorry spectacle presented in the persons of the old pair of lovers (his own wife and his old friend, who had thrown away their careers in the enthusiasm of an infatuation years ago) would prevent the young pair, his son's wife and her lover, following their example. You can imagine the uneasiness of an English audience left with such a doubt in their minds when the curtain falls. Is this a *happy* ending? No answer. It is an ending, and hardly that—rather a recurring decimal dot. Life repeats itself; experience does not make for wisdom; men and women revolve in a 'circle.'

Mr Maugham has not shown his usual skill in bringing us at once in touch with the situation in the first few minutes. The situation is this: A young married couple (fine country house; husband—young politician and amateur of furniture and bric-a-brac; wife—bored, active and restless) find themselves confronted with an extremely delicate situation. The young wife has asked her mother-in-law and Lord Porteous to stay with them. Her husband has not seen his mother for thirty years, not since she ran away from his father with Lord Porteous to Italy, where they have lived as exiles in a demoralised society ever since. It was not Arnold Champion-Cheney's idea that they should be invited, but Elizabeth's. She has conceived a romantic idea of this disgraced beautiful mother-in-law of hers, and has insisted that Arnold should at last forgive his mother. The real explanation of her insistence is that she has a strong fellow-feeling with the reckless Lady Kitty, and has half a mind to follow her example. Now, just as the interesting pair are about to arrive Mr Champion-Cheney the elder unexpectedly turns up. Elizabeth breaks the situation to him, and he is about to withdraw discreetly when he perceives the half-unconscious motive which actuated Elizabeth. He decides to stay. The arrival of the ex-Mrs Champion-Cheney (Miss Lottie Venne—admirable she is) means a great disillusionment for Elizabeth, for instead of meeting a sad, beautiful, dignified woman she sees a frivolous sparrow-minded, painted old creature, highly ridiculous and full of petty temper, while her heroic lover has become a testy, nagging old man. Their flaming, shining love-affair has guttered down to a sordid sort of marriage. Mr Champion-Cheney takes every opportunity of promoting squabbles between them and holding them up as object-lessons to his romantic daughter-in-law. She sees what he is doing; it depresses her, but it does not prevent her listening to her lover. Even Miss Lottie Venne's confession that on the whole, in the long run, their glorious elopement had been a failure, though it shakes her does not stop her, and Mr Champion-Cheney's last card, his instructions to his son to simulate the generosity of unselfish love by offering to get divorced and take the blame himself, fails, too. Off the young people go. The old lovers, though they know the young ones are fools, are moved to tears and laughter by a scene which recalls so vividly their own first careless rapture—besides, perhaps, these young creatures are made of finer stuff than they were, and they may make a success of it. The play ends with the toot of their departing motor and old Mr Champion-Cheney entering and explaining with great complacency how he has succeeded in disentangling the lovers. All the three old people roar with laughter.

Now, the weak point in the play is the character of Lord Porteous, who is conventionally drawn and common-place and uninteresting, and the weak point in the acting, which otherwise is first-rate throughout, is Miss Fay Compton. Her version of

Elizabeth is neither restless, nervous, nor intense. Mr Thesiger is quite admirable as the husband. There is one admirable scene between the two young lovers, but their love relation is spoilt by a serious defect. Mr Maugham is insensitive to shades of feeling and to language. Affection and passion may and often do in life find expression in words of abuse, 'you little devil,' 'you boiled owl,' etc., even in uglier phrases, 'you dirty dog,' etc., but this alters the quality of the emotion, and when such expressions are exchanged between lovers at the most serious moments, an impression is made of a deep-seated vulgarity and obtuseness of feeling. I had an uncomfortable sensation that Mr Maugham liked to hear them talk like that and expected us to enjoy it, too. Still *The Circle* represents a decided step forward on the road towards the creation of his genuine cynical masterpiece—May I live to see it.

82. W.J. Turner, review, *London Mercury*

III, April 1921, 663–4

Walter James Redfern Turner (1889–1946) was an Australian-born poet, novelist and critic. Turner supported himself by unremitting effort as a free-lance arts journalist. He was at various times music critic of the *New Statesman*, drama critic of the *London Mercury* and literary editor of the *Spectator*. He was also an industrious book-reviewer and broadcaster. His novels include *The Duchess of Popocatapetl* (1939); and among his verse *Songs and Incantations* appeared in 1936.

The article, of which the following is an extract, deals with a miscellany of nine plays.

Mr Somerset Maugham has always been one of the most interesting of our successful playwrights, and *The Circle* is one of the best of recent comedies and deserves a long run, not only because it is an excellent play brilliantly acted, but also because it is much more intelligent than the average successful comedy.

The plot is simple: a wife runs away with her husband's best friend, leaving her son of five years old. Thirty years later the son's wife is also contemplating leaving her husband, and has persuaded him to invite his mother—whom he has never seen since she left his father—down to their house. His mother and the man she ran away with arrive and also, unexpectedly, his father. This situation is handled in a remarkably straightforward fashion, with an absence of sentimentality or humbug, that could only be called cynical by those who pass by the experiences of life in blinkers. The father, who is a selfish, cold-blooded, astute person, quickly realises that his son's wife is on the brink of repeating his own wife's performance, and determines to prevent her by making his wife and her lover appear as odious as possible, egging them on to quarrel, and so forth. When the crisis comes he gives his son, who is a cold-blooded prig like himself, some Machiavellian advice on the tactics to employ, and by an appearance of extraordinary nobility the son nearly succeeds in making his wife sacrifice her love. The lover, however, triumphs by sheer honesty and directness, and the play ends happily. The dialogue is often extremely good, the character-drawing is excellent, except that the mother is not consistently drawn, and the acting is superb, as might be expected from a cast including Miss Fay Compton, Miss Lottie Venne, Mr Allan Aynesworth, Mr Holman Clark, Mr Ernest Thesiger, and Mr Leon Quartermaine. *The Circle* is one of the few plays on the London stage that persons of ordinary wit can go to without having their intelligence insulted.

EAST OF SUEZ

His Majesty's Theatre, London, 2 September 1922
(209 performances)
[Written 1922. Published London, September 1922; New York,
November 1922]

The background to this 'spectacular' derives from material
gathered during Maugham's journey to China in 1919/20.

---

83. James Agate, 'West of Suez',
Saturday Review (London)
CXXXIV, 9 September 1922, 374–5

James Evershed Agate (1887–1947) was a leading London
dramatic critic from the time he first began to write for the
Sunday Times in 1923 to his death, one of the few who
wielded the power to make or break a production. Agate was
Manchester-trained, fluent in French, sensitive to serious
music, a fastidious stylist and a pugnacious advocate of his
own opinions. All these attributes combine to make the nine
volumes of his journal, *Ego*, an entertaining record of his life.

Dipping, one day this week, into the sixpenny box of a
second-hand bookseller, I came across an old account of the
London stage. Therein I read the sad story of *Nitocris*, the great
Egyptian spectacle-drama; how the Nile was turned into a grotto to
drown a bunch of conspirators, but without arousing enthusiasm;
how all the gods of Egypt were carried in procession, but to no
popular purpose. Drury Lane had hissed and in the *Examiner* next

morning Henry Morley advised the author to turn the thing into a pantomime and get rid of the words. I was to visit His Majesty's that evening, and I trembled. Would Mr Dean avoid the old mistake of drowning the play in excess of spectacle? True that he had spoken of restoring this theatre to a state of lesser absurdity; yet those hordes of real Chinamen threatened disquietingly.

My apprehensions were ill-founded. In *East of Suez* it was the play which swamped the spectacle. 'The man recovered of the bite, the dog it was that died.' The beginning was most promising. The overture, for which the lights were scrupulously lowered, turned out to be a most ingenious piece of musical leg-pulling. Mr Goossens had made no pretence of absorbing China as Mackenzie did the British Empire and Sibelius Finland, and then giving his emotions back in terms of his own art. He had simply reproduced the cat-calls of the East on Western stops and strings, and left the task of regurgitation to the audience. To Western ears this is not music, although to the Celestials it may make an exquisite tone-poem. One needed, to hear sympathetically, a Chinese dressing-gown, or at some Promenade Concert under Peking skies to watch the chopstick of a Hen Ri Wu. There are, however, always a number of people who, the less they understand, the more they are impressed. (See any German shopkeeper confronted with Goethe's *Faust*.) The simple, musically speaking, among the audience at His Majesty's doubtless took this cleverly executed little joke of Mr Goossens for the sublimer recondities, and disposed themselves to mystery. The curtain rose upon a scene of babel of which no word reached our comprehension. Orientals, adorned with the bowler of European culture and chattering from the teeth outwards, proffered their extortionate bargains in cheap watches, picture post-cards, the meaningless frippery of the Occident. They looked a secret and as wise as monkeys. From time to time a white man would be thrown up on this yellow flood, concealing by the grave carriage of his body on the natural defects of his European mind. The shopkeepers put up their shutters. One of them, belated, is mildly admonished by the native policeman. A British sailor yields to a street-walker. 'Good-bye' the native policeman calls after them from the shadow of the gateway. It is night. I do not know if this is like China; but I do know that it is extraordinarily like the old port at Marseilles. At this point alas! we took leave of Mr Dean. His frontispiece pointed to a tale of Loti;

the drama was to stray no further than Streatham.

And now I am in a difficulty. Mr Somerset Maugham is a writer of great distinction, yet he has written a quite insincere play. I am convinced that Mr Maugham knows China or, at least, that China is not Europe. I feel he realizes very definitely that the root of the trouble between English men and Eurasian women is the English code of morals. But his play shows that he distrusts his medium, that he is aware he must not say openly that what is the matter with these mixed unions is their legality. He does say it, ultimately, but then only by implication. In the meantime there are three hours to be filled in after a fashion which shall be acceptable to Streatham. This, of course, spells sentimentality, in which Mr Maugham is not in the least interested; and this, I think, explains why *East of Suez* rings so exceedingly untrue. If you may not speak truth one artificiality is as good as another. To the artist there is little discriminating in insincerities, and Mr Maugham, who can be an extraordinarily fine and fastidious artist when he likes, has here turned on the oldest of conventions. The two commonplace Englishmen in this play, each morally worth, to us who believe in their code, the whole jabbering crew of the first scene, are yet dramatically less interesting. Those others elude us, we know what these will do. One upright fellow will insist upon marriage with the Eurasian woman who, unknown to him, has been the mistress of a Chinaman and has also been engaged to his best friend. That other upright fellow will, after a thousand protestations, court the lady again, and shoot himself upon discovery. There is a model for plays about women who, for any reason, are *déclassées*, and Mr Maugham has used it. 'You may dive into many waters, but there is *one* social Dead Sea—!' is what, in effect, the new Cayley Drummle says to the friend who is about to announce his forthcoming marriage. And later, 'I should like to express my regret, Aubrey, for the way in which I spoke of George Orreyed's marriage.' Only the names are altered. At its vital point Mr Maugham, like Pinero, burks the issue. Paula's ruin springs not from the fact that she is a courtesan at heart but from a coincidence; Daisy is defeated not because she is a Eurasian, but because she is Daisy. Yet both plays set out to prove that if the class is 'not nice' you cannot afford to have anything to do with it. Touch pitch and you will be defiled. Both plays seek to prove the general from the particular. But Streatham doesn't want to know about a particular

Daisy; it wants to hear that all marriages with Eurasians are fatal, and so keep its menfolk. Above all it wants to shut its eyes to the way in which they may be kept. That at which Mr Maugham hints, and would say if he dare, is that the passion of both men is not unreasonable but anti-social, not unlawful but inexpedient. Very few things are immoral which are sincere, and the real point of view of European ladies is not that they object to the inevitable, which is silly, but to the recognition of it entailed by marriage. We feel that if Daisy had been mistress instead of wife, the lover would not have betrayed his friend, so strange is the European code. The betrayer shoots himself, not because of his sin against morality, but on behalf of the *convenances*. He blushes to do openly that of which he is not, at heart, ashamed. He fears social ostracism. Daisy's passion is to entwine her arms about her lover and with him to sit upon a hill-side watching the rice grow, 'for ever,' as the poet puts it, 'in a deliberate bliss, a spirit sliding through tranquillity.' That tranquillity is to be induced, she carefully explains, by opium. Whereupon the pistol-shot. What Mr Maugham is careful not to explain is that the lover was quite willing to sit on the hill-side for such time as he could do so under the cover of adultery. It is a curious situation. Streatham hopes that by doing away with these marriages the mingling of races will come to an end. Mr Maugham knows that strange desire will persist, but that if there is to be no bother there must be no marriage. He knows too that between such outspokenness and the British stage are arrayed all the forces of law and order, the censorship and public opinion, army, navy and the police. And all the time that fascinating crowd from the docks, about whom Mr Maugham could tell us so much, is idle. I do not blame the author, but the theatre to which he conforms.

The play was perfectly acted by our friends, who had no European conventions to contend against, and exceedingly well by the English actors within those conventions. But I should have dearly liked to know what the impassive Oriental thought of the hysterical Englishman whose mouth is as full of 'love' as a dressmaker's is of pins.

84. Desmond MacCarthy, review, *New Statesman*

XX, 7 October 1922, 14

His Majesty's is the home of pageant-drama; for any other purpose its huge stage is not only useless but a drawback. On those wide boards an actor must needs take exercise to convey even a slight impression of restlessness; from those distant galleries human faces are scarcely more expressive than the oval keys beneath a group picture. Subtleties of acting, and therefore subtleties of situation, are physically impossible upon it, and, moreover, a vast crowded auditorium is psychologically a sounding board only for certain dramatic effects. The dramatist writing for such a theatre should take this into account, and consequently the critic of his play that he has had to do so. His Majesty's is the stage for the display of plain, popular emotions; the situations presented to so large an audience should be striking and easy. The majestic dramatist should borrow his technique from the opera and melodrama. He may, if he can, put even as much drawing into his characters as Shakespeare did, but like Shakespeare's, his situations must stand out comprehensible and arresting, even if ancillary touches are wasted and escape notice. I was impressed by the grasp Mr Somerset Maugham's *East of Suez* exhibited of these conditions. In the prologue he uses the capacity of the stage to present realistically a picture of swarming streets of Pekin, a scene not without bearing on his theme; in the last moment of the last act, when his half-cast heroine, whose father was an English merchant, is absorbed again into her maternal China, he has unblushingly and properly had recourse to a symbolic tableau. There Miss Meggie Albanesi sits as the curtain falls, hieratic and impassible in Chinese robes, with her beguiled, desperate, but infatuate English husband kneeling at her feet. The three acts in between have illustrated, in terms emphatic and easy, the clash between Eastern and English temperaments and ethics. The marriage of Harry Anderson (Mr Malcolm Keen) with the half-cast beauty Daisy is 'an international episode'; the love between Daisy and George Conway (Mr Basil Rathbone), conscience-stricken on his part unscrupulous on hers, is a deft piece of romantic magazine literature; both are tough, serviceable strands for tethering attention. I noticed on comparing the play as performed with the published text that a good deal of the crudity, as I supposed, of the preparation was due to cutting, but—and here is the proof that Mr Somerset Maugham knew his business thoroughly—such omissions left the situations, so far as the incurious were concerned, solid and striking.

He has drawn Daisy well, and she is well acted. The characteristic which he wisely shows from the moment she comes on to the stage is her insensibility to the claims of loyalty and straightforwardness. So far it would be gross partiality to describe her as Oriental; it is only the lengths she is presently prepared to go in order to satisfy her passion for George, namely, her easy consent to the removal of her husband at the suggestion of her mother and her Chinese ex-lover, and her gradual transformation from a bewildered, pitiable little adventuress of the common type to something harder, more primitive, conscienceless and simple, which illustrate the theme of the play, that East is East and West is West and never the twain shall meet—except to their mutual discomfiture.

The most admirable invention in the play is Daisy's grotesque, ever-present nurse, who turns out to be her mother, most vividly played by Miss Maire Ault. She represents the Oriental conception of loyalty, unscrupulous towards all except the object of devotion. The effect of the narrow yet philosophic tenacity of this hideous old woman and of grim, placid Lee Tai Cheng, Daisy's ex-master, is to make the fervid emotional passions of the Europeans seem flimsy and childish. Mr Somerset Maugham has not drawn George well. He has not been sufficiently interested in him. As I have taken the opportunity of observing whenever I have criticised one of his plays, the angle from which he sees deepest into life and character is cynical. He has, for obvious reasons, represented George as the high-minded, generous English gentleman, who is miserable at having yielded to his passion for his friend's wife; but the conventionality of the result shows that the dramatist's sympathies lie elsewhere. The scene in which George yields to the passion of Daisy is an almost comic reversal of masculine and feminine parts: 'Don't, don't. Oh, this is madness!'. . . . 'Oh, I've been here too long! Daisy, I beseech you let me go. . . . I know how good and kind you have been. . . . My precious'—these exclamations wrung from the distracted George echo in my memory. Mr Maugham goes near to suggesting that George chucked Daisy for the uninteresting, eligible Sylva Knox, but—unfortunately he boggles at this sensible and coherent conclusion, and Daisy's revenge is left on our hands as a mere piece of misguided vindictiveness.

THE CONSTANT WIFE

Maxine Elliott Theatre, New York, 29 November 1926
(295 performances)
Strand Theatre, London, 6 April 1927 (70 performances)
[Written 1926. Published New York, April 1927; London,
September 1927]

This is a sardonic reworking of the theme developed in
Maugham's earlier play *Penelope* (1909)

85. Robert Benchley, 'Something Good', *Life*

LXXXVIII, 16 December 1926, 19

Robert Charles Benchley (1889–1945) was an actor, humorist
and author. In the 1920s he edited *Life*, for which he also
wrote theatre criticism. He was theatre critic of the *New
Yorker* from 1929 to 1940. He is best known for his series of
witty sketches concerning the average man.

If, at this late date, there should be any doubt as to the truth of the old
saying that blood (unlike the daisies) will tell, it can easily be
dispelled by a visit to the Maxine Elliott Theatre, where Ethel
Barrymore is playing in Somerset Maugham's *The Constant Wife*.

If ever there was a patrician performance, here it is. All the
Barrymores and Drews that have ever graced the theatre are
contributors to each tilt of the chin, and they have every reason to
be proud of their contribution, for never have we seen a chin tilted
with such distinction.

This does not mean that Miss Barrymore's comedy methods are those of Colley Cibber and his age. They are, in fact, highly modern and informal. When, explaining a knee-disorder of her rival, she says: 'It slips,' the delivery and intonation are indubitably those of 1926 and yet in the background stands the shade of some Katharine ready to emerge if the occasion should demand.

Mr Maugham's play, while far from perfect, has a great many lines of high comedy and not a few of wisdom. It should be the despair of American playwrights to hear what these English can do with one word in the structure of comedy. When Mabel Terry-Lewis (another shining example of the existence of a stage aristocracy) remarks on husbands who are 'systematically' unfaithful, Mr Maugham has Miss Barrymore ask if 'systematically' is not a rather *grim* word to use. Or again, when it has been suggested that an unfaithful husband makes his wife ridiculous, it is Miss Terry-Lewis who is allowed the remark: 'If every unfaithful husband made his wife ridiculous there would be a great deal more merriment in the world than there is to-day.' By the use of these two words, 'grim' and 'merriment,' Mr Maugham has transformed two lines which might otherwise have been just lines into delectable comedy. It is very discouraging to those of us who would never have thought of using those words in a hundred years. It is a gift that even the most humble English writers seem to have, and something ought to be done about it.

86. Ivor Brown, 'Heartless House', *Saturday Review* (London)

CXLIII, 16 April 1927, 598–9

Mr Maugham is usually to be thanked for his relentlessness, like the consuls who did not spare the republic. He conceives humanity almost in terms of metal; so they are forged and so they endure. His new characters, like many of his old, are without emotion. My qualification 'almost' is due to their possession of, or by, desire. The men want women and the women, a shade more ambitious, want men and pearls. As they are all in the comfortable set and have never come within working distance of oven or dish-cloth, they can hardly be said to want comfort. It is there and it is theirs. For the rest, they seem to want heaven as little as they fear hell. Ardours, endurances, and ecstasies are not for them. Like the rakes of Restoration drama they are touched by a single impulse and even here one is forced to doubt sincerity. Did Wycherley's Mr Horner really desire all his victims or did he merely desire the thought of conquest? I often think that all that chatter about cuckolds was rather less serious to Horner than golf-talk to ourselves. Eagerness to excel is natural and the current mode of supremacy was in clandestine adultery. Now a prosperous citizen has his alternative at Walton Heath. He has other lists than those of the Divorce Court in which to joust with his neighbour, but in both cases a pastime and a passion are confused.

Mr Horner was genuine in wanting to be champion of his craft. But what of Mr Maugham's Mr Middleton, famous surgeon of Harley Street? He did not seem to be a grand lover or a regular Turk. Had he been in the habit of contributing poetic truth to inquisitive books of reference he could hardly have begun 'Priapus my father, Libitina my mother.' One did not conceive him on that scale. Yet he would lie to his attractive and intelligent wife in order to visit the idiotic Mrs Durham. Was he happily, whole-heartedly faithless? One hardly thought so. His amorous adventures seemed only an affectation. Had somebody prompted him he might have fallen more deeply in love with a mashie. That is a pity, for there is something dull about casual lechery untouched by Horner's diablerie or a Don Juanish conviction.

Constance, Mrs Middleton, on the other hand, had convictions. Though undoubtedly voicing the last cry in her clothes, she had, after hard process of thought, reached an intellectual position. It was the kind of position that might have been established by a formidable young Fabian round about 1890. Marriage, she thought, is my trade. John Middleton has bought me. If he can afford to pay for a mistress as well, it is his right. But if I can earn a living and can afford to pay my whack of the bills, then I can take a lover. It is my right. On this economic interpretation of holy wedlock she acted. When John was in hot water with Mr Durham *re* Mrs Durham, Constance stooped to fish him out. Then she went into the business of household decoration on fashionable and remarkably remunerative lines and, having made fourteen-hundred pounds in the first year, paid John a thousand for the house expenses and went off to Italy with her lover and the odd four hundred in her pocket, vowing to return in six weeks. For a moment or two John's blood became tepid, but he soon cooled and offered to accept her conditions and begin another matrimonial term after the vacation.

Is it worth arguing over such a collection of inhumans? Would ever a wife live up (or down) to her logic like Constance Middleton, who took her husband's adultery without a touch of emotion and even rescued him by lying in public merely to uphold an abstract equation of marriage and money? The Middletons had a child at school. Yet for neither parent did the existence of the child appear to have the least consequence. Fay's mother used to drop in periodically in order to announce that men were deceivers ever and that only a foolish wife would bother for a moment about a mistress or a covey of mistresses behind the arras. Is it in the least use protesting that it is not done, that even Mr Horner's company, with its rivalries of concupiscence, is more natural than this ungallant clique for whom fire is ice and ice has lost its sheen?

It must be said on Mr Maugham's behalf that he does not turn his ice into ice-cream. Nothing is more dismal (and few things are more common) than the play or book in which the author who has come to shock remains to soothe. Mr Maugham is not of that kind. There are no cowardly mitigations. He abides by his Heartless House; when he elects to be sardonic he sees it through. He is as true to his convention of characterless character as Constance Middleton is true to her financial computations about man and wife. *The Constant Wife* suffers nothing by inconstancy in the writer. But the dramatist who thus rejects reality must have the substitute. A seeming originality of plot, a new and notable turn of phrase, a peculiar pungency of wit, or a miraculous gloss upon the acting—any of these may save him. But Mr Maugham was out of form when he wrote *The Constant Wife*. The dialogue does not crackle. Mr Dean's production was neat, but it could not cure a deficient vitality in epigrams which suffered from over-crowding. Moreover, the play was miscast.

Miss Fay Compton and Mr Leon Quartermaine have given us

some extremely fine stage-partnerships. He has a leaping flame of style, she a gentle radiance. If we are to see them at their best he must attack and she defend. But on this occasion she must be as cool and callous a customer as ever tied up her marriage-lines in a syllogism and turned the Book of Love into a primer of financial arithmetic, while he has simply to philander without conviction and surrender without a fight. Nothing more, perhaps, could have been done with the empty, ugly part of John Middleton. In that case a fine actor was wasted. For the highly argumentative Constance, who has a tiresome and reiterative part, a harder personality than Miss Compton's was needed. The others had an easier time. Miss Marda Vanne is an actress of extreme flexibility. She changes style, looks, and mood for every part she plays, and again she was brilliantly not herself. Miss Heather Thatcher, as Mrs Durham, was entertaining in vapidity, Miss Mary Jerrold was sharp in worldly wisdom, while Mr Paul Cavanagh gave substance to a shadow as the lover bought and paid for by Mrs Middleton.

THE LETTER

Playhouse, London, 24 February 1927 (338 performances)
[Written 1926. Published London, June 1927; New York,
September 1927]

This is a dramatisation of the story of the same name included
in *The Casuarina Tree* (1926).

87. Unsigned review, *Times*

25 February 1927, 12

Strength of will, a perfect self-control, an extraordinary power of
swift decision—these are Mrs Crosbie. Her character is plain at the
outset. No weak woman in a panic could have shot Hammond
with such determination, no woman to whom hatred did not lend
the strength of madmen could have poured six bullets into him,
have dropped the revolver beside his body, and have given orders,
in Mrs Crosbie's tone and manner, to her Chinese servants. When
her friends come, her story is ready for them. She was alone in the
bungalow; Hammond appeared, talked, drank, attempted to rape
her; she killed him in self-defence. The story—and it is a long
one—is told clearly and smoothly. It is interrupted now and then
by an emotional breakdown, but its coherence is, in the circumstances, remarkable. Crosbie, who loves his wife, never doubts it.
Young Withers also believes it. Joyce, Crosbie's friend and lawyer,
wondering why in self-defence she emptied her revolver into a man
already dead, thinks that her tale is almost too coherent. Perhaps he
thought, and with reason, that it was a trifle theatrical as well.

Suspicion of her is in his mind and ours. To all others she is as
innocent as she is beautiful, and it is certain that, when she takes her

trial in Singapore, the jury will acquit her. We, then, are to watch suspicion grow to certainty, to observe, under Mr Maugham's psychological microscope, her strength of will fight with her increasing terror. Ong Chi Seng, Joyce's confidential clerk—a little masterpiece of smug, half-Westernized orientalism in Mr George Carr's hands—knows that there exists, in the possession of Hammond's Chinese mistress, a letter in which Mrs Crosbie implored Hammond to come to her bungalow on the night of the murder. It conflicts with her whole defence; it is, Joyce knows, enough to hang her. He taxes her with it in prison. She denies and denies having written it: then confesses. It has to be bought. Its contents have to be concealed from her husband. But it has to be bought with money that her husband will presently have to repay.

After the acquittal they all return to the bungalow. It has seemed a triumph; there are friends to arrange flowers for them: Crosbie is already talking of new work they will do and new happiness they will enjoy together. But Mr Maugham is not a sentimentalist. He is logical and just. The truth comes out, and there is nothing in the play more impressive than Mr Nigel Bruce's brilliant outburst of despair when Crosbie learns that his wife was Hammond's mistress, and yet cannot cease to love her. Mr Leslie Faber's opportunity, taken with admirable quietness, is principally in his gentle but determined cross-examination of Mrs Crosbie in prison; and Miss Cooper, though she is perhaps inclined to over-emphasize the theatricalism of her narrative in the first act, exhibits Mrs Crosbie's character with consistent insight and genuine strength. What a feat of dexterity the whole play is! With what economy and with what understanding of the uses of the stage it is written! It never pauses or falters; not an outline is blurred. It is very conspicuously the work of Mr Maugham and of none other.

·

88. Ivor Brown, 'Here Are Tigers', *Saturday Review* (London)

CXLIII, 5 March 1927, 350–1

This is an extract from an article reviewing two plays.

The fauna of the Federated Malay States still includes tigers and, as Mr Maugham reminds us, a man-eating female of tigerish humour may be found in the bungalow of as decent a fellow as ever failed in Responsions and took to planting rubber. I have no authority for stating that Robert Crosbie failed to satisfy the examiners, but, had he presented himself for that rather humble ordeal, I feel that he might have borne the impress of 'the plough.' He might, on the other hand, have been so capable at scrum-half that examiners would have taken note of the fact and tempered justice with loyalty to the larger interests of the University. However, here are Robert Crosbie, decent fellow, and Leslie his wife, in a Malayan bungalow, whose verandah looks on to rows of those trees so coveted by Mr Harvey Firestone and other voluble citizens of the U.S.A. Robert's eyes may be all for the adorable Leslie, but they are not remarkably sharp. The perfect wife has a lover, Hammond, in the next plantation and, should business call Robert to Singapore, opportunities are not neglected. Hammond, however, tires of Leslie and takes a new mistress from the Chinese settlement. Leslie's claws grow visibly, for Robert, poor innocent, has married a tigress, a fact which Hammond painfully discovers when she 'plugs' him with all six barrels as a lesson to unfaithful adulterers. Leslie, when jealousy cools, has to lie for her life, and she invents an assault made by the dead man. Her lawyer, Mr Joyce, seems doubtful from the first (she told her tale a shade too well) and he soon discovers from his Chinese clerk, who combines the study of Herbert Spencer with a nonchalant style in blackmail, that Hammond's new Chinese mistress has possession of a letter from Leslie begging the deceased to come to her on the night that her husband was in Singapore. Either Leslie goes down at the trial, or the letter must be bought at the very stiff price which an education at Hong Kong University and post-graduate study of the English philosophers suggest to the Chinese clerk as sweetly reasonable. Joyce defeats his own scruples on the 'Can a Lawyer Buy?' issue, but he has to purchase the letter on the security of Robert Crosbie's estate. Result, public acquittal with honour for Leslie and private discovery without it; Robert, decent as ever, will forgive his tigress her treachery, though he can hardly feel comfortable about the false charge of rape which now stands proven over the grave of a murdered man. Leslie's penalty is to know that she has killed the man whom she really loves. Going a stage further than Catullus, who hated while he loved, she can worship and kill and then worship memory. The curtain falls on considerable potentialities of distress.

Mr Maugham has told his bleak tale quietly, and Sir Gerald du Maurier has produced it with that muted vigour which is the trade-mark of his own style in acting and presentation.... Crosbie, Joyce, and Hammond have all been trained at the best English schools how not to make a fuss. Mr Allan Monkhouse, reviewing the performance of Macbeth by a too demonstrative actor, once asked whether murder could be as serious as all that. A connoisseur of the old-fashioned, full-throated acting might ask on this occasion whether murder could be so trivial. But the tensity is there, if the noise is not, and the counterfeit of the inexpressive Englishman is subtly conceived and sustained. Miss Gladys Cooper plays the tigress with a compression of fury and despair, whose utterance can have no rhetoric, and does it with high ability. In the first act, where she tells her false story about Hammond's assault, she has of course, to act at acting, and the way in which she left her audience just not credulous was the measure of her success. Knowing playgoers might observe: 'Of course, the woman's lying. Otherwise there'll be no play. They've engaged S. J. Warmington for Hammond's part, and so far he's only been instantaneously murdered. You don't have a good man like that for a super's job, so they'll have to put in a "throw-back" scene for him to come in again.' But discount this cunning and the effect of Miss Cooper's story on the audience is, I feel sure, exactly that produced on the lawyer Joyce, which is a supreme tribute to her simulation of simulation. Mr Leslie Faber and Mr Nigel Bruce are sahibs beyond reproach, and Mr George Carr is immensely entertaining as the slant-eyed Spencerian from Hong Kong. The whole affair is as adroit as the professional theatre can make it. The ending makes Crosbie's bungalow the bleakest of bleak houses—and the tigerish start was not riotously cheerful. Yet the public which announces its hatred of a depressing show will flock lusting to see it. The theatre is an odd place and adroitness can be magical.

THE SACRED FLAME

Henry Miller Theatre, New York 19 November 1928
(24 performances)
Playhouse, London, 8 February 1929 (209 performances)
[Written 1928. Published New York, November 1928; London,
February 1929]

89. J. Brooks Atkinson, 'Murder Will Out at 11', *New York Times*

20 November 1928, 28

Justin Brooks Atkinson (b. 1894) was drama critic on the *New York Times*, editor and author. In 1947 he received the Pulitzer Prize for his work as a news correspondent in Moscow.

Another of Mr Maugham's highly cultivated shilling-shockers has come to the stage of Henry Miller's Theatre, where *The Sacred Flame* was acted last evening. Toward 11 o'clock the murderer confesses with a sweet, maternal beneficence that almost transfigures her. Mary Jerrold plays that part so tenderly, with so much unassumed beauty, that you wish she might not have to squander so much radiance on a sterile piece. For despite Mr Maugham's rather weary adequacy and competence in the company of the sprightly and the well-heeled, *The Sacred Flame* seems to this skeptical observer a well-bred bore. Mr Maugham's heart is not in it. No one's heart is in it. Papier-maché is papier-maché, no matter how skillfully you mold it.

Into the dull existence of an English family Mr Maugham

255

introduces first a murder and then an illegally expectant mother. She is, in fact, wife of the perpetual invalid whose death suddenly appears to be from unnatural causes; the father is his brother. The accuser is Nurse Wayland, an admittedly chaste woman, who is disagreeable enough to demand a coroner's inquest. One act, prolix to the point of discomfort, prepares the situation. Two more acts talk it blue in the face. Ultimately, the mother confesses that she helped her invalid son on his way to eternity in order that passionate youth might have its fling unencumbered.

So long has Mr Maugham been finding his way around the stage that you are astonished he has not constructed a sounder play with his puppets. As it is, there is a thin plausibility about all the circumstances that almost persuades you to believe them. The mother appears to have done something extraordinarily fine. The unfaithful wife and the treacherous brother appear to have loved for the best of all concerned. When the mother confesses to her crime every one is quite properly embarrassed by the selfless rectitude, the exalted uprightness, of her deed. For such is the privilege of melodrama no matter how well or ill it speaks the King's English.

What is more astonishing is that so practiced a hand as Mr Maugham's should have dipped into so much mawkish sentimentality. While the private hearing is in progress in the elegantly furnished drawing room, wistful minds are forever running off on the beauties and wonders of the universe—the stars and the rivers, no less. These homilies are expertly worded and neatly spoken. Mr Maugham and his actors know their trades. But the style does not mask the hollowness of the phrasing and does not spare you the distress of suspecting the virtue of its literary antecedents.

All the actors speak with grace and behave themselves decently. Even in the presence of murder they do not repudiate their manners. As the nurse, professionally accoutred, Clare Eames seems to overact the heroics and to endow melodrama with the splendid coloring of Greek tragedy. It is perilous, in the acting, to adorn dramatic trifles with tragic substance; it gives the secret away. Miss Jerrold does *The Sacred Flame* a better service by avoiding ostentation in her part.

90. J.T. Grein, 'Three Leading Ladies', *Illustrated London News*

CLXXIV, 23 February 1929, 318

There was a charming scene on the stage of the Playhouse after the curtain had fallen on Mr Somerset Maugham's fine play, *The Sacred Flame*—perhaps his finest since *The Circle*. The audience, breathless through the whole of the third act, burst forth in an ovation of unmistakable portent. It was their tribute to the playwright and the players; and as Mr Maugham, who had watched his work from a corner, had suddenly disappeared, the actors came in for the friendly tornado, only to be stemmed by a speech. Meanwhile, from the gallery came shouts of 'Cooper!' 'Jerrold!' 'Eames!' Then happened a pretty incident, almost unique in our theatre. Miss Gladys Cooper came forward, tendered her right hand to Miss Mary Jerrold, her left to Miss Clare Eames, and in a few cordial words returned thanks for 'myself and my two leading ladies.' The action was all the more appealing since it exactly expressed what everyone felt. Here was a case in which there was not one star, but three.

Miss Gladys Cooper's own performance was charming and full of feeling. She looked younger and more beautiful than ever. She let us feel, by gentle restraint, that she realised to the full the dilemma of the young wife, between pity for her disabled husband and passion—bridled by discretion—for her lover. Rightly, she perceived that this was not an opportunity for flamboyancy, but for repression. If we were to sympathise with her as the author intended, she had, as it were, to remain in the background, for around her the battle was fought by the two women who duelled for her fate—her husband's mother for her salvation, the nurse for her destruction. Between the twain she was the quarry, and the more passively suffering she appeared, the more intensely would her performance appeal to our sympathy. This realisation was the beauty of her portrayal.

To Miss Jerrold fell the part of the mother—a *mater dolorosa* if ever there was one. To her the situation was no secret. She knew what tortured the soul of the young wife: she had herself in younger days known the pangs of love for another man. She had struggled and won, and in that self-denial she had learned great understanding and tolerance; she would stop short at nothing to give that happiness to others dear to her which had been denied to herself. That led her to tender to her son the draught of deliverance which made her a murderess in the eyes of the law and religion. She was aware of it, but she did not rue it. I would not here discuss whether her act was defensible; I would only deal with Miss Jerrold's vitalisation of the character, with her art and with the subtle suavity with which she veneered an ominous proposition. And her portrayal was superb. There was not a soul in that house which did not go out in sympathy to that sweet, vivid, simple, tender little mother, who showed her strength in fighting for her son and daughter-in-law; who defied the nurse, and mellowed that formidable opponent by a confession so frank, so heartfelt, so convincing that she, the murderess by law, won over her adversary, who apparently stood up for righteousness, but inwardly was impelled by love unanswered.

If Miss Jerrold was all femininity and gentleness, the nurse of Miss Clare Eames was outwardly all sternness and stolidity. Only the very careful observer saw in the first act that by a glance, a furtive twitch of features, she betrayed her feelings for the moribund man. Throughout, in a part most difficult, complex, and almost repellently unsympathetic, Miss Eames never flinched in her conception. She seemed to pace through the action, a stony character relentlessly moving towards the goal of revenge. Yet all the while jealousy, passion, and—it was most delicately indicated by the artist—the ideal craving for the fulness of life, were raging within her. She husbanded all her emotional power until the right moment; and then she carried all before her.

THE BREADWINNER

Vaudeville Theatre, London, 30 September 1930
(158 performances)
[Written 1930. Published London, September 1930; New York,
October 1931]

91. Desmond MacCarthy, 'Two Comedies', *New Statesman*

XXXVI, 11 October 1930, 14–15

This review contrasts Maugham's *The Breadwinner* with Noël
Coward's *Private Lives*, also first produced in London in
September 1930.

Mr Somerset Maugham is not an Ibsen, and Mr Noël Coward's
resemblance to Tolstoy is not striking, but the themes of *The
Breadwinner* and *Private Lives* resemble respectively those of *A
Doll's House* and *The Kreutzer Sonata*; only they are brought up to
date and turned topsy-turvy. In *The Breadwinner* a husband, not a
wife, leaves a 'doll's house' to live and learn, and in *Private Lives* we
are invited (most successfully) to laugh over—yes, and to
envy—the violent alternations from tenderness to exasperation and
back again, which between man and woman, husband and wife,
Tolstoy felt to be so loathsomely hideous and humiliating that he
saw no cure for them but to stamp sex out of life altogether.
Hopeless remedy, of course—quite hopeless.

These two comedies now running in London, and with every
prospect of continuing to please, are symptomatic of the times. It is
not the Noras who now excite the sympathy of dramatists and

audiences but the Helmers—the predicament of 'breadwinners', not of wives. Isn't the slavery, we now ask ourselves, of the breadwinner to his job often as humiliating as that of woman to 'the home'? If she kicks, why should not he? And when 'Norval,' as I shall continue to think of him, slips into freedom from a home in which he has been for years a mere breadwinner, slips away, after exposing the selfishness of his wife and children, the sympathies of the modern audience appeared to go with him, as they once went with Nora when she slammed behind her the door of the 'doll's house'.

This shift of sympathy is significant. But the comparison between *The Kreutzer Sonata* and *Private Lives* is still more significant. To do Tolstoy's contemporaries justice, they never thought that story one of his good books. There was a fanaticism in it far from admirable, and the deduction of a sweeping conclusion from a particular case shocked common sense. What is interesting is that Mr Noël Coward and Tolstoy agree about the nature of passion, only while the old prophet says, 'Look, isn't it ignoble and the very opposite of love?', the young comic dramatist, who does not pretend to be a thinker but, as a matter of fact, has a clearer view of life than many who pretend to teach, says, 'Isn't it exciting and amusing?'

In *Private Lives* two honeymoons are entertainingly contrasted. The relation between Amanda Prynne and Elyot Chase is based upon the kind of attraction which alone, according to the dramatist, matters between man and woman, while their respective relations to their lawful spouses are unreal and conventional. A moment's reflection shows the weakness of both *The Kreutzer Sonata* and of *Private Lives* as pictures of life. The former is based on blind fear of lust, and in *Private Lives* we only see the beginning of the story. The worst is to come. We hear what chapter one of the lives of Amanda and Elyot was like. Their marriage ended after exasperated quarrels in divorce and remarriage to others. Though we only watch the first three days of their lives after they have bilked their just-wedded partners and come together again, these show that chapter two will probably repeat chapter one. We watch scenes of rapturous tenderness modulate into the exchange of such sentiments between them as 'You damned sadistic bully!' 'You loose-living wicked little beast!' and finally into a scrimmage on the floor. True, the curtain falls on reconcilement and thus the audience is sent smiling away. *That* shindy has not mattered. Why should it? It is not the first or the second or the fifth that does. But anyone who has watched human nature knows that soon, and often very soon, shindies destroy the beautiful and tender overtones of passion and that mutual confidence which makes even its momentary satisfaction satisfying. So, although the play apparently ends happily, and the story is so deftly and amusingly conducted that the audience envies Mr Coward's lovers, no one, if he or she reflects, can agree with Amanda's pronouncement upon her lover and herself: 'We may be all right in the eyes of heaven, but we look like being in a hell of a mess socially.' No: they are in a hell of a mess all round. It is not the least of Mr Coward's achievements that he has thus disguised the grimness of his play and that his conception of love is really desolating.

I wonder, if these lines catch his eye, what he will think of this analysis of his airy, quick little play? That I am dissecting a butterfly which was just meant to amuse us with its flutterings, and have rubbed off its bloom? Perhaps. Let me assure him that I enjoyed its flutterings and bright changing colours very much.

The interpretation of character and scene throughout was admirable. What a talent Miss Gertrude Lawrence has! If you want unflagging vivacity in an actor or actress look for him or her among Variety Artists. They have 'go' and sparkling finish. They must have them, also the faculty of making much out of mere hints. They have to hold attention, often alone on the stage, by making the best of comic and sentimental hints often of the barest and most perfunctory kind. They learn to be collaborators rather than interpreters. Mr Coward himself is almost as good as Miss Lawrence (what praise!) and Miss Adrienne Allen and Mr Olivier played their parts as they should have been played. They understood and showed it. Mr Coward's great gift as a dramatist, as I have occasion to repeat whenever I write about him, is that his dialogue has the rhythm of life, and the rhythm of modern life is more broken and much quicker than that of twenty years ago. He understands, too, that it is more important that a joke on the stage should be spontaneous than perfect. If it is a brilliant piece of wit so much the better, but it must be first exactly in the right key. Mr Maugham is not nearly so deft at catching that life-rhythm, and his wit is deliberate rather than quick. Consequently when it is not first-rate, it disappoints. On the other hand he has a firmer grip of what he is writing about, and all the implications of his subject. He always knows where he is. He is adept in making his characters betray themselves in typical lines. Sometimes he abuses this power, and you think, 'But if that person could say *that*, he or she would know more about themselves than the dramatist intends them to.' But at others he puts into their mouths a line which illuminates the character naturally, as well as the situation from beginning to end. He has a firmer grasp of ultimate futilities.

His works can hardly be described as the harvest of an indulgent eye. His best jokes have ever a grim underside; his best drawn characters are exposures. His good people are apt to be conventional figures or hazy in outline; and he has evidently been much struck on his journey through the world by the impudent selfishness of certain types of women. In a sense he approves of selfishness, for he sees it masquerading everywhere, and he comes to preferring it naked and unashamed. But really some women carry selfishness too far! They are such bilkers too, taking without giving, and without a notion of fair play.

The Breadwinner is a play about a man who threw his top-hat over the windmill; turned on his family (leaving them a genteel subsistence), and said, 'I don't see the point of slaving for you any more. You are not fond of me and I am not fond of you; you think I'm an old bore and I, too, find you boring.' The comedy lies in this family, who have never felt under the smallest obligation to him, who have criticised him freely, suddenly discovering that they mean as little to him as he does to them. It is a shock. What! he doesn't think it worth his while to keep them in cars and comfort! Of course the young can't be expected to enjoy his company, but that he shouldn't delight in theirs or in seeing them enjoy themselves—well, that is almost incredible!

It is quite a good idea for a comedy, but *The Breadwinner* is not quite a good play. In the first act the dialogue is not nearly entertaining enough. That act is occupied in showing the attitude of the young towards their parents. There are two pairs of them, male and female, and all four are cousins. The consensus of opinion among them is that after forty their elders, who have had their innings, ought to make room for the young. The dramatist's object is not only to show in this act their want of affection and gratitude, but also that these bright young things are deplorably silly and boring. He succeeds only too well. We are glad when the act is over. But the last two hold the attention, and he was blessed in Mr Squire, with his Hawtrey methods, as his interpreter for the placid but firm Mr Battle, also in Miss Marie Löhr who plays Mrs Battle. The outspoken English rose seemed to shock the audience a little. Well, she exists.

92. J.B. Priestley, 'A Letter from England', *Saturday Review of Literature* (New York)

VII, 1 November 1930, 299

John Boynton Priestley (1894–1984) was a Bradford-born novelist, playwright, essayist and critic who rivalled Maugham in versatility, industry and popular acclaim. They tended to steer clear of each other in their professional lives, while offering each other's writings a guarded respect. Maugham represented cosmopolitan urbanity, Priestley rooted provincialism. Priestley's fiction includes *The Good Companions* (1929), *Angel Pavement* (1930), *Bright Day* (1946); and among his plays, *Dangerous Corner* (1932), *When We Are Married* (1938) and *An Inspector Calls* (1947) are still occasionally revived. Both men regarded themselves as professional writers, firmly agreeing with Dr Johnson that 'No man but a blockhead ever wrote except for money'.

These last two or three weeks, the spotlight has been on Somerset Maugham, who has brought out both a new play and a new novel. The play is *The Breadwinner*, a very sardonic comedy of a stockbroker who allows himself to be 'hammered,' that is, publicly cast out of reputable business, because he is bored with his wife, his son, and his daughter, and sees no reason why he should go on working for them. He has twenty thousand pounds—it really should go to his creditors—and he gives his wife and family fifteen thousand and keeps the remaining five for himself. It is a clever, cynical little piece—with one or two awkward patches of sentiment in it—and represents, of course, a reversal of the conventional revolt-of-youth theme. Indeed, I think the best passage is that in which the defaulting father calmly points out to his astonished son and daughter that they bore him with their tedious chatter. But I agree with the dramatic critic who wrote that this was not a complete rounded comedy but only the beginning of one. Instead of three acts (the action is continuous throughout the play), showing how father left home, there ought to have been only one, the first, and then there ought to have been two more acts showing us what happened afterwards. How did the wife and children behave with their fifteen thousand pounds? What became of the former stockbroker after he retired to the continent on an income of five pounds a week?

The novel has attracted more attention than the play in literary circles. I am surprised, though, that there has not been a bigger rumpus, for when I read the novel before publication I anticipated a colossal row. *Cakes and Ale, or The Skeleton in the Cupboard*, is the title of this novel. It is told by a writer, one Ashenden, who has figured in Maugham's fiction before and bears a very close resemblance to Maugham himself. Ashenden describes his relations with Edward Driffield, a very distinguished novelist who lived to become the Grand Old Man of Letters. When Ashenden was a mere boy and Driffield was a struggling writer, recently married to an ex-barmaid who was anything but faithful to him, the two became acquainted. Later, in London, when Driffield was beginning to make a name, they met again, and Ashenden, like several other young men in the set, made love very successfully to Mrs Driffield. Then Mrs Driffield ran away with an old flame of hers to America. Driffield, after some years, married again, this time with the nurse who had looked after him, and settled down, not always very comfortably, to become a Grand Old Man. At the end of the book, we have a last glimpse of the first Mrs Driffield, now a widow in America and as sprightly as ever, though a very old woman. This first Mrs Driffield seems to me the only real character in the book, and she is an interesting study of the easy-going a-moral woman, who out of good nature allows any friend to enjoy her beautiful body. Driffield himself is a far more shadowy figure, and not very successful. For the rest, there is, as usual, some very good writing in the book, and some amusing and sardonic comments on the literary life.

But why should there be a rumpus? For this reason, that it is impossible to escape the feeling that Driffield is intended as a portrait of Hardy. The reader who jumps to this conclusion has every excuse. Hardy, like Driffield, was born and bred in the country, was fond of cycling and rubbing old church brasses, was a long time before he received adequate recognition, had one of his best novels banned, married twice, returned to the country to be a

Grand Old Man, was given the O.M. On being taxed with this, Somerset Maugham has declared that he did not intend this to be a portrait of Hardy, that he only met Hardy once and knew very little about him, and that he had a perfect right to invent a distinguished novelist and give him any traits that he pleased. And here, it seems to me, is revealed a very pretty little problem in literary ethics, and one that is likely to become more and more important as the tendency to find material for fiction in real life increases, as it seems likely to do. Maugham's case is simple enough. He would say that no reader has any right to decide that Edward Driffield is Thomas Hardy and then to attack him, Maugham, because Driffield has certain unpleasant characteristics not found in Hardy. It is the reader and not Somerset Maugham who has turned Driffield into Hardy and Hardy into Driffield. That sounds convincing, but I for one do not think the matter is so easily settled. While deploring this habit of finding 'keys' to characters and actions in fiction, I think the novelist must take upon himself a certain responsibility. If, for example, Maugham did not intend his readers to be reminded of Hardy, then he acted with a strange stupidity (and a less stupid man than Somerset Maugham never put pen to paper) when he set to work to create the figure of Edward Driffield. There are far too many coincidences of fact.

Suppose that I wrote a rather scandalous story of contemporary literary life, and made the chief character in it a distinguished novelist and dramatist, a man who lived in a beautiful villa on the Riviera, who had once been a medical student, and who in many other ways had a curious resemblance to Mr W. Somerset Maugham. I think Mr Maugham would protest, or if he did not, his friends would. I could reply, with perfect truth, that I had simply written a novel, that I had never exchanged a word with Mr Maugham and had only set eyes on him once, and that if people were foolish enough to think that I had been writing about Somerset Maugham when I had been merely writing about my fictitious Aloysius Jones, it was their affair and not mine. But I do not think that Mr Maugham or his friends would be satisfied. He and they would feel that I had started something unpleasant that I could not stop, and that my lack of tact—to say the least of it—looked like working a good deal of mischief. For once, Sir Toby's sublime retort does not convince me: 'Dost thou think, because thou art virtuous, there shall be no more cakes and ale?' I think it would be better if there was no more of this *Cakes and Ale*.

Two of our most distinguished novelists, both senior to Maugham, were agreeing in my presence the other day that Maugham was greatly undervalued as a novelist here. In America, where *Of Human Bondage*, his most ambitious novel, has long commanded a huge public (and I have heard it maliciously stated that this is because it is a study of an inferiority complex), I fancy that he enjoys the reputation he deserves as a novelist. If he does not here, I do not think it is from any failure to appreciate the individual worth of any of his stories, though it may be that his somewhat dry, hard manner, more French than English in its fine frugality, is not quite to the taste of the general English reading public. (I think the English, even at this late date, still prefer a copious gusto in their novelists, for that is the tradition.) I should say at a venture that he is undervalued as a novelist simply because he has been so successful as a dramatist. Versatility in an art is always regarded with slight suspicion in England, unfortunately, and some writers—Maurice Hewlett was one and Hilaire Belloc is another—have paid dearly for their interest in many different forms. And it has always been especially difficult for a writer to command equal attention and respect both inside and outside of the theater. Thus, once Barrie was accepted as a dramatist, people lost interest in him as a novelist. Arnold Bennett has always been seriously accepted as a novelist but not as a dramatist. Galsworthy has combined both reputations, but I fancy that even he has been rather 'out' in one capacity when he has been very much 'in' in another. St John Ervine and Clemence Dane have both written some excellent fiction, but nobody bothers about it much. Now Somerset Maugham's stage successes have been enormous, and I think they have overshadowed, by the sheer glare of theatrical publicity thrown on them, what seems to be the far more solid merit of his fiction. He himself, I understand, takes his novels and other non-theatrical prose work (for *The Gentleman in the Parlour* showed him to be an essayist of travel of extraordinary merit) far more seriously than he does his plays. His comedies are astonishingly clever, but the best of his fiction is more than clever and I think it will be enjoyed and studied long after his plays have been swept from the stage by some succeeding fashion in drama, less brilliant than this work perhaps but at once more robust and truer to ordinary life.

FOR SERVICES RENDERED

Globe Theatre, London, 1 November 1932; transferred to Queen's
Theatre, London (78 performances)
[Written 1932. Published London, December 1932; New York,
April 1933]

93. Peter Fleming, review, *Spectator*

CXLIX, 11 November 1932, 659

Robert Peter Fleming (1907–71) was a traveller, journalist,
historian, essayist and critic. As a young man down from
Oxford he became special correspondent of *The Times*. His
travels resulted in such books as *Brazilian Adventure* (1933)
and *News from Tartary* (1941). His work on the *Spectator*
included drama criticism and a regular column under the
pen-name 'Strix'. He was married to actress Celia Johnson,
who played Elizabeth in the 1931 revival of *The Circle* at the
Vaudeville Theatre, London.

As Mr Maugham sees it, Rambleston, where the Ardsleys live in a
faithfully observed atmosphere of Landseers and lawn tennis, is still
part of the devastated area. The guns in France have been silent for
a decade and a half, but for the Ardsleys the interest in catastrophe
has been accumulating. Sydney, the son, is blind and bitter, too
ready by half to let the world see what lies behind his mask of
resignation. Eva, who lost a lover in the war, faces in pitiful and
ill-controlled apprehension the knowledge that it is now almost too
late to find another. Ethel is heroically making the best of her
marriage to a sot in a Sam Browne. Collie Stratton, who
commanded a cruiser with distinction, is heading for disaster as
manager of a garage. These are, directly, the victims of war. If they

are not all in the same boat, they are all survivors of the same shipwreck.

But Mr Maugham has piled on a good deal of extraneous agony—extraneous, that is, if we read a text into his title and follow his implied intentions by regarding the piece as an arraignment of the nation's ingratitude. *Post bellum* is not necessarily *propter bellum*. If the war decreed that Mrs Ardsley should find post-war life a sad and silly business, no longer in the best of taste, it is not the war's fault that she must shortly leave it. And if, for the twenty-six-year-old Lois, there are fewer gentlemen than ex-officers, and a tragic shortage of both, her shoddy method of making good her want of a husband can hardly be charged to the account of Mars. As for the Cedars, the Great War was no more responsible than the Black Death for making their folly unsavoury.

By blaming everything on the dogs of war, Mr Maugham weakens the force of his argument. His 'outers' detract from the effect of his 'bulls'. For Sydney, Eva, Ethel and Stratton the war has been the ultimate cause of tragedy; but for most of the rest it is no more than a fairly good excuse for not averting fiasco. They are like flies drearily buzzing out their lives against a window pane: always the same window pane. It does not occur to them that another window in the room may be open.

The first two acts drag. Lois vacillates too long between her bounder and her boor. It is not till the third act that the play comes savagely to life, and the curtain falls on horrors more truly dreadful (though not much nearer to high tragedy) than anything in the twilit charnels of the Elizabethans.

There is brilliant acting from Mr S.J. Warmington as Cedar, the helpless, domineering sensualist, and from Miss Flora Robson as the girl desperately trying to retrieve on the roundabouts of peace her heart's losses on the swings of war. Mr Cronin Wilson plays Howard Bartlett with well-judged gusto, and Miss Diana Hamilton beautifully sketches the resignation of his wife. Mr Cedric Hardwicke as Sydney, Miss Louise Hampton as his mother, and especially Miss Marda Vanne in the awkward part of Mrs Cedar are others whom one would like to praise at length. Mr Ayliff's production had moments of clumsiness, and was not quite up to the impeccable standard of Mr Shelving's scenery.

But let no one say that this play, however well its temper suits our times, is Mr Maugham's best.

94. J.T. Grein, 'Two Gifted Pessimists', *Illustrated London News*

CLXXXI, 26 November 1932, 854

This review contrasts Maugham's *For Services Rendered* with A.A. Milne's *Other People's Lives*.

Two of our foremost playwrights—Mr W. Somerset Maugham and Mr A.A. Milne—have given us the fruit of their contemplation of two paramount actualities. Mr Maugham has expressed himself in bitter plaint; Mr Milne in lighter, satirical vein, with a dramatic touch at the end. In both cases the keynote is—frustration. Frustration, the fate of the post-war generation; frustration, the outcome of the vain efforts of our young contemporaries to ameliorate 'other people's lives' as a pastime fraught with disastrous consequences. Mr Milne begins gaily enough. The first act is a masterly exposition and exposure of the bright young people of to-day who, having nothing to do 'twixt cocktail and dinner, or after a dance all too early finished, talk in their futile way about the world in general and themselves in particular, evolving from the general exchange of thought a novel mission for the benefit of their neighbours. These conversations are wonderfully brilliant. Mr Milne has a wit all his own. He gathers his coruscating sayings seemingly from nowhere, and yet they not only hit home every time, but they prompt the wonderment whence they came, and how it is possible thus to flit from twig to branch with rarely a miss. It would seem that Mr Milne has the inventive sort of mind that seeks humour in every direction, and lets go without worrying whether his public is quick enough in the uptake to relish its keenness. Candid playgoers would often answer a 'Why did you laugh?' with 'I don't know; it sounded funny and it seemed to fit in'. Sure of his public, Mr Milne amuses himself by watching the amusement he produces in others. Yet sometimes (I should say rarely) it leads him too far, and in his heedless canters he forgets the obstacles on his way, he forgets the dramatic conflict that he treated all too lightly.

Thus in *Other People's Lives*, which are so banefully played with by their youthful would-be reformers, he makes us believe that a dignitary of the Church, bent on increasing the population of Canada, would barter a stalwart young girl's emigration (because she promises to be a bountiful wife) for the mother's operation by his half-brother, a distinguished surgeon. Such a pact is unthinkable, yet Mr Milne handles it banteringly, and drowns its fateful significance in a welter of conversation, only cut short by the mute sorrow of her afflicted husband when he hears of his wife's death. It ended the well-meant efforts of the young people to reform these tranquil little lives that vegetated in their unpretentious simplicity and only asked to be left alone. It was, indeed, the inevitable end, and yet, unfortunately, it was unskilfully brought about, and it marred all the ingenuity that had preceded it. Up to the middle of the second act, we felt in harmony with the author; we expected some kind of disillusioning solution, but we saw it otherwise. The leap from comedy to drama was too sudden, and it was brought about by a *tour de force* instead of a logical, acceptable turn of events.

When the play, after its very successful trial-trip at the Arts, comes to a regular theatre—a dead certainty, if ever there was one—this transition referred to will have to be altered. One can have too much even of sparkling talk, and in the third act the last scene is merely a *réchauffé* of the very first, when the young people formed their society for the reform of the Tillings that ended fatally for both parties—in death on the one side, in rue on the other. Later on I shall have an opportunity to speak at greater length about the actors, but one performance should and will be remembered above all, and that is the figure of Tilling, the simple little clerk who, after the day's toil, laboriously penned novels in his admiring family circle which surely no publisher would accept. That character of gentle tolerance and sincerity is played by Mr Lawrence Hanray in his inimitable, human way. With the lawyer's clerk in *Justice*, and the magistrate in *The Silver Box*, this portrayal forms a trilogy of characterisation superb in conception and elaboration. It has—at length—raised Mr Hanray to the front rank of English actors, to which, by rights, but unrecognised, he has belonged for many years.

As regards Mr Somerset Maugham's play, *For Services Rendered*, I find myself in a somewhat difficult position. I am a deep admirer of Mr Maugham. I value him as one of our very foremost novelists and playwrights. Yet on the first night I could not endorse the opinion, expressed next day in many quarters, that this play is great, and, more specifically, that it represents a distinct picture of the *état d'âme* of little people in a hinterland township. There is the blind ex-soldier, whose meanderings and worrying tyranny in the household are a post-war product; there is the sad fate of the naval commander who, incompetent in business, commits acts of indelicacy threatening him with imprisonment and driving him to suicide. These two are examples of that frustration which has been the lot of so many derelicts. Mr Maugham draws them with pathos dipped in embitterment. But the other characters—the unquenched virgin driven to frenzy; the younger girl who, bored to extinction in the mustiness of her surroundings, flees to illicit freedom with the man who tempts her; the other sister who bears her bondage of marriage to a drunkard until she seeks outlet in hysteria; the mother who falls a victim to fell disease; the father who vegetates in the house in blinded optimism—are they victims of the aftermath of war? Are they not representatives of the drab lives that eke out a cloistered, monotonous, hopeless existence in countless provincial cities? Do they not belong to the same kind which, years before the war, the late Mr Stanley Houghton depicted in *Hindle Wakes*?

Certainly Mr Maugham, after opening with a static first act in which he merely draws a picture of the family, lets events take a more dramatic turn, and the deeper he goes into it, the more bitter becomes the pessimism inoculated in the characters. But even the great climax, the paroxysmal outburst of the eldest girl, who sees her last hope gone and envisages her perennial condemnation to spinsterhood, is not a post-war aftermath. True, the man she desired, the commander, commits suicide; but under all circumstances her fate would have been the same. She was one of those whom no man would have, who was destined to live unkissed and unwooed. True, in the third act, the scene of nature's revolt in the elderly girl's miserable existence created a deep impression; it was sprung upon us as a surprise; it was handled by the author with great dexterity. But, on reflextion, was it the 'explosion' that moved us so deeply, or was it the acting of Miss Flora Robson, who unsparingly poured out her wrath and her soul? When I recall this play in its details, I can but see a faint wraith of war-influence; but I cannot follow why it should be exalted above many others Mr Maugham has written, and which, both in structure and penetration, were of greater dramatic value.

SHEPPEY

Wyndham's Theatre, London, 14 September 1933
(83 performances)
[Written 1933. Published London, November 1933]

For the theme of his last play Maugham adapted the plot of
one of his two earliest-written short stories, 'A Bad Example', which was included in *Orientations* (1899).

95. Desmond MacCarthy, 'Mr Maugham's New Play', *New Statesman*

n.s. VI, 16 September 1933, 325–6

Yes, it is a comedy, but a comedy which borders upon drama and
even upon religious drama. It begins in the saloon of a fashionable
hairdresser's shop in Jermyn Street, and it ends with a dialogue
between a hairdresser's assistant and Death. In Act I and II comedy
predominates, but the drama lies in the contrast between the spirit of
Christian charity and what passes for the Christian religion in the
world. Some of the humour is grim. You could not have a much
bitterer joke than a young daughter clasping her pretty little hands
in an agony of supplication and imploring, 'Oh God, make father
potty.' But most of the humour lies in lines, revealing selfish
snobbishness and genteel aspirations, and spoken by those who do
not realise what they have betrayed. Here Mr Maugham has always
excelled.

In earlier days I would have expected that Mr Somerset
Maugham in treating such a theme would have written more out of

273

his contempt for what he disliked than out of his sympathy for whatever contrasted with it. Contempt for human nature, and an indulgence towards it equally scornful, has hitherto been his strongest suit whenever he has deviated from comedy proper. The reason why that admirable play *For Services Rendered* did not hold the public for long (many enjoyed it and admired it—under protest) was that positive sympathy, as contrasted with satirical exposure, found in it no counterbalancing expression. For the discerning and tough-minded this did not detract from their response to the play, but there was no character in it on which the popular imagination could rest with complete satisfaction. Here, in this play, it is not so. The character in it which is most vividly conceived is 'Sheppey' the barber, who is compact of natural kindliness and goodness. No qualities are more moving on the stage than these, but they are exceedingly difficult to handle without tipping over into sentiment. The dramatist must avoid showing that he is touched by them himself. Mr Maugham has not sentimentalised Sheppey, even when his inexhaustible and spontaneous 'charity' approaches the gospel ideal. Sheppey is not a saviour of souls; he cannot save the petty thief or the public-house tart. He is not interested in them because they have immortal souls, let alone as citizens, but because he cannot help liking them as they are, even when he wishes they were different. He is shocked by misery and unhappiness but he cannot be disgusted by human beings, whatever they do. As one of the characters remarks, Sheppey has no moral sense whatever. Galsworthy once drew such a character. Wellwyn in *The Pigeon*, which, to my mind, was one of his best pieces of work.

How does Mr Maugham modulate from a fashionable hairdresser's shop to the theme of Christian charity? It is deftly done, and there are two points about the management of the transition which will excite the admiration of those who know anything about the playwright's craft.

First, the character of Sheppey, revealed to us while he is shaving customers and chatting with the other assistants, is (though at the time no such interest enters our heads) exactly the right soil out of which the flower of Christian charity might plausibly spring, granted some sudden opening, illumination or religious conversion—or whatever you like to call it—takes place. What made Sheppey the perfect barber, and the soul of the establishment he served, was his *humility*; that old-fashioned but important virtue, and the one, oddly enough, which often makes a man trust his intuitions against the judgment of the world. Without drawing our attention to it directly the playwright has suggested Sheppey's natural humility, by exhibiting his wholehearted devotion to his little job; and it was this quality which Mr Richardson's admirable impersonation of every side of Sheppey's character, brought out so well. Not long ago we saw Mr Richardson in *Wild Decembers* as the curate who wooed Charlotte Brontë—successfully at last. Once again he shows a rare understanding of human goodness, and a rare restraint in expressing it; Mr Richardson is again a perfect interpreter of a dramatist's subtler intentions, and in a part, too, which requires a nice adjustment between humour and deep feeling.

The second point about Mr Maugham's transition is the ingenious use of what may be described as 'the red herring.'

Two very important things happened to Sheppey that morning in Jermyn Street. He had had to attend the police court as the principal witness in the case of a man who stole an overcoat from a car; and while listening to his own and other cases he had been strangely upset. The criminals and outcasts of society are human beings like himself and as amiable as his customers! Hunger and misery had made them what they were; Sheppey is so disturbed by this discovery that he cannot help chatting about his amazement.

The second, is the news that he has won £8,500 in the Irish Sweepstake. When the curtain falls on the establishment drinking Sheppey's health in champagne, we are naturally left guessing how his luck is going to affect him. I must mention that he has brought in with him a woman from the public house opposite, with whom he had often had a little friendly talk, discovering now she is hungry and exhausted; and that when he and she are left alone together, he has a slight fit—probably the result of suppressed excitement. Well, how is his sweepstake luck going to affect him and the story? I do not suppose a single person in the theatre anticipated the actual consequences. I know several alternatives, each in Mr Maugham's vein, occurred to me, and not one of them proved right: he might be paralysed by another stroke and his 'luck' turn out a curse, or his wife, whom we had not seen, might be a tiresome silly woman who would destroy the contented life he had hitherto led by her pursuit of silly social ambitions, or she might be furiously jealous of the woman who brought him home that night; or again, the money might spoil Sheppey himself—in his middle-age he might turn vulgar-gay and rush to ruin.

But Act II shows Mrs Sheppey to be charming, sensible, steady; and, gradually, it is disclosed that Sheppey's experience in the police court, together with his fit (probably this was accompanied by some strange spiritual illumination as with Dostoievsky), have together implanted in him a very different longing. He has forgotten his day-dreams of buying a nice little house and providing a slap-up wedding for his daughter, who is engaged to a pushful young schoolmaster in a county council school; he is resolved instead to give his money to all and sundry who clearly need it more than he does.

The conflict is not between husband and wife, but between Sheppey and the young couple, who see whisked away before their eyes the blessed chance of attaining the gentility they covet. Their dismay, their despair, are without bounds. No honeymoon trip to Paris for them; no marriage even perhaps for Sheppey's daughter (excellently played by Miss Angela Baddeley)—for she understands her Ernest, who conceals beneath the tags of a pretentious education and devotion to public service, the passions of a little arrivist. Ernest's arguments, and her violent clutch upon the money, make excellent comedy in contrast to Sheppey's buoyant insistence that the outcasts, the thief and the prostitute should come and live with them, and his determination (he only knows that this makes him happy) to scatter his fortune. Such a sudden conversion to the ethics of the New Testament must be madness! He has failed to redeem the thief—who steals from him, or the prostitute—who runs off to the streets again, but these things matter not to Sheppey. He has obeyed his inmost impulse. If only the doctors would certify him! Mrs Sheppey also is deeply perturbed, especially when her husband turns down an offer of a partnership in the hair-dressing business, which in old days he had coveted before all things. Her husband is certainly in a queer state. But when the doctors diagnose his case as one of religious paranoia she is dismayed. (Here Mr Maugham indulges in some over-charged but effective satire of mental specialists.) Again we are left in doubt as to what will happen in the last act; a Strindberg ending of a loving woman fixing a strait-waistcoat on 'the father' seems a possibility. But Sheppey is lucky to the last.

96. J.T. Grein, 'Somerset Maugham's New Play', *Illustrated London News*

CLXXXIII, 30 September 1933, 498

The production of a new play by Mr Somerset Maugham in our theatre is an event of first importance claiming serious attention and demanding considered criticism. Not only is he a novelist of universal distinction, but an established dramatist whose powers of characterisation and narrative are in themselves a justification for lively anticipation and a promise that the movement on the stage will not lack effectiveness or credibility. The outlook centered in the end of the brilliant opening act of *Sheppey*, at Wyndham's, stimulated anticipation into excitement; for had he not essayed a theme so great, a subject so profound in its dramatic possibilities, a problem so significant for our present generation, that at once both hope and doubt arose as to whether the playwright could bring it to fulfilment? This figure of Sheppey was no shadowy outline, no sentimental creature, no mere crank or fool which we must suffer for the sake of the subject, but a plain, honest hairdresser's assistant in Jermyn Street who has the luck to win an Irish Sweepstake prize. The character is wholly vital; his simple, homely lovable nature is evident from the outset, and his conversion is as comprehensible as his character. Like Saul of Tarsus on the way to Damascus, under the impact of shock he too sees a white light from Heaven and is transfigured. Now we are aware of the sublimity of the subject, for this is none other than a Jesus of Nazareth in our present-day world. It is a subject that playwrights have attempted, but never more than theatrical effectiveness has been attained. Mr Maugham surmounted the first difficulty—that of creating a living human being who could fit the idealisation—with conquering power and craftsmanship. The greater difficulty was to come.

And what are the gifts Mr Maugham brings to his work? An incisive pen that will not suffer thought to be clouded by woolly platitudes nor permit character to be undermined by false accents, a grip of character that penetrates beneath the surface and gets down to the roots of being, a swift sense of narrative which keeps a story continually interesting, and a mastery of craftsmanship that can take full advantage of every opportunity and exploit every situation. To these must be added a caustic wit and a passionate indignation. Are these gifts enough? Idealism demands more than the equipment of the satirist if it is to tread the stage. Mr Maugham's genius is at its best when he whips human folly and stupidity; and in *Sheppey* this is the drift of his aim. It is here that the promise of the play goes on the rocks. The spirit, the potentiality, and the vision which set the action in motion give place to satire and gall. Sheppey was only to be sustained by a miracle of sympathetic imagination, by an illumination of his soul influencing his surroundings. 'To touch the hem of His garment' should have been the spiritual desire. But the power is not with him, but is transferred to those around him. The whole character of the play changes and the tone drops, so that instead of awe there is only levity, and the beauty of Sheppey's character is only disfigured. What a soulless unregenerate world Sheppey lives in, and its worst expression is through the daughter. There are no reliefs in this uncompromising study. Miss Angela Baddeley and Mr Eric Portman as the son-in-law are fierce to the point of violent dislike, but Miss Cecily Oates offers, as the wife, redeeming virtues that make her more than a theatrical foil. Mr Ralph Richardson builds up a portrait of an idealist that is only robbed of sublimity by the author's mood. It is a rare performance by the actor, yet we do not chiefly remember it. And why? Because too often dialogue offends by its aggressiveness, too often sensibilities are outraged by utterances that shock, for hysteria blots the theme. There are sanctities that should be safe from such assaults. Admit the play's theatrical merits—its structural strength, its subtle Scriptural parallels, its astute juxtaposition of characters, its biographical history of Sheppey down to the moving yet enigmatic death scene, its highlights skilfully employed by Miss Laura Cowie with vivid effect—admit all these and more, yet *Sheppey* somehow falls below its promise; for tragedy is reduced to irony and poetry to adroit prose. As a piece for the theatre it is brilliantly done; as a drama it fails to realise the sublimity of the Gospel story wherein it is rooted, and in place of exaltation offers only a disillusion born of despair.

PART V
BOOKS
(1934–1959)

EAST AND WEST
New York, August 1934

ALTOGETHER
London, August 1934

In this volume were collected Maugham's five books of short stories: *The Trembling of a Leaf* (1921), *The Casuarina Tree* (1926), *Ashenden* (1928), *First Person Singular* (1931) and *Ah King* (1933).

97. Louis Kronenberger, 'The Story-Telling Art of Mr Maugham', *New York Times*

12 August 1934, 2

Louis Kronenberger (1904–80) was a historian, literary critic and editor, and an authority on eighteenth-century England.

This book makes very interesting and very disappointing reading. One finds one's self in the presence of an astounding story-teller and passes from each of these stories to the next with the impatient zest that only expert story-telling can foster. It is not conceivable that anybody should be bored reading Mr Maugham; he is the sort of writer who can choose a subject in which you have no interest, who can indeed choose a subject that you definitely dislike, and yet by his gift for narrative compel you to read on to the end. He is perhaps the least dull writer, for the largest body of readers, of his generation: both the man who reads Tolstoy and the man who reads Sabatini can read Maugham with understanding and relish. Among living writers in English only Kipling and Tarkington, it seems to me, can equally share that honor.

Nor is this kinship with Kipling and Tarkington in any sense fortuitous: there is a very marked reason why all three men can attract everybody from the man in the street up to the genuine highbrow. All three are men of great natural talent with an astonishing power of story-telling, and all three are men whose sense of values lags far behind their ability. The picture they give us of life plainly has nothing in common with the skill they display in painting it. For those who are content with the picture the skill shown in painting it is of course an extraordinary boon. But for those who are not content with the picture the skilled brushwork becomes, sooner or later, an object of dissatisfaction. It seems more than wasteful; it seems almost immoral. For to see talent glorifying shoddiness, particularly when in the same hands you have seen it glorify truth, is a pretty unpleasant business. But certainly in most of Kipling's work one looks in vain for the light that shines through his half dozen best stories; in most of Tarkington's work one looks in vain for the conviction carried by *Alice Adams*, and in all of Maugham's later writing one looks in vain for the realistic promise of the early novels and the unchallenged reality of *Of Human Bondage*.

These thirty stories, most of them quite long as short stories go, are the products of the past fifteen years. The first of them, 'Rain,' was written in the same year that Maugham published his last satisfactory book, *The Moon and Sixpence*; and they very definitely represent the arrived and mature man. Since it took him almost no time at all to master the short-story medium, we can at once dismiss from our inquiry any considerations of technique. Maugham started off writing short stories with a great deal of skill and gradually acquired a great deal more; on the technical side there is nothing further to say. But in all the years he has spent in writing these stories he has acquired nothing beyond additional skill; he began with a catchpenny and spectacular tale that lies all on the surface, and nothing he did afterward can be regarded as really more important or substantial. His themes, when you come to think about them, are remarkably varied, his locales are diversified, his story-telling is flexible; and yet for all their variety these tales seem altogether alike and produce an altogether like effect. The curse of a common point of view, and a very unsatisfying point of view, lies heavily upon them. The curse of a solved, tabloid outlook on life disfigures, belittles, desiccates them. It is not quite the outlook or point of view of the fairly well educated reader who may be described as Maugham's most enthusiastic audience; Maugham himself is on the one hand too superior, on the other hand too clever, to succumb to that outlook. But it is that outlook fortified by an immense worldliness—a worldliness so cynical, so adaptable, so penetrable that it lends to the provincial mind its own cosmopolitan eyes; and with those eyes one can see a great deal further than usual without seeing the least bit deeper. Maugham has dowered these stories with all his sophistication and wit and social presence, but he has made his gifts ornamental, not useful: nowhere has brilliance served to uncover depth—it has been turned into a kaleidoscope, not into a light.

While damning Chekhov with faint praise in a preface that often sounds like an apologia, Maugham remarks that 'the pleasure of recognition, which is the pleasure [Chekhov] thus aimed at, is the lowest of all esthetic pleasures.' In that one statement I think he gives himself away as fully as he does in all the succeeding stories. And acting on such a belief, Mr Maugham in most of these narratives has set to work to dazzle us with surprise; in one story after another we are cheated of recognizing life as we know it to enjoy the banal and meretricious surprises, the swift melodrama, the cynical paradoxes of a writer who wants to make us gasp; and that is all. We gasp at 'Rain' but we are not convinced; the trick was far better done by Anatole France in *Thaïs*. There is a momentary catch in our throats at the end of 'The Alien Corn'; the next moment we feel emotionally duped. And once the spell is broken, it is broken forever; nothing in the world can make us believe Mr Maugham's contrived illusion again.

It is because, in every respect, Maugham is so much the reverse of a fool that all 900 pages of this book have so insidious a quality. His shrewdness is staggering; his objectivity, his 'tolerance' are faultless. He doesn't point a moral; he doesn't take sides. Both the parties to his drama may be wrong-headed or prejudiced or idiotic; he plays no favorites. There is a real worldliness in such stories of human deadlock as 'The Door of Opportunity,' 'The Human Element,' 'The Book-Bag,' 'The Outstation'; the situations they evolve are the situations of real life, and Maugham has let them be played out in a credible and suitable fashion. Yet those stories uncover nothing for the reader, release nothing in him. He accepts without participating; it is mathematics Maugham is giving him, not humanity. And this seems all the more strange when one considers how much drama and suspense Maugham has put into such stories, until one realizes how much emotion, how much intimate reality he has left out.

Maugham points out in his preface that, though many of these stories are told in the first person, they are in no way to be thought of as his own experiences. Yet the constant play of the 'I' throughout this book has a very disconcerting effect. For the 'I' is always a well-off and poised novelist who moves in the smartest society—a tiresome sort of narrator who presently grows into a very snobbish symbol. It is a calculated snobbery which is doubtless not true of Mr Maugham himself, but which adds a further touch of worldly glamour to the very clever story-teller who would rather impress magazine readers than add to his stature as a writer. The same touch, for me, often spoils the lighter stories, which—since they are written frankly to amuse—are the best things in the book. Some of them are much in the manner of Max Beerbohm, but for a number of reasons they fall short of Beerbohm's success. For Beerbohm is much wittier and much more delicate, and he uses the artistic scene in a subtler way. Also the snob in him is based on a temperament, and is revealed with disarming playfulness. At heart Maugham is perhaps less of a snob, but on paper he seems much more of one.

Here is, beyond doubt, one of the most readable books that have been published in a very long time. But here too is the wreck of a very considerable talent, and it is a wreck in no way splendid. In their poorer work most writers of merit offer less completely and satisfyingly some traces and signs of themselves at their best; but whoever can find in these brilliantly flashy pieces any evidence of the solid worth of Philip Carey's journey through life, or even of the honest grossness and humor of *Liza of Lambeth*, has much deeper insight than I have. The Maugham of these pages seems to me an entirely different person.

98. Raymond Mortimer, 'Re-reading Mr Maugham', *New Statesman and Nation*

n.s. VIII, 25 August 1934, 243–4

Raymond Mortimer (1895–1980) was a leading English literary critic. For many years on the staff of the *New Statesman and Nation*, he succeeded Desmond MacCarthy as its literary editor, and then went on to join him as a regular lead book-reviewer on the *Sunday Times*. Two collections of his reviews were published, *Channel Packet* (1942) and *Try Anything Once* (1976).

Mr Somerset Maugham thinks that the critics have not given him a square deal, so the thirty stories in this volume are sandwiched between a preface by the author and a reprinted article by Mr Desmond MacCarthy. The reviewer will find in the preface a warning of what he ought not to say, and in the article, which is almost wholly laudatory, an example of what he ought. The stories themselves are most of them told by a disillusioned man of the world who remains superbly objective in face of cruelty, treachery and murder, but for whom the highbrow is something he resents even more than he does the missionary: something to be treated with not only detestation but contempt. (Indeed 'The Creative Instinct' [*sic*] seems to me the weakest story in the volume, in spite of its charming plot, because the author's hatred of highbrows has goaded him into unconvincing caricature.) It is odd that Mr Maugham, who is, I suppose, the most successful living writer, should let his calm be ruffled by the criticisms of persons he believes to be so petty, gullible and insincere.

> Is one mocked by an elf,
> Is one baffled by toad or by rat?
> The graveman's in that!

But if one is a highbrow it is little use pretending not to be, even to escape Mr Maugham's contempt; and so I shall parade the cloven hoof by trying to criticise his stories by the highest standard I know.

In his preface Mr Maugham implies, I think justly, that the critics have been cold to him largely because his stories derive rather from Maupassant than from the more fashionable Tchehov. (His remarks on these writers reveal him as a most acute critic.) Actually the stories of Tchehov have been too indiscriminately praised: many of them are mere jottings, and both he and Maupassant wrote too much. Mr Maugham lives much more conscientiously up to his own highest level. To illustrate his methods he transcribes in his preface the working notes, made from observation, on which the story 'Rain' was constructed. 'They are written in hackneyed and slipshod phrases without grace' he says, 'for nature has not endowed me with the happy gift of hitting instinctively upon the perfect word to indicate an object and the unusual, but apt, adjective to describe it.' In view of this statement it is interesting to find that in the story itself most of these 'hackneyed and slipshod phrases' are repeated without alteration. Mr Maugham complains that reviewers call his work 'competent,' and supposes that he is damned with this faint praise because of the definiteness of form in his stories. Lord knows there has rarely been a less incompetent writer, but I think it is true to say that he does not hit, either instinctively or on reflection, the perfect word to indicate an object. It would be difficult to find examples of clumsy writing in Mr Maugham's late work (though he sometimes trips into such surprising *clichés* as calling a woman 'exquisitely gowned'), but it would be equally difficult to find passages in which the words had a life of their own. Possibly a fresher, less business-like style would slacken the pace of the stories by side-tracking the reader's attention from the design to the texture, but I do miss vividness in Mr Maugham's descriptive passages. After reading many—too many—stories with a Malay setting, I have no clear impression of the atmosphere of Malaya: I have merely become bored with the sarongs and padangs and kampongs which serve for local colour. On the other hand, Mr Maugham describes persons prodigiously well by the phrases he puts into their mouths. In a scrap of dialogue we have their social background, their pretensions, and the passions they seek to conceal. As a result, when re-reading these stories I have been surprised not by their excellence as stories (which I remembered) but by the suspense in which they held me, although I already knew how they would end. In this respect he beats Maupassant, whose stories depend too often on surprise. For in Maupassant the characters are created for the plot: in Maugham the plot is created by the characters. 'Honolulu' is one of the very few stories which are just stories: and afterwards in 'P.&.O.,' where he uses a similar plot, the interest has shifted from the action to the reaction which it has upon the spectators' characters. Very often the point is the revelation of some wholly unexpected trait, a 'degrading' passion in an ambassador or a society beauty, or the ability to murder in apparently commonplace persons, as in 'The Letter,' 'Before the Party,' and 'Footprints in the Jungle.' Mr Maugham delights in uncovering the heel of Achilles—that is why he is called a cynic—and there are no wholehearted heroes or villains in his work. His extraordinary knowledge of human beings is like that of an experienced confessor, and as a result of it he is never shocked. This comprehension of the essential piebaldness of human character gives his stories a peculiar virtue. As examples of his method take 'Mackintosh' and 'The Outstation': in each case two incompatible men are isolated, with the result that one becomes accessory to the other's murder. The murders, though their circumstances are arranged with admirable skill, are merely logical deductions from the confrontation of characters, and the interest of each story lies chiefly not in the violent conclusion but in the subtly stated premises. And in both of them the reader's sympathies are made to waver delicately in the balance by the calculated mixture of qualities in each of the antagonists. Mr Maugham has developed in the narrow room of the short story a richness of characterisation hardly previously found except in the novel.

Ultimately these stories are the work of a comic writer. 'Life is really very fantastic,' he says in one of them, 'and one has to have a peculiar sense of humour to see the fun of it.' Mr Maugham has this himself. Most of the stories 'end unhappily,' but they are devised to excite irony rather than pity. Almost the only character treated with tenderness is the scoundrelly old Walker at the end of 'Mackintosh,' and here the tenderness seems to me just off the note—in fact, to be sentimentality. Yet Rosie in *Cakes and Ale* proves that Mr Maugham can be tender. In fact, his last two novels show that he is a writer of promise. *Of Human Bondage* is so far his most solid achievement, because of the passion behind it; and I suspect it is a better book than *The Old Wives' Tale*, for instance, or any other of the realistic novels of the decade before the war. But in the meanwhile Mr Maugham, who is not a natural writer, I think, in the sense of having a gift for handling language as a *matière*, has learnt a great deal about writing; and in *The Narrow Corner* he put his acquired skill to new uses, so that it is probably true to say that his last book was also his most perfect.

Mr Maugham lacks the gift which is not necessary to immortality but which alone can make it certain: he does not possess a poetic vision of the world. But he has the good taste not to pretend to it, and does not offer us electro-plate in lieu of silver. There are few purple passages in his work, and it would be better if there were none. Though the critics have praised him less than he deserves, the public have appreciated him more than he could reasonably expect, for he has done nothing to placate them: his irony and amorality are the qualities which usually they most dislike. He would wish the critic, I gather, to praise his stories for their shapeliness, and indeed each of these thirty is a model of construction. But I humbly recommend them for what seems to me rarer and more important than shapeliness, for the first and essential literary virtue, a virtue which they possess in the highest degree and the lack of which stamps some supposed masterpieces of form as fraudulent—the power to seize and hold the reader's attention.

99. Graham Greene, 'Maugham's Short Stories', *Spectator*

CLIII, 31 August 1934, 297

Graham Greene was born in 1904. In addition to his outstanding career as a novelist, short-story writer, and playwright, Greene has a sizeable collection of weekly journalism to his credit as a book and film critic. This is the first of several reviews he wrote of Maugham's work.

Mr Somerset Maugham's tales are so well known to all who are interested in the art of the short story that a reviewer may be forgiven for dwelling chiefly on the preface Mr Maugham has contributed to this beautifully produced volume. It is a finely written, delightfully 'sensible' essay on the short story, and it is the more valuable because it represents a point of view not common to many English writers. Mr Maugham represents Maupassant's influence when most English short-story writers of any merit represent Chekov's.

Mr Maugham can write nothing without inspiring confidence; he is a writer of great deliberation even when his style is most careless ('burning mouth,' 'nakedness of soul,' 'mouth like a scarlet wound'); he will never, one feels, lose his head; he has a steady point of view. The banality of the phrases I have noted do not indicate an emotional abandonment; they indicate a rather blasé attitude towards the details of his stories; narrative is something which has to be got through before the point of his anecdote appears, and Mr Maugham is sometimes a little bored and off-hand in the process. The anecdote to Mr Maugham is very nearly everything; the anecdote, and not the characters, not the 'atmosphere,' not the style, is primarily responsible for conveying Mr Maugham's attitude; and it is anecdote as contrasted with spiritual analysis: Maupassant with Chekov: that he discusses in his preface with great justice to the opposite school.

I do not know that anyone but Chekov has so poignantly been able to represent spirit communing with spirit. It is this that makes one feel that Maupassant in comparison is obvious and vulgar. The strange, the terrible thing is that, looking at man in their different ways, these two great writers, Maupassant and Chekov, saw eye to eye. One was content to look upon the flesh, while the other, more nobly and subtly, surveyed the spirit; but they agreed that life was tedious and insignificant and that men were base, unintelligent and pitiful.

This comes very generously from a disciple of Maupassant, and Mr Maugham's praise of his master is never exaggerated. 'Maupassant's stories are good stories. The anecdote is interesting apart from the narration, so that it would secure attention if it were told over the dinner table; and that seems to me a very great merit indeed.' The best of Mr Maugham's stories too are anecdotes, the best are worthy of Maupassant, and his failure really to reach Maupassant's rank is partly his failure to stick to the anecdote. Too many of his short stories sprawl into the proper region of the novel. Take for example 'The Pool,' where the scene changes from the South Seas to Scotland and back to the South Seas, where the action covers years, and of which the subject is the marriage of white and half-caste. Nor did Maupassant's preference for the anecdote imply a method which Mr Maugham finds only too necessary: the method of the 'yarn,' of the first person singular. He defends the convention ably in his preface, but in a collected volume the monotony of the method becomes apparent. One has only to remember how this convention of the first person was transformed by Conrad, to realize a strange limitation to Mr Maugham's interest in his craft.

This air of being at ease in a Sion which he so candidly and rightly despises is rather pronounced in his defence of the popular magazines. As he explains in his preface, he came to the short story late in his career, he was already well known as a dramatist, and it is not surprising that his stories have always been welcomed by the magazines. His good fortune has blinded him to the demands which the popular magazine makes on its less famous writers. When he remarks: 'It has never been known yet that a good writer was unable to write his best owing to the conditions under which alone he could gain a public for his work,' he has been misled, I think, by his own success. Writers belonging to a less easily appreciated school than the anecdotal, who depend for their market on the intellectual magazine, are lucky if they can earn £20 by a short story, while the writer who fits the taste of the popular magazine may well earn £200. It is seldom that financial worry is a condition for the best work.

DON FERNANDO

London, June 1935; New York, July 1935

When *Don Fernando* was reissued in the Collected Edition of his work Maugham made substantial revisions in order to meet objections made by Raymond Mortimer in his *New Statesman* review (No. 101 below) and by Desmond MacCarthy in his *Sunday Times* review of *The Summing Up* (1938).

---

100. Graham Greene, 'Spanish Gold', *Spectator*

CLIV, 21 June 1935, 1076

'A writer,' Mr Maugham declares in these 'variations on some Spanish themes,' 'is not made by one book, but by a body of work. It will not be of equal value; his books will be tentative while he is learning the technique and developing his powers; and if, as most writers do, for it is a healthy occupation, he lives too long, his later work will show the decline due to advancing years; but there will be a period during which he will bring forth what he had it in him to bring forth in the perfection of which he is capable.' To this last-mentioned period *Don Fernando* belongs; it is Mr Maugham's best book.

It will be an unexpected book for those to whom Mr Maugham still primarily means: adultery in China, murder in Malaya, suicide in the South Seas, the coloured violent stories which have so appreciably raised the level of the popular magazine. But there is a more important Mr Maugham than that: the shrewd critical humane observer of *Cakes and Ale*, of the best Ashenden stories, of the preface to the collected tales. The characteristic most evident in these books and in *Don Fernando* is honesty. It has emerged slowly out of the cynical and romantic past; there are passages in *The Trembling of a Leaf* and *The Painted Veil* which Mr Maugham must find acutely embarrassing to remember, and it is interesting to learn in *Don Fernando* that Mr Maugham's extensive knowledge of Spanish literature was accumulated when he was young, to provide him with material for a romantic Juanesque novel which he never wrote. Instead of Don Juan then we have Don Fernando, the innkeeper and curio dealer who forced Mr Maugham unwillingly to buy an old life of Ignatius Loyola and it is with this life that his study of old Spain starts.

I have never read a book with more excitement and amusement. The contrast is peculiarly piquant between the opulence of the material (the fierce asceticisms of Loyola and St Peter of Alcantara, the conceits of Lope de Vega, the ribaldry of the picaresque novelists, the food and the architecture and the painters of Spain, the grim bright goaty land) and Mr Maugham's honest unenthusiastic mind. I do not mean pedantic or unimaginative. Honesty is a form of sensitivity, and you need a very sensitive ear to detect in the verbose plays of Calderon 'faintly audible, while this or the other is happening, the sinister drums of unseen powers.' Conrad defined art as 'a single-minded attempt to render the highest kind of justice to the visible universe,' and Mr Maugham here at the peak of his achievement as an artist renders it all the time. One may smile at the idea of Mr Maugham doing one of Loyola's 'Spiritual Exercises' and finding it extremely severe ('I thought I was going to be sick'), but it is that quality of honest experience which gives his style such vividness.

Tarragona has a cathedral that is grey and austere, very plain, with immense, severe pillars; it is like a fortress; a place of worship for headstrong, violent and cruel men. The night falls early within its walls and then the columns in the aisles seem to squat down on themselves and darkness shrouds the Gothic arches. It terrifies you. It is like a dungeon. I was there last on a Monday in Holy Week and from the pulpit a preacher was delivering a Lenten sermon. Two or three naked electric globes threw a cold light that cut the outline of the columns against the darkness as though with scissors.... Each angry, florid phrase was like a blow and one blow followed another with vicious insistence. From the farthest end of the majestic church, winding about the columns and curling round the groining of the arches, down the great austere nave and along the dungeon-like aisles, that rasping, shrewish voice pursued you.

Don Fernando may be superficially discursive; Mr Maugham is in turns critic, tourist, biographer (to find short lives as shrewd and amusing we must go back to Anthony à Wood and Aubrey), but he is working steadily forward towards the statement of his main argument: 'It looks as though all the energy, all the originality, of this vigorous race had been disposed to one end and one end only, the creation of man. It is not in art that they excelled, they excelled in what is greater than art—in man.' To that man Mr Maugham has rendered the highest kind of justice, whether he is the playwright of artificial situations or the unknown sailor who, when the Armenian bishop, Martyr, begged a passage, replied, 'I will take him in my ship; but tell him that I go to range the universal sea.'

101. Raymond Mortimer, 'Mr Maugham', *New Statesman and Nation*

n.s. IX, 29 June 1935, 966

Mr Somerset Maugham in his new book places a word upon a variety of subjects, Spanish saints and landscapes and writers, the aesthetic emotion, European food, mysticism, Baroque architecture and the human heart. To impose some appearance of unity upon his treatment of these subjects he has chosen a most curious form: *Don Fernando* is supposed to be the history of studies made by the author in preparation for a historical novel which he at last decided not to write. (It was about a young man who, after a life of picaresque adventure, became a monk, a theme very similar to that of one of his earliest books, *The Making of a Saint*.) Gide's *Journal des Faux Monnayeurs*, in which he describes the processes by which he made his great novel, is a book important to anyone professionally interested in literature; and a similar journal about an imaginary book would, in Mr Maugham's hands, be enthralling. Unluckily he has been content to use the form as a ramshackle framework, which seems to me to add very little to the book. Indeed the whole business of this unwritten novel is made so unconvincing that I begin to wonder if after all it is not true: if it were fiction, a novelist of Mr Maugham's accomplishment would have made it more probable.

Mr Maugham loves the Spaniards, but has no illusions about them. Not having illusions is, after all, one of his *spécialités de la maison*.

They have added surprisingly little to the great stock of thought that forms the working material of our world. They have produced neither a philosopher nor a man of science of the first rank. . . . The history of Spain in the Golden Age is a history of the abysmal ineptitude of which the human race is capable.

Moreover, 'Edgar Wallace is better than all the picaresque novelists put together,' and having read twenty-four plays by Lope de Vega and a dozen by Calderon, Mr Maugham has not much good to say of either. Of *Don Quixote* he declares that it is a very great work, but that it would be hard to find one of so much importance that had so many glaring defects. Incidentally he reveals the fact, unknown, I think, to most of us, that Cervantes lived on the immoral earnings of his sisters and daughter. Here is his comment:

I do not believe that there is any man who if the whole truth were known of him would not seem a monster of depravity; and also I believe that there are very few who have not at the same time virtue, goodness and beauty.

It is this view, behind a narrative skill most patiently developed, which has made Mr Maugham one of the few important novelists alive. Incidentally it is a profoundly civilised view, for nothing has caused more cruelty than the illusion that men are white or black, whereas really they are varying shades of grey. It is a view which has given Mr Maugham his reputation for cynicism, and the sentence quoted, therefore, seems to me perhaps the most significant in the book. For, eventually, one is less interested in what Mr Maugham tells us about Spain than in what he reveals about himself. He is notoriously the most enigmatic of our prominent writers. He never delights Pen Club dinners with whimsical speeches about his own character, nor does he even give the newspapers the benefit of his opinions on the Modern Girl, the Quantum Theory, and the composition of the Test Match Eleven. In his admirable stories he has perfected the use of the first person singular, but we are not expected to take as a self-portrait the bland *raconteur* at whose knees the sturdy planters confess their sins. I think there is more of Maugham himself in *Don Fernando* than in any of his books since *Of Human Bondage*. Even here he sometimes draws a red herring across the track: of Lope de Vega, for instance, he says that he 'was a good-natured, normal, sensual man. In fact he was exactly what a dramatist should be if he is to have success.' I think of our four most successful dramatists, Shaw, Barrie, Mr Coward, Maugham himself; and I wonder whether irony cannot be overdone. Here is another curious sentence:

I should say that the three essentials of good writing are lucidity, euphony, and simplicity; and their importance is according to the order in which I have placed them.

Evidently this knocks out Aeschylus, Tacitus, Shakespeare, Browne, Saint Simon, Browning, Kierkegaard, Rimbaud, Henry James, Proust, and in fact most of the best poets and a good proportion of the best prose-writers. But at least it squares with the author's practice: his prose is lucid almost to the point of colourlessness, and euphonious almost to the point of banality. We hardly notice the medium of communication; a thought arrests us, but very rarely a word. Mr Maugham has indeed brought this self-effacing technique almost to perfection. Stendhal, Maupassant, and Norman Douglas seem to have a similar aim, but their prose remains more personal than Mr Maugham's. It is an excellent method of writing, and has been used by some of the greatest. But it is not the only one.

Mr Maugham makes admirable remarks on Baroque architecture, including this most felicitous comment: 'Mass is but an instant in the unending curve of movement.' And here is an equally happy account, straight from the horse's mouth, of a view of the artist very like Mr Max Eastman's:

The work of art, whether the artist intended it or not—and for my part I think he seldom does—proffers a communication. This has nothing to do with the artist. From his standpoint it may only be a by-product of his activity: so the esculent swallows build nests for their young and are unaware that for their aphrodisiac qualities they will go to make soup for the enfeebled but amative Chinese.

The book is indeed packed with sentences which one would like to quote. One of the best passages describes the author's experience when he attempted one of the Spiritual Exercises of St Ignatius. I should have liked a fuller account of St Teresa—who combined with her mysticism a Machiavellian cunning in practical affairs to which Mr Maugham does less than justice. The most remarkable part of his book is that devoted to El Greco, whom he portrays as a clever and luxury-loving Levantine, never acclimatised in Spain, a sardonic humorist, a sceptic and at the same time a mystic. 'He stands on the bank, aloof and ironical, and watches the river of life flow on. He is persuaded that opinion is no more than prejudice.' Can it be that Mr Maugham when studying Greco's pictures sometimes saw his own face reflected in the glass?

Don Fernando is evidently and eminently a book written by Mr Maugham for his own pleasure. Parts of it are rather dull, notably seventeen pages, where seven would have been enough, of a Sixteenth Century Dialogue which he has disinterred. Presumably a considerable proportion of Mr Maugham's admirers will be disappointed—St John of the Cross is not everyone's cup of tea. This is a book for educated persons, written by one of the most intelligent men alive. Perhaps I should add, since stupidity is increasingly well thought of, that 'intelligent' seems to me one of the strongest epithets of praise.

102. Terence Holliday, 'The Love Story of Mr Maugham and Spain', *New York Herald Tribune*

21 July 1935, 7

Don Fernando is the triumphant record of a failure of a novel that never came to be written. It narrates the struggle of an artist who was seized by his material, at first exclusively engaged by it over a period of years, then partially preoccupied with it for a further period, and at last completely defeated by it. In a sense, *Don Fernando* is a disjected though happy love story, a reflection of the many facets of Mr Maugham's love of Spain, under whose enchantment he fell in his earliest and most impressionable writing years and whose glamour the passing of time has served only to deepen and intensify. But if the artist was disabled in his attempt to project his mistress into the objective realm of imaginative literature, the lover was the more eager to record and cherish and brood upon her beauties; the result, in this present volume, is an incomparably intimate, informed and revealing treatment of the Spanish genius, its palaces and churches, arts and letters, food and drink, mystics and picaroons.

Readers who recall Mr Maugham's earlier book on Spain, *The Land of the Blessed Virgin*, may note with surprise the author's present attitude toward it:

I am bitterly conscious of its defects.... In those days, at the end of the nineteenth century, the young were more immature than at present; they had not the knowing, clever way of concealing their ignorance that now fills with admiration those who have occasion to read their works.

These two sentences have been chosen with great care as characteristic of Mr Maugham's habitual approach to his material, as indicative of his detachment, candor and critical wit. For it must be observed that *Don Fernando* is by no means an exercise in rhetorical rhapsody. It includes no *con amore* obbligatos to sunsets or scenery. Instead, there are cool but deeply felt and often austere passages of great beauty, having their source in a mature awareness of things often seen with ever-increasing appreciation of their loveliness.

As writer, Mr Maugham is professional to the last degree; as traveler, reader, observer of painting and architecture, he has never lost the saving, distinguishing touch of the amateur. Who, save those who must, would endure another academic or pious dissertation on Cervantes or St Ignatius Loyola, St Teresa or Lope de Vega, Vicente Espinel or Fray Luis de Leon? These formidable figures, stiffened and formalized by age and conventional handling, come delightfully alive under Mr Maugham's fresh, invigorating touch, and yield an unexpected pleasure to the most casual and uninstructed reader.

Consider for a moment Don Fernando himself, he who gives the book its title, tavern-keeper of Seville in the street called Guzman el Bueno, wine-seller and dealer in curios, purveyor of a manzanilla that frequently tempted Mr Maugham out of his way. Don Fernando's exceptional taste included not only wines but the silver, lace, old fans, paste ornaments and antique rings that he solicited from the shabby-genteel among his neighbors and offered to the tourist. Amiable and even cordial relations were at once established between Don Fernando and Mr Maugham, and these endured until the appearance of

...the book...an ugly little volume, much too thick for its height, and the parchment with which it was bound was crinkled and yellow.

'I'll give it you for thirty pesetas; I lose five on it, but I want you to have it.'
'But I don't want the book,' I cried.
'Twenty-five pesetas.'
'No.'
'You needn't read it. Put it in your library.'
'I haven't got a library.'
'But you ought to have a library. Start your library with this book. It's a beautiful book.'
'It isn't a beautiful book.'
And it wasn't.

It was finally thrown in to make up the difference between the bid and asked price of a seventeenth-century wooden statuette of St Anthony, carried home by the reluctant and conquered buyer, and forgotten. And then one rainy afternoon Mr Maugham picked it up in an idle moment, turned a few pages and began to read. What followed, here translated and set down in Mr Maugham's superb style, is the strangest and most moving story in all the literature of Spain: the early life of Don Iñigo de Oñaz, better known as St Ignatius Loyola, as related not long after his death by Father Pedro de Ribadeneyra of the Company of Jesus.

A more moderate enthusiasm appears in the estimate of St Teresa's talents and accomplishments, and even the glories of the Spanish drama and picaresque romance are criticized with some severity and praised with restraint. But the extended consideration of El Greco is the most notable section of the book, and on this pregnant topic Mr Maugham offers a number of original and arresting judgments. These will be read with pained astonishment by those who have been content to accept at second hand the estimates of the more popular esthetic specialists. Mr Maugham has familiarized himself with the scanty records of El Greco's life, and has repeatedly observed and considered the paintings at first hand; the spell of that curious, baffling and sinister genius has stimulated his imagination and intelligence to the formulation of several highly unconventional opinions. Mr Maugham's own genius is too skeptical, ironic and humane to allow the suggestion that his findings are conclusive.

It would be the height of impertinence at this late date to praise, or even to enumerate, Mr Maugham's merits as a master of the writer's craft; in *Don Fernando* he has much to say on the subject of literary technique. So not only must this book be heartily commended to the Hispanophile and the general reader who enjoys the play of a lively, sophisticated and civilized intelligence, but it must be urged particularly on the young, the inexperienced or beginning writer. Mr Maugham is himself on the side of the professional. But he adds:

It is, however, true that the amateur has some advantages that may give his work charm. The occasions of his life may provide him with a subject that is in itself interesting. He may have an attractive freshness. If his character is engaging or odd, his inexperience may allow him to reveal it so unaffectedly that his work has a quality of delight. Sincerity and a natural distinction sometimes enable him to string words together with clearness and elegance. But this is rare. To write simply is as difficult as to be good.

103. Osbert Sitwell, 'The Spain of Somerset Maugham', *London Mercury*

XXXII, September 1935, 485–6

(Sir) Osbert Sitwell (1892–1969) is best known for his autobiographical memoirs, *Left Hand! Right Hand!* (1945) and the four further volumes. He was also the author of books of verse, *Wrack at Tidesend* (1952), *On the Continent* (1958), short stories and travel-writing.

Mr Somerset Maugham and Mr W.B. Yeats, artists so different in their outlook and in the nature of their work, are yet alike in this one respect; that they are the only writers with a reputation established for many years who never for a moment rest on their laurels, but continually aspire to new perfection and to a fresh technique. Here, certainly, the similarity ends; for one is rich in satire, and the other, perhaps, with all his magnificent gifts, possesses it to a lesser degree. Yet, in this new and exciting book, *Don Fernando*, Mr Maugham carefully controls his sense of satire, and reveals what, to many, will be a new vein.

The first thing to be said about *Don Fernando* is that it is an intensely orginal work, as pleasant to read, as quickly read, as any book that has taken but a tenth of the thought and feeling that must have gone to the making of this one. It has the curious, controlled easiness, the limpid, effortless phraseology, that have given Mr Maugham his great public, and have, at the same time, tended to make those persons to whom the difficulty of a work constitutes its virtue underrate his value as a writer. Nobody, you would have thought, could be so dense as to underrate the value of such books as *Of Human Bondage, On a Chinese Screen* or *Cakes and Ale*; such rich and varied work. And yet, just as people exist who, because they see no ripple of muscles behind the expert movement of a trained athlete, do not seize the virtuosity of it, so there are those who seem to take Mr Maugham at his own modest value. This book should certainly dispel their illusions.

What other author could have given us this particular work, so simple, so complicated, and leaving behind it such a strong flavour of Spain; of Spain as it really is, and really was; a book as full of national character as Borrow's, but owing nothing to previous English writers on Spain? ...Perhaps it is necessary, if you would write about the Peninsula, to find a formula which enables you to digress. His queer trade supplied this formula to Borrow: but Mr Maugham, with his novelist who went to Spain to write a book, has contrived one for himself. (Alas! now that he has found this personal recipe, it is certain that others, ungifted, will follow him.)

How illuminating, too, are his side-shots: his few remarks, for example, upon Zurbaran; an artist whom no one unacquainted with the south of Spain can appreciate; 'Zurbaran is not a painter for whom many people feel enthusiasm. You have to know him well, and study him, to realise how remarkable an artist he was. He

had power, and that is a quality you seldom find in painters. But this is not the place to say much of him, and my immediate business is only with these portraits' (of Carthusian monks)....
'They are painted with the tightness that characterized him. Those white robes do not seem made of wool, but of a material as rigid as baize, and the folds have none of the yielding quality of stuff; they might be carved in wood. But the harshness, the stiffness, of the manner gives you rather a curious feeling. It may be repellent, but it does not leave you indifferent.'

The reviewer of this book has travelled often in Spain, and stayed many months there. To him at any rate, *Don Fernando* has brought back a thousand incidents he had forgotten, and explained a thousand small happenings that he had not understood. The book is as full of character as are the landscapes, the wines, the food or the persons Mr Maugham describes. It is, moreover, rich in information of the most interesting kind, but so politely presented—without any of the 'look what I know!' airs of the minor writer—that the reader feels he has put himself in possession of the facts.

COSMOPOLITANS

New York, February 1936; London, March 1936

Although these brief sketches, when compared with Maugham's previous five volumes of short stories which make up the content of *East and West* (*Altogether*), cannot properly be described as 'the mixture as before', the title the *Times* reviewer gave to his review of *Cosmopolitans*, Maugham used the phrase as the title of his next collection of stories (1940).

104. Florence Haxton Britten, review, *New York Herald Tribune*

23 February 1936, 10

Cosmopolitans is a smartly named collection of what are known to the trade as short-shorts. Mr W. Somerset Maugham, most competent of story tellers, wrote them between 1924 and 1929 to make double-page spreads for the late Mr Ray Long's *Cosmopolitan Magazine*. These little stories are cosmopolitans in another sense. 'I am of a roving disposition,' the narrator announces in the first sentence of one of them—and speaks most accurately for Mr Maugham himself. For the *mise en scene* of these fictive excursions ranges from Vladivostok to Seville, from Thursday Island to Claridge's, and from Capri and Paris to Guatemala City and Shanghai.

It would be impossible for Mr Maugham to write a dull story, or an incompetent one. But in this collection of twenty-nine little anecdotes of the wide, wide world and the seven seas he comes as close to going over the edge about twenty-nine times as Charlie Chaplin on roller skates does in *Modern Times*. His recoveries—like Charlie's—are occasionally superb.

Mr Maugham at his best conveys a sense of the enjoyment of an infinite leisure in which to observe, with detachment and cynical amusement, the absurd yet somehow always appropriate foibles of human kind. In *Cosmopolitans* his usual fascinating verbosity is sharply checked. In the first two or three stories, particularly, the feeling of compression is positively painful. As he adjusts himself to the limitations of space, Mr Maugham is able occasionally to stretch a bit and stroll up and down the scene in a few paragraphs of introduction or of witty *obiter dicta*. ('They were very rich old men and that was a bond between them,' he says—for example—in 'Straight Flush.' 'The rich feel at ease,' he goes on, 'in one another's company. They know that money means merit. Their experience of the poor is that they always want something. It is true that the poor admire the rich and it is pleasant to be admired, but they envy them as well and this prevents their admiration from being quite candid....')

But for all his sardonic worldliness peering through the lines, the total effect of *Cosmopolitans* is one of triviality. It is as though an important actor were stepping out of his extended role to appear before the curtain in a little *entr'acte* patter. Mr Maugham has not the knack of building up a quick, inevitable surprise plot (the very best use to which the short-short story can be turned) nor is he able, like Kay Boyle, for instance, to give a tremendous sense of the integrity of her theme and her relation to it in what amounts almost to a swatch of her goods. Mr Maugham tries both these methods and, for the most part, fails.

And apologizes, it seems to me, both in context and introduction for the slightness of his present accomplishment. He speaks, in 'A String of Beads,' of another story contained in the collection. '"We've all heard [says his dinner companion] of wives palming off on their husbands as false a string of pearls that was real and expensive. That story is as old as the hills."' '"Thank you," I said, thinking of a little narrative of my own.'

And in a very interesting but, I think, arguable preface he says: 'I could not waste a word. I had to be succinct. I was surprised to find out how many adverbs and adjectives I could leave out without harm to the matter or the manner. One often writes needless words because they give the phrase a better ring.'

One does indeed. But I fancy that when a sense of parsimony creeps into any piece of creative work which is not apropos of the thing itself, then the work, both in idea and form, is likely to be scamped. And it seems to me that *Cosmopolitans*, a merely—though quite—acceptable series of short stories by one of the most brilliant story tellers of our day, is a case in point. A delay of seven years in getting these tales between covers is in itself, I presume, an acknowledgment.

105. Unsigned review, 'Mr Maugham's Mixture as Before', *Times*

31 March 1936, 10

These twenty-nine 'very short stories' owe their brevity to journalistic exigence. Mr Maugham tells us that he had to adapt himself to his new medium, but his technique remains very much what it has been in his longer stories: the 'beginning, middle and end' that he insists on remain the almost (but never quite) irrelevant beginning, in which atmosphere is gently suggested by Narrator No. 1; the essential middle, in which Narrator No. 2 reveals the sting of the tale; and, finally, the fading away that is never either bathos or anticlimax.

But Mr Maugham does not wish us to bother much about technique. 'Entertainment' is the criterion by which he would have the reader judge him—('I ask nothing from him but that he should find them amusing')—and amusing entertainment the majority of these very short stories certainly provide. (There are a few tragedies—the break-up of the profound but comic friendship of four fat Dutchmen, and more than one broken marriage.) Mr Maugham's 'cosmopolitans' belong, as usual, to every quarter of the terrestrial globe (even, in one instance, to the celestial spheres): a full-blooded Italian chef in Asia minor; an American doctor hidden in Italy by a wife with social aspirations in London; a

London verger who, sacked for illiteracy, made a fortune as a tobacconist; card-sharpers (if such they were) in Peking; 'German Harry,' a Danish hermit in the Torres Straits; a sponger in Guatemala; a beggar in Vera Cruz—and other denizens of ports, east and west, where travelling novelists drink 'gin pahits' over their cards waiting for ships great or small. The stories are all very slight and may not add greatly to the author's reputation; but if read 'one or two now and then,' as directed, they will not noticeably diminish it.

THEATRE

New York, London, March 1937

106. Bernard DeVoto, 'Master of Two Dimensions', *Saturday Review of Literature* (New York)

XV, 6 March 1937, 3

Bernard Augustine DeVoto (1897–1955) was professor of English at Northwestern University and Harvard, and editor of the *Saturday Review of Literature*. He was an authority on Mark Twain.

Mr Maugham's new novel is well named. Quite apart from the fact that its principal characters are actors, it has the speed, smoothness, and entertainment of an expert theater piece. One reads it with complete absorption, surrendered to the skill of a novelist who has mastered his trade. The effects are prepared in precisely the right way and occur with the utmost naturalness, the timing is sure, the dialogue is superb. Structurally and thematically it is journeyman work without a flaw, as fine a specimen of the well made novel as this generation has seen. Mr Maugham is a professional novelist, he is competent in all the instrumentalities of his craft, and he manipulates them with a disciplined suavity that has the pleasure of the reader always in mind. A well made novel, however, is like a well made play: one rises from it thankful for being amused but beginning to forget what happened in the first act.

Mr Maugham, who has always practised a severe economy of ideas, is here occupied with the superficial and even the second rate.

His heroine, Julia Gosselyn, the great actress who projects into her own life the emotions, attitudes, and effects she has learned in the theater, belongs to a type long exploited even by the popular magazines; and though Mr Maugham refines the type and fluffs it up with his magnificent dialogue, he neither adds to it nor gives it life. Her husband, Michael, the handsome, hard-working, vain and unintelligent actor-manager, and her kept lover, Thomas Fennell, the young man on the make, are types from the earlier theater of Mr Maugham. He makes a lively and varied display of these, and of other puppets labeled 'fool' and 'cad.' His hand is much quicker than the eye, it is all brisk, revelatory, and epigrammatic, and it goes to show that we are nowhere near so fine and clever as we think, and, when you come down to it, we are just animals after all. Mr Maugham enjoys himself pointing out the splendors we haven't got, and never breathes deeply. But, a specialist in emptiness and pretense, he never gets to important vacuums and illusions, and even when he has his characters in bed, where he is at his best, his comedy consists in avoiding rather than utilizing the sources of comedy.

The result is excellent entertainment, a skillful and self-conscious fantasia on vanity, cupidity, jealousy, spite, stupidity, histrionism, minor brutalities, sexual possessiveness, and the no longer secret power of personal odors to inspire passion—in short, Noel Coward without tears. That it is no more, that in spite of Mr Maugham's cherished boutonniere of cynicism he does not write robust comedy, is due to his inability to respect the integrity of his characters' emotions. Even in this puppet-show it sometimes becomes necessary for Julia to feel an emotion, and then the play goes flat. Mr Maugham can only tell us that she fell in love, experienced ecstasy, or was plunged into despair: he cannot endow her with the feeling. He tells us that her consequent behavior was pretty funny but it is only theater; and you can no more be cynical about emotions you don't believe in than you can be heartbroken about them. Mr Maugham's attitude robs his comedy of edge, for perfunctory ignobility is just as ham as perfunctory nobility, and the reader ends by admiring the dexterity of the derision but glad to get out of the playhouse into the street, where the profanity of taxi-drivers is heartfelt. *Theatre* is first-rate hammock reading for people with high I.Q.'s.

107. Elizabeth Bowen, 'A Straight Novel', *New Statesman and Nation*

n.s. XIII, 27 March 1937, 525

Elizabeth Bowen (1899–1973), one of the leading English novelists and story-writers of her generation, wrote a weekly book review in the *Tatler* for many years and occasionally, as here, reviewed for the *New Statesman* (when Raymond Mortimer was literary editor). Her books include: *The Hotel* (1927), *Joining Charles* (1929), *The Death of the Heart* (1938) and *The Little Girls* (1964).

Mr Somerset Maugham still writes the classic, or straight, novel: there is nothing tricky about his construction; he does not make telling cuts, shoot from unlikely angles or vary his distance from the object in view. *Theatre* is straight narrative, not photography: he has an almost hypnotic command of narrative style; not a sentence stops the mind and each leads on to another in a rapid overlap. This is a style that is neutral, functional, and fully efficient, the servant not the mistress of the writer's invention, a method perfected (within its own limits) not a preoccupation. Not a phrase is there for its own sake; transparency to meaning is the object, not colour; not a phrase obtrudes romantic complexity. For its activity, Mr Maugham's style is stripped: there is no atmosphere, no American cuteness, no attempted poetry: it is professional writing, without a touch of amateur privilege—and this is pretty rare now. Rare also—a good deal too rare—is a novel not setting up to be anything but a novel, not made the parade-ground of indignation or fantasy. It might not be well to make Mr Maugham a model, but he should set a precept: he might correct our tendencies to maunder, to exhibit or to denounce. With first-rate ability, but without high-class fuss, he drops a plumb-line into the subject. Here is a personality so positive, so pickled in experience it attracted, that it can use style impersonally. The professional has not time for stunts.

Theatre is a story told from one point of view—that of the actress heroine, Julia Lambert. This centralising of the story in one person, a person at the same time visible to the reader, makes for emotional unity and brings the other characters into scale so satisfactorily that one wonders why the method has, lately, lapsed. It is possible that only the accomplished writer can hope to sustain what might be monotony. Julia's values—assessed by the author with satirical coldness or, still more coldly, made to assess themselves—alone give the action significance, and so make the plot. Her blunders and limitations are used (like *Emma's*) to let counterplot appear: her shrewdness is at fault when emotion twists it, or vanity. That a good deal is going on that *she* does not, cannot or will not perceive, is obvious: the reader, at an impassive glance from the author, picks up inferences, signals she overlooks. Hence the excitement of this exciting book: it is like a film in which someone will not see what is coming. But the element of surprise is always present: you were not so much in on the joke as you had thought.

This is comedy on a rather painful plane, with a few bad moments, some grand ones, and embarrassments that bring the heart to the mouth. Julia Lambert, in private life Mrs Michael Gosselyn, portrayed with good-tempered malice, some sympathy and an occasional tightening of Mr Maugham's cruelty, is a forceful, engaging, never romantic figure. Her interior monologue, some of her conversation, is energetic and bawdy; she has a touch of the trooper; her behaviour in love or society is controlled, languid, artful in the exact sense—it may be said to be dictated, as a religious person's behaviour is dictated. Success and massage have preserved her youth for her up to forty-six: her heart, when she meets Tom—a dim young man from an office, brought home to lunch by her husband—is both young and free. She brings her life to her acting, on one occasion, with what looked like being fatal results for a play, but she can always borrow her acting for her life, save her face, bluff in impossible situations or retrieve some dangerous spontaneity. In her naivety, her ruthlessness, her coarseness, her impatience with her own suffering, the major artist appears: she hates (though abides by) dieting, and likes love. Her duplicity is natural and automatic—she is two people: seldom are both present. It is possible that the profession of acting may sublimate in the female the falsity, insatiable monomania and anti-human vanity that Mr Maugham so detests: at all events, Julia is one of his most agreeable heroines.

Theatre is not a documentary novel of back-stage life, an analysis of its glamour or of its hopes and fears. This is theatre life at its suavest, most settled and least Bohemian—for which I, for one, am thankful. The cast of the novel are already successful people, full of shrewdness and energy, without waste emotion, subject in one case only to the aberrations of love. Massage and the siesta, dressing-room comforts, cutlets and creamed spinach, costly respectable pleasures, photographers and reposing riverside week-ends are the routine. Julia (except once in her lover's arms) seldom thinks of the theatre: she *is* the theatre. Outside that intense existence, never quite interrupted, life is a mesh of detail through which her placid husband, her disconcerting son, her dresser, her rich woman friend, her platonic lover appear. Only Tom, or her passion for him, cuts near the quick of her life and begins to impinge on art.

Julia's first and last stage appearances inside the bounds of the novel, before and after the love-affair, have the same calm:

Having addressed the envelope she threw the card in the wastepaper basket and was ready to slip into her first-act dress. The call-boy came round knocking at the dressing-room doors.

'Beginners, please.'

Those words, though heaven only knew how often she had heard them, still gave her a thrill. They braced her like a tonic. Life acquired significance. She was about to step from the world of make-believe into the world of reality.

The mature woman's infatuation for a young lover, the distinguished person's obsession with a nonentity, sounds a stale enough subject: here it takes new irony and—by Julia's control of the situation from her disadvantageous position—a curious bold grace. Julia's eagerness for love and royal high-handedness expose her to a string of humiliations from the recalcitrant, muddled and common Tom, avid for luxury but suspicious of being bought up. He hurts her a little deliberately, but—as with most objects of misguided affection—his main power to hurt is in his stupidity. Every degree of that torture inflicted by stupid beloveds on highly organised lovers is noted by Mr Maugham. Julia is not on the Proust scale, but her suffering, her ironic sense of the falseness of the position, is in the Swann and Charlus tradition. By making Julia something more than a woman, giving her the artist's bi-sexuality, Mr Maugham has been able to generalise her love. Julia is so far masculine in that love with her has an aesthetic element: she fell out of love with her husband when his beauty was over; Tom's extreme youth, with its particular attributes, is a strong factor in her feeling for him. Her lack of bunk about this, her unreflecting pleasure at the affair's outset, and her personal greatness—as much greatness at least as Mr Maugham will allow her—make her affair with Tom, for all its humiliations, grandiose and unsordid. Her doubleness, the Phoenix vitality of the actress side of her nature, make it impossible for her to be wholly trapped: at the same time, these contribute to Tom's uneasiness. The situation between them, its phases and variations, is magnificently realised—and generalised.

The sum of *Theatre* is: an astringent tragi-comedy, with twin subjects, love and art. Mr Maugham anatomises emotion without emotion; he handles without pity a world where he finds no pity. His disabused clearness and hardness do, it is true, diminish any subject a little. If great art has to have an inherent kindness, his is not great art. But what a writer he is!

THE SUMMING UP

London, January 1938; New York, March 1938

108. Montgomery Belgion, review, *Criterion*

XVII, 1938, 748–52

Harold Montgomery Belgion (1892–1973) was in his youth a
journalist (chief sub-editor *Westminster Gazette*, 1924–5).
After service in two world wars he became known as a man
of letters with right-wing views and an intimate knowledge
of modern French culture. His books include *The Humanist
Parrot* (1937), *News of the French* (1938) and *The Worship of
Quantity: A Study of Megapolitics* (1969), and studies of
modern writers including Poe, H.G. Wells and Malraux.

News is treated and presented in the English popular press very
differently to-day from twenty-five years ago. Instead of being
expected to attend for the length of a column or half-a-column to
the details of single events, the reader can pass from item to item
without pause. The shortness of reports and the way both they and
their headings overlap and vie with one another imply a belief on
the part of those who produce our newspapers that the reader of
1938 demands a constant shift of attention and that only he who
jumps will read. It is a belief which has begun to spread to the
purveyors of books. Now, albeit for different reasons, the book
too tends to be an affair of snippets. The volume of disjointed
reminiscences and gossip was of course already familiar. But to-day
heterogeneity of content is appearing in literary *genres* where

cohesion and a homogeneous subject-matter had seemed essential. Mr André Malraux's latest production, *L'Espoir*—of which an English translation is likely to be available by the time these words are published—is labelled a novel. But it is neither the study of character nor the account of how a certain situation arose and was resolved which a novel commonly proves to be. The hero, so to speak, of *L'Espoir* is the Spanish civil war. Mr Malraux has wished to convey the atmosphere on the Republican side. He himself has been in Spain; but he has relied on his imagination and on what he may have been told as much as, if not more than, on what he can have seen. He has not written a diary. His field is too wide to have been encompassed by any single personal experience. But he has entirely dispensed with plot. *L'Espoir*, therefore, is at least of technical interest. In it a novel has been given much of the snippety form of the contemporary English newspaper. Mr Maugham's book has the same relation to an autobiography that *L'Espoir* has to a novel proper. It stands midway between the autobiographical *genre* and such a collection of seemingly haphazard reminiscences as Dr Halliday Sutherland's *The Arches of the Years*. It is an arrangement of snippets.

This is not pointed out with any intent of reproach. A newspaper is not put together by chance; and that Dr Sutherland in *The Arches of the Years* selected with art his two subsequent volumes have made very evident. In any case, Mr Maugham no more wished to write an autobiography than Mr Malraux a conventional novel. Some time ago Mr Malraux remarked that a recent instalment of Mr Gide's *Journal* afforded an instance of how a *document* could sometimes succeed better than fiction in communicating the feel of actual life. In *L'Espoir*, then, he must obviously have intended to produce an imaginative *document*. In the same way, Mr Maugham has wanted to set down his reflections 'on the subjects that have chiefly interested' him 'during the course of' his life. The subjects range from the rich and powerful with whom he came in contact upon attaining celebrity to truth, beauty, and goodness. There are sections on producing a play and on actors. But the greater part of the book is about writing. The striking thing is that whereas *L'Espoir* must be pronounced dull,* *The Summing Up* is continuously entertaining from the first to almost the last of its 317

* However, it entrances Mr. Gide. Cf. *Nouvelle Revue française* (May).

pages and (as I shall indicate) in many sections instructive as well. Its having been a 'best-seller' was only to be expected.

What makes that striking is that to inject the quality of *continuous* readability into a collection of snippets cannot be easy. According to Mr Maugham, the most effective and the easiest way of securing a reader's attention for the whole of a book is to supply what he calls 'direction of interest'; it is, that is to say, to employ—in his own words—'the method by which an author causes you to concern yourself with the fortunes of certain people under certain conditions and keeps you attached to them till he has reached his solution'. Needless to say, the method is the same for the fortunes of one person as for those of a group. But employing this 'direction of interest' is just what Mr Maugham had to forgo in not writing an autobiography even as Mr Malraux in not writing a real novel. It is true that as Mr Malraux does precariously hold together his otherwise discrete incidents or episodes by always making the participants in them one or the other of two small recurring groups of characters, so Mr Maugham gives some cohesion to his reflections by being frequently autobiographical in passing. He mentions that he was born and spent his childhood in Paris, that he was early left an orphan. He specifies the stages of his formal education. He indicates whither he has travelled. He records the fortunes of his early novels, his experiences with plays, his turning to the short story. He wrote six full-length plays and waited ten years before obtaining production on the commercial stage, and then he had four plays running at once. He says what he did during the War. He analyses his powers. He discloses peculiarities, such as that he once stammered and that he has 'never experienced the bliss of requited love'. (The latter statement is illuminating. It shows that Mr Maugham has written so frequently about a one-sided passion, not simply because he considers that situation effective, but because he looks on it as particularly true to life.) And also in passing he, as it were unconsciously, portrays himself, leading the reader to see him as industrious, persevering, full of common sense, and agreeably unassuming. But in spite of the autobiographical cement, there can be no doubt that in producing so admirable a book with his chosen material he has accomplished a feat.

The feat emphasizes a truth not generally recognized. It is that of all living prose writers Mr Maugham is the one the aspirant of letters who desires to be read, who wants

not to please the cook's taste but the guests,

must find it most profitable to study. For nearly everything that has come from Mr Maugham's pen is in the nature of a feat. None of his novels is without momentum, but most of them will not seem more substantial for being dissected. The incidents composing *Mrs Craddock*, for instance, do not of themselves form a climax, they might well be in another order; and the supervening crisis is imposed on rather than begotten by what precedes. So in *The Moon and Sixpence*, once the narrator has run down Charles Strickland in Paris and has heard from Stroeve that Strickland's paintings are the work of a genius, the tale is over. What follows is but a succession of scraps. Indeed, *The Moon and Sixpence*—as Mr Maugham acknowledges in the preface to the current edition—had to be eked out with material taken from a magazine. Even in *Of Human Bondage*, which is deemed his best novel and is more nearly than any of the others a connected whole, the picture of life is very one-sided and fragmentary. It might seem that he is not so much a novelist as a writer of short stories. Yet many of the short stories fail to move the reader owing to their artificiality, and there is about the solution of their plots a monotonous sameness. He remarks in *The Summing Up* that he has had 'variety of invention' but 'small power of imagination'. That is borne out by those stories of his which vary in plot but are identical in theme. Likewise the material of his plays, as he would no doubt be the first to admit, is usually very slight. The coldness which met the most ambitious of them—*Sheppey* and *For Services Rendered*—is not due to the public's want of perception. The author has not been profound enough for what he wanted to attempt. Really Mr Maugham has never had anything to say beyond that people are not all of a piece, that although the most violent sexual passion may be unreciprocated women are gross and easily fall a prey to their senses, and that numerous wives hate their husbands and numerous husbands their wives. If, then, he has been able to win the admiration as well as the favour of the public, it can only be that whether he is constructing a play, telling a short story, or *beginning* a novel, he does his job to perfection. As regards his plays in particular, Racine would certainly have approved the skill with which in *Home and Beauty*, for example, he has made *quelque chose de rien*; and at the same time as this farce is built out of nothing its neat and highly absurd third act is in the tradition of that *Silent Woman* of Ben Jonson's which Dryden extols. In short, Mr Maugham is a first-rate craftsman. And with him this means not only that he has given value for the fortune which his work has brought him, not only that there must be assigned to him a high place in contemporary letters. It means also that he has always treated writing as a profession. That, he remarks in *The Summing Up*, is what every one should do who would be an author. It might be thought that there he is at variance with Coleridge, who declared—out of his own experience—that the writer courts wretchedness if he relies on the pen as his sole means of support. But he is not. In insisting that the writer should be professional, he simply means that 'to write must be the main object of the author's life'; and he adds: 'Swift with his deanery, Wordsworth with his sinecure, were just as much professional writers as Balzac and Dickens.'

What accordingly he has to say in *The Summing Up* about writing is the accumulated wisdom of a successful professional writer in this sense, and it is there that both the main interest and the importance of the book lie. The concluding sections on truth, beauty, and goodness, and also on God and immortality, are negligible. Of course those momentous problems have fascinated him and he is aware that at times they more or less fascinate us all. But it is odd that, after putting such a strong case for professionalism in authorship, he should not have realized that metaphysics are better professional too. He says himself:

It is very unlikely that the dramatist who is lucky enough to have been born with the faculty of putting things so that they carry across the footlights will also be an original thinker.

No wonder, then, that where he would be metaphysical he is hardly as much as an amateur! This does not prevent the book as a whole from being the model of a form in which it is difficult to hold the reader's attention. For that reason it will repay being closely examined by those who try to handle a pen. Furthermore, although Mr Maugham, as he says, at first took to writing as a duck to water, it was to dawn on him presently that writing is 'a delicate art' needing to be 'painfully acquired', and he proceeded to study it. Because this experience governs what he has to say on the subject, and also especially because the philosophy of authorship which he expresses in the course of these pages is above all professional and practical, he must be said to have provided on writing and the writer the best treatise of our time.

109. Graham Greene, 'Maugham's Pattern', *Spectator*

CLX, 14 January 1938, 59

Kinglake once referred to 'that nearly immutable law which compels a man with a pen in his hand to be uttering every now and then some sentiment not his own,' and compared an author with a French peasant under the old *régime*, bound to perform a certain amount of work upon the public highways. I doubt if any author has done—of recent years—less highway labour than Mr Maugham. I say 'of recent years' because, as he himself admits in this summing-up of his life and work, he passed like other writers through the stage of tutelage—and to the most unlikely people, the translators of the Bible and Jeremy Taylor. That stage lasted longer with Mr Maugham than with most men of equal talent—there is at the heart of his work a humility and a self-distrust rather deadening in their effects, and his stories as late as *The Painted Veil* were a curious mixture of independent judgement when he was dealing with action and of *clichés* when he was expressing emotion.

An author of talent is his own best critic—the ability to criticise his own work is inseparably bound up with his talent: it *is* his talent, and Mr Maugham defines his limitations perfectly: 'I knew that I had no lyrical quality. I had a small vocabulary and no efforts that I could make to enlarge it much availed me. I had little gift of metaphor; the original and striking simile seldom occurred to me,' and in a passage—which is an excellent example of his hard-won style at its best, clear, colloquial, honest—he relates his limitations to his character:

It did not seem to me enough merely to write. I wanted to make a pattern of my life, in which writing would be an essential element, but which would include all the other activities proper to man...I had many disabilities. I was small; I had endurance but little physical strength; I stammered; I was shy; I had poor health. I had no facility for games, which play so great a part in the normal life of Englishmen; and I had, whether for any of these reasons or from nature I do not know, an instinctive shrinking from my fellow-men that has made it difficult for me to enter into any familiarity with them ... Though in the course of years I have learned to assume an air of heartiness when forced into contact with a stranger, I have never liked anyone at first sight. I do not think I have ever addressed someone I did not know in a railway carriage or spoken to a fellow-passenger on board ship unless he first spoke to me. ... These are grave disadvantages both to the writer and the man. I have had to make the best of them. I have followed the pattern I have made with persistence.... I think it was the best I could hope for in the circumstances and with the very limited powers that were granted to me by nature.'

'It did not seem enough to me merely to write,' and even in this personal book the author is unwilling to communicate more than belongs to his authorship; he does not, like a professional autobiographer, take us with commercial promptitude into his confidence. His life has contained material for dramatisation, and he has used it for *fiction*. There is the pattern in his writing and we are not encouraged to look for its reverse in life: the hospital career (the public pattern is in *Liza of Lambeth*); the secret agent in Geneva (we can turn to *Ashenden*); the traveller—there are many books. The sense of privacy, so rare and attractive a quality in an author, deepens in the bare references to secret service experience in Russia, just before the Revolution, of which we find no direct trace in his stories.

The nearest Mr Maugham comes to a confidence is in the description of his religious belief—if you can call agnosticism a belief, and the fact that on this subject he is ready to speak to strangers makes one pause. There are signs of muddle, contradictions...hints of an inhibition. Otherwise one might trace here the deepest source of his limitations, for creative art seems to remain a function of the religious mind. Mr Maugham the agnostic is forced to minimise—pain, vice, the importance of his fellowmen. He cannot believe in a God who punishes and he cannot therefore believe in the importance of a human action. 'It is not difficult,' he writes, 'to forgive people their sins'—it sounds like charity, but it may be only contempt. In another passage he refers with

understandable scorn to writers who are 'grandiloquent to tell you
whether or no a little trollop shall hop into bed with a
commonplace young man.' That is a plot as old as *Troilus and
Cressida*, but to the religious sixteenth-century mind there was no
such thing as a commonplace young man or an unimportant sin;
the creative writers of that time drew human characters with a
clarity we have never regained (we had to go to Russia for it later)
because they were lit with the glare and significance that war lends.
Rob human beings of their heavenly and their infernal importance,
and you rob characters of their individuality ('What should a
Socialist woman do?'), and it has never been Mr Maugham's
characters that we have remembered so much as the narrator, with
his contempt for human life, his unhappy honesty.

110. Stephen Vincent Benét, 'A Self-Taught Trade', *Saturday Review of Literature* (New York)

XVII, 16 April 1938, 3–4

Stephen Vincent Benét (1898–1943) was a Pulitzer Prize-
winning poet whose work includes *John Brown's Body* (1928)
and *The Devil and Daniel Webster* (1937).

Time brings its revenges and, somehow or other, the characterization of Mr Maugham, by his publishers, on the jacket of his last
book, as 'the dean of living English novelists,' brings with it a
certain sense of shock. For the record is there for anybody to look
at—and yet deans are deans. They may be bland or irate—great
men or small—but it is a little difficult to see Mr Maugham in that
particular cabbage-patch. It is rather like calling a very efficient
tiger the oldest lion in the zoo.

For Mr Maugham is that anomaly among English novelists—a
professional writer who has known the precise uses of his skill and

thought a great deal about its exercise. He has seldom tried to be lyric, he has never been a reformer. He has never, to my knowledge, pulled out either the patriotic or the sentimental stop. The love of the English countryside, the humors of rustics, the rambling roominess of the English novel—these are absent from his work in great quantities. Yet he has been able, in his greatest book, to portray human passion, aspiration, and defeat, and to do so without cant or exaggeration. That is a good deal for any writer to have done.

Now, most young writers have a burning desire to know how the trick is done—or any part of it. But there are very few ways of their finding out, for writing is a self-taught trade. And few textbooks on the subject give anything worth the getting. They do not because their authors lack, for the most part, one essential—an individual creative impulse sufficiently strong to write, successfully, other things besides textbooks. But when a skilled man talks about his own ways of work, with candor, he is always worth listening to, even if you intend to do an entirely different sort of work yourself.

There has not been very much of that sort of talk in English letters since Fielding's prefatory essays in *Tom Jones*—talk at once instructed and wise. And, on the whole, the poets have done rather better at it than the prose writers. But, among the recent books of autobiography or semi-autobiography, there are two which, it seems to me, would be extremely valuable to any young writer. One is Maugham's *The Summing Up* and the other is Kipling's *Something of Myself.*

To say so is neither to compare the two books and the two men—nor to say that, by reading them, you will immediately be able to write *Of Human Bondage* or *Puck of Pook's Hill* in five easy lessons. But both books have one thing which most textbooks lack—the actual, professional point of view of the professional writer, and—less in Kipling, more in Maugham—a good deal of description of the actual work involved in becoming a writer at all. For most of us begin by thinking we can do it all on desire, and are horribly disappointed when we fail. The drawer in the table sticks—the house is lopsided—and yet we had such a fine idea of a house. Why didn't it turn out like that—isn't writing just a business of putting down a number of words on paper? Well, no, it is a little more than that—and why it is more than that, both books very clearly show.

Sometimes, too, they say the same things—or their approximate—and it is interesting to note the likeness. It is interesting to compare Kipling's 'Mercifully, the mere act of writing was, and always has been, a physical pleasure to me,' with Maugham's 'When I began to write I did so as though it were the most natural thing in the world. I took to it as a duck takes to water;'—to compare again Kipling's statement, 'There is no line of my verse or prose which has not been mouthed till the tongue has made all smooth and memory, after many recitals, has mechanically skipped the grosser superfluities,' with Maugham's 'I had a logical sense, and if no great feeling for the richness and strangeness of words, at all events a lively appreciation of their sound...it seemed to me that I must aim at lucidity, simplicity and euphony.' I should like to underline the word 'sound' in the Maugham paragraph—otherwise the reader might miss it, and there are too many tone-deaf writers as it is. It would be interesting, too, to compare the identical advice that these two very different writers give about 'following up a success.' The advice, by the way, is 'Don't,' and it is worth heeding, in spite of editors and publishers. And, some day, a graduate student may trace the French influence upon both of them—and discuss the whole field of the short story. For the moment, it is enough to say that both give professional advice, the kind of advice you can only get from the tried craftsman. Let us get back to Mr Maugham and *The Summing Up*.

A body of work, an *oeuvre*, is the result of long-continued and resolute effort.

The writer is free to work in whatever place and at whatever time he chooses; he is free to be idle if he feels ill or dispirited. But it is a profession that has disadvantages. One is that though the whole world, with everyone in it and all its sights and events, is your material, you yourself can only deal with what corresponds to some secret spring in your own nature. The mine is incalculably rich, but each one of us can get from it only a definite amount of ore.

The writer does not copy his originals; he takes what he wants from them, a few traits that have caught his attention, a turn of mind that has fired his imagination, and therefrom constructs his character. He is not concerned whether it is a truthful likeness; he is concerned only to create a plausible harmony convenient for his own purposes. So different may be the finished product from the original that it must be a common experience of authors to be accused of having drawn a lifelike portrait of a certain person when they had in mind someone quite different.

I am doing violence, course, to *The Summing Up* by quoting such
individual passages as the above. But they are worth thinking
about—not only for the beginning writer. And the whole book
gives a picture of the progress and development of a craftsman that
is truly remarkable in its intellectual frankness.

Mr Maugham has written for money, he has written for fame.
He has also and essentially written because he had to write—and he
scamps neither aspect of his career. The gifts of the gods were not
handed to him on a silver platter—he began with 'a natural lucidity
and a knack for writing easy dialogue.' But he remarks of himself
unsparingly 'My language was commonplace, my vocabulary
limited, my grammar shaky and my phrases hackneyed.' We can all
recognize ourselves in that horrid little description—what is more
important, perhaps, for the young writer, is that Mr Maugham was
able to recognize it and then go on. In other words, he did not sit
down and consider himself an unappreciated genius on the ground
of his defects. He worked. He tried for a florid prose and richness of
texture—he studied the Song of Solomon and Jeremy Taylor.
They were highly recommended but they didn't happen to fit him.
And, having learned his first lesson—that the admired style of the
period is not always the one for you—he worked. He made an
unexpected success with a novel and thought his fortune was made.
It was not. He turned to writing plays—had a *succès d'estime* with
one, but had to wait ten years and write six others, before his first
sensational success as a dramatist came. Well, there are a good
many writers who would like that sort of success—four plays
running in London at once and three of them substantial hits. But it
is not done by telling other writers that you have a wonderful idea
for a play.

Yes, *The Summing Up* is worth studying—worth studying if it
contained nothing more than the few pages that concern the
writing of *Of Human Bondage*. For, when it was written, Mr
Maugham had both money and fame. He could have gone on as a
playwright, and cashed in. But he did not because he could not.

I was but just firmly established as a popular playwright when I began to
be obsessed by the teeming memories of my past life.... It all came back to
me so pressingly, in my sleep, on my walks, when I was rehearsing plays,
when I was at a party, it became such a burden to me that I made up my
mind I could only regain my peace by writing it all down in the form of a
novel. I knew it would be a long one and I wanted to be undisturbed, so I

refused the contracts managers were anxious to give me and temporarily retired from the stage.

It would be hard to put the matter more clearly and simply—or with greater effectiveness. That is what you have to do for the best work—you have to do it because you can do no otherwise—and to do it demands integrity as well as skill.

I remember very well the first shock of reading *Of Human Bondage*—the realization that here was somebody telling the truth. You might not like it but you could not deny it—here was the truth as one man had found it to be. And it is this intellectual honesty—often dispassionate but always civilized—that runs like a vein of iron through all of Maugham's best work. He has never taken human beings for granted—they are there to be observed, not judged or belabored. He can, it is true, employ malice upon a character as easily as a cat uses its claws—but the best of his work still strikes me as singularly unmalicious. The worst is as ephemeral as a good Martini, and as well-mixed. Even in such an essentially empty book as *Theatre*, the pieces fall into place with a satisfying click, the expected surprises come off. The incision is so neat that one ceases to wonder, looking on, whether the operation was really necessary. A great craftsman—a great operator—and something more.

For it would be worth anybody's while—especially the hypothetical young writer's—to look at certain things. To notice, for instance, the ease of the transition between past and present and back again in *Cakes and Ale*—to meditate over the self-revelation in such a line as Lady Kitty's in *The Circle*—'Notwithstanding all my temptations I've been absolutely faithful to Hughie in spirit'—with the chill it brings to the enthusiasms of the heart. Or, for that matter, to notice the form of the short stories—the casual beginning that is not quite so casual as it seems. Mr Maugham writes stories that have a beginning, a middle, and an end, and you can see the point of departure, but not at first. I admit that much of the work has a bitter taste, but it is never brackish. And I doubt if a writer should be penalized for his skill. It is part of his business to be skillful, though his way may not be your way.

As regards women, Mr Maugham has created at least three living ones. Thackeray did not do more and Bennett created two. It seems odd to think of him as 'the dean of living English novelists'—the title, with its implications, belongs to a different sort of man. But what are you to do? If he had not written *Of Human Bondage*, a handful of the short stories, and some of the other work—you may choose as you will—it would be very easy to dismiss him as a clever and adept French writer in English—something between the early W.L. George and a superior and sharper Pinero. I mean, if you were a youthful critic and used to dismissing elder writers. But, unfortunately, the work is there, and there to be judged. I do not know what the final judgment will be and I doubt if Mr Maugham would be entirely interested. But perhaps this much may be said. It includes one masterpiece, in its scale and for its time. It includes no work, since the very early work, that is not the work of a professional. It includes an autobiography of extreme intellectual honesty, by a man who wished to make a certain thing of his life and has worked it out to that pattern. It is honest, in the field of its lens. And for consistent clarity and consistent ease, it is hard to match in contemporary writing.

I should like, if I had room, to comment upon certain other remarks of Mr Maugham's in *The Summing Up*—his remarks about style, for instance, his remarks about success. But I cannot, and you had better read the book instead. You will not find the complete portrait of a man, in the Rousseau style. But you will find the portrait of a mind and the portrait of a writer. And, if you want to know how certain things are achieved in writing—well, here is how one man did them, if you can read and remember.

111. Malcolm Cowley, 'The Maugham Enigma', *New Republic*

XCIV, 30 March 1938, 227–8

Malcolm Cowley (b. 1898) is a poet, critic and historian of modern American writing. His works include *The Literary Situation* (1954), *A Second Flowering* (1973) and *The Dream of the Golden Mountain* (1980).

There is a Somerset Maugham enigma, one that has always puzzled me. Why has he never written another book that was half so good as *Of Human Bondage*? Since 1897 he has been a professional writer, since 1907 a successful playwright, since 1916 a famous novelist. On the flyleaf of his latest book is a list of thirty-eight that preceded it—best-selling novels, short stories, travels, plays that were smash hits in London, New York, Berlin—and these are only the books he wants to remember; there are half a dozen others he is willing to forget. More than a collection of separate works, he has produced a unified body of work, an *oeuvre*, something that very few living writers have achieved in our language. Yet there has been a suspicion among critics that the *oeuvre* was artificial and the production of a second or a third-rate artist. The critics have usually been unjust to Maugham; they have neglected his great achievements as a craftsman. He has never fallen so low as Arnold Bennett at his worst or Sinclair Lewis at his third-best. Even when writing for the sort of public he despised, he was upheld by the strict morality of the prostitute who told him years ago that she was proud of always giving honest value. Still there were times when his heart wasn't in the work. Why did he write one book that was full of candor and human warmth? Why did he never climb back to the same level?

In *The Summing Up* he gives a partial and indirect but still a convincing answer to these questions. Of course that wasn't his aim in writing the book. Having reached the age of sixty-three, he wanted to take an inventory—'to sort out my thoughts on the subjects that have chiefly interested me during the course of my life.' He didn't propose to write an autobiography or a book of confessions—'I have no desire to lay bare my heart, and I put limits to the intimacy that I wish the reader to enter upon with me.' But without being frank, in the cant use of the word, he intended to be personal and completely truthful; and the result is the most interesting book he has published for twenty years. Incidentally it tells us a great deal about the sources and the psychological effects of his one great novel.

Of Human Bondage was written when Maugham was forty years old; his literary apprenticeship was over. He had learned four languages and studied masterpieces in all of them; he had worked to develop a prose style; he had written several novels, most of which were pure technical exercises; he had enjoyed the rare experience of having four plays running during a single London season. But in the midst of his success as a popular playwright, he began to be obsessed—the word is his own—by the teeming memories of his past life. 'It all came back to me so pressingly, in my sleep, on my walks, when I was rehearsing plays, when I was at a party, it became such a burden to me that I made up my mind that I could only regain my peace by writing it all down in the form of a novel. I knew it would be a long one and I wanted to be undisturbed, so I refused the contracts managers were anxious to give me and temporarily retired from the stage.'

Novels written after such an apprenticeship and out of such a necessity are almost certain to be good novels. But why didn't Maugham produce others of the same rank?

There are at least two answers and one of them is purely psychological. The clue to it lies in his use of the word 'obsessed.' Maugham was obsessed, haunted by the past—by his mother, kind and beautiful, who died when he was eight; by his lonely boyhood in the vicarage at Blackstable; by his schoolmates jeering at his stammer (which was the psychological equivalent of Philip Carey's clubfoot); by the suffering humanity he saw at St Thomas's Hospital; and finally, I should guess, by a love affair as prolonged and unhappy as Philip Carey's love for Mildred. He was under a compulsion to tell the whole story, to perform the rite of public confession and so receive absolution. 'The book,' he says, 'did for me what I wanted, and when it was issued to the world...I found myself free forever from those pains and unhappy recollections. I put into it everything I then knew and having at last finished it prepared to make a fresh start.' He would never again return to the material that was closest to his heart.

But there is a second answer that lies in a field between the psychological and the social. The coldness and externality of Maugham's later novels was partly a result of his success—'the greatest danger that besets the professional author':

Success...often bears within itself the seed of destruction, for it may very well cut the author off from the material that was its occasion. He enters a new world. He is made much of. He must be almost superhuman if he is not captivated by the notice taken of him by the great and remains insensible to the attractions of beautiful women. He grows accustomed to another way of life.... How difficult it is for him then to move freely still in the circles to which he has been accustomed and which have given him his subjects! His success has changed him in the eyes of his old associates and they are no longer at home with him. They may look upon him with envy or admiration, but no longer as one of themselves. The new world into which his success has brought him excites his admiration and he writes about it, but he sees it from the outside and can never so penetrate it as to become a part of it. No better example of this can be given than Arnold Bennett. . . .

But Maugham himself is another example of the author separated by success from the circles that gave him his best subjects. They were not the upper-middle-class circle with which his later books have dealt. He was born into the upper middle class—his father was solicitor for the British Embassy in Paris—and he will die in it too, but he has never felt at home with its members. Except in a few early plays like *Jack Straw*, he has always observed them as a faintly hostile stranger. His best subjects were the poor people he met when he was a down-at-the-heels medical student and a starving writer.

There is a story here with which his future biographer will have to struggle. My own idea is that when Maugham left Paris at the age of ten, an orphan speaking broken English—when he was neglected by his uncle the vicar and tormented by his schoolmates because of his timidity and his stammer—he became psychologically alienated not only from church and school but from his own class in English society. A few years later, at St Thomas's Hospital, he met the people who lived in the Lambeth slums and all hostility vanished. Philip Carey had the same experience in *Of Human Bondage*; he found that 'he was less shy with these people than he had ever been with others; he felt not exactly sympathy, for sympathy suggests condescension; but he felt at home with them.'

At this point the path of the hero diverged from that of the novelist. Philip Carey fell violently in love with a waitress, lost her and married a seamstress instead. After becoming a doctor he chose to practise in a poor fishing village, partly because it was his first opening but also because he liked the people and they liked him in return. Somerset Maugham, as soon as his plays made money, bought a house in Mayfair, but only because he liked the neighborhood as a symbol of success; he was irritated by the people. And that, I should guess, is the trouble with his work during the last twenty years. He has been writing stories—accurate and workmanlike and dramatic stories—about a class from which he has been spiritually alienated, and about people with whom he doesn't care to live. One reads in his character an impulse toward generosity and fellow-feeling that he hasn't given himself much chance to display. The faintly disagreeable aftertaste in his books can be defined in half a dozen words. It is the milk of human kindness, half-soured.

CHRISTMAS HOLIDAY

London, February 1939; New York, October 1939

112. Evelyn Waugh, 'The Technician', *Spectator*

CLXII, 17 February 1939, 274

It is often amusing when reading the book of an established writer to pretend to oneself that his name is unknown, and that one has casually picked up a first novel, and to ask whether, if one were a publisher's reader, one would recommend its acceptance without misgivings; if one were a critic, whether one would foretell its author's brilliant future. The result is sometimes illuminating. In the case of Mr Maugham, however, this kind of make-belief fails in the first page. One realises immediately that one is dealing with the work of a highly experienced writer, and one reads it with a feeling of increasing respect for his mastery of his trade. One has the same delight as in watching a first-class cabinet-maker cutting dovetails; in the days of dictated 'thinking-aloud' writing Mr Maugham's accomplishment is yearly more exhilarating. He is, I believe, the only living studio-master under whom one can study with profit. He has no marked idiosyncrasies which threaten the pupil with bad habits. His virtues of accuracy, economy, and control are those most lacking today among his juniors.

For pure technical felicity I think his new novel is his best. It is the story of a Christmas holiday in Paris of a well-to-do, well-mannered, mildly cultured and quite exceptionally charming young Englishman. The important point about the hero is that he is not a prig. It is a common complaint that in modern novels there are too few likeable characters. Well, here is Charley. He goes to

Paris for a few days' treat. The boy, Simon, who, until a year or two before, had been his best friend, is living there as a journalist. One of Charley's motives in coming is to renew their friendship. He finds a monomaniac. Simon had had an unhappy upbringing. Charley, in fact, was the sole being who had given him affection, and he had returned it fully. Now the perverse conditions of his childhood have reasserted their importance. He has developed a lust for power which takes the form of the ambition to be chief of the secret police under the political régime which he foresees in England—a régime to be established by communists, but in Simon's eyes bereft of all features except power.

To fit himself for this career he adopts a kind of satanic asceticism, physical and spiritual. No monk struggled more ruthlessly to expel sin than Simon struggles to expel goodness. His love for Charley is one of the things he is seeking to turn out of his life. Outrageous as his character is, and ludicrous as he would appear in other hands than Mr Maugham's, he is here completely convincing. Not unnaturally Charley finds the encounter an unhappy prelude to the good time he has promised himself. At a house of ill-fame—whose *sous-maîtresse* deliciously says, 'Sometimes I think the life we lead is a little narrow'—he meets a Russian with whom, platonically and reluctantly, he spends the whole of his little holiday. She is the wife of a murderer, and she is working as a prostitute with the preposterous belief that she can thus expiate her husband's crime—preposterous, but again absolutely convincing. Mr Maugham has elsewhere, more than once, given evidence of the belief that association with a Russian is a necessary part of an Englishman's adult education. Lydia teaches Charley to admire Chardin—at least she teaches him by her own intense response to Chardin what it is to look at a picture. She tells him the story of her own disastrous marriage to a habitual criminal. This recitation occupies the greater part of the book. It is brilliantly done and needs studying closely in detail; the transitions from direct speech to stylised narrative, the change of narrator as Simon takes up part of the story, the suspense that is created even though the reader already knows what the climax will be, are models of technique. Charley meets in her company two returned convicts from Cayenne, one of whom has stayed on an extra two years in order to befriend his companion. He has some further conversations with Simon, ending in a brutal parting. Then rather glumly he returns home. His family receive him with joy; his father with a kind of vicarious lubricity. The last sentence is this: 'Only one thing had happened to him, it was rather curious when you came to think of it, and he didn't just then quite know what to do about it: the bottom had fallen out of his world'.

But what has really happened is that the bottom has fallen out of Mr Maugham's book in this prodigious piece of bathos. All that inimitable artistry to end in this climax? For what does it amount to? Charley had led what is called a sheltered life, meeting mostly people who led the same kind of life, or who accepted it as normal. In Paris he has been rather roughly introduced to some people with quite different ideas and habits. He must have known, intellectually, that they existed; he must have known that there were head-hunters in Borneo and monks in Tibet and lunatics in asylums who had totally different views of the universe. What was before an intellectual abstraction is now real and concrete to him. All he had learned is the heterogeneity of mankind. It is a valuable lesson; some people never learn it. But his own virtues of kindness and tolerance and humour and honesty are still virtues, his bed is still as comfortable and his dinner as satisfying, he has not received any compelling call, such as does apparently from time to time change people's lives, to any different destiny. He has lost a friend who, anyway, has not meant much to him in recent years; otherwise he has merely had an instructive and profitable holiday, and he will be just the same kind of fellow in future with a slightly wider and wiser outlook.

113. Richard A. Cordell, 'Five-Day Adventure', *Saturday Review of Literature* (New York)

XX, 21 October 1939, 10

Richard Albert Cordell (b. 1896) is a professor of English, lecturer in Japan and Formosa, and author of *Somerset Maugham: A Biographical and Critical Study* (1961).

First of all, it must be said without quibbling reservations that *Christmas Holiday* is a first-rate novel, almost the best of the fifteen novels Somerset Maugham has written during the past forty-two years. It lacks the intense sincerity, the sweep, the autobiographical power of *Of Human Bondage*, but is its superior in form and style. *Christmas Holiday* is a short novel—really an extended anecdote—brilliantly written, and enriched by Maugham's peculiar gifts: a never-failing lucidity and a frequent beauty of style, the astringent humor, the easy summoning to life of a group of diverse characters, a gripping story, and an unobtrusive, gently ironic, but never captious interpretation of character and event.

In other words *Christmas Holiday* conforms perfectly to the author's conception of a good novel, often expressed and defined in his critical prefaces: it has an absorbing story, an agreeable style free of irritating eccentricities, a group of living and diversified characters who are interesting in themselves, the whole novel quietly stamped with the author's private view of the universe. Somerset Maugham does not write his novels in a vacuum. In *Christmas Holiday* he shows, for instance, that he is aware of the nature of dictators and dictatorships, and of threatening economic and social revolutions in this brave or cowardly new world; he implies a shrewd understanding of the important cultural forces of our day. But the emphasis is almost altogether on men and women, on the dark places of the soul, on the unaccountability of human nature.

Because of the detective-story interest of the plot little must be

331

said of the story itself. It is sufficient to say that the young hero on a five-day holiday in Paris has a shattering experience that knocks the bottom out of his seemingly secure and elegantly mannered way of life. Coming from a London home of elegance and conscious culture, he is thrust into a breath-taking, sordid, and harrowing adventure that upsets all his nicely collocated values of art, music, and morality, and destroys his complacent satisfaction in his enviable, well-ordered existence. The somewhat crashing final sentence completes the pattern of the novel and makes unequivocally clear the import of the story.

Some readers will object to a digression in the story—a caricaturing of the hero's parents, their artiness, their self-conscious culture and magnanimity, their glitter and shallowness. But the digression is justified on two counts: it fills out for the purpose of dramatic contrast the hero's environment; moreover it is so highly entertaining in itself that it does not seem to slacken the pace of the narrative.

Admirers of Somerset Maugham—may their tribe increase—can not afford to miss *Christmas Holiday*.

BOOKS AND YOU

London, New York, March 1940

These essays were first printed in the *Saturday Evening Post*.

---

114. Lorine Pruette, 'How to Like to Read', *New York Herald Tribune*

14 April 1940, 21

Lorine Livingston Pruette (b. 1896) is the author of *Saint in Ivory* (1927), *School for Love* (1936), and *Working with Words* (1951).

Here are the three essays which appeared some months ago in *The Saturday Evening Post*, plus some amendments and extensions given in a preface. Many who read these essays must have wished for this more permanent form. Everything that Somerset Maugham writes has to an extraordinary degree the quality which he praises in the great books of his present consideration, that of being readable. He writes a lean and supple prose, so agreeably organized that it seems to proceed upon its way less from organization than from inevitability. You can surely read these essays with both the pleasure and the profit which he hopes we shall all find in some of the books he is recommending to our attention.

The lists of books, English, European and American, are of course interesting and important, in their own right and because of the critical intelligence which has selected them. But of even greater interest is the statement of Mr Maugham's approach to literature,

333

which begins in a defense of pleasure—in itself 'a great good, all pleasure'—and proceeds to the position that many famous writings of the past should be no longer read, except by scholars. Reading is praised as a sport in which you can engage practically all your life, in solitude, and at little expense. 'To acquire the habit of reading is to construct for yourself a refuge from almost all the miseries of life.'

The author mentions his own reading customs. In the morning before starting work he reads for a while in science or philosophy, something that requires a fresh and attentive brain. Later on, when his work is done, he reads history, essays, criticism or biography, and in the evening a novel. In addition he keeps on hand a volume of poetry in case he feels in the mood for it, and by his bedside he keeps one of those books into which you can dip at any place. It happens at the moment that my own bedside book is Maugham's own collection, the 1,600-page *Traveller's Library*.

In selecting the great works which he feels he would have been the poorer not to have read, Mr Maugham naturally covers much familiar territory. Less customary are his endorsements of Gibbon's *Autobiography*, Boswell's *The Journal of a Tour to the Hebrides* and Goethe's *Wilhelm Meister*. There are some judgments here of *David Copperfield* as Dickens's best novel and Dickens as England's greatest novelist, of Hazlitt's 'My First Acquaintance With Poets' as the finest essay in the English language, of Balzac as the greatest novelist who ever lived, of Benjamin Franklin as the typical American just as Doctor Johnson is the typical Englishman.

Among the American writings there are several great reputations which he finds unjustified, including that of Emily Dickinson. The reasons why each book has been selected are given with economy and effectiveness, and more is told about many of the books than you would believe possible in so short a space. Many phrases beg for quotation, including the deflation of people who say proudly that they cannot read novels, implying that their minds are occupied with greater things. But one short paragraph must be quoted, because it sums up the author's approach and is such an appropriate reminder for our time.

But literature is an art. It is not philosophy, it is not science, it is not social economy, it is not politics; it is an art. And art is for delight.

The coolly distinguished, informal but never intimate essay

seems particularly appropriate to Somerset Maugham. Perhaps, as well as having a time of day for different kinds of reading, he has a time of life for different kinds of writing, and *Books and You* will prove the modest and delightful prelude to a full volume of criticism.

THE MIXTURE AS BEFORE

London, June 1940; New York, July 1940

For the title of this collection of short stories, see headnote to No. 105.

115. V.S. Pritchett, review, *New Statesman and Nation*

n.s. XIX, 15 June 1940

(Sir) Victor Sawdon Pritchett (b. 1900) is a novelist, short-story writer, critic, autobiographer, and a regular literary journalist for many years on the *New Statesman*, of which he has been both literary editor and a director.

Society lags behind its writers and takes sometimes a generation to catch up with them. It is a fact, for example, that although two wars stand between us and everything Mr Maugham has to say, he is established as one of the most distinguished and most readable of the older writers. Accomplishment has always been sneered at in English letters and readability has become a sneer too; yet these two qualities, cultivated with an unequalled scrupulousness by Mr Maugham, have at least made their impression. By them and by the combination of bitterness and tolerance (or, in his lower manner, cynicism and *laissez faire*), he has managed to convince an enormous public which has grown more and more embittered, disillusioned, tolerant and even frivolous, that he is their man, the tailor's mirror of the moment. And, since society lags, so to a great extent, he is. He has also had luck. The last forty years of the

English novel have seen an enormous and optimistic social preoccupation, a cheerful, complacent or sensitive dismembering of tabus which released the individual. The present war has, on the short view, dashed all that and Maugham, the sceptic, who would have nothing to do with it all either in politics or belief, survives among the wreckage of public Utopias and private sensibilities. At least, one of the two Maughams survives; the other, in dinner jacket and holding the Ritz cocktail, looks rather tawdry, like that *crème de menthe* spattered dress suit at the surrealist exhibition.

Novelists have a multiple personality in their work and a dual personality in their profession. In the latter they divide simply into God and Mammon. Maugham begins as the austere, impersonal, sceptical, and even pitying God, walking among men and women, and watching them sedulously creating their misery and illusions. Tired of walking, he takes a seat at the café and, comfortable, finds scepticism become cynicism, austerity become chic, pity becoming the indulgence of the man of the world, morality a trick. He plays Iago to humanity's bellowing Othello and, disdaining disorderliness and anarchy, as Iago did, he creates an imaginary human being, an efficient, orderly, removed and sensible one, who has put money in his purse and has learned to live in a world of illusion without illusions. Iago, after all, was a very civilized man, cruel no doubt and probably frustrated, but a great deal pleasanter to live with than the rhetorical Moor.

Writers do not commonly add anything new to the ideas which dominated them in their twenties. The Maugham strain can be found in his contemporaries—Shaw, Kipling, and Galsworthy—in the former two particularly. Writers were reacting to the new financiers' British Empire, the gentleman myth, the aestheticism of the decade, and all attacking sexual tabus and convention. To the modern reader the words 'gentleman' and 'convention' seem an obsession in Maugham and Shaw; Shaw is all for tearing up the Empire, Kipling for expanding it until it becomes mystical; Maugham succeeds him as the debunker of the white man's burden which usually turns out to be his wife's adultery. Maugham is Kipling, turned inside out, discovering alcohol, beachcombing and middle-class sex, where Kipling portrayed the Roman overlord and evoked the secret, savage hierarchy of the jungle. The jungle is not usually savage in Maugham; it is, strangely enough, something pictorially extravagant which surrounds the judicious aesthete.

People go to pieces in the Maugham jungle and, living happily as wreckage, disconcert the conventional; they do not, as in Kipling, discover the masonic ritualism of the animals. Of the two writers it is hard to say who is the more romantic, the more masochistic, the more knowing. Kipling's saving quality was his cunning, Maugham's his common sense; both have an embarrassment before emotion, a gnawing sense of imminent evil.

But really Maugham has more in common with Shaw. He has the Shaw trick of turning things upside down, but it is a trick which does not come into its own until Maugham begins to write short stories. The form invites that artifice. You wrote a story about a gentleman and showed he was a cad, you divulged the acidity in what 'the world' calls virtue and the humanity in what it calls vice. Good women turn out to be bitches; if you redeem the prostitute it is because you lust after her ('Rain'). This topsy-turvy became fantasy in Shaw; but Maugham's imagination is defective there. He is unexcitable. Shaw drunk might sing sentimentally 'The Harp that Once on Tara's Walls'; Maugham, one feels, would choose the more moderate languors of 'The Lily of Laguna.' What begins as an attack on convention in Maugham, and especially on the lady and gentleman convention, spreads and deepens into a general philosophy of life (at first dramatic and finally tolerant and ironical) that everything turns into its opposite. People are destroyed by their virtues as well as by their vices.

Take the new collection of stories, The Mixture as Before (said, one hopes mistakenly, to be his last). The theory is illustrated frivolously in the tale of how three fat women, living on a starvation diet at Antibes, decide to guzzle once more when a thin woman whom they grow to hate, comes along and crams down as much as she can hold without fear for her figure. The gentleman preoccupation: an actor palms himself off as a sahib and, after he is exposed, behaves with the fantastic gallantry of the sahib magazines; a lie has turned into truth. The moral question: a murderer is supposed to suffer pangs of conscience, but here is a murderer who has no pangs but actually was driven to a wicked crime by his conscience. The aesthetic question: the 'nineties' great preoccupation with the artist as the social antithesis of the gentleman—this is the theme of many Maugham novels and stories, Theatre, The Moon and Sixpence, etc.— is illustrated by the vulgar horror of a great singer's life contrasted with the sublimity of her art. The problem of happiness: the happiest man in the French convict settlement is one who has just been made executioner; preparing for his first execution, he enjoys the scenery like an honest man properly content with the world, unaware that he is about to be murdered. This story, 'An Official Position,' and another, 'The Facts of Life,' are Maugham at his best. The last is brilliant comedy of extraordinary ingenuity and narrative skill.

Mr Maugham has often written about the position of the artist but has obviously his period's stress on the pure artist. This may be all right for painters and musicians, but for novelists it is dubious doctrine. Maugham's own common sense has rejected the cultural snobbery of the art hounds and, without discarding a belief in the isolation of writers, he has nevertheless had the wisdom to recognise that he is a moralist who works, as moralists must, within their limits. At least, he is drawn now towards the middle-class clubman's common sense; and now towards a monklike asceticism. He is the unshockable and the detached. Yet there are no detached people. If detachment means attachment to the search for truth, one cannot say Mr Maugham *is* altogether attached to this search. In two-thirds of *Of Human Bondage* perhaps; but not in the stories. He is attached there to his pattern which is what remains for him of that early addiction to 'art for art's sake', which he confessed to and disapproved of in *The Summing Up*. And pattern is the trick. For this reason a brilliant piece of macabre narrative like the executioner's story has the enormous readability, the exact, lucid if slightly perfunctory prose, of the best Maugham manner, and carries one to the most savage height of irony, yet makes no profound impression at all. A moralist, he has displayed not a curious and horrifying fragment of life, but an argument. On the other hand, a purely artificial story like 'The Facts of Life' in which a young man goes to Paris and, heedless of his father's warnings of the awful consequences, gambles, lends money to a stranger and picks up a woman, and comes back having committed all these follies without damage, indeed having made 6,000 francs on the deal, produces a lasting impression on the reader. It has not merely exposed the fatal weakness of the moralist position; it is perfect artificial comedy without pretending to be otherwise.

There is another sense in which the Maugham detachment is skin deep. His scepticism has the virtues of pity, tolerance, humanity, an eye for humbug and a love of the diversity of human nature. But his real attachment is to his class. Where his contemporaries became sociologists and prophets; or, uneasy in their class and unanchored, tossed about like pretty boats in the harbours of their own private sensibilities, Maugham, insisting on a writer's duty, assumed the stability and immortality of the world he lived in. Hence the capacity to see an unruly world at one remove, the dapper and detached figure in the Ritz bar. (He knows, as his last novel, *Christmas Holiday*, showed, the bar may get a bomb in it, but it was characteristic that he sought to teach a modern young hero a lesson by the pure Symons-Wilde device of making him spend a *nuit blanche* with a prostitute vicariously expiating sin. Oh 1890!) We feel today the need of being more direct, less reflective in narrative because it is impossible to keep the world at one remove from the middle classes any more.

Two novels of Maugham's stand out, one by God and the other by Mammon. *Of Human Bondage* did for its time what is more popular in French literature than in English owing to our fear of priggishness: the honest portrait of a young man. Thackeray had tried it in *Pendennis*—a novel which ought to be re-read. Maugham does not in the least mind admitting the two great English shames: snobbishness and priggishness. Mammon blossomed perfectly in the classic merriment of *Cakes and Ale*. These books, like all of Maugham's—this is due to his devotion to technique—improve on re-reading. He has always kept his head; in *Cakes and Ale* he kept his heart. The sentimentality of the man whose mask of disappointment has become second nature does not show here. Iago has ceased to moralise. He seems to have felt; and yet to have retained his wits.

116. Iris Barry, 'Midsummer Nights' Fare', *New York Herald Tribune*

14 July 1940, 4

Iris Barry (1895–1969) was a film historian and critic, and author of *D.W. Griffith: American Film Master*.

With a writer who can do no wrong, like Mr Somerset Maugham, one's critical faculties are edged in a special and possibly deceptive fashion. Actually he promises no more in this book of short stories then a mere level of competence and a hint of amusement, interest and emotional stimulus. But to a very large extent the competence alone is enough. It is like being satisfied by hearing a great executant play Czerny's exercises perfectly and enjoying the quite mistaken impression that one sees, for the moment, the tricks and devices by which that perfection is achieved. For instance, in these stories even a reader who has done nothing more literary than write a few letters may very well observe that they are made up of the least pretentious and often quite brief sentences. 'He was a fearful snob.' 'I was seized with rage, and with all my might I hit her over the head with my Indian club.' 'He was found one morning on the mountainside lying quite peacefully as though he had died in his sleep.' There is nothing more startling about the whole perform-ance than that, except the discretion, the experience and the artistry with which it is managed. The simple sentences build up into a pre-designed whole and communicate exactly as much as the author intended.

None of these stories, perhaps, could be called important, not even that most heartfelt one, 'The Lotus Eater,' which concerns a mild little man who had been a bank manager, but resigned and bought an annuity in order to spend twenty-five years of his life at Capri. That was the bargain he had made with life: so much happiness for so long, and then the end. Either life or he did not keep the pact, for he lived on beyond the allotted time... however, that and the character of the man make the story itself.

Another alarmingly vivid portrait-study is that of the Englishman who acted as though he were a gentleman and then died as if he really had been one. Even more penetrating is the story of the convict who, years after he had killed his totally unregretted wife, is still remorseful about a shabby trick he had once played on a boyhood friend. All of them, to a remarkable degree, give one the sensation of being shown the inside mechanism of human behaviour by a man who is truly an expert on the subject though he is possibly one whose attitude is that of scientific interest and detachment rather than love. Only in 'The Three Fat Women of Antibes' is there complete humor and affection as well as shrewdness. It is a simple enough account of the effect that a slender woman had on three stout contemporaries.

There is really nothing in it except food and bridge, but the observation is brilliant, and, with all its reticence and apparent superficiality, the whole story is a triumph of craftsmanship. All the characters, for example, distinctly exist outside the particular limits of the tale itself, and Mr Maugham (or so he is clever enough to make you think) merely obliges you with a little revealing glimpse of them at one particularly trying moment of their lives. There are not many short-story writers who can suggest this impression of permanence in their figures. The same effect obtains to some extent with regard to young Garnet, who went to Monte Carlo to play tennis, and there so brilliantly disregarded his father's advice concerning gambling, lending money and frequenting women. One could very well predict what the future held for him, although the story teller himself suggests nothing whatever about it.

As with all books of short stories, precautions should be taken with this one so that its contents are not swallowed whole; there should be a law against reading such a book right through and thus spoiling it. But even consumed in that greedy fashion, it still leaves the reader hoping that Mr Maugham's publishers will not seriously abide by the threat which its preface contains. The stories are perfect midsummer nights' fare, and it would be a pity not to have more of that.

UP AT THE VILLA

New York, April 1941; London, May 1941

This novelette was originally written as a short story titled 'A June Night', which remains unpublished.

117. Morton Dauwen Zabel, 'A Cool Hand', *Nation* (New York)

CLII, 3 May 1941, 534–6

Morton Dauwen Zabel (1901–64) was professor of English at the University of Chicago and author of several works of criticism including *Forms in Modern Fiction* (1949), *Craft and Character in Modern Fiction* (1957) and *The Art of Ruth Draper* (1959).

This novel, as unmitigated a specimen of fictional drivel as has appeared under respectable authorship within living memory, might be fitly dismissed as the latest triumph of servant-girl's literature were it not for the phenomenal value that still attaches to Maugham's name among modern authors. The standard argument on his case is familiar. He is the complete Cool Hand and Technical Expert among writers; he has never been taken in by literary gangdom, aesthetic pretensions, or anything else in the life around him; he is a walking model of his own no-nonsense, fact-facing, smooth-tooled heroes; he is always perfectly aware of what he is doing and is as fully in control of his faculties when turning out a piece of trash as when producing a masterpiece. This reputation has been as carefully fostered by himself as by his admirers. *The Summing Up* was a deftly calculated exercise in his favorite virtue—professional sincerity; so superbly calculated, indeed, that even its author seemed unaware that his elaborately cold-blooded realism gave his show away more readily than the bewildered ardors and protestations we usually get in literary memoirs. Popular critics are always pushovers for the cool kind of aesthetic amorality Maugham professes. 'His cynicism has advanced so far as to become candor,' exclaims Mr Fadiman: 'It's a positive pleasure to be sold so smooth and shiny a gold brick.' We are also used to hearing Maugham called 'the greatest living English novelist,' the implication always being conveyed that were he so disposed he could, at any time he feels like it, produce another *Cakes and Ale* or *Of Human Bondage*.

One is moved to ask: then why doesn't he do so? For ten years now, since *Cakes and Ale* in 1930, he has turned out a succession of luxurious pot-boilers, *Cosmopolitan* thrillers, and Hollywood slick-jobs equaled only by the similar procession of banalities that followed *Of Human Bondage* in 1915. His plays, expertly carpentered actor-pieces and drawing-room comedies in the fagged line of Pinero, are hard to discuss seriously even among the arid wastes of modern drama; one has only to see them in revival a few years after their glamorous first nights and shorn of their original stars to realize the prodigies of mechanical contrivance, mawkish dialogue, and trumped-up moral pretension they encompass. Modern fiction, especially in England, has mostly represented a triumph of higher journalism, but Bennett, Wells, and Galsworthy at least respected the more serious social sympathies, class conflicts, and psychological interests of their time. Maugham has never let these worries run away with him. He has brought high gifts—in story-telling, in humane observation, in suspense, in humor, and even in more serious matters of passion or decadence—to the most trivial of uses. His two notable books have issued from the only two experiences in which he has allowed himself to be deeply or personally implicated: his youthful sufferings in love, thought, and physical disability and his ordeal of moral exoneration as a professional writer. The first struggle he sublimated by a patient, disillusioned, laborious, unoriginal, but convincing realism; the second by a brilliant feat of satire. Yet one has only to look at the conclusions at which those books arrive to understand why he lapsed into a perfect model of the literary journeyman, hostile to artistic risk or innovation, invulnerable to the serious claims of his profession, and apparently without conscience when it comes to lending his remarkable equipment to the highest sales values that tawdry smartness and banality command.

If any doubt remains on this scope, *Up at the Villa* should dismiss it. The screaming falseness of its dialogue (on pages 39–43 or 87–99, for instance) should alone be enough to turn the stomachs of even moderately sensitive readers; it would put to shame the humblest employee of the Hollywood script-mills. Perhaps one exaggerates the importance of all this. But Maugham is influential; his claim to importance is highly respected in schools, rental libraries, and newspaper columns; he figures as a guide for ambitious talents. His career in the fashionable drawing-rooms and international cocktail sets of Europe, in Riviera villas, in theatrical circles, on P. & O. liners, or among the glamorous places of the Orient is a model of envy to innumerable aspirants who take this kind of success as a symptom of serious literary distinction. And it is quite in line with his elaborately groomed, no-nonsense attitude toward art that he should in recent months have used his current pulpit in the *Saturday Evening Post* to disseminate a large skepticism about modern literature, to expound his man-to-man common sense on the aesthetics of the mystery thriller, and to reduce the labors of Henry James to an ultimate refinement of futility. The motive behind these Literary Lessons for Rotarians is not difficult to glimpse: no man likes to be shown up by his betters quite as ruthlessly as the slightest comparison between the work of James and Maugham shows up Maugham. At the age of sixty-seven James had not only written an almost unbroken succession of subtle and profoundly original novels (in which, contrary to the opinion of Maugham and Van Wyck Brooks, he was taken in by *nothing* in the world of sham and ambition in which he mixed) but was writing, in the fulness of his age and wisdom, one of the most searchingly pathetic and beautifully wrought stories ever set on paper, 'The Bench of Desolation.' At the age of sixty-seven Maugham turns out *Up at the Villa* for the delectation of drugstore readers, movie audiences, and the boudoirs. One of its features that provides Mr Fadiman with special pleasure is that it does not contain 'a wasted word.' The fact has seldom been more deftly reversed. *All the words are wasted!*

And incidentally, if the title of 'greatest living English novelist' is to be thrown around any further, it is time it landed in the right quarter. The greatest living English novelist is E.M. Forster.

118. Pamela Hansford Johnson, 'Bread and Circuses', *Books of the Month*

XI, June 1941, 18–19

Pamela Hansford Johnson (1912–81) was a novelist and book-reviewer whose fiction includes *This Bed Thy Centre* (1935), *The Unspeakable Skipton* (1959), *The Good Listener* (1975) and *The Bonfire* (1981). She also wrote a series of *Six Proust Reconstructions* which were broadcast by the BBC on radio and a book of literary memoirs, *Important to Me* (1974). Her second husband was the novelist C.P. Snow.

How pleasant—always—to meet Mr Somerset Maugham! But *Up at the Villa* is not his best work. It is, of course, fascinating and elegant; it could not be otherwise; but the theme just borders on the footling. It might be said with some justification that Mr Maugham's master, Maupassant, also thought up some footling plots at times; but he did apply to them the acrid lick of colour that brought up the picture, however banal, into morbid relief. Mr Maugham has, up to now, done the same thing, but in this short novel, which has only 150 pages odd, he has run into what is for him a high degree of sentiment. Mary Panton, a lovely young widow living in Italy, is on the point of marrying a kindly but depressingly wooden diplomat when, acting one night on impulse, she invites a young down-and-out Austrian musician in to her home, permits him to make love to her and through her unintentional callousness in dismissing him when she considers the hour for loving is over, causes him to commit suicide. Frantic with fear, she invites the help of a young bad hat, a notorious cad with women, in disposing of the body. This achieved, she finds herself compelled to confess the incident to the diplomat, who is so gentlemanly and forgiving about it, yet so shocked that she thinks after all it might be better to marry the bad hat. She would certainly be safer, and she might easily be happier. The weakness in this book is that Mr Maugham seems blinded by affection where his heroine is concerned. She is a trying and useless young woman, so far as I can see, but no Maugham guns are trained on her. She gets off scot-free and quite unillumined by criticism. For all that, *Up at the Villa* is attractive and binding from the first page to the last; naturally.

THE HOUR BEFORE THE DAWN
New York, June 1942

Written as British war propaganda during Maugham's residence in America during World War II, this novel has never been published in England.

119. Unsigned review, *Nation* (New York)
CLV, 4 July 1942, 18

The twilight hour of Mr Maugham's professional life is dark indeed. His latest novel, written with his chin up, his tongue in his cheek, and his eye on Hollywood, lacks the old cynicism, but it lacks, too, the old craftsmanship. However, in a stock story of how the war affects the lives of a typical English county family there is a point worth comment, that Mr Maugham has a single refugee in the book, a young Austrian girl who turns out to be a Nazi spy and betrays the family and country that gave her refuge. It seems strange to have to remind the author of *Of H-m-n B-nd-ge* that to kindle suspicion of refugees in the minds of his large audience is scarcely cricket.

120. R. Ellis Roberts, 'The Art of Somerset Maugham', *Saturday Review of Literature* (New York)

XXV, 27 June 1942, 6

At his best—and this novel of a county family in war-time England is, except for a few slight infelicities of phrase, Maugham at his best—Somerset Maugham can establish his characters with an economic precision very few of his rivals can approach. These characters are quick, vivid, idiosyncratic, and the shadows which they throw are symbolic of more than these men and women, blundering, heroic, enduring, humorous, and intolerably suffering. Here is a cross-section of England at war, given with understanding, wit, love, and a reserved passion that is the more effective because Mr Maugham has not often allowed himself to be indignantly passionate.

The Hendersons have lived on their estate in Sussex, Graveney Holt, for some two hundred years. They are not, that is, an old family and belong to that upper middle-class which has for centuries rescued the older aristocracy from the canker of age-long privilege. The Hendersons are 'Army' as well as 'county.' General Henderson is retired; his eldest son, Roger, is on the active list of Military Intelligence; Jane, the daughter, noble-hearted, is married to Ian Forster, once in the Grenadiers, now very fat and in the forties; Jim is at Oxford and a member of the Peace Pledge Union and the youngest son, Tommy, is still at school. The whole family is assembled at Graveney Holt for Mrs Henderson's fifty third birthday on the 31st of August, 1939. Mrs Henderson is a wonderfully successful portrait of a woman in whom natural wisdom breeds justice and that sense so rare that mankind, desperately hankering after it, has agreed to call it 'common.' There is one other at the birthday—Dora Friedberg, an Austrian whose father has been killed in a concentration camp in Germany.

Too many novelists, writing about the war, are unable to persuade us of the truth that personal tragedies, personal problems do not cease in wartime, are indeed heightened among people whose lives and traditions are free. Mr Maugham has no such difficulty. The book opens with May's request to Roger for release from a marriage to which he has brought care, respect, affection but not that overwhelming attention her romantic temperament demands. The news of war stops any idea of divorce. The arrival of war turns Jim's pacificism—dismissed by his family (except his mother) as callow idealism, into a grim, hard reality; with war, Jane has the agony of seeing her Ian, unfit, out of training, worry his way back into the army; the old General has pride and anxiety in Roger and Ian, deep disapproval and bewilderment for Jim who works as a farm-laborer.

Exquisitely, Mr Maugham portrays the private and domestic tragedies in the light of the great public tragedy of the war—the long-drawn-out prologue when, after Poland, nothing seems to happen: then the speed and terror of the tramping feet, the thrusting tanks, the diving air-planes, ruthless, unconquerable whether resisted or unresisted, a ghastly maelstrom of effective destruction—never stopped. Only at Dunkirk the men who are machines, the machines who are gods are for a moment baffled: for once they are not fed. The prey escapes: and England, stripped of its equipment, wakes to know herself alone.

Then come the months of the air-raids, of the threatened invasion.

At Graveney Holt the great house is full of refugee children from London, whom Mrs Henderson, May, and Dora look after. Jane lives on in Westminster, a focus of reckless gaiety and courage for the tired men who fight and work. Jim keeps to his principles. Roger only just escapes from Dunkirk—the story of that flight is one of the best things in the book as, in its simple lines, the characterization of his Cockney companion is one of the best portraits. The final tragedy in the lives of these people is provided by Dora; no doubt Mr Maugham will be accused of melodrama— there are critics who detest the catastrophical, the accidental in fiction. I don't agree with them. There are traitors and liars in the world; and such people as the Hendersons (remember their kind 'appeased' the enemy) are taken in by them. There is nothing incredible in the deaths of Dora and Jim—and the violence of that episode mirrors the gigantic violence that causes it, and Jim's idealism is at once justified and annulled by Dora's death.

The story stops—there can be no end yet—in the spring of last year; perhaps Mr Maugham will give us one day his story of the dawn which is even now breaking.

THE RAZOR'S EDGE
New York, April 1944; London, July 1944

The basic plot structure for this novel was taken from Maugham's play *The Road Uphill*, written in 1924, which has never been produced or published.

121. Joseph Warren Beach, 'Maugham Considers Mystics', *New York Times*
23 April 1944, 3

Joseph Warren Beach (1880–1957) was professor of English at the University of Minnesota and a literary critic. He was the author of critical books on Meredith (1911), James (1918), Hardy (1922) and Auden (1957).

The startling regression to savagery which has marked our time is a challenge to the spirit which literature cannot ignore. We may look in fiction as elsewhere for efforts to set up a faith that can stand against the tides of history, supporting the will and conscience of man against all dismal demonstrations of Malthusian economics and Machiavellian ethics. It is not surprising that one of the first of these should come from the hand of an English writer whose early novels and tales were written before the Boer War, whose Oscar-Wildean comedies were on the boards before Sarajevo, and whose most famous novel, *Of Human Bondage*, dates from 1915. While Maugham was one of the stalwarts of realism who gave the *coup de grâce* to Victorian complacency, his cool blood was warmed by an afterglow of Victorianism and he never seriously questioned the basic premises of that nineteenth-century culture of which he was a distinguished exponent. With all his irony, his cynicism, his uncanny faculty for reducing human motives to their lowest common denominator, he has long stood for a humanism which cherished the surface values of civilization even when it could not quite recall the grounds on which they were based.

It is out of that remote and fading world that his voice now comes to us in a philosophical novel whose theme will suggest men of a later generation, Charles Morgan and Aldous Huxley, as well as an earlier Tolstoy or Dostoevsky. His central character is an American youth, who as a flier in the first World War has looked on death, and who gives up the life of love and money-making for that of the Hindu Vedanta, and, like Christian Wahnschaffe in Wassermann's famous novel, disappears in the end behind the veils of 'calmness, forbearance, compassion, selflessness and continence.' But so long as he remains within the range of human visibility, the Indian saintliness of Larry Darrell stands in relief against the materialism and worldliness of Elliott Templeton (prince of snobs), Gray Maturin (financier), Isabel Bradley and Suzanne Rouvier (representing the feminine cult of social security), not to speak of the Babylonish frivolity and corruption whose name is Paris, in the delineation of which Mr Maugham is such a past master. Then finally there is Sophie Macdonald, a spirit akin to Larry's, whose vision of Evil is too much for her, and drives her the way of sin and death where Larry goes the way of life and sanctity.

Mr Maugham would resent this description of his book as a novel of ideas—a literary type of which in *The Summing Up* he has spoken with disparagement. But that is the way the reading world is bound to take it if they are to take it as anything more than another example of his large resourcefulness as an entertainer. They are bound to welcome it as a contribution to the problem: how may the spirit maintain its life in a world of corruption? A timely reminder of the ancient truth: 'He that loseth his life shall find it.'

Those of us who are not much taken by the notion of sainthood *in vacuo*, nor easily impressed by selflessness except where it is shown working in a *medium*, are not likely to hail this oriental model of spirituality as the true antithesis to pork-packing, stock-gambling materialism. We should have preferred something more in the way of positive goodness, employed on some of the tangible objects of goodness, such as—shall we say?—social justice. And it does not help much for Mr Maugham to have put himself into the story as one of the characters by way of offering his own type of humane hedonism as an alternative to Hindu mysticism.

And yet, an urbane personal intrusion into his narrative is one of those happy technical inspirations in which Maugham is so prolific. For one thing, it enables him to get away with the pretense that the characters in the story are people he has actually known—a pleasing reversal of the customary legal fiction that the characters are wholly invented by the author and without models in the actual world.

The story is carried forward with Maugham's usual deftness and ingenuity of manipulation. Everything has been provided for from the start: no loose ends are left trailing. In some points the technique is tiresome and outmoded—the set elaborate descriptions of persons and places, nothing left to the imagination, and the stark materiality of every circumstance, a heritage from the French realists of the age of positivism. The writing is direct and idiomatic, without affectation or 'Impressionism' and almost without flavor. Where nature and feeling are concerned, there is no attempt to avoid the conventional turn; the reader has no impulse to dwell on a passage for its special rightness of phrasing or perception. In Maugham there are few intentions that lie much deeper than the surface. The dialogue is but another phase of his own style. The people say just what they mean, no more and no less; they speak by the book. And, except where he is laying on the colors of American slang or of French bourgeois elegance, there is little to distinguish one person's speech from another.

Manners and character are Maugham's forte, and here the provision is lavish and unfailing. 'Society' and snobbery he has studied with the passion of a Proust. No American writer knows better this Chicago-in-Paris. His irony never sleeps. The ceremonial death of Elliott Templeton and his laying out (in the costume of a noble ancestor, borrowed from Velasquez) make one of the unforgettable scenes of English comedy. Unforgettable at least, till something comes along more truly memorable.

122. Diana Trilling, review, *Nation* (New York)

CLVIII, 6 May 1944, 547

Diana Trilling (b. 1905) is an essayist on literary and topical subjects whose books include *Claremont Essays* (1964) and *Mrs Harris* (1981), an account of a murder trial. She was married to Lionel Trilling, who died in 1975.

W. Somerset Maugham's *The Razor's Edge* is subtitled 'The story of a man who found a faith,' but it is not a religious novel. It is not even a mystical novel, really, despite the fact that one of its chief characters is the man who finds faith, in India, in the mystical worship of the Absolute. For Maugham's concern with the realm of the unworldly—and it is not a new concern—is scarcely more serious than his purely mundane concerns. He has an amateur's interest in the spirit which is perhaps only the natural counterpart of his ever-waning interest in the fruitful human possibility. 'A chill went down my spine as it strangely does when I am confronted with deep and genuine emotion. I find it terrible and rather awe-inspiring,' he says of himself in *The Razor's Edge*, and he reveals the flirtatious nature of his occasional excursions into mysticism just as he suggests the reason for the failure of his whole literary career. Mysticism, that is, is bound to be inviting to the person who is afraid of the deep emotions; yet it can never fully win him, any more than humanity can fully win him. All the characters in Maugham's latest novel inevitably inhabit the non-dimensional universe which is all that is left when the deep emotions have been disavowed.

123. Kate O'Brien, review, *Spectator*

CLXXIII, 21 July 1944, 64, 66

Kate O'Brien (1897–1974) was an Irish playwright and novelist, some of whose work was performed in the London theatre before World War II. She published ten novels including *The Ante-Room* (1934) and *The Last of Summer* (1943), and travel books set in Spain and Ireland.

Discriminating novel-readers will sigh with relief to find this present patch of fictional dullness lighted up by a new Maugham— all the more as we had been told by the master some time ago, I think, that he would never again give us a novel. There will be much rejoicing at his change of resolution, and this solid, skilful, accurately calculated book will not only give pleasure and food for reflection to a great number of people, but must also re-stir critical consideration of a formidable talent, a formidable sum of talents.

All who care for the novel seriously must have their blind spots among novelists. Save in some of his shorter pieces, I have never been able to feel any warm enthusiasm for Balzac—since amazement before stupendousness is not at all the same thing as enthusiasm; all through my life I can return at any time to any volume of Turgeniev and read it through with something more than my first delight, but I notice that I do not return to Dostoevsky; I read Trollope with admiration, but only with tepid pleasure—there is a difference; and save over the forever enchanting *Emma* I have never been able to become anything approximating to a 'Janeite.' Among the greater of my contemporaries, too, I draw some blanks which very likely do my taste no honour; but whatever the reasons for these they seem to lack correspondence, and do not explain why I am unable to appreciate with full pleasure the maturer works of Mr Maugham. His technique in the construction of a story is almost perfect, I suppose, and he brings all the easier graces to adorn his austere outline; precision, tact, irony, and that beautiful negative thing which in so good a writer becomes positive—total, but *total*, absence of pomposity; he is

356

never solemn and he is never facetious, and these two seemingly opposed manners are great traps for the pompous. He strips everything down to the reasonable; he is always cool, always detached, and he observes relentlessly.

My trouble is that, accepting the fine accomplishment of his manner, I find I never care for the matter of his books. Often it seems just worldly stuff that has been done as well, or less well, before; but sometimes—as in this new novel—we find that in fact it is serious, with individualism and trouble in its seed, but that Mr Maugham is simply not going to be flurried out of his beautifully finished technique to deal as he should, and could, with its potentialities. This story, for instance, is of a young American man, a brilliant air ace of the 1914–18 war, who returns to Chicago to find that he cannot live the life his rich friends and relatives have mapped out for him there, cannot marry the nice girl he has long been in love with, but cannot at first say more of what he really means than that he wants to 'loaf.' He is, in fact, searching for the good life, the ideal of the saints. He sets out after it, and the pattern of his search is most skilfully woven against the worldly design of the lives of his relations; they, pursuing their supremely materialistic way in Chicago, London, Paris and the Riviera; he, crossing with them often, going his from Montparnasse to a Belgian coal mine, thence *via* a German farm and a Benedictine monastery to the Hindu temples and hermitages of India. He finds what he wants, and goes back to America to be a taxi-driver and try to live like a saint; and his one-time girl and her husband, and all the others of the story, find what they want—for, as the author says, he has written 'nothing more nor less than a success story.' But he has written it from the outside; gracefully, sympathetically, and with a sufficiency of bitterness—but using Larry too easily throughout, as a beautiful symbol, and never attempting to hack down to the bones of the man himself; spreading over all the rest of the story too, and even over Larry a bit, that gloss, that convenient, amusing *chic*, that curious *Champs Elysées décor* which this author finds irresistible and which he does so well; indeed, excessively, sterilisingly well.

124. Cyril Connolly, 'The Art of Being Good', *New Statesman and Nation*

n.s. XXVIII, 26 August 1944, 140

Cyril Vernon Connolly (1903–74) was a leading English literary journalist, editor of the magazine *Horizon* (1940–50). He was the author of a novel, *The Rock Pool* (1936); a critical-cum-autobiographical study, *Enemies of Promise* (1938); and *The Unquiet Grave* (1944).

This is Mr Maugham's best novel since *Cakes and Ale*, and, appearing at a time when the decline in literary quality is fairly matched by the decline in literary taste, it breathes the atmosphere of another world.

The novel is a considerable addition to the literature of non-attachment, and ranks with Huxley's *Grey Eminence* and Heard's *Man the Master* as powerful propaganda for the new faith or, rather, new version of an old faith, which is called by various names; neo-Brahmanism, or the Vedanta of the West—and which has made its home in somewhat macabre proximity to Hollywood. This does not mean that Mr Maugham 'has been converted by Gerald Heard' and so forth, for in all his previous work there has always been a strong inclination to mysticism and an ill-concealed sympathy for those who turn their back on the world. Mr Maugham's gallery of bums and beachcombers, his sanguine study in *The Moon and Sixpence*, his interest in the Spanish mystics in *Don Fernando*, and in various Eastern types of holy man, proclaim this obsession through all his work. He is the worldliest of our novelists, and yet is fascinated by those who renounce the world, whether to do nothing, to become artists, to be a Communist as in *Christmas Holiday*, or a Saint as in *The Razor's Edge*. The book is indeed a study in pre-sanctity in the early years of a man whom the author hints is capable of saving the world, if it will ever listen—and it is part of his sanctity that Larry should be in many ways very like everybody else, a delightful simple single-minded

Krishnamurti from the Middle West. Since he is to be tempted, we have also pictures of the World and the Flesh: the world in the form of Elliott Templeton, most perfectly drawn of all the characters; the genial infinitely painstaking romantic snob, with Catholic and discreetly homosexual leanings, whose magnificent but empty career of social success Mr Maugham paints with lingering tenderness, right down to the wonderful death-scene which is a kind of farewell offering to his old corrupt world of Paris and the Riviera, whose eclipse he would seem here both to acknowledge and to regret.

The flesh appears in the guise of three women: Isabel, Elliott's niece, an admirably drawn American girl, charming and sensitive when first engaged to Larry, but moulded by the conditions of moneyed American life into a chic, beautiful, greedy, heartless woman, typical of all well-dressed, noisy, yet withal warm and honest, machine-tooled cosmopolitans. It is Isabel's tragedy to know that Larry, whom she rejected as a suitor because he was poor, is the only man who really attracts her and can bring out her own potentialities. The two other women are Sophie Macdonald, the type of American girl gone to the bad—drink, drugs, sailors—out of the violence of her disappointment with life; and Suzanne Rouvier, Mr Maugham's familiar female character, the honest whore. She represents the charm and common sense, the fundamentally worthwhile values of French civilisation, as contrasted with the depravity of American, as typified by the worldly Elliott, the savage Isabel, the nymphomaniac Sophie, and Isabel's simple, money-making husband, Gray. These are the material the young saint (who, however, is also an American) has got to work on. On the whole, he is not a success, for in this pre-sanctity stage, in his commonplace, somewhat priggish, larval form, he is chiefly concerned with getting away from people like these and trying to find the truth by reading and travel, manual labour and meditation. He is enlightened by a holy man in Southern India, and the lovely descriptions of this country make some of the pleasantest reading in the book. They also present Mr Maugham with his hardest problem, that of conveying the mystical experience, that explosive which has so far defied all rational analysis. I think that, on the whole, for a writer who is not a mystic, he has managed to do this: he conveys well the passionate quest for truth which consumes Larry's whole life and which originates in his experiences as a pilot in the last war, when he made the discovery that 'the dead look so terribly dead when they're dead.' Thus the moment of faith to which it leads up comes as no surprise. But of what faith? This seems to me the real difficulty: to a sceptical mind it seems doubtful whether human beings actually possess the apparatus which can discover truth, and when they pin it down in a doctrine there is always a sense of disappointment. Now, the neo-brahmins of Hollywood have a doctrine, and that doctrine embraces a considerable amount of Hindu religion and Yoga mysticisms, so Larry has to believe in the transmigration of souls, in Brahma, Vishnu and Siva, and Mr Maugham's attempt to make this convincing seems far more disastrous than the mystical experience or the penetrating criticisms of Christianity which he previously describes. A ridiculous hypnotic trick, an example of suggestion, is made use of as a 'sign' of power, and the vision of Larry's previous selves also fails to come off. It would have been better for the novel not to have confined Larry to any known religious system: to let him have his revelation and then leave it at that.

The Razor's Edge shows a great technical improvement on the author's recent novels. He handles his four or five characters to perfection, and includes himself—not as a fictional character, but as the flesh-and-blood Willie Maugham of real life—with complete mastery. Here is a novelist right inside his own novel, not a mere stooge or onlooker, or larger than life, as a *deus ex machina*, but on the same plane as all the other characters, not more real nor less—a brilliant feat, carried off with quiet mastery. The too short staccato sentences which often mar his style have also been expanded; there is less of 'I have a notion,' and the writing is delightfully flexible, vivid and easy. Everything appears haphazard, yet everything is to the point. Maugham is the greatest living short-story writer, and so one expects his handling of plot to force one into a breathless, non-stop reading from the first page to the last, and his character-drawing and observation to be in the fine tradition—but one would not expect to be so captivated by the brilliant fluency of the writing. Here at last is a great writer, on the threshold of old age, determined to tell the truth in a form which releases all the possibilities of his art. His comments and asides excite us in their justice, and sometimes by their rancour. He has, for example, a note of particular asperity whenever there is any question of the standing of writers in the social world. If there is one thing to regret about this novel it is that it is written not for us but for Americans: one detects a considerable amount of playing down to the transatlantic common man and a faintly disapproving attitude to Europe and this country. Mr Maugham has never been a master of words; he has always preferred the *mot moyen* to the *mot juste*; he is incapable of those flights of vocabulary which we find in the great living stylists: Logan Pearsall Smith, E.M. Forster, Max Beerbohm—but even he should know better than to use 'exquisitely gowned' or various slangy expressions (not in dialogue but in the author's musings) which are already out of date. Yet if his book is written for Americans, it is certainly a tract for them! Never have their weak points been so tactfully yet remorselessly suggested—Mr Maugham never forgets the spiritual dust-bowl which every American carries within him, and which he vainly tries to irrigate with alcohol, statistics or labour-saving devices. 'I have a notion,' Mr Maugham seems to say, 'that the new Messiah is going to have his work cut out.' Here is his final judgment:—

Larry has been absorbed, as he wished, into that tumultuous conglomeration of humanity, distracted by so many conflicting interests, so lost in the world's confusion, so wishful of good, so cocksure on the outside, so diffident within, so kind, so hard, so trustful and so cagey, so mean and so generous, which is the people of the United States.

It has puzzled me, considering the sheer delight that I and all my friends have received from this novel, that it has been so uncharitably reviewed. Are we becoming incapable of recognising excellence when we see it? I think prejudice is to blame, prejudice against any book which so perfectly recaptures the graces that have vanished, and against any writer who is so obviously not content with the banal routine of self-esteem and habit, graced by occasional orgies of nationalism and herd-celebrations, with which most of us, from the lovely Isabels and exquisite Elliott Templetons, down to the tame gravel-throwing apes of Fleet Street, fidget away our one-and-only lives.

THEN AND NOW

London, New York, May 1946

For the sub-plot of this historical novel Maugham adapted the plot of *La Mandragola*, a comedy by Machiavelli (1469–1527), the novel's protagonist.

125. V.C. Clinton-Baddeley, review, *Spectator*

CLXXVI, 17 May 1946, 514

Victor Vaughan Reynolds Geraint Clinton Clinton-Baddeley (d. 1970) was an author and theatrical historian whose works include *The Burlesque Tradition in the English Theatre after 1660* (1952), *All Right on the Night* (1954) and *The Written and the Spoken Word* (1965). His sister Angela Baddeley, the actress, played the role of Florrie in the original production of *Sheppey* at Wyndham's Theatre in 1933.

The only convincing historical dialogue is that which is sufficiently alive of itself to convey the spirit of a period without relying on the Dutch courage of fancy language. It can be successfully written only by a man who so perfectly understands what he is writing about that the period is implicit in every sentence, marked not in the words but in the habit of thought which lies behind them. Somerset Maugham's new book is a historical novel and a first-class example of brilliant dialogue-writing. It describes the embassy of Machiavelli to the court of Caesar Borgia, and in plain economic modern English it draws a picture of Renaissance politics as cleanly edged as the neat figures and landscapes in an Italian picture. Machiavelli goes to Caesar Borgia to play a temporising part on behalf of the Signory of Florence. He is present at the most serious crisis in Caesar's affairs, and at the massacre of the smaller princes at Sinigaglia. It is all as exciting as any gangster story of modern politics, and parallel with it runs a counter-plot as good as any tale of gallantry from Boccaccio. Machiavelli is the observer of the first and the victim of the second story, the two being held together in the nicest balance, farce weighed against drama, and laughter against treachery.

This book is a study both of the man who wrote *The Prince* and of the man who was his model, and they stand here in exactly that relationship, the Duke in supreme authority and the Florentine envoy anxiously trying to guess his mind, and not always guessing right. During their first interview the Duke sentences two Gascon soldiers to be hanged for looting. Machiavelli laughs to himself, convinced that the whole affair is a piece of play-acting intended to impress him. The reader is amused by this elaborate device and pleased with Machiavelli's sharpness in detecting it, until nine pages later he comes upon the two soldiers hanging in the market-place. 'It hadn't been a comedy then. Machiavelli stood stock still and stared with dismay.' The reader is halted, too, for it is a fine point, beautifully scored. The characters of both men have suddenly disclosed an unexpected curve.

These two portraits are so well done that if it were not for the *Decameron* counter-plot one could almost consider the book as a biographical study. It is short, but it has not been lightly undertaken. Indeed, it must have entailed considerable research. On the other hand, it does not show Mr Maugham in as new a light as might naturally be supposed. Caesar Borgia and Machiavelli are both characters very much in his country—and the title of the book, without any further explanation in preface or text, is *Then and Now*.

126. Edmund Wilson, 'Somerset Maugham and an Antidote', *New Yorker*

XXII, 8 June 1946, 96–9

Edmund Wilson (1895–1972) is America's leading man of letters of the modern period. His works include volumes of fiction, drama, poetry, travel-writing, but he is known primarily for his polished critical essays published in collections such as *Axel's Castle* (1931), *The Triple Thinkers* (1938, revised 1948) and *To the Finland Station* (1940). Wilson was the regular book-reviewer on the *New Yorker* from 1944 to 1948. Since his death his *Diaries*, covering decades from the 1920s through to the 1950s, have been published, edited by Leon Edel.

In this article Wilson went on to review Newton Arvin's edition of *Hawthorne's Short Stories*, which he contrasted with Maugham's *Introduction to Modern English and American Literature*.

It has happened to me from time to time to run into some person of taste who tells me that I ought to take Somerset Maugham seriously, yet I have never been able to convince myself that he was anything but second-rate. His swelling reputation in America, which culminated the other day in his solemn presentation to the Library of Congress of the manuscript of *Of Human Bondage*, seems to me a conspicuous sign of the general decline of our standards. Thirty or thirty-five years ago the English novelists that were read in America were at least men like Wells and Bennett, who, though not quite of top rank, were at least by vocation real writers. Mr Maugham, it seems to me, is not, in the sense of 'having the métier,' really a writer at all. There are real writers, like Balzac and Dreiser, who may be said to write badly. Dreiser handles words abominably, but his prose has a compelling rhythm, which is his style and which induces the emotions that give his story its poetic meaning. But Mr Maugham, whose use of words is banal, has no personal rhythm at all, nor can he create for us a poetic world.

Now, unless I read for information, I find it extremely difficult to get through books that are not 'written.' I can read Compton Mackenzie, for example, of the second rank though he is, because he has, as a writer, real gifts of a not too common kind. But my experience has always been with Maugham that he disappoints my literary appetite and discourages me from going on. His new novel—*Then and Now*—seemed to me, all through its first half, one of the most tasteless and unreadable books from which I had ever hoped to derive enjoyment, and nothing but the necessity of supplying this review could ever have taken me through it. *Then and Now* is a historical novel: it deals with Machiavelli and tells the story of his mission, as envoy from Florence, to the headquarters of Caesar Borgia, when the latter, in his campaign of domination, appeared to be at his most effective and most menacing. The way in which this promising subject is handled suggested, I was shocked to discover, one of the less brilliant contributions to a prep-school magazine. Here are Machiavelli and Borgia confronting one another: 'Although he had but briefly seen him at Urbino, Machiavelli had been deeply impressed by him. He had heard there how the Duke Guidobaldo da Montefeltro, confiding in Caesar Borgia's friendship, had lost his state and barely escaped with his life; and though he recognized that Il Valentino had acted with shocking perfidy he could not but admire the energy and adroit planning with which he had conducted the enterprise. This was a man of parts, fearless, unscrupulous, ruthless and intelligent, not only a brilliant general but a capable organizer and an astute politician. A sarcastic smile played upon Machiavelli's thin lips and his eyes gleamed, for the prospect of matching his wits with such an antagonist excited him.' This narrative from time to time is obstructed by the introduction of thick chunks of historical background that sound as if they had been copied out—so compressed and indigestible are they, so untouched by imagination—from some textbook in the history classroom: 'In June of the year with which this narrative is concerned, Arezzo, a city subject to Florence, revolted and declared itself independent. Vitellozzo Vitelli, the ablest of Il Valentino's commanders and bitter enemy of the Florentines because they had executed his brother Paolo, and Baglioni, Lord of Perugia, went to the support of the rebellious citizens and defeated the forces of the Republic,' etc., etc. As will be seen from the above sentence, in which, if we glide over the comma, we are at first misled into supposing that Baglioni was executed, before we find that he went with Vitelli, the writing is amateurish. The book is full of ill-composed sentences, bulging with disproportionate clauses that prevent them from coming out right, or confused by 'he's, 'him's, and 'his's that apply to different antecedents: a kind of thing that an English master would have been sure to bluepencil in the young student's themes. The language is such a tissue of clichés that one's wonder is finally aroused at the writer's ability to assemble so many and at his unfailing inability to put anything in an individual way: 'But Il Valentino appeared to be well pleased. It looked as though he were prepared to let bygones be bygones and restore the repentant rebels to his confidence.... But whatever sinister plans he turned round in that handsome head of his, the Duke was evidently not ready to resort to more than veiled threats to induce the Florentines to accede to his demands.... The Duke gazed at him thoughtfully. You might have imagined that he was asking himself what kind of a man this was, but with no ulterior motive, from idle curiosity rather.... The truth, the unpalatable truth, stared him in the face.... He had taken him on this trip from sheer good nature, he had done everything for him, he had introduced him to persons worth knowing, he had done his best to form him, to show him how to behave, to civilize him, in short; he had not spared his wit and wisdom to teach him the ways of the world, how to make friends and influence people. And this was his reward, to have his girl snatched away from under his very nose.' This dullness is only relieved by an occasional dim sparkle of the Wildean wit that made comedies like *Our Betters* amusing without investing them with that distinction which, in Wilde, is the product of style: 'If only she knew as much about life as he did she would know that it is not the temptations you have succumbed to that you regret, but those you have resisted.' But even this kind of thing would not be beyond the competence of a schoolboy.

About halfway through the book, however, we find that what the author has been doing, in his tiresome piling up of dead incident, is introducing the elements of a plot. This plot is pretty well contrived; it could hardly have been worked out by a schoolboy, for it shows a practiced hand, and it carries us through the rest of the book. We find here, furthermore, that the scheming of Caesar to accomplish his political ends is connected, not merely through ingenuities of plot but also by moral implication, with Machiavelli's scheming to make a conquest of the wife of a friend. Machiavelli as well as Borgia is cynical about human motives; Machiavelli (though politically a patriot working for republican Florence) is aiming in his personal relations at power for the sake of power, just as Borgia is. And the victims of both are equally cynics, equally double-dealers. The upshot of the whole affair is that Machiavelli, returning home with a certain admiration for Borgia but in a rage over the duplicity practiced on him by the young wife and her associates, meditates upon his experience and finds in it the material for *Il Principe*, his treatise on Realpolitik, and for his comedy *La Mandragola*. This, too, shows more knowledge of the world than a schoolboy would have been likely to acquire, but that schoolboy, grownup and much travelled and somehow diverted from his normal career of law, medicine, diplomacy, or parliament, might have written—did, in fact, write—such a novel as *Then and Now*. With a certain amount of interest in the drama of human behavior, he had no special talent for literature, and he ought really to have stopped with the school magazine, but for some reason he kept on writing, and the result has been Somerset Maugham.

The admirers of Mr Maugham will tell me that he is 'old and tired' now, and that historical novels are not his forte—that it is quite unfair to judge him by *Then and Now*, which is one of the least of his books. I know that he has done better stories, but I am not sure that it *is* quite unfair to judge his quality by the quality of *Then and Now*. This quality is never, it seems to me, that either of a literary artist or of a first-rate critic of morals; and it may be worth while to say this at a moment when a tendency seems to be prevalent to step up Mr Maugham's standing into the higher ranks of English fiction. What stirs one particularly to protest is a certain disposition on the part of Mr Maugham himself to take advantage of his popularity for the purpose of disparaging his betters. Though Mr Maugham's claims for himself are always carefully and correctly modest, he usually manages to sound invidious when he is speaking of his top-drawer contemporaries. In an anthology which he edited a few years ago, *Introduction to Modern English and American Literature*—a mixture of good writing and tripe that sets the teeth on edge—we find him patronizing, in what seems to me an insufferable way (and with his customary buzz of clichés), such writers as Henry James, James Joyce, and W.B. Yeats. 'His influence on fiction,' he writes of James, 'especially in England, has been great, and though I happen to think it has been a bad influence, its enduring power makes him an important figure.... He never succeeded in coming to grips with life.... This story ['The Beast in the Jungle'] reads to me like a lamentable admission of his own failure.' Of *Ulysses*: 'I have read it twice, so I cannot say that I find it unreadable, but...like many of his countrymen, Joyce never discovered that enough is as good as a feast, and his prolixity is exhausting.' Of Yeats: 'Though he could at times be very good company, he was a pompous, vain man; to hear him read his own verses was as excruciating a torture as anyone could be exposed to.' Well, it is quite true of Henry James that his experience was incomplete and that he wrote about his own deficiencies, and that Joyce is sometimes too prolix, and it may be true that Yeats was sometimes prompous. And Mr Maugham mingles praise with his detraction, but, from reading this *Introduction*, you would never be able to discover that all these men belong to a different plane from that of Michael Arlen and Katharine Brush, whose work is also included—a plane on which Somerset Maugham does not exist at all. Mr Maugham would give us the impression that all novelists are entertainers who differ only in being more or less boring (though he grants, with a marked lack of enthusiasm, that Henry James supplied, 'if not an incentive, at least an encouragement to those who came after him...to aim consciously at giving fiction the form and significance that may sometimes make it something more than the pastime of an idle hour'). We get the impression of a malcontent eye cocked up from the brackish waters of the *Cosmopolitan* magazine, and an insistent and peevish grumbling. There is something going on, on the higher ground, that halfway impresses and charms him, but he does not quite understand what it is, and in any case he can never get up there.

Even when Mr Maugham is able to admire more cordially the kind of work that is done on this higher plane, his way of talking about it betrays his lack of real appreciation and almost always gives the impression of impertinence. So, in his speech at the Library of Congress, we find the following remarks about Proust: 'Proust, as we know, was enormously influenced by the now largely discredited philosophy of Henri Bergson and great stretches of his work turn upon it. I suppose we all read with a thrill of excitement Proust's volumes as they came out, but now when we reread them in a calmer mood I think what we find to admire in them is his wonderful humor and the extraordinarily vivid and interesting characters that he created in profusion. We skip his philosophical disquisitions and we skip them without loss.' Now, it is perfectly obvious here that Mr Maugham does not know what he is talking about. Some aspects of Bergson's philosophy are still taken very seriously by first-rate philosophers of certain schools; and even if Bergson's whole system were regarded with universal disapproval, that might not affect the validity of the artistic use that Proust has made of one of its features. This feature—the difference between 'time' and 'duration': how long something takes by the clock and how long it seems while it is going on—is itself only one of the features of Proust's metaphysical picture, which in general has more in common with the implications of relativistic physics than with the Creative Evolution of Bergson. It is this exploitation of the principle of relativity in the social and personal fields that gives Proust his philosophical interest and that makes his novel, I suppose, the greatest work of philosophical fiction ever written. In *A la Recherche du Temps Perdu*, the philosophy so pervades the narrative that it is difficult to see how you could skip it: if you jumped over the 'disquisitions,' you could still not escape from Proust, in a thousand intimations and asides, expounding his relativistic theory; and since the unexpected development of the characters, the astonishing reversals of relationships, all the paradoxes and contrasts that provide the main interest of the story, are dramatizations of this theory, it is difficult to understand how a reader can 'admire' the former and yet disregard the latter. The inability of Mr Maugham to realize what there is in Proust helps to explain why he has not put more into a novel like *Then and Now*.

CREATURES OF CIRCUMSTANCE
London, New York, July 1947

This was Maugham's last collection of short stories.

127. Olivia Manning, review, *Spectator*
CLXXIX, 8 August 1947, 188

Olivia Manning (1908–80) was a novelist and fiction-reviewer. Her reputation rests on two three-novel sequences, *The Balkan Trilogy* and *The Levant Trilogy*, published between 1960 and 1980, which trace the fortunes of Guy and Harriet Pringle in Romania, Greece and Egypt in the wake of advancing armies during World War II. They were based on her own experiences and those of her husband, R.D. Smith, who worked for the British Council, and for the BBC as a features producer.

This article also reviews volumes of short stories by A.L. Barker, Graham Greene and John Sommerfield.

Mr Somerset Maugham's age and reputation place him above the criticism of the young, so I can only say that for those who, like myself, delight in his commonplace middle-aged characters with pasts of remarkable passion and violence, *Creatures of Circumstance* gives us the mixture as more than once before. I do not think Mr Maugham intends these short stories to be more than entertaining, and anyone who does not find them that must be hard to entertain.

128. Charles Lee, 'Mr Maugham, Still Urbane', *New York Times*

27 July 1947, 4, 23

Charles Lee (b. 1913) was a newspaper editor and academic, and author of *How to Enjoy Reading* (1936) and *An Almanac of Reading* (1940).

It is not overstating matters to say that here is a volume of short stories that would have had Scheherazade herself holding her tongue. In one or two cases she might have nodded a bit. But for the most part, the nodding would have taken its opposite and more flattering form, that of a vigorous gesture of approval. Mr Maugham not only has good stories to tell; he knows how to tell them well. His narrative technique has about it the grace of all finely executed art. He unreels his spell with the same well lubricated assurance as the most cunning angler does his line: and the quarry stays hooked.

In an introduction Mr Maugham rightfully emphasises the story element of his offering. He opposes the fuzzy obliqueness of modernists who

think it enough if they have described a mood, or given an impression or drawn a character. That is all very well, but it is not a story and I do not think it satisfies the reader. . . . There is also today a fear of incident. The result is this spate of drab stories in which nothing happens.

In the fifteen stories of *Creatures of Circumstance* very nearly everything happens. People fall in and out of love, discover infidelities, shoot and knife their rivals, murder their fathers, their children or their children's sweethearts, go mad, abandon society, kill for 'honor' and, occasionally, come to pacific terms with their fellows. These conflicts (witty, touching, melodramatic or fantastic as the case may be) are waged on a broad geographical front: England, France, Borneo, Spain, Italy, America, Scotland and the high seas. Mr Maugham is nothing if not generous.

371

Sheer story-telling virtuosity, in keeping with his own estimate, will probably be allowed as the main element of his charm. Another is his poise, his attitude of mellow maturity in the very midst of commotion. His note of amused tolerance at the unexpected vagaries of the human animal was never more urbanely maintained than in his new book. This tone of sophistication, of been-around intelligence—combined, as it is, with an air of tweeds, good brandies, long Havanas and after-dinner ease—is perhaps the major component of his appeal.

Allied to all this is his acute understanding of human beings. It is all very well for Mr Maugham to accent the gift of story. But without his perspicacity, his suave searchings of motives, his ironic asides, in short his expressed or implied 'readings of life,' his stories would lose their unique authority and substance. It takes a special point of view, perhaps an old Roman philosopher's detachment fused with modern psychological probing, to observe so coolly and wisely that life's bus is no more wayward than its passengers.

An over-all description of the people in this book can be made in the words of his title. The characters are creatures of circumstance. But they are more than automatons: they provide causes as well as respond to effects. They *make* circumstances.

Thus, pompous George Peregrine, in 'The Colonel's Lady,' discovers that his drab and demure little wife has placed him in awkward social circumstances with the publication of a volume of poems describing a love affair with a young man. But Peregrine's blinding vanities created the prior circumstances that made her disloyalty inevitable. Typically, Maugham's story, teasing and absorbing as pure narrative, is other things besides: a study of sex and marriage, of the spiritual sag of middle age, of subtle vengeance, of human arrogance and indifference, of double standards.

'The Colonel's Lady' is but one of several outstanding stories which tomorrow's anthologists will collect. Others due to find posterity around the corner are 'Appearance and Reality,' a spiced and sparkling comedy of French love; 'Sanatorium', a shrewd study of love, hate and suffering among varitempered patients in a Scottish health resort (this one is really a compressed novel in the *Grand Hotel* pattern); and 'A Casual Affair,' a poignant tale of a man wrecked by a great passion.

Nor is this all. In the semicomic 'Winter Crusade' [*sic*] you will discover how the officers of a German passenger freighter finally silenced a garrulous tea-room proprietress enamored of her own conversation and young men; in 'The Mother' you will see how a pathological possessiveness turned a mother into a monster of hate; in 'Episode' you will read of an odd postman who rang on love once too often; in 'The Happy Couple' you will meet a woman who would engage in murder but not in illicit love with the man of her heart; in 'The Unconquered,' a powerful story of the war, you will observe revenge in one of its most ruthless and brutally noble forms; in 'The Kite' you will hear the Freudian case of a man whose apron string was two miles long.

And in the end, if you are discerning, you will also meet yourself: for you, too, Mr Maugham would have you remember, are one of the creatures of circumstance.

CATALINA

London, August 1948; New York, October 1948

Maugham's last novel, set in seventeenth-century Spain, was based on a legend concerning the miraculous, not to be found in his earlier Spanish book *Don Fernando* (1935).

---

129. Paul Bloomfield, review, *Manchester Guardian*

20 August 1948, 3

Paul Bloomfield (b. 1898) is the author of works of literary and social history, *Imaginary Worlds or the Evolution of Utopia* (1932), *The Many and the Few or Culture and Destiny* (1942), novels and biographies. He was a book-reviewer for the *Listener* and *Time and Tide*.

The article also reviews other fiction.

Catalina might have been written under a Mediterranean sun by a Frenchman, a sceptical deist, a reluctantly renegade Catholic, a member of the Academy. Actually the author is Somerset Maugham. Mr Maugham once said that writing a play was 'as easy as falling off a log.' Reading this diverting 'romance,' as he calls it, one feels that he found writing it no harder than that. Catalina is the subject of a miraculous cure in Spain in the Golden Century. The intrigues the event gives rise to are very funny. The gracious shadow of St Teresa falls across her path. Towards the end of the story, when she has been properly married to her Diego, she meets no less a person than Don Quixote. Though the ease of Mr Maugham's style is perfect—and what a delight!—all the way through, the admirable structure a little goes to pieces after the Virgin's second intervention in Catalina's life. But in spite of the faster tempo at the end readers will lay the book down with no sense of fatigue: on the contrary, they will heave a sigh of regret that these Anglo-Voltairean larks do not run to a second volume. A trifle, to be sure, but brilliantly clever and amusing.

130. Orville Prescott, review, *New York Times*

26 October 1948, 29

Orville Prescott (b. 1906) was literary editor of *Eve* magazine 1936–47, a columnist and a lecturer on literature. He was also co-editor of the *New York Times* Books of the Times.

It has been a long time since Somerset Maugham has written a novel as good as *Catalina*, not since *Cakes and Ale*, which was published in 1930. *Catalina* is not nearly as good as that brilliant and maliciously amusing novel; but it is greatly superior to such flabby potboilers as *Then and Now*, *The Hour Before the Dawn* and *Up at the Villa*, and greatly superior also to the pretentious, machine-made mysticism of *The Razor's Edge*. *Catalina* is a gay and light-hearted romance which flirts mischievously with several serious subjects. It cannot be taken seriously and, I'm sure, was not intended to be so taken. But it is a sleekly clever book, a cynically and cold-bloodedly clever book. In the seventy-fifth year of his age Somerset Maugham still regards the human comedy as a diverting spectacle, a suitable target for impudent jests. The tragic elements in it he refuses to regard tragically; the farcical delight him.

After a long and spectacularly successful career as a playwright, short-story writer and novelist, Mr Maugham turned in his declining years to the historical past and produced *Then and Now*, an unfortunately flat tale about Machiavelli and Cesare Borgia. In

Catalina Mr Maugham has continued to focus his mocking eye upon historical human aberrations, shifting from the deplorable conduct of a Borgia to the deplorable fanaticism of the Spanish Inquisition. His romance and his comedy take place against a backdrop of burning heretics.

This deft and completely unrealistic romance is many things at once: a fairy tale which follows faithfully a popular and ancient formula; a moral parable in which sundry incontestable arguments in favor of tolerance, humility and loving kindness are presented; a fantasy in which miracles play a major role, not only miraculous cures through the intercession of the Blessed Virgin, but providential little miracles designed to promote and protect chastity and to foster the honorable estate of holy matrimony. It is also a repository for numerous typical Maugham gems of cynical worldly wisdom...

...no previous experience with fairy tales can prepare readers of *Catalina* for what followed Catalina's cure, the contest between the lusty young woman, who wanted to get married, and Dona Beatriz, prioress of the Carmelite Convent, who wanted to make a nun of her and perhaps a saint. Dona Beatriz, that efficient, haughty, scheming woman, is the object of some of Mr Maugham's most malicious irony. The Bishop, who was as sincerely religious as Dona Beatriz was not, comes in for his share of Mr Maugham's ridicule, too. But it is ridicule touched by pity. The Bishop's belief may have brought suffering to others; but it was genuine and he suffered for it himself.

Catalina, which Mr Maugham has written throughout with his tongue in his cheek, in a spirit of mock-heroic comedy, collapses into outright farce in its closing pages when Catalina becomes a successful actress and many times a mother, thus escaping the designs of Dona Beatriz, and when she meets a sorrowful knight not quite right in his head, a forlorn refugee from another and a more enduring comedy about human folly.

An example of the worldly wisdom of Somerset Maugham: 'He had learned in his short life that a man should never excuse himself, and she, young though she was, knew that it is vain to reproach a man. However heinous his offenses, it only irritates him to have them thrown in his teeth. A sensible woman is content to let them weigh on his conscience if he has one, and if he hasn't, recrimination is wasted.'

GREAT NOVELISTS AND THEIR NOVELS
Philadelphia, Toronto, September 1948

TEN NOVELS AND THEIR AUTHORS
London, October 1954

First printed in 1947/48 as articles in the American magazine *Atlantic Monthly* under the title 'Ten Best Novels', they appeared in 1948 both as introductions to the ten novels in abridged form and as a collection of essays, in Philadelphia and Toronto. Extensively revised, the essays were published in England, after serialisation in the *Sunday Times*, in 1954.

131. John W. Aldridge, 'Mr Maugham's Ten Sheared Candidates', *Saturday Review of Literature* (New York)
XXXI, 2 October 1948, 23–4

John Watson Aldridge (b. 1922) is a professor and critic. His books include *After the Lost Generation* (1951) and noval, *The Party at Granton* (1960).

Mr Maugham wrote the essays in this collection to introduce the set of ten best novels which the Winston Company is now publishing. The reissuance of such standard works as *War and Peace, Old Man Goriot, Tom Jones, Pride and Prejudice, The Red and the Black, Wuthering Heights, Madame Bovary, David Copperfield, The Brothers Karamazov,* and *Moby Dick* may seem an extravagance at a time when nearly all of them are or have been available in regular and Modern Library editions, but it is justified, Mr Maugham feels, because not only are they his choice of the ten best novels of the world brought together for the first time as a series, but with the elimination from each of 'the portions it is wise to skip,' they have been made immensely more readable and, consequently, available to a wider audience than they have enjoyed in recent years.

The seasoned reader of Maugham the novelist and teller of tales may be expected to approach these essays with some uneasiness. The transition from fiction to criticism can be a painful one for an author, especially when he undertakes to make it in late career and is the sort of author Maugham is, and it can be even more painful for his admirers if, like Maugham's, they have grown accustomed to looking to him for the same old brand of pleasure served up in the same old way year after year and if they expect him to have the good sense to stay clear of matters that are properly none of his business. Fortunately, Mr Maugham makes the great novelists and their novels his business with as little pain to himself and to his readers and with as much good sense as he has made the ways and foibles of the world his business for the last three or four decades.

Actually his approach is not, in the pure sense, critical at all. He views the novels he has selected with the practised eye of the professional writer and the keen sense for appreciating the best in them of the professional reader. His standards are those he has evolved over the years of his experience with his craft; and they are valid in so far as he has found them applicable to himself. Like most writers, he appreciates in the work of others the qualities he sees in his own and does not generally concern himself with those which he has been unable to acquire. This might easily be a major weakness if it were not for the fact that he has chosen to call great ten novels which fit his specifications closely and which, because they have survived both time and generations of critical appraisal, serve as excellent endorsements of them.

It seems to Mr Maugham that a great novel should be, above all else, entertaining; that it should have a widely interesting theme, a 'coherent and persuasive' story, probability, clarity, vividness, and simplicity, and that, in varying degrees, the novels under discussion have all of these qualities. In his biographical sketches of the authors he applies the personality to the work and the work to the personality and comes through with some penetrating conclusions. Unfortunately, the parallel cannot always be clearly drawn, and it is on the occasions when it cannot—as in the case of Melville—that the sketches become pure biography and the evaluations merely speculative. It may be that Mr Maugham's novelist's interest in character and idiosyncrasy about ideas handicapped him here, for he often gives us more details on the authors' lives than many of them deserve and fewer than would be helpful on the works themselves. The studies of Tolstoy, Emily Brontë, Dostoievsky, and Balzac seem to me the most successful. In them he strikes an effective balance of the two.

It would be incorrect to say that Mr Maugham has made final judgments of the novels and novelists he has chosen as the greatest, or even that he has argued a wholly air-tight case for their selection over a hundred others. What he has given us is his opinion, carefully considered and based on long experience, and he has written it down with his customary grace, in essays that are as pleasing to read as the books they are intended to introduce.

132. Noël Annan, review, *New Statesman and Nation*

n.s. XLVIII, 13 November 1954, 61–2

Noël Gilroy Annan (b. 1916) is a historian of ideas, an academic administrator, and a literary critic. His works include *Leslie Stephen: His Thought and Character in Relation to His Time* (1951, revised 1984). He was created a life peer in 1965 and has been Provost of University College, London, since 1966.

Foreigners tell us that Englishmen always remain schoolboys and I sometimes visualise English society as an ancient school taught by its authors. The classical and Christian Sixth is taken, of course, by Mr Eliot, his rival Mr Forster teaches the modern Sixth, and Mr Amis and Mr Wain have recently been engaged to take the Remove. There is also an indolent form where the rich boys while away their time. It is known as café society and its form-master has always pretended not to be an usher at all. This is Mr Somerset Maugham, who sets up as a worldly observer older than the rocks on which he sits and his eyelids more than a little weary. But he cannot disguise his vocation. He, too, is a schoolmaster of the sort that wears well-cut tweeds and stays with the mothers of his rich young pupils during the holidays; and his mission is to civilise the upper classes. How could he help teaching? He grew up at a time when writers seemed naturally to gravitate to pedagogy. Kipling, Wells and Shaw were followed by Galsworthy, Belloc and Chesterton, and Mr Maugham had the sense to know whom he could teach best. He is one of our best didactic writers, ever ready to point the moral to adorn his tale. The Sixth have never cared for him, but then what are the plaudits of little swots to those of Pop? Mr Maugham has written for Pop, written very well and scored all along the line. He has taught them to tolerate the behaviour of queer fish and not to be surprised if one of their own friends turns out to be rather odd after his sixth martini. But today their lesson is to be not only life but literature: the ten greatest novels.

So it says on the time-table, but in fact the lesson is mainly about life. Mr Maugham is really at a well-known pedagogic game— scoring off the other beaks. We are told that unless a critic is a man of the world his ignorance of life will lead him to make asinine judgments; and unless he is a novelist his ignorance of technique may well be a fatal handicap. This leaves Mr Maugham, who is both, in a pretty strong position. He will modestly acknowledge his debt to a scholar for all his factual information, but his warm handshake is a deceptive judo grip which enables him after a few sentences to send the scholar flying across the room. When Mr Maugham murmurs 'I cannot but think . . .' we know that the critic is in for trouble. He beats the ears off a Doctor of Divinity and Master of an Oxford College for trying to whitewash Fielding's amiable sensuality in two volumes, and time and again he points out that the critics who try to explain away this or that scene in a

novel or quirk in the author's character betray their ignorance of
human beings. I enjoy the spectacle of Mr Maugham gently
extending his claws from the soft fur of his infinitely readable style
and deprecating priggish attempts to paint the great writers
without their warts and protect them against charges which only a
professor would consider discreditable. Mr Maugham is very right.
Dons are singularly inept in their remarks about life; and since, as
everyone knows, they never cheat, lie, get into debt, shake with
passion, nor, their wives being neuter, have any experience of sex,
academic wisdom about human nature is sadly wanting.

Yet is worldly wisdom always so much better? Mr Maugham
thinks that the incident in *Persuasion* where Louisa falls on her head
on the Cobb at Lyme Regis is clumsy. Why should a naval officer
'who has seen action and made a fortune in prize-money' become
paralysed with horror because a girl is stunned? Surely he has
observed that naval officers are curiously shy with well-bred ladies,
and though they have seen death in battle can easily be flummoxed
by a girl in a fainting fit. Then he thinks that Dostoevsky's
psychology is at fault when Nastasia cannot forgive Totsky for
seducing her.

The particular value attached to virginity is a fabrication of the male, due
partly to superstition, partly to masculine vanity and partly, of course, to a
disinclination to father someone else's child. Women, I should say, have
ascribed importance to it chiefly because of the value that men place upon
it, and also from fear of the consequences. . . . I cannot bring myself to
believe that when a virgin 'gives herself' to a man to whom she is
indifferent or actually averse, it is anything but an unpleasant and painful
experience. That it should rankle for years and alter her whole character
seems to me incredible.

I cannot but think that Mr Maugham's knowledge of virgins is
sadly rusty. Has he never heard that many (not all) girls who
surrender their virginity fall passionately in love with the man who
seduces them, a love which can turn to hate particularly if
prolonged and desperate unhappiness ensues? Even on the Riviera
the little dears resent being whisked into bed by clumsy or untender
performers: and it requires only a little imagination to realise that in
nineteenth-century Russia a girl might feel rather more strongly.
Mr Maugham has fallen into a fallacy, which he condemns in
others, of thinking that what he believes to be reasonable must be a
fact.

Then he cannot resist the delights of conjecture, a game as dangerous for him as it is for others. He says that one should not suppose that Emily Brontë's love poems were merely a literary exercise—I did not know that anyone did—and that likely enough she fell in love with one of the mistresses or girls at the school in Halifax where she taught and wrote most of these poems. Here Mr Maugham seems to me to be *narrow-minded*. It is narrow-minded to think that all strong emotion must spring from a direct experience; and everything we know about Emily Brontë suggests that while her feeling for Nature came from direct experience, her feelings about people sprang from the fictitious Kingdoms which existed in her imagination and not from the world about her. Explanations of an author's work in terms of his psychology are rarely satisfactory. They neither tell us what the work is about, nor how far the author achieved what he set out to do, nor why it suceeds or fails. After a time a dreadful fear assails us that these biographies are a device for evading that difficult and unhappy task of getting to grips with the ten greatest novels themselves.

To come to grips with *The Brothers Karamazov* is difficult for a master of naturalism such as Mr Maugham. His cool, rational worldly spirit is repelled by the idea that spiritual suffering cleanses the soul; to him all suffering is evil and the characters of those who suffer are not cured but distorted still further. Such a comment is really meaningless because he is denying that suffering makes people happier, which Dostoevsky was never asserting; the ideals of the novelist and the critic are hopelessly at variance. And when he says that Ivan is more interesting than Dmitri, when he fails to see that the diabolic influence in Dostoevsky's eyes is Ivan's atheism, which is the clue to his extraordinary behaviour at Dmitri's trial, then one is almost (but not quite) persuaded that a Doctor of Divinity would have understood the work better. It is not enough to add that the characters 'palpitate with life.'

Still, he is quite right to teach us to admire palpitation, and his views, which at first appear old-fashioned, are not only sensible but look as if they will soon be accepted even by some of the austerer critics. Entertainment and readability, he says, are among the greatest virtues of the novel; the characters should be convincing and interesting; dialogue exists to bring them to life and advance the story; and vigour, vitality and creative force are more important than a consistently good prose style which few of the great novelists possessed. Moreover, Mr Maugham stands on those liberal principles which need to be reiterated today when he drily asks for some latitude to be used when defining novels as moral or immoral. His remarks need to be taken to heart not so much by the critics as by the politicians and lawyers.

Indeed, I can think of no greater public service that his publishers could render than to send a copy of this humane book *gratis* to Sir Theobald Mathew, the Director of Public Prosecutions. Mr Maugham writes very simply and he should be able to understand it. He and the late Home Secretary remind one of prefects who have slogged their way up the school by sheer strength of character and now urge their monitors to stop smut being talked in the changing-rooms. The present purity campaign is a fascinating spectacle. Every stop in the organ of Good Form, of hypocritical English life, is being pulled out. Novels are declared to be obscene, but sadistic comics for children must not be prohibited for that would interfere with the freedom of the Press; seaside holiday-makers enjoy buying vulgar postcards—that must be stopped at once; and publishers are sagely advised at luncheon not to protest against these prosecutions lest a censorship of literature comparable to that which is exercised over the theatre and cinema might be established. Meanwhile a plaque to Wilde is put up in Tite Street and we all glow with righteous indignation against the savage sentence which he received at the hands of the Victorians, well knowing that he would receive precisely the same sentence today. Indeed, it was only those courageous institutions, Sir Robert Booth-by and the Church of England, who pushed the late Home Secretary from behind and compelled him to set up a committee to investigate sexual offences. But of course we are told that amidst all this no one would dream of censoring real literature.

Why not? The Swindon magistrates when they ordered the *Decameron* to be burnt were only acting in accordance with official notions of purity. Art is frequently pornographic. Like Boucher's enchanting picture of *La Petite Morphil* at Munich, many poems and passages in novels are designed to stimulate the sensual appetites. And very enjoyable they are, too. It is cant to suggest that because every stanza or paragraph is not equally stimulating they are somehow neutralised. Sir Theobald Mathew, poor fellow, has probably not had time to read much literature (except the *Decamer-*

on); but a short anthology could easily be prepared which would give him a sleepless night. The question remains what harm is done by these lascivious writings? Mr Maugham has given the artist's defence:

If you asked him how he could defend himself against the charge of corrupting the young, he would answer that it is very well for the young to learn what sort of world it is that they will have to cope with. The result may be disastrous if they expect too much. If the realist can teach them to expect little from others; to realise from the beginning that each one's main interest is in himself; if he can teach them that, in some way or other, they will have to pay for everything they get, be it place, fortune, honour, love, reputation; and that a great part of wisdom is not to pay for anything more than it is worth, he will have done more than all the pedagogues and preachers to enable them to make the best of this difficult business of living.

Will Sir Theobald and his minions please ponder on these words written by a Companion of Honour?

A WRITER'S NOTEBOOK

London, New York, October 1949

This is a selection from the entries made in the numerous journals kept by Maugham throughout his writing life, which he then destroyed along with most of the remainder of his accumulated private papers.

---

133. Charles Morgan, 'Maugham's Workshop', *Spectator*

CLXXXIII, 7 October 1949, 468

Charles Langbridge Morgan (1894–1958) was a novelist, playwright and a dramatic and literary critic. His theatre reviews appeared anonymously in *The Times* from 1926 to 1939 and have never been collected. His novels include *The Fountain* (1932), *Sparkenbroke* (1936), *The Judge's Story* (1947) and *The River Line* (1949). One of the best-known writers in Britain and France before World War II, Morgan has not yet emerged from a long period of neglect.

Since he was eighteen Mr Maugham has kept notebooks in which he has recorded emotions, ideas and observations of men and things which might afterwards be useful to him as a writer. Some of this material, already used in his books and plays, has been excluded from this volume; the rest appears in it. The result is fascinating in its variety, its candour and, sometimes, its self-repression.

The epigrams of callow youth in the early 'nineties, when the author was in fashionable revolt, have not been shut out. As the years pass, they appear less often and become less wilfully decorative, but the young man's eagerness to shock himself and the world continues surprisingly long. As late as 1901, when his age is twenty-seven, a careful and shrewd assessment of Matthew Arnold's style is followed by this:

I'm glad I don't believe in God. When I look at the misery of the world and its bitterness, I think that no belief can be more ignoble.

The next year yields this note:

Bed. No woman is worth more than a fiver unless you're in love with her. Then she is worth all she costs you.

This is the so-called 'cynicism' of the period, corresponding to the smartness of the chromium-plated or hard-boiled generation two decades later. But Mr Maugham was not writing only this. Almost at the same time, in a comment on Jeremy Taylor, with whom he was by no means in complete sympathy, he could write: 'One cannot turn a page without finding some felicitous expression, some new order of simple words which seems to give them a new value,' and simplicity is the quality in Jeremy Taylor which most critics miss. Mr Maugham saw it unerringly, and, being himself a writer by instinct, was not deterred by any differences of theological opinion from proclaiming it. This is why the book is valuable. It is what it says it is: a *writer's* notebook, not an ideology masquerading as criticism or an autobiography pretending to final wisdom.

It is interesting, in the first place, that Mr Maugham should have kept these notebooks at all. For an imaginative writer, the method is of debatable value, and in his preface he debates it, fully aware of the danger that you may rely overmuch on your notes 'and so lose the even and natural flow of your writing which comes from allowing the unconscious that full activity which is somewhat pompously known as inspiration.' But there is another danger which he does not speak of—namely, that the habitual note-taker may lose the even and natural flow, not of his writing only, but of his experience itself; he may become unable to resist a temptation to reach for a pencil while his lady's smile is still incomplete. And this tendency to see life in terms of art—though it will be despised as 'cold blooded' by those only who do not know what imaginative writing is—can be perilous if the process of transmutation is too swift.

Experience, if given a chance, performs for an artist a miraculous pre-selection among her riches before submitting them to his conscious selectiveness. His notebook, if it becomes habitual and clamorous, may interfere with the miracle by demanding too much, too soon. Of this a writer of Mr Maugham's quality is necessarily aware. Nevertheless, he has kept notebooks for nearly sixty years. The reason is the only good one: that for him the advantages were greater than the disadvantages. Vineyards are not uniform, nor are their processes. His grape-juice of experience was best matured in this way. If he had been primarily a poet, if he had been nearer to Turgenev than to Flaubert, the balance might have swung the other way, but he is an analytical observer, and his notebooks were necessary to him as store-houses of material for analysis.

Scenes and people in the Pacific, in Russia, in India, in the United States; sketches of character, outlines of stories, passages of criticism, reflections on a host of subjects from the Absolute to the destiny of France: all are preserved with an admirable detachment, as if the writer had said to himself as each was put away, 'Perhaps not, but one never knows the value of material until one has treated it.' Nor is the material 'raw'. This is no scribbling of notes at random. Preliminary treatment has been applied. Some of the outlines are indeed such masterpieces of brevity that their own perfection may well have forbidden the development which was at first intended.

Mr Maugham's 'self-repression' has been spoken of, and the word needs to be explained. There is in his writing a quality which has been miscalled 'cynicism.' A cynic, by Wilde's definition, is 'a man who knows the price of everything and the value of nothing,' but a cynic is bleaker than that—he is one for whom the problem of values is boring or non-existent. For Mr Maugham it is of perpetual interest; either directly, or, in his notes on religious subjects, indirectly, he continually reverts to it. 'Though the turn of my mind,' he says, 'is concrete and my intelligence moves inactively among abstractions, I have a passion for metaphysics....' His self-repression consists in a refusal to allow that passion to have effect.

I do not wish to raise any question of agreement or disagreement with his interpretation of Epicureanism, but only to remark that his lucid and discerning mind, whenever it approaches the abstract, has a disconcerting habit of suddenly refusing a fence and swerving into irrelevance. For example, he turns away from the concept of Absolute Beauty by asking, 'What sort of absolute is it that is affected by personal idiosyncrasy, training, fashion, habit, sex and novelty?' The answer is that the absolute is not affected. Though we attain to the concept of it through our various and stumbling perceptions of things we call beautiful, its being is not in those things and is not diminished either by our ceasing to value them or even by their annihilation. The idea of Absolute Beauty may or may not be delusory; but it certainly cannot be invalidated by the destruction of Chartres cathedral or by our coming to think that the cathedral is ugly.

Mr Maugham again refuses a fence in his discussion of the nature of the soul. Character, he has said, is the soul's sensible manifestation. Character is affected by the accidents of the body. Therefore, he argues, again confusing the idea with one of the things through which it may be apprehended, the soul must be affected by the accidents of the body; and he adds: 'I find it then impossible to believe that the soul thus contingent on the accidents of the body can exist in separation from it. When you see the dead it can hardly fail to occur to you that they do look awfully dead.' Something prevents him from seeing that his final sentence, far from clinching his argument, re-opens it. Might it not be that a body looks 'awfully dead' precisely because the soul is separated from it?

The greater a reader's respect for Mr Maugham, not as a master-craftsman only but as an artist, the stronger will his desire be to do more than cover this book with urbane compliments. He will be led, as I have been, to grapple with it in an attempt to discover that special tension which gives character and vitality to the author's work. This tension arises, I think, from a conflict between his 'passion for metaphysics' and his determination not to give himself or his characters the benefit of the doubt. If he has an affectation or mannerism it is of ruthlessness. This is partly honesty and courage, but partly fear. Fear of what? Of sentimentality? Of being duped? Of self-deception? Honourable fears, but still fears, and fears are conditions of the imagination which criticism too seldom attempts to understand. They run like a shudder across these pages. They are among the winds that drive Mr Maugham's powerful ship.

134. V.S. Pritchett, review, *New Statesman and Nation*

n.s. XXXVIII, 8 October 1949, 401

'My object is to find a rule of conduct for the average man under the normal conditions of the present day.' That is the kind of sentence we might expect to find in the autobiography of Benjamin Franklin; it was written down in his notebook during his very early twenties by Mr Somerset Maugham, when he was making his way out of a sheltered and conventional upbringing and sharpening his teeth on the world. It is unfair to make much of the juvenilia of writers, though Mr Maugham, with his usual detachment, has let his early moralisings stand, but occasionally an early phrase will cast a long shadow: already the paradox of Mr Maugham's character is displayed in its austere quest for worldly wisdom. Those who discover they do not believe in God had better begin a search for what they do believe in. And over fifty years later, among the rules in the same notebook, we notice this echo from Dr Johnson:

> There is no need for the writer to eat a whole sheep to be able to tell you what mutton tastes like. It is enough if he eats a cutlet. *But he should do that.*

The italics of the last, powerful and operative phrase are mine. Mr Maugham lies between the whole sheep eaters and the Lotus eaters: he has kept, wisely, to the moralist's cutlet.

And so, his notebooks—the random collection of a lifetime's moralisings, epigrams, portraits of people, jottings for stories, descriptions of scenes, which a novelist is bound to keep, hoping that they will be eventually useful—are as agreeable to read as any of his set pieces. Uncertain and sententious in his early years, at the time of moral crisis, they quickly grow into the familiar manner, so suave and yet with the fine cutting edge, when the success he confidently expected arrives. What is lacking is the transforming passion which is the impulse of creative writing; what is always active: his integrity as a writer. Honesty has his vanity as an author—his desire, like Mérimée's, is neither to dupe nor to be duped—and his honesty has been, one suspects, a desire to get questions settled and to make time and place for the continuous demands of his talents. That is to say he is probably more ruthless than honest, a practical rather than a seeking moralist. One has only to compare his notes with Gide's—though we must admit the difference between a journal of private life and a writer's working notes—to see that Maugham's are of the kind that seal off or put an end to what he is discussing:

It may be that it is the I in us which is the cause of our wickedness, but it is the cause too of our music, our painting, our poetry. And so what?

or

I don't know why it is that the religious never ascribe common sense to God.

Again, to compare him with two other note-takers: Jules Renard, whose *Journal* led Mr Maugham, albeit with humility, to publish these notes, and with Henry James. To the former Mr Maugham denies creative power, by which he means the power to enlarge his material. This seems to me a narrow use of the words: Gide came closer to Renard when he said that Renard was 'not a stream but a distillery.' And of fierce spirits, indeed. Of course, Renard lacked invention, and yet, to judge by the quarrels caused by his *Journal*, he was thought inventive enough. There is a creative power which is in the seeing and which may amount to a reduction and not an enlargement of the subject. It is a dangerous argument to say that Renard's theories were simply justifications of his shortcomings as a 'novelist' who was obliged, by lack of invention, to stick to his own experience. The originality of many writers has come from the bold use of their weaknesses. The bad writers are those who have never known their own limits or weaknesses, and have never had the patience and the art to turn them to account.

Nor, after Renard, shall we find in Mr Maugham's notes those ecstatic soliloquies of Henry James, crooning alone in his room

390

among his precious particles, his *données* and *dénouements*, and comically caught in the tremendous mystification of moving, say, Maisie from Sir Claude to Mrs Wix, and then, in sublime infatuation, back again. Mr Maugham's notes have a natural lack of such intimacies. Like his epigrams, his notes close doors. What went on in his imagination when he used this note or that we shall not know until we make the jump from fact to invention.

He is a well-mannered writer. What he writes, even if it is only a note, is finished and well done. It can be perfunctory: forty years later this became 'The Colonel's Lady':

> They were talking about V.F. whom they'd all known. She published a volume of passionate love poems, obviously not addressed to her husband. It made them laugh to think that she'd carried on a long affair under his nose, and they'd have given anything to know what he felt when at last he read them.

Or extensive, but factual, like the original note for 'Rain'. Here is one passage:

> The lodging house. It is a two storey frame house with verandas on both floors, and it is about five minutes walk from the dock, on the Broad Road, and faces the sea. Below is a store in which are sold canned goods, pork and beans, beef, hamburger steak, canned asparagus, peaches and apricots, and cotton goods, lava-lavas, hats, raincoats and the like. The owner is a half-caste with a native wife surrounded by little brown children. The rooms are almost bare of furniture, a poor iron bed with a ragged mosquito curtain, a ricketty chair and a washstand. The rain rattles down on the corrugated iron roof. No meals are provided.

That description has been a little cut for the story. The portraits of the tart, the missionary and his wife have been taken almost word for word from the notes.

Like most novelists, Maugham has not used the greater part of his notes. They are the environment rather than the material, and they disclose that part of a writer which is really the traveller, the cutlet-eater. The portraits are of two kinds: those of people so immediately interesting that, maddeningly, they are complete and there is nothing to be done with them; those of uninteresting people, the decent man, the pleasant woman whom the author feverishly catalogues hoping to overcome his repugnance to the normal, hypnotised by a hopeless attraction to it. For the featureless presents a challenge to the novelist. Cannot he provoke one phrase? There is the Flemish innkeeper with 'his fat, tardy laugh.' That was worth catching. A shy and difficult acquaintance, he produced, heavily and slowly, this apology for consulting his wife before he agreed to serve his customer: '*Il faut bien que je la demande puisque je couche avec.*' There is a description of a scene in a makeshift hospital in France in 1914, which is as powerful as any of Whitman's notes on the Civil War, and leaves one with the regret that Mr Maugham, whose real subject has always been pain, should have drifted away to the sociable and the bizarre. The gain to urbanity has been a loss to passion. Two other grim sets of notes, those on the convict settlement in Martinique (the scene of one of his best stories of the middle period) and on life in Bermondsey before the war, confirm the impression.

Bermondsey. Dan has been out of work for months. He is miserable and humiliated, and his brother Bert, who is in work, bullies him. He throws it in Dan's face that he keeps him. To take it out of him he makes him do odd jobs for him. Dan is so wretched that he feels he'd like to make an end of himself, and it requires all his mother's persuasion to get him to wait till something turns up. The mother, Mrs Bailey, is a charwoman who works in a Government office in Whitehall. She goes out at six in the morning and doesn't get back till six at night. One day Bert comes home and because Dan hasn't fetched his other shirt from the laundry and he wants to go out, he swears at him. They have a fight and Dan, smaller, weaker, ill fed, gets a thrashing. Mrs Bailey comes in and stops the fight. She roundly abuses Bert. He says he's sick of it all and he's going to be married. They are horrified; without his week's money, with Dan earning nothing, it's impossible for Mrs Bailey to support herself, Dan and the two younger children. It means starvation. They tell Bert he can't get married, at least not till Dan gets work; he says he must, his girl's going to have a baby. He flings out. They are all crying. Mrs Bailey goes down on her knees and makes the others, Dan and the two children, do so too, and she prays God to have mercy on them and help them. They are still praying when Bert comes back with the shirt he has just fetched for himself. He looks at them angrily.

'Oh, all right, all right,' he shouts. 'I'll give her ten bob to get rid of the little bastard.'

The Bermondsey novel was never written; the interesting thing about that note is its intimate, factual accuracy, the lack of any spoiling suggestion from a view of art that would be hostile to it. But seeing these few Bermondsey pages among the innumerable comments on travel in the East, in Russia and America, among the sea of faces which Mr Maugham has put down, it is hard to see how they could have stood their ground among the distractions of civility. Mainly Mr Maugham has been drawn to the romantic disappointment, and not to the tragedy where no illusion or expectation lay in the first place.

Dozens of notes in this book bring to mind the seriousness of Mr Maugham's vocation, the austerity that lies within the worldliness. His description of Kerensky during the revolution is a brilliant piece of character-drawing and one of the most direct accounts of the beginning of the upheaval that I have ever read. His richness, at his best, is like Mérimée's (I don't quite understand how the comparison with Maupassant was ever made; the notes contain an amusing attack on Maupassant and Turgenev and a surprising defence of Chehov which he has let stand, though now his opinion is very different). For like Mérimée he is masked, if not altogether self-effacing; and in observation he is like a cool hunter. He is far less an aesthete than Mérimée and, of course, no poet; he believes that the value of art is to be judged by 'the right action,' to which, in the philosopher's sense, it leads; but, like Mérimée, he injects irony to close subjects, to paralyse wounds. His notes do not add, for this reason, a new sensation to our lives, or open us to new experience. They suggest, rather, the price he has paid for his. It is a tribute to the quickness of his curiosity that they should have the immediate and diverse readableness of his finished work.

135. W.H. Auden, 'Notebooks of Somerset Maugham', *New York Times*

23 October 1949, 1, 22

Wystan Hugh Auden (1907–73) was a major English poet, critic and (in collaboration with Christopher Isherwood) dramatist, a leading figure in the literary movement which came into prominence in England in the 1930s. He settled in

America in 1939, receiving American citizenship in 1946. In a note in an anthology Maugham edited in 1943 he wrote, not very appropriately, of 'the savagery of W.H. Auden's poetry'.

A career as long, as productive and as successful as Somerset Maugham's earns a writer his membership in that select and curious group which Jean Cocteau has aptly named *Les monstres sacrés*. When Maugham publishes a new book, therefore, it would be dishonest of the critic to pretend that he either can or wishes to read it as if it were by an unknown writer or to judge it by esthetic standards alone; in addition to any literary merit, it has inevitably and, I think, quite properly a historic interest as the act of a person in whom one has long been interested. Having for us a history, the author has become not only a novelist but also a character in our novel, and a platitude or a blind spot is scarcely less revealing (and therefore fascinating) than an insight or an area of enthusiasm.

In describing *A Writer's Notebook* it may be as well to begin by saying what it is not. It is not—no one who is familiar with Maugham's work would expect it to be— a series of personal confessions. I have found only five in the whole book: that he always expected to be successful, that he has a recurrent dream of the City of God, that the famous rumor of his fainting at the sight of the Yogi is untrue, that he can never remember the order of the letters in the alphabet, and that he still has twenty-six of his own teeth. Nor is it a collection of practical tips for the would-be writer; I have found only one and that for his parents—'Give him a hundred and fifty a year [pre-war pounds] for five years and tell him to go to the devil.'

It is the condensation of fifteen volumes of notes begun when he was 18 years old in which, as he says in his preface (which contains, by the way, an acute comparison of the English and the French literary life): 'I never made a note of anything that I did not think would be useful to me at one time or another in my work, and though, especially in the early notebooks, I jotted down all kinds of thoughts and emotions of a personal nature, it was only with the intention of ascribing them sooner or later to the creatures of my invention. I meant my notebooks to be a storehouse of materials for future use and nothing else.'

Their primary fascination for any reader of a younger generation than Somerset Maugham's derives from the fact that, while the problem of every man and writer is at all times essentially the same, namely, first to learn to be himself and then to learn to be not himself, its specific content changes rapidly and radically.

For example, Maugham grew up during the Eighteen Nineties, when the fashion in literature was the Wildean epigram and the Pateresque jeweled prose, for neither of which, as it happened, he had a talent, yet began by trying dutifully to produce, as a young writer today might attempt the stichomythia of Hemingway or the dialectic of Kafka. Gradually, through his own experience of life and his contact with other styles like those of Voltaire and Matthew Arnold he learns where his real interests lie and what he can do well. Even more striking, perhaps, than the difference in literary climate is the difference in the theological and moral world climate between the bourgeois, Erastian, largely deist Anglicanism of the prosperous England in which he was raised and the pseudo-scientific nihilism of the ruins which surround us now.

No young writer today would set down as a significant reflection—'Even if it held that pure unselfishness without after-thought gives most pleasure and brings the greatest rewards, that pleasure and those rewards are still its justifications'—not because hedonism is any less true or false than it then was, but because it is no longer a battle-cry of liberation from hypocritical relatives but merely an echo of the flat, dreadful, familiar voice of our jailers. Similarly, he will scarcely find it necessary to demand more sexual freedom; his aphorisms, if he makes them at all, are much more likely to concern the lack of a limiting principle to give his passions order and meaning. (How few of us have the strength of character to be even capable of the sustained folly of the hero in *Of Human Bondage*?)

Of himself as a writer Maugham says: 'My native gifts are not remarkable, but I have a certain force of character which has enabled me in a measure to supplement my deficiencies. I have common sense. Most people cannot see anything, but I can see what is part of my nose with extreme clearness; the greatest writers can see through a brick wall. My vision is not so penetrating.'

Like nearly all self-analyses, this is at once too modest as regards the gifts and too proud as regards the character, for what lies in

395

front of one's nose depends upon the direction in which one chooses to look. The greatest writer cannot see through a brick wall, but, unlike the rest of us, he refuses to erect them. The writer to whom we find it most difficult to be fair, whom we accuse of knowing nothing about 'Life'—in Maugham's case he seems to be Henry James—is the one whose particular brick wall happens to be different from one's own wall, which stands unrecognized behind our vision precisely because it is self-made or unconsciously inherited.

The criticism which can be made of Maugham, as it must of all but the great masters, is that, having succeeded in becoming himself, he has been, as a writer and on the whole, content to remain so.

All through *A Writer's Notebook* there appear Theophrastian character sketches and anecdotes recorded because they struck the author as potential material for stories. What strikes the reader is their similarity. The ironic contradiction of character occurs time and time again: the teetotal philanthropist turns out to be a secret drinker, the brutal resident in Malaya becomes genteel in Cheltenham, the formidable mother-in-law is found naked in a hotel, murdered by a piece of trade—such are typical of the kind of 'life' which he succeeds in portraying.

There are indications, however, that they are not the only kind of story he would like to tell. 'Fiction,' he says, 'has never enriched the world with a more delightful character than Alyosha Karamazov,' and one suspects that the deepest wish of a writer who has so often been called cynical has, all along, been to write a story about heroic goodness. He notes down the suggestions for such and in both cases, with an honesty as admirable as it must, for him, be sad, adds a note : 'It was too difficult for me to cope with and I never wrote it.'

I think many readers are going to be surprised—I certainly was—to learn that Somerset Maugham, of all people, believes 'that the value of art lies in its effects...not in beauty but in right action.'

A Writer's Notebook ends on a valedictory note: 'I am like a passenger waiting for his ship at a wartime port. I do not know on which day it will sail, but I am ready to embark at a moment's notice...I read the papers and flip the pages of a magazine, but when someone offers to lend me a book I refuse because I may not

have time to finish it, and in any case with this journey before me I
am not of a mind to interest myself in it. I strike up acquaintances at
the bar or the cardtable, but I do not try to make friends with
people from whom I shall so soon be parted, I am on the wing.'

To which we can only answer: 'We shall miss you. Of course we
shall find new writers to read, but art, like friendship, is personal,
that is, unique, and no writer is replaceable by or even comparable
with another. Thank you for having given us so much pleasure for
so long, for having never been tedious'—and so wish him
Godspeed.

136. S.N. Behrman, 'The Notes of a Popular Pessimist', *New Yorker*

XXV, 29 October 1949, 88, 91–4

Samuel Nathaniel Behrman (1893–1973) was a playwright
whose plays include *Jane*, a dramatisation of Maugham's
short story of that title, which was produced in London in
1947 and in New York in 1952. His memoirs of growing up
in Massachusetts were published in *The Worcester Account*
(1954). He was a regular contributor to the *New Yorker* after
World War II.

In the summer of 1908 there were four plays by W. Somerset
Maugham running simultaneously in London. Nothing like that
had ever happened before, and *Punch* published a cartoon showing
four posters announcing the Maugham plays and, huddled before
them, the figure of William Shakespeare, enviously scowling and
biting his fingernails. When Maugham quit as a playwright,
because, as he put it, he would no longer endure the 'indignity' of
the theatre, he was an immensely popular dramatist, played all over
the world. Last year, at seventy-five, he saw his books, in English
and in translation, sell two million copies. In addition to having a
huge public in the United States, he is adored in France, in the

Scandinavian countries, and in his own favorite country, Spain. Except by the critics, he is almost universally read. This unusual popularity is surprising, considering that Maugham's outlook— just as clearly expressed in his *A Writer's Notebook* as it is in the earliest of his short stories—is profoundly pessimistic. Often in his *Notebook*, which contains notes he has made over the past fifty-seven years, he complains of the authors—the Russians, especially—who have no sunshine in them. Yet there is no sunshine in Maugham; there is plenty of heat but no sunshine, in the sense in which he uses the word. There is a minimum of hope, no joie de vivre; the pervading tone is sardonic, fatalistic, sombre. His characters have almost no chance against fate. In his funny stories—and he has written some very funny ones—the tone is decidedly astringent. There is no 'lift' in Maugham. With him, love is not an ecstasy; it's an agony, a humiliation, a penalty. It is rather paradoxical that a writer of whom these things may be said should have attained a popularity so staggering. I think the answer lies in the fact that his personality comes through in all his work and fascinates his readers, as it does those who have encountered it in person. It is a personality at once frankly revealed and withdrawn (he will tell you everything, up to a point); he manages to be at once candid and enigmatic. He is a patrician with a disdain for all forms of snobbery, remote from others in essence but close to them in common sense. Common sense is his fetish; in the *Notebook*, he reproaches the French, whom he loves, and God, whom he does not love, for being deficient in it. As for his fame, he is perfectly willing, as an exemplar of common sense, to enjoy its emoluments to the full while deprecating the process that gave it to him as one of the blind and unpredictable forces that make up the sometimes entertaining but generally frustrating huggermugger of life. This subject furnishes one of the last of his notes:

Gushing, she said to me: 'What does it feel like to be famous?' I suppose I've been asked the question twenty times and I never could think how to answer, but today, too late, it suddenly occurred to me. 'It's like having a string of pearls given you. It's nice, but after a while, if you think of it at all, it's only to wonder if they're real or cultured.' And now that I have my reply ready I don't expect anyone will ever put the question to me again.

Maugham has come to treat his own personality and career as he does those of the characters in his stories—with humorous irony.

'When my obituary notice at last appears in the *Times*, and they say: "What! I thought he died years ago," my ghost will gently chuckle,' he writes. A Parisian painter engaged on a portrait of André Gide, who was living near Maugham's villa on the French Riviera, came to lunch with Maugham one day last spring. He asked Maugham if he knew Gide. Maugham said that he had never met him, although he had once shared a railway compartment with him on the Golden Arrow between London and Paris. The painter was surprised that Maugham had not introduced himself. 'It might have been embarrassing!' said his host. 'It might have run like this: "M. Gide, I'm Somerset Maugham," and M. Gide might well have asked, "Who?" Wouldn't risk it.' He risks it in his books, though, and countless readers have come to feel that in him they have an acquaintance who is somewhat off the beaten path. For the sophisticates of the international set he is, of course, one of themselves, but for the innumerable others he is a close observer who travels everywhere, knows everybody, and could belong to the best clubs if he wanted to. He doesn't want to, because he realizes that the members are bores. This is a comfort to the millions whose exclusion is involuntary.

All this is very well, but it leaves out a major ingredient in Maugham's popularity—his remarkable storytelling gift. Storytelling is a firm and severe craft, and his *Notebook* gives some insight into its workings. Maugham is aware, without being too much disturbed by it, of the criticism that he has written too much. 'The trouble is,' he admits, without any apology, 'that I could never write fast enough to get my ideas down.' The *Notebook* contains outlines for at least twenty unwritten Maugham stories. (It would be interesting to see if anyone else could write them.) Those loathsome interstices 'between ideas' that torture other writers seem never to have existed for Maugham; the *Notebook* is a repository of overflow. One may belong to the group of writers who think that he is the greatest master of the short story since Maupassant; one may belong to that other group of writers— Glenway Wescott wrote amusingly about them in an article entitled 'Somerset Maugham and Posterity' (Mr Wescott is much more sanguine about Maugham's chances with the unborn set than Maugham is)—who are driven crazy by his existence and by his sales; but if one is at all interested in fiction as a commodity that may have some intrinsic value even if it is salable, one may find out in Maugham's current volume of self-revelation a good deal about how it is produced. Since he doesn't intend to use it any more, he gives other writers the run of his workshop. His craft hints fall into three categories: notes from which he subsequently molded successful stories; stories that undoubtedly would have been successful had he found the time to write them; and, finally, stories that he didn't write because (a) he didn't know how to handle them or (b) they didn't fit his particular formula. In three notes written in Pago Pago in 1916, you find the raw material from which 'Rain' was made; a short paragraph written in 1901 gave him 'The Colonel's Lady' in 1941. But it is too late for authors in search of an idea to do anything about these; Maugham anticipated them. However, here is one of perhaps twenty or thirty stories in the book that Maugham didn't have the time to write and that writers with more leisure might take a fling at:

They're both dead now. They were brothers. One was a painter and the other a doctor. The painter was convinced that he had genius. He was arrogant, irascible, and vain, and he despised his brother as a philistine and a sentimentalist. But he earned practically nothing and would have starved except for the money his brother gave him. The strange thing was that though bearish and uncouth in manner and appearance he painted pretty-pretty pictures. Now and then he managed to have an exhibition and always sold a couple of canvases. Never more. At last the doctor grew conscious of the fact that his brother wasn't a genius after all, but only a second-rate painter. It was hard for him after all the scrifices he'd made. He kept his discovery to himself. Then he died, leaving all he had to his brother. The painter found in the doctor's house all the pictures he had sold to unknown buyers for twenty-five years. At first he couldn't understand. After thinking it over he hit upon the explanation: the cunning fellow had wished to make a good investment.

Here is another, which Maugham didn't write because of his strong views on what a short story should be (his comment on why he didn't write it is interesting):

A week or two ago someone related an incident to me with the suggestion that I should write a story on it, and since then I have been thinking it over. I don't see what to do. The incident is as follows: Two young fellows were working on a tea plantation in the hills and the mail had to be fetched from a good way off, so that they only got it at rather long intervals. One of the young fellows, let us call him A., used to get a lot of letters by every mail, ten or twelve and sometimes more, but the other, B., never got one. He used to watch A. enviously as he took his bundle and started to read, he hankered to have a letter, just one letter, and one day, when they were expecting the mail, he said to A.: 'Look here, you always have a packet of letters and I never get any. I'll give you five pounds if you'll let me have one of yours.' 'Right-ho', said A. and when the mail came in he handed B. his letters and said to him: 'Take whichever you like.' B. gave him a five-pound note, looked over the letters, chose one and returned the rest. In the evening, when they were having a whisky and soda after dinner, A. asked casually: 'By the way, what was that letter about?' 'I'm not going to tell you,' said B. A., somewhat taken aback, said: 'Well, who was it from?' 'That's my business,' answered B. They had a bit of an argument, but B. stood on his rights and refused to say anything about the letter that he had bought. A. began to fret, and as the weeks went by he did all he could to persuade B. to let him see the letter. B. continued to refuse. At length A., anxious, worried, curious, felt he couldn't bear it any longer, so he went to B. and said: 'Look here, here's your five pounds, let me have my letter back again.' 'Not on your life,' said B. 'I bought and paid for it, it's my letter and I'm not going to give it up.'

That's all. I suppose if I belonged to the modern school of story writers, I should write it just as it is and leave it. It goes against the grain with me. I want a story to have form, and I don't see how you can give it that unless you can bring it to a conclusion that leaves no legitimate room for questioning. But even if you could bring yourself to leave the reader up in the air you don't want to leave yourself up in the air with him.

A great part of *A Writer's Notebook* is concerned with philosophical and religious questions; Maugham has a teleological obsession. The abiding passion of his life, he says at the end, has been the study of philosophy. As an amateur philosopher, he has a certain status; an American professional, who was staying with him at his villa a few months ago, reports that a longish critique of Kant's *Critique*, which Maugham wrote for his guest's scrutiny and edification, is, within its narrow limits, very original; it is a closely reasoned attempt to dig out of the Sage of Königsberg a code of life and thought that will meet Maugham's exiguous standards of common sense. The American professional has, on the strength of this essay, invited the British amateur to lecture here on Kant before a gathering of professional philosophers. Maugham discusses many abstruse questions, but never in language that is not easily comprehensible to any intelligent reader. Nor is he ever inhibited from setting down a thought by the reflection that others have had it before; his sole interest is the process by which he arrived at it. Oddly, there is something about his preoccupation with a personal God that gives this part of the book a faintly Victorian flavor.

Maugham writes constantly about God as about someone he hasn't met and never expects to meet but dislikes intensely by reputation. Here is a characteristic passage, from near the end, about the soul:

But what is the soul? From Plato onwards many answers have been given to this question, and most of them are but modifications of his conjectures. We use the word constantly, and it must be presumed that we mean something by it. Christianity has accepted it as an article of faith that the soul is a simple spiritual substance created by God and immortal. One may not believe that and yet attach some signification to the word. When I ask myself what I mean by it I can only answer that I mean by it my consciousness of myself, the I in me, the personality which is me; and that personality is compounded of my thoughts, my feelings, my experiences, and the accidents of my body. I think many people shrink from the notion that the accidents of the body can have an effect on the constitution of the soul. There is nothing of which for my own part I am more assured. My soul would have been quite different if I had not stammered or if I had been four or five inches taller; I am slightly prognathous, in my childhood they did not know that this could be remedied by a gold band worn while the jaw is still malleable; if they had, my countenance would have borne a different cast, the reaction toward me of my fellows would have been different, and therefore my disposition, my attitude to them, would have been different too. But what sort of thing is this soul that can be modified by a dental apparatus? We all know how greatly changed our lives would have been if we had not by what seems mere chance met such and such a person or if we had not been at a particular moment at a particular place; and so our character, and so our soul, would have been other than they are.

In 1896, in a note set down in Capri, when he was twenty-two, Maugham wrote:

I wander about alone, forever asking myself the same questions: What is the meaning of life? Has it any object or end? Is there such a thing as morality? How ought one to conduct oneself in life? What guide is there? Is there one road better than another?... I could make nothing out of it all; it seemed to me one big tangle. In desperation, I cried out: I can't understand it. I don't know, I don't know.

More than half a century later, in the lovely villa that, after long wandering, he has made his home and that is as carefully constructed for his way of life as are his best stories, he still queries and still discovers no answer. The price one has to pay for life is, for him, too high; the consolation others find in art, he denies himself: 'Some have ascribed to art a value which is its own justification and persuaded themselves that the wretched lot of the common run of men was not too high a price to pay for the radiant productions of painter and poet. I look askance at such an attitude.... Art, unless it leads to right action, is no more than the opium of an intelligentsia.' If there is any assuagement, Maugham finds it in the contemplation of heroic conduct—in 'the defiant gesture of Paddy Finucane when, plunging to his death, he transmitted the message to the airmen in his squadron: "This is it, chaps."' It is characteristic that in his whole *Notebook* Maugham seldom mentions any of his celebrated friends. Innumerable famous people, from Kipling to Winston Churchill, have stayed at his villa, but Maugham is really interested in ordinary, rather than in what he calls 'notorious,' people. That Maugham's readers feel a personal relationship with him is attested by his fan mail, which, another recent visitor to his villa reports, is voluminous and incessant, and comes from all over the world. Maugham thinks that the reason people take the trouble to write him is that they are lonely. He answers all except the unanswerable. A lady wrote from Cleveland to confide in him that she was in love, that she wondered how she could get her man, and, even more, how if she got him, she could hold him. Maugham answered crisply, 'The way to get a man is to be sexually attractive; the way to hold him is to be sexually satisfactory.'

This *Notebook* is, in a sense, Maugham's valedictory. He summarizes the advantages of old age, but he admits they are cold comfort. This is his last word:

I am like a passenger waiting for his ship at a wartime port. I do not know on which day it will sail, but I am ready to embark at a moment's notice. I leave the sights of the city unvisited. I do not want to see the fine new speedway along which I shall never drive, nor the grand new theatre, with all its modern appliances, in which I shall never sit. I read the papers and flip the pages of a magazine, but when someone offers to lend me a book I refuse because I may not have time to finish it, and in any case with this journey before me I am not of a mind to interest myself in it. I strike up acquaintances at the bar or the card-table, but I do not try to make friends with people from whom I shall so soon be parted. I am on the wing.

From his will and from the force of his character, Maugham has created a way of life that has served him, and a long shelf of books. It has been an extraordinary exercise in craftsmanship. Now, as he approaches the end, he manages to endow it too, if not with sunshine, at least with suspense.

THE VAGRANT MOOD

London, New York, October 1952

---

137. Sir John Squire, 'Somerset Maugham as Essayist', *Illustrated London News*

CCXXI, 15 November 1952, 802

John Collings Squire (1884–1958) was a poet, essayist, anthologist, parodist and editor. His books include *Poems in One Volume* (1926), and his autobiography *The Honeysuckle and the Bee* (1937). As a literary journalist he moved from the *New Statesman* to found the *London Mercury* in 1918, which he edited until 1933. The periodical provided a platform for the 'Georgian' school of poets, of whom Squire was the champion. He was knighted in 1933.

Mr Somerset Maugham has had a long, full and variegated life. He began his adult education as a medical student, and his literary career as a novelist with *Liza of Lambeth*. In that first phase he was recognised as a man of unusual talent by a small circle of people. He then switched to the theatre and had a rapid success as a playwright who could turn easily from caustic social satire to jolly farce—in which last connection I must say that I wish that I could see a revival of *Jack Straw*, even though Charles Hawtrey is not still alive to play the principal part. I trust to memory, and I may be a few years out in my dates, but I seem to remember that it was even before the 1914 war that he had five plays running in London at once, with his name picked out in bright lights over the porticos of five theatres. However that may be, there came a time when, though continuing the production of plays, he resumed the practice of fiction. He wrote novels, he wrote short stories, but the plays went on. Then there came a point at which he produced what I think the sincerest and the most deeply felt of all his plays, *Sheppey*; one that began with a very cunningly contrived comic first act and then got down to fundamentals and gave us a glimpse of the romantic concealed beneath the surface of this reputedly cynical worldling. It failed. Unless I am mistaken, with that play Mr Maugham bade farewell to the stage, thinking: 'If they won't take my pearls they shan't have any more husks.' But to stop writing; that was too much for him. More novels followed; and then a reticent, precise volume of reminiscences; and now there comes a collection of literary essays.

They are of varying quality: the chapter entitled 'Some Novelists I Have Known' is rather flimsy, and contains a rather unkind passage about Arnold Bennett, whom the author liked, but whom, I think, he didn't quite understand: though he does realise what a barrier Bennett's stammer was between Bennett and the world. But the other chapters are all extremely good, and deal so acutely with subjects so various that it is evident that, had he never been what Bennett used to call 'a creative artist,' he might have been an extremely penetrating and catholic critic along the lines of Sainte-Beuve. He writes of Augustus Hare (whom he knew in youth), of Zurbaran, of the 'Decline and Fall of the Detective Story,' of Burke, and of the philosopher Kant. All these chapters have led me to think that Maugham would be a delightful man to discuss things with and to differ from—if only about ending sentences with prepositions.

It is rather difficult to review a book which has so many subjects as this. Had Mr Maugham devoted himself entirely to Augustus Hare, to the Detective Story, to Burke (and I am horrified as I realise that Burke and Hare have once more been brought together) or to Kant, one could have concentrated on one theme and have said something about the subject and Mr Maugham's attitude to it. Had he written only about Augustus Hare, that industrious cicerone and snob, who wrote so voluminous an autobiography and was so complacent, it would have been possible to write a whole page about Hare. What a man to write about! Mr Maugham writes of his elder: 'I was accustomed to family prayers and I noticed that some of the prayers Augustus read sounded strangely in my ears. Then I discovered that he had neatly inked out many lines in the Prayer Book he read from. I asked him why.

'"I've crossed out all the passages in glorification of God," he said. "God is certainly a gentleman, and no gentleman cares to be praised to his face. It is tactless, impertinent and vulgar. I think all that fulsome adulation must be highly offensive to him."' But—though Hare will doubtless have monographs devoted to him later, and was certainly a zealous explorer both of ancient Rome and of fashionable England—no sooner has Mr Maugham whetted our appetite for Hare than he switches to Zurbaran.

His chapter about Zurbaran is very illuminating. He gives whatever information there is to be given about that great artist—great at moments, competent at all times—who is so little known in England. He betrays a sympathy with historic Spain. And, as it were, incidentally, he reveals his deeper feelings in a manner which is not customary with him: 'I cannot expect the reader to have noticed that I have not claimed that any of the pictures I have spoken of had beauty. Beauty is a grave word. It is a word of high import. It is used lightly now—of the weather, of a smile, of a frock or the fit of a shoe, of a bracelet, of a garden, of a syllogism; beautiful serves as a synonym for good or pretty or pleasing or nice or engaging or interesting. But beauty is none of these. It is much more. It is very rare. It is a force. It is an enravishment. It is not a figure of speech when people say it takes their breath away; in certain cases it may give you the same suffocating shock as when you dive into ice-cold water. And after that first shock your heart throbs like a prisoner's when the jail gate clangs behind him and he breathes again the clean air of freedom. The impact of beauty is to make you feel greater than you are, so that for a moment you seem to walk on air; and the exhilaration and the release are such that nothing in the world matters any more. You are wrenched out of yourself into a world of pure spirit. It is like falling in love. It *is* falling in love. It is an ecstasy matching the ecstasy of the mystics. When I think of the works of art that have filled me with this intense emotion I think of the first glance at the Taj Mahal, the St Maurice of El Greco, seen again after long years, the Adam with his outstretched arm in the Sistine Chapel, Night and Day and the brooding figure of Guiliano on the tombs of the Medici and Titian's *Entombment of Christ*. Such an emotion I, for my part, have never received from the highly competent, well-painted, well-drawn, dignified, thoughtful canvases which Zurbaran painted for the altars of churches and the sacristies of convents. They have great qualities, but they appeal to the mind, to the intelligent appreciation, rather than to the heart and nerves which are thrilled and shattered by the rapture of pure beauty.'

Later, he qualifies: he finds that in certain pictures Zurbaran did achieve pure beauty. Then, since the book is a miscellany, he turns to Edmund Burke (appreciating the nobility of his prose and his sentiments and the soundness of his political views but coming no nearer the core of the man than anybody ever has come), to the philosopher Kant, who wrote a disquisition on aesthetics but turned up his nose at Beauty underneath his nose, and to the Detective Story.

I don't think that Mr Maugham has ever written a Detective Story: if he has I must apologise. But I doubt whether, unless he might rise to a challenge, he could write one now. For he says that this *genre* has been completely exhausted, and has been superseded by the hard-boiled story in which tough guys conspire with or cosh gangsters' molls. 'Every background has been utilised—the country house party in Sussex, Long Island or Florida, the quiet village in which nothing has happened since the Battle of Waterloo, the castle in the Hebrides isolated by a storm. So have clues—fingerprints, foot-prints, cigarette-ends, perfume, powder. So have unbreakable alibis which the detective breaks, the dog that does not bark, thus pointing to the fact that it was familiar with the murderer (this was first used, I think, by Conan Doyle), the code letter which the detective deciphers, the identical twins and secret passages.... Every method of murder, every finesse of detection, every guile to throw the reader off the scent, every scene of action in every class of life, has been used again and again. The story of pure deduction has run to seed.'

All this Mr Maugham says. As an author and a critic he says: 'I do not see who can succeed Raymond Chandler. I believe the detective story, both the story of pure deduction and the hard-boiled story, is dead'—and he calls Sherlock Holmes, that most living of all imaginary characters, a lay-figure. Yet he ends with: 'But that will not prevent a multitude of authors from continuing to write such stories, nor will it prevent me from continuing to read them.'

Thank goodness the man's human!

138. Christopher Morley, 'The Maugham Seesaw', *New York Times*

5 April 1953, 5

Christopher Darlington Morley (1890–1957) was an author and journalist. His novels include *Parnassus on Wheels* (1917) and *The Haunted Bookshop* (1919).

I had a strong sensation of seesaw in rereading Mr Maugham's agreeable book; what dear old Dr Johnson in one of his prayers called 'vacillation and vagrancy of mind.' No wonder; perhaps a kind of telekinesis? For I first read the book last November, aboard my favorite S. S. Media, crossing the North Atlantic in what the chief officer's daily bulletins described as a long, very heavy westerly swell. The English edition was then just published and I had bought a copy (12s 6d) as viaticum. You know the tiffin routine aboard a British ship: after plenty of cold beef with mustard, and those huge baked Idahos buttered with red pepper, and a glass of ordinaire at a shilling, you totter up to the corridor of A deck. From your station amidship you see Media's poop mightily soaring and sinking. You fall into your comfortable thwartship berth and in a few minutes—soothed both by Mr Maugham and perhaps a slab of treacle tart—you are off for such siesta as needs an ocean voyage to attain. About 5 P.M. you creep again into the corridor; and observe, through the open door to the after deck, how wildly she oscillates in the gigantic marching swells.

So I felt this again, and remembered how the ship's doctor (he happened to be, like Mr Maugham, a graduate of St Thomas' Hospital) hurried through the book I lent him, because (he said) it was probably the only thing that could reprieve one of our table-mates from her desolating seasickness.

I have always envied Mr Maugham his 'eminent readability' (which he shrewdly calls the novelist's most precious gift). He learned it

408

from Hazlitt; I envy him also his possession of Hazlitt's Complete Works. He learned that happy talent (mixing the general with the intimate) from Hazlitt. I always intended to learn it too, but when that great swatch of a dozen volumes was on the *Saturday Review* shelves, and I was casting sheep's (or Lamb's?) eyes on them, they were prioritied by the editor—who hasn't, as I've often told him, a corpuscle of Hazlitt's bloodstream in him. One of the things I used to sleep with, in our stormy little Media, was the idea of telling Maugham the various ways in which a set of Hazlitt has been one of my supreme frustrations. To own that large-paper suite is a patent of nobility.

I told the nauseated lady (she was Scottish) that what I liked most in Mr Maugham's book were his pieces on Burke and Hare. She was old enough, or ill enough, to cry: 'No! the body-snatchers?' Which showed she had read her R. L. S. But Mr Maugham's choices were Edmund Burke and Augustus Hare. In analyzing Burke's style, his rhetoric, his prose cadences both conscious and unconscious, both oral and written, Mr Maugham is in the professional vein I relish most. Shop talk is always the best, and its connoisseurs see the little *jeux de fantaisie* never suspected by the brutish mass-consumer. I fell asleep with special happiness on Mr Maugham's remark (about Burke) 'something of an old-fashioned air he has by his frequent use of an inverted construction.' This has the slyness enjoyable. Sometimes I went asleep with less luxury because Mr Maugham (like Hazlitt, on whom he tutored himself too stringently) falls off-ear in his sentence-ends, apodoses. But as the ship's doctor said, he has the perfect negative charm: he delights you because he makes it so plain he doesn't care whether you like it or not. To use one of his favorite words, you are often exasperated.

But about Augustus Hare, of whom only such tuitioned grandchildren of the Victorian era as myself are likely to know the name, Mr Maugham uses him in his showpiece to describe the daily routine of a nineteenth-century household. What kept me awake longer than Cunard protocol was his saying that at 8 A. M., in the Victorian country house, 'a maid in a rustling print dress and a cap with streamers came into your room with a cup of tea,' etc. I am wondering whether possibly Mr Maugham's memory is at fault. Did housemaids, parlormaids, ever wear streamers for their early duty? Weren't streamers (viz. long white dangletapes) always for outdoors, and specially for nursemaid display? My memory only goes back to about 1897; but, though American born and bred, I had unusual chance to observe the freaks of British behavior around the twist of the century. Tell me about this.

How much, while passing unconscious aboard the plunging Media, I'd have enjoyed to argue with Mr Maugham. His theme on the decline of detective stories: of course he's quite right, but evidently he's only read the corny two-bit stinkeroos, with their carnal lithography. He praises Hammett and Chandler, whom I believe rather coarse fare. The readables are still not the whodunits, but the *how*dunits, followed from Dr Thorndyke. As a chance example, which I've just reread, Francis Iles' *Malice Aforethought*. In a story of that genre the reader knows all, yet the co-efficient of anxiety is very high.

Mr Maugham in these random essays seesaws like the Media; but no one has better earned the right to compose as he chooses. The essay on Kant (apparently a 'colloquium' for the philosophical seminar at Columbia) is on the upper swing; though I think he should have given a dexterous wave to De Quincey. The beam tips fairly low in his anecdotes of novelists he has known (James, Wells, Bennett, etc.), though I confess I love a forward pass as well as anyone. I'm not even abashed to learn that one of Wells' mistresses said his body smelled like honey; or that Arnold Bennett wanted to rent his own petite amie two nights a week. Like Mr Maugham I haven't much sense of veneration, but the writers I most fully admire have subtly shown it. If you were a collector you'd enjoy putting side by side the jacket blurbs for the English and American editions of *The Vagrant Mood*. You'd hardly guess they were the same book. In England the book-buying taste has slid down to Mr Maugham: in the States it has crawled up to it. So, bless his indomitable and exasperated heart, it's good for him both ways.

139. Frank Kermode, 'Eminently Readable', *Manchester Guardian*

11 November 1958, 2

John Frank Kermode (b. 1919) is a scholar, literary critic and academic, Fellow of King's College, Cambridge, King Edward VII Professor of English Literature at Cambridge, and a Visiting Professor at Columbia University. His published works range from Shakespeare criticism to studies of contemporary authors as in his *Modern Essays* (1971). Latterly he has become sympathetic to the 'structuralist' approach to a text and has directed his critical attention to the Bible in *The Genesis of Secrecy* (1979).

A prefatory note in this book informs us that it is the last Mr Maugham proposes to publish, after a career lasting some sixty years. Its relaxed, discursive manner is what might be expected of an author at once so old and so self-possessed; no one would have supposed him to be the kind of writer who finishes in a sudden blaze of triumph, despair, or mystery. He has not invented a strange old-man's style, but gone on as urbanely as ever, always concerned with leisurely unfolding, never with brilliance or concentration of texture—a potent, unruffled opponent of what others choose to regard as the central tradition of modern letters. The genre to which these essays belong is indeed obsolescent; they might have been called 'Hours in a Library' or 'Through My Study Window.' Wonderfully indifferent to the fashion, Mr Maugham is one of the few living critics who would dare, without irony, to call an author 'eminently readable' (he uses this phrase of Tillotson). He can do so because of his confidence that eminent readability is a prime virtue, and that he possesses it; which of course he does, as all, with or without irony, would agree.

The five essays concern Goethe as a novelist, an Indian saint, Tillotson, the Short Story, and finally three French 'journalists,' the Goncourt brothers, Renard, and Léautaud. A large proportion of the book consists of leisurely biography (there are solid biographical accounts of Goethe, Tillotson, Katherine Mansfield, Chekhov, and the three French writers, together with summaries of their books). These accounts do occasionally include judgments of value, and very consistent these are. Mr Maugham dislikes fiction that gives itself airs, and dismisses James, Forster, and Gide because they were not good at 'mere stories.' In a long account of Renard he refrains from saying much more about his value than that some think L'Ecornifleur a pretty good book. With these French writers of what has been called the 'syphilitico-pessimistic age' one would hardly expect Mr Maugham—in spite of Of Human Bondage—to have much sympathy, and in fact he registers his distaste for their eccentricity and squalor. It is not altogether easy to see why he thought the Goncourts worth writing about. Even in his long passage on Chekhov he denies us the chance of hearing one prolific story writer on another by confining himself to general praise of Chekhov's constructive power.

The book is not, then, valuable as criticism. 'The Saint' has the value of a clear record of an interesting figure, prefaced by a characteristically lucid and level account of Indian religion; but in some ways the Tillotson essay is the most interesting. Mr Maugham does not claim to be an authority on the subject, and his essay begins as frank belles lettres. But he finds Tillotson's prose interesting (though whether 'simple and honest' is a good account of it may be questioned) because Tillotson is historically one of the founders of the plain style; Dryden acknowledged his debt, and Addison regarded him as 'the chief standard of our language.' Now Mr Maugham, though he suggests a few corrections or adjustments in a passage he quotes, finds in this literary ancestor something to admire. Still, one wonders if Addison's comment means quite the same thing as 'eminently readable.'

These essays are of course designed to entertain, and are not for those who feel hot for critical certainties. Some of them contain long digressions; the one on the Short Story is a bit of a rag-bag. But one gets through them with such remarkable ease and pace that this matters less than it would in criticism that tries to establish something. To all who enjoy easy and informative literary talk it will give an enjoyable evening; this is Mr Maugham's true intent, and he fulfils it with all his usual skill.

140. Karl G. Pfeiffer, 'Mr Maugham's Valedictory', *New York Herald Tribune*

31 May 1959, 8

Karl Graham Pfeiffer, an American professor, contributed articles to various magazines. He is the author of *Somerset Maugham: A Candid Portrait* (1959).

Points of view, a collection of five essays mostly on writers and written, its author tells us, as his last word. As Mr Maugham is a man of his word who never speaks carelessly, we must regretfully accept his statement as fact. Maugham's last book is also an uncommonly good one. True, it is the mixture as before, but the ingredients are better than those from which he fashioned *The Vagrant Mood*, six essays he wrote when he was only seventy-eight.

The new collection is better than *The Vagrant Mood* chiefly because it devotes more space to a discussion of writers and Maugham's special qualification as a critic is his insight into the working of the writer's mind during the act of creation. He is himself not only a master craftsman but more than most writers a conscious one, well aware of how he gets his effects. He can therefore breathe new life into a tired old masterpiece by focusing attention on some of the problems its author faced and explaining how he solved them. When he recounts plots he is not much more entertaining than the rest of us who engage in that tiresome practice. But he is fascinating when he distills the writer from his writing, and that is what he does in most of these essays.

Maugham is admirably consistent. Age has wrought no perceptible change in his point of view. He is still as tolerant of amoral behaviour as a man young enough to enjoy it. Nor has he unexpectedly erred on the side of charity. These portraits of Goethe, Katherine Mansfield, Jules Renard, Paul Léautaud, and the Goncourt brothers are savage. In most of them there is at least one startling resemblance to himself, and one wonders whether that is what attracted him to them.

'The Saint' and 'Prose and Dr Tillotson,' the two shortest essays, are portraits of good men and provide judicious contrast. They show Maugham equally at home in the world of the spirit and the world of the flesh. 'The Saint' also contains an admirably clear and Maugham-like exposition of the complexities of Hindu philosophy. Who but Maugham would explain the necessity of evil in the world by analogy with the vermouth in a dry martini?

In his 'last' book Maugham is austerely unsentimental. He is a little kinder to Chekhov than he used to be, but he continues to damn Henry James with faint praise. He warns us again to beware the insidious poison of charm. He still finds in a man's social class the soundest clue to what makes him tick. And he is still sensitive to the charge that it ill becomes an artist to make a fortune from the practice of his art.

Points of View also reveals Maugham's unique merits as a writer: the smooth-flowing, euphonious style, the bits and pieces of autobiography that escape his reticence ('What makes old age hard to bear is not the failing of one's faculties, mental and physical, but the burden of one's memories'), the pungent flavor of the Maugham personality, and the uncompromising integrity of the man who, as Richard Aldington put it, 'refuses to conform to anybody's idea of what is right to think and feel and do, and has labored with the utmost sincerity to discover what he really does think and feel'.

141. J.P. Collins, 'W. Somerset Maugham, Playwright and Novelist', *Bookman* (London)

LVII, October 1919, 12–15

Mr Somerset Maugham has stood for years among my arrears of conscience. That is to say, after a working acquaintance as an old reviewer with his half-dozen novels, and as an old and grateful playgoer with his score or more of comedies, the fancy came of late to go through them again and see if they would pass on second or third reading. So far from proving a holiday task, they gave the holiday a double zest, and I can heartily recommend a run through Mr Maugham's writings as a post-war tonic. The thing to stipulate is that the reader must be modern-minded and the reverse of squeamish, especially about the seventh commandment. So much said, it remains to give the best advice of all, and that is to read Mr Maugham, as I have done, in the green core of his own breezy county of Kent.

The first book Mr Maugham launched upon the public could hardly have been, considering its slight dimensions, a clearer indication of the fearless line he was to follow. *Liza of Lambeth* came at a time when Gissing and Morrison were still a force, and the odour of mean streets was accepted as synonymous with literary honesty and courage. There is certainly no lack of either about his idyll of Elizabeth Kemp of the lissom limbs and auburn hair, but with all allowance for the racy dialect, the frolics of

415

Chingford 'beano,' the rueful futility of the faithful Thomas, and the engaging callousness of Liza's mother, the effect upon the reader is one of crudity of set purpose, and an interval of twenty years' acquaintance only makes it, on repeated reading, seem cruder still. No artist of experience setting out upon a traverse from gaiety to gloom would allow his hand to appear so flagrantly; and no practitioner who wanted to do anything but make our flesh creep would admit such a double blow, to the reader and the heroine alike, as occurs at the climax of Jim Blakiston's hefty love-making. Every time one reads of the downfall of 'Liza,' one cannot help feeling that if she had perished in manuscript under a veto from the publisher's adviser, the lesson might have spurred the author to gain that mastery in fiction which he seems somehow to have disdained. And his next study in feminine portraiture showed how far he could travel towards perfection.

Mrs Craddock—which I take to be Mr Maugham's best work as a novelist—is a sex-satire punctuated by four curtains, two of tragedy, and two of comedy. This mixture of opposites should be enough to damn it in the eyes of a public intent upon classifying everything by means of labels, and on making everything so classified stick to its label like grim death. Yet the unclassifiable may flourish, and does, when its merit is beyond dispute. It is so long, reckoned by the 'speedometer' of war and peace, since the nineties when *Mrs Craddock* made her bow in covers, that one forgets the kind of reception she met; the only safe thing to bet is that she was fully a decade ahead of her time. Victorian influences were still alive, and the modern cry for well-to-do women to occupy themselves with something to justify their existence was still in the nature of a novelty, so that this lay-sermon against the intellectual lady-idler may have seemed less *à propos* than we know it to be now. If Mr Maugham were writing it again, he would pack Edward Craddock off to France as a major of Territorials, and invest his wife with a posthumous decoration instead of sending him to his death in a fox-chase, and her to a contrite widowhood. But then there would be even chances that Gerald, the dissolute boy, might go out and perish afield with just as much credit, and the heroine be left to torture memory as fiercely as ever on the dilemma of romance and remorse. It is likelier still that, in these morbid days, Mr Maugham would have given himself rather more rein with Bertha Craddock's disappointment as a mother—

the one episode which satisfies us by the test of probability and exalts her for the moment from a self-tormenting neurotic into a kind of Niobe.

Even in the fuller light of experience, however, he could hardly have bettered this study of an impulsive and exigent woman rising at the outset to the height of a bold and womanly choice in defiance of social prejudice and family tradition, and then relapsing under the disillusions of marriage into the worst and weakest failings of her class. The love that might have saved her, steadily evaporates; the child that might have drawn the ill-assorted pair together, proves to be still-born; and the success that comes to Edward as a land-holder and a local magnate makes him all the more odious and misunderstood to this embittered wife of his. Whether or not the author wrote the story as an experiment in alienation of sympathy, it would be hard to say; but he certainly succeeds in shifting the reader's sympathy from wife to husband, and in restoring the true balance between character and mere culture. The process gains immensely by the exquisite chapter of farce in which Mrs Craddock is forced to hear her worthy spouse go stodging through a political speech which stamps him in her eyes a hopeless clodpate, and then to hear the haughty dames whose criticism she has always dreaded, acclaim him as a patriot and a saviour of his country. After that the fox-chase finish comes by way of an anti-climax, like the watery ending of *Beauchamp's Career*, and one's sense of irony would have been satisfied by a lighter crisis, say, the promotion of Edward to administrative honours as an agriculturist, and a life peerage, so as to complete the discomfiture of Bertha's ancestral pride. In the days when he wrote this novel Mr Maugham may have shied at the device of a title as something hackneyed and impossible, but a death in the hunting-field was very little better, and it is not improved by the rather poor premonition which dawns upon us earlier in the chapter. What is worse, it seems clumsy and resourceless compared with the ironic key of the book at its best, such as rings, for instance, in a passage half-way through:

Mr Craddock's principles, of course, were quite right; he had given her plenty of run and ignored her cackle, and now she had come home to roost. There is nothing like a knowledge of farming, and an acquaintance with the habits of domestic animals, to teach a man how to manage his wife.

One hears one's feminine acquaintance snorting at boomerang comments like these, but they will do well to read this book steadily through. I would even make it a textbook in post-graduate courses, alongside *The Egoist*, or some such corrective of sex vanity. Sometimes I wonder how on earth the pundits of Paris could sit all day for months and yawn over protocols and Leagues about reconciling nations and adjusting tariffs, when the crucial question of the race is the approximation and mutual comprehension of the sexes. It might not improve the girl-graduate's opinion of mere man to have him pictured like the smug eupeptic that Edward Craddock is, but at least it would cure her of the folly of asking for honeymoons to be made of evergreen cheese.

If *Liza of Lambeth*, as we have seen, was a raid into realism, and *Mrs Craddock* a successful venture into sex-psychology, it was tolerably certain we should find other experiments among Mr Maugham's other novels, and of these the most ambitious is *Under Human Bondage* [sic]. The title in itself is typical of the author's determination not to mince matters or camouflage his wares with sugar 'icing' or the bravery of the poster. Nor is the work less laborious than the title threatens. A chronicle of three hundred thousand words is not lightly written or lightly read, and the story of Philip Carey unmistakably belongs to the school of the panoramic story which has come in secular waves with *Clarissa* and *Wilhelm Meister*, with *Le Juif Errant* and *Jean Christophe*. Centrifugal energy may account for these lava-breaks on the part of authorship, nor is the public likely to object so long as it remains addicted to 'the lumping penn'orth.' But there is no real vitality in this kind of megalomania, and the rules of economics will prevent publishers in the end from encouraging authors to combine a maximum of letterpress with a minimum of plot. The vogue of *Sinister Street* is already dead, you may say, because its aim was to accumulate detail and eliminate invention or relief.

Mr Maugham's book excels most of its rivals because it has at least an outward shape which they have not, and those who read it attentively will find no difficulty in marking off its undenoted sections—Canterbury, Heidelberg, Montmartre, Mildred, Medicine, Millinery, and Marriage. Something like a hundred pages goes to each division but the last, and this supplies a welcome pretext for the story's stopping like a clock. There was no earthly reason why we should be debarred from the connubial confidences of Sally Athelney any more than we were from the intimacy of her several predecessors in Philip's affections; but even abrupt respectability has its claims, and Philip is nothing if not a creature of impulse. At every stage of the story you rub your eyes to discover whether the club-foot is a key to his character or merely a plea for sympathy; but at no stage do you discover enough evolution in the man to justify the story's length. Its best passages are the wrangles about art and morality, the sharp contrast between environments, and the longings to get away to that dreamland, Spain. One almost sees that if the author had not already written an Andalusian travel-book, it is to Spain the story would have taken us, and it might easily have made a better background for Philip than the studio-slums of Paris or the purlieus of Vauxhall. As it is, he strikes us as a Christian who is no Christian, making a Progress which is no Progress, and preferring the slough of dilettantism and self-reproach to anything in the way of steady effort and self-control. When he emerges from the medical morgues of St Thomas's and drops into Mildred's tea-shop, you would never dream, if you didn't know your London, that there intervenes all the wonder and inspiration of Westminster Bridge. An exclusion of healthy 'reflexes' is characteristic of the book and its class. It remains a kind of descriptive quarry for lesser men to plunder, rich in violent emotionalism, eccentric episodes, range of character, and unbridled dialogue.

To couple Mr Maugham's novels and plays together by what divines call the 'synoptic' method is to come to the inexorable conclusion that he has made the one a stepping-stone for the other. He has used fiction, in a word, as the roughing-in ground, the modelling clay, for the more assured perfection of his work upon the stage. No one can read the two versions of *The Explorer* without seeing the process and admitting the point. Other men have produced play first and published the story afterwards, but who has ever met any such instance without feeling that the story had been the anterior form—in a fallow and unwritten condition perhaps, but still pre-existent to the play? *The Merry-Go-Round* is another of Mr Maugham's stories written almost idly in disregard of plot, it seems to me, since the book is simply a fagotage of ill-assorted couples where the women invariably get the worst of it, and the men never labour under the slightest sense of expiation, except perhaps in the way of discomfort or insolvency. The middle chapters yield more than one episode which the author has turned to account in the way of drama. Some expert book on stagecraft years ago, I remember, praised the last act in *Landed Gentry* for the dexterity with which Grace is spared the shame of an awkward disclosure, and there may have been ill-humoured and undiscerning critics who explained the device away as dictated by regard for the sentimental pit or a search for novelty. But when you turn from the text of the play to the seventh chapter of *The Merry-Go-Round*, you see how much the position has gained from restraint and elaboration. So far as concerns the issues at stake, the predominance of caste and code over natural feeling, the two versions are about equal; and in so far as the author has not had to consider the emotional scope of a particular actress, the novel has a marked advantage. But in point of artistry the play has finish and superiority, and the story seems unlicked and hasty by comparison, though no one can surely hold that *Landed Gentry* is a finished piece of work by any means. It is inferior, for instance, to *The Tenth Man* in power and reality of appeal, in the clash of character, and in legitimately framed effect. Here again Mr Maugham has drawn for his climax upon a scene in *The Merry-Go-Round* and made true metal of what had been merely ore in the rough. Thus at point after point one is forced to the conclusion that he has expended patience and skill upon the theatre which he might have very well bestowed in fairer measure on his stories.

Curiously it is in *The Explorer*, one of the slightest of his books, that he shows what an easy command he possesses over the story-form pure and simple. It is hard to accept Helen's [sic] attitude, first of disbelief in her hero, and then of surrender. You feel that there is somehow no sufficient pretext for her second change, since a woman so deep-set in her principles would hardly waive them for the sake of an affection she had abjured. At any rate, the book is much more than the study of a strong man trampling on calumny, or even the outcrop of hereditary taint in character under new conditions; and if one were asked to name an example in English of the finished shorter novel, such as French fiction has produced so brilliantly and so often, *The Explorer* might very well stand. It is certainly a long way ahead of a clever extravaganza like *The Moon and Sixpence*, which draws for its lightness and humour chiefly upon its title, and for its invention chiefly upon an insufferable whimsicality. Ranking last in order of chronology, it may fitly conclude this survey of a remarkable and original tale of work, one which suffers not from any want of consistent and versatile ability behind its author's pen, but simply because he has given too many of his book-creations impulse instead of motive, and casual shape instead of artistic form. They are effects without a cause, and possibly that is why so many of their actions are the same. Mr Maugham's books are transcripts, not of life as a tolerable whole, but of phases which suit his rather arbitrary treatment, and if we fall into impatience with them now and then, it is because he seems to take impatience as the note of the age in which we live. After all, if you get out of temper with one of his novels, there is an excellent remedy: you can always read the play.

142. H. E. Bates on the modern short story

1941

Herbert Ernest Bates (1905–74) was a prolific writer of short stories and novels. His World War II stories, published under the pen-name of 'Flying Officer X,' were widely read. Among his many other works are *The Poacher* (1935), *The Jacaranda Tree* (1949) and *Love for Lydia* (1952).

The following is an extract from chapter VI of *The Modern Short Story* (London: Thomas Nelson and Sons, 1941, 142–6).

... To the young writers of post-war England [Conrad] had little to offer.

Nor, rather surprisingly, had Maugham. Maugham is at once an attractive and a rather disconcerting figure. Beginning as a writer with, as it were, no ear for words, Maugham had very early to choose a stylistic model which his own limitations would permit him to follow without embarrassment. To have chosen a pretentious, poetical, highly coloured writer would have been fatal. Maugham chose Maupassant, and throughout his career has stuck to Maupassant. It is interesting to recall here that Maupassant has been described as 'the born popular writer, battered by Flaubert into austerity,' and perhaps Maugham is an example of the sort of writer, popular, cosmopolitan, commercial and yet in some way distinguished, that Maupassant might have been if left alone. Maugham is now, at his best, as in *Cakes and Ale*, a master of cultivated acidity. The spare sere detachment of his prose may, with the exception of recurrent lapses into appalling sentimentality, be safely offered as a sound foundation course in commercial-literary craftsmanship.

One other influence, not I believe admitted by Maugham, seems to have shaped his craft. Repeatedly throughout his work, speaking both for himself and through his characters, Maugham reveals an ironic impatience with the stuffiness of literary and moral conventions (see the delicious dissection of the pompous social-climbing novelist in *Cakes and Ale*), and is constantly administering the acid corrective. The parallel for this side of Maugham's method is not Maupassant, but *The Way of All Flesh*, a book for which Maugham is admirably fitted to write a modern counterpart. Here are two quotations:

Like other rich men at the beginning of this century he ate and drank a good deal more than was enough to keep him in health. Even his excellent constitution was not proof against a prolonged course of overfeeding and what we should now consider overdrinking. His liver would not unfrequently get out of order, and he would come down to breakfast looking yellow about the eyes.

I fancy that life is more amusing now than it was forty years ago and I have a notion that people are more amiable. They may have been worthier then, possessed of more substantial knowledge; I do not know. I know they were more cantankerous; they ate too much, many of them drank too much, and they took too little exercise. Their livers were out of order and their digestions often impaired.

The account of the first paragraph, which is Butler, is pitched in a key identical with that of the second, which is Maugham. The effect in both is gained by a series of apparently matter-of-fact statements, made almost off-hand, with a sort of casual formality, qualified by a sort of airy, 'Of course I don't really know. Don't go and take my word for it,' which in reality injects the note of irony. Maugham and Butler again and again use this trick of creating

ironic effect by disclaiming all trustworthy knowledge of what
they are talking about, and by pitching their remarks in a negative
key. The effect is delicious; butter won't melt in these acid mouths.
The Way of All Flesh and *Cakes and Ale* will, in fact, repay some
pretty close comparative study, and will show, I think, that
Maugham found a far more profitable and compatible influence in
Butler than in Maupassant.

It is my contention in fact that if Maugham had, as a writer of
stories, rejected Maupassant as a model and kept more closely to
Butler, we should have been presented with the first full-length
English short-story writer worthy of comparison with the best
continental figures. Unfortunately Maugham, in spite of an
excellent eye, a dispassionate steadiness, a genius for the diagnosis
of human frailty, and a cosmopolitan temperament, lacks one very
great and supremely important quality. Unlike Tchehov and
Maupassant, in whom he professes to see great differences but who
were much alike at least in this respect, Maugham lacks compassion. He has no heart, and in place of that heart one has the
impression that he uses a piece of clockwork. It is this, I think, that
gives Maugham's work the frequent impression of cheapness. This
effect is heightened by something else. Maugham, having mastered
the art of irony, mistakenly supposed himself to be a cynic. But
throughout Maugham's work, and notably in the stories, there
exists a pile of evidence to show that Maugham the cynic is in
reality a tin-foil wrapping for Maugham the sentimentalist.
Maugham's cynicism indeed peels off under too-close examination,
thin, extraneous, tinny, revealing underneath a man who is afraid
of trusting and finally of revealing his true emotions.

There would be little point, here, in doing more than summarize
the quality of Maugham's stories. They are easily available,
pleasantly readable; they tell a story—in the sense, that is, that what
they have to say can be expressed anecdotally; they deal largely
with romantic places, for Maugham, like Kipling and Conrad,
loves the East, and to his talent for painting its scenery and people
he owes, as they do, much of his popular success. He delights in
exposing human frailty, particularly amorous and marital frailty,
and the humbug of convention; he is suave and urbane; he has the
keenest sense of dramatic situations and delights in leaving the
reader, as Maupassant and O. Henry did, with the point of the
story neatly sharpened and vinegared in his hands. His natural sense

of poetry is nil; his methods are as objective as the newspaper report of a court case, and sometimes as bad; he wisely refrains, except on rare occasions, from the purple passage, yet he has apparently never discovered any conscious and simple method of detecting himself in the act of using a cliché. When he is good, like the little girl, he is very good; and similarly when he is bad he is horrid.

Maugham indeed, though presenting the interesting case of a man who (on his own confession) evolved an attractively individual style without the help of a natural ear for words, has nothing new to offer. He simply perpetuates a tradition of straightforward, objective story-telling, largely derived from French naturalism, that is already well-known. Thus Maugham's influence is not, and never has been, wide or important.....

143. Sewell Stokes, 'W. Somerset Maugham', *Theatre Arts* (New York)

XXIX, No. 2, February 1945

Sewell Stokes (1902–79) was a British arts journalist who became a close friend of Isadora Duncan. His memoir of her was the basis for the film of her life. His articles were collected into books with titles like *Hear the Lions Roar* and *Are They the Same at Home?* With his brother Leslie, Stokes wrote a successful Broadway play about Oscar Wilde. During World War II he became a probation officer and wrote books out of that experience, as well as a biography of Gladys Cooper, *Without Veils (1953)*, to which Maugham contributed an Introduction, reprinted in *A Traveller in Romance* (London, 1984).

The apocryphal story most often related about Somerset Maugham finds the distinguished author and dramatist in gentle argument with a friend—the subject of the argument being his own merit as an artist. Evidently the friend believes that Maugham does not do himself justice in this respect, and says so; to which criticism the accused replies as follows: 'Would you rather I wrote books like *War and Peace* and lived in modest comfort—or am I to be allowed to write the popular stuff I do, and by it earn the luxury I enjoy?' The answer to that one, of course, is that Maugham couldn't write books like Tolstoi's masterpiece if he tried; and what is more, nobody is as keenly aware of this fact as Maugham himself. It is doubtful if there ever lived a man with fewer illusions about his own work; and possibly it is just because he never loses an opportunity of indulging in self criticism—a habit singularly few authors manage to acquire—that a number of professional critics, out of sheer perversity, insist upon elevating him to a position in the literary world that is hardly justified by his achievements, brilliant as these often are. Indeed, there is a school of thought in England that regards Maugham as the Grand Old Man of Letters; but against this are numerous admirers of his, who, with the best will in the world, can describe him as nothing more than a master of magazine fiction. And so it is with Maugham the dramatist. Arguments about his place in the theatre never cease, despite the fact that the subject of the argument has not only given up writing plays, but has firmly stated his reason for doing so.

Unlike those popular dramatists, Henry Arthur Jones and Arthur Wing Pinero—both of whom outlived their popularity, and died bitterly reproaching a public that dared to find them hopelessly outmoded, and quite boring—Maugham gracefully retired from the stage in 1933, and since that time has always referred to himself as an ex-dramatist. Would it not be kinder, therefore, to respect his wish that the plays be allowed to die a natural death, instead of reviving their memory by insisting upon their shortcomings? Much kinder; and wiser, too, seeing that none of them—with perhaps two exceptions—is likely even to be noticed by historians of the early twentieth-century theatre in England. And yet, such a provocative figure has Maugham become, largely because of his objective attitude towards his work, that a critical estimate of him ought almost certainly to produce implications whose significance must be of interest, of value, even, to students of the theatre in our time. When writers who have failed to master dramatic technique—Henry James and George Moore, for example—declare the stage too crude a medium for the interpretation of their ideas, one does not pay them too much attention. But precisely the same declaration, coming from a playwright who has been a favorite with audiences for over forty years, is a very different matter; and what we ask ourselves, then, is why the author of thirty plays, nearly all of them hits, should turn at last with a sigh of relief from the workshop that has appeared for so long to be his natural home. For it is not even as if Maugham, at the age of sixty, laid aside his pen with a tear of regret for the glorious days that were past. Not at all. Once he had made up his mind to leave for good the theatre that had so richly rewarded him, his feelings were more akin to those of a man suddenly released from a long term of imprisonment. Here, in his own carefully chosen words, is what amounts to nothing less than an expression of gratitude for his deliverance:

When for days you have been going through a mountain pass, a moment comes when you are sure that after wandering round the great mass of rock in front of you, you will come upon the plain; but instead you are faced with another huge crag and the weary trail continues; surely after this you will see the plain; no; the path winds on and another mountain bars your way. And then suddenly it lies before you. Your heart exults; there it stretches wide and sunny; the oppression of the mountain is lifted from your shoulders and with exhilaration you breathe the more spacious air. So I felt when I had done my last play.... I had won great notoriety and perhaps even a passing fame. I might have been satisfied. But there was one thing more I wanted to achieve and this it seemed to me I could not hope to reach in the drama. Perfection.

To judge a man accurately, one needs some knowledge of his antecedents; and whereas we are most often denied this in the case of the average citizen, with a professional man, and particularly with a man whose profession is the theatre, we have the advantage of dealing with someone whose life has been lived more or less in public. This is so in Maugham's case; and we shall not be wasting our time, therefore, if before attempting to discover what lesson is to be learned from his attitude to the drama, we examine in some detail the experiences through which he has passed, and which must in some degree be responsible for the conclusions he has come to at the end of a long career as a playwright.

Born exactly seventy years ago, Maugham had what is considered an excellent education: King's School, Canterbury; Heidelberg University; and St Thomas' Hospital—where for a time he was a medical student. He was a student at a time when Oscar Wilde's plays were drawing all London, and it is fairly safe to assume that the Irishman's wit, and the brilliant success it was having, had something to do with the young man's decision to give up medicine and become a dramatist himself. What is certain is that once he had chosen to devote a part of his time to the theatre—the rest he gave to his novels and stories—Maugham lost no time in finding out how the trick was done; for a trick, and little more than a trick, he believed it to be—and here he was again following the Irishman's example, since Wilde himself is alleged to have said that, in order to learn the technique of writing for the stage, he shut himself up alone for a week-end with the works of the most popular French dramatists, and on emerging from his seclusion, knew all that they had to teach him. As it happened, the youthful Maugham was even more painstaking than his master, for he not only read other people's plays in an endeavour to discover the secret of their success, but even went so far as to copy them out in his own hand. This laborious exercise, he told the present writer long ago, he found extremely useful as a guide on many points relating to dramatic construction. One can believe him. The pity is that more aspiring dramatists do not strive as diligently to master their craft. If they did, fewer manuscripts whose shapelessness makes them useless for stage presentation would litter the offices of the managers. At the same time, admirable though this method of self-instruction is, its adoption by Maugham in his prentice days at once gives a clue as to what *kind* of dramatist he started out to be. Unlike Chekhov, Shaw, O'Casey and Saroyan—men who preferred to invent their own technique, and by doing so risked failure—he made an obvious bid for success. His ambition was to become a successful playwright; not a playwright who might, if chance favoured him, turn out to be a success. And how well he succeeded in this endeavour was proved in 1908, by which time he had four original plays running in London concurrently: *Lady Frederick*, *Jack Straw*, *Mrs Dot* and *The Explorer*.

No doubt remains that Maugham, from the start, set himself up in business as a playwright. Had he inserted in the newspapers an advertisement which read: 'You want the best plays—I write them!', he would have spoken no less than the truth. A manufacturer of smart plays for smart audiences, is what he quickly became; and his speciality was what is known as High Comedy. Instinctively, he knew the value of an amusing epigram, and if a finished work of his had not a sufficient number of these, he decorated the manuscript with additional ones, as easily as a dressmaker adds sequins to a gown that needs brightening up.' One can imagine him smiling—less from satisfaction at his own brilliance, than from the knowledge that he had the trick of getting a stage laugh when he needed it—as he set down such a neatly contrived little piece of dialogue as this utterance of Lady Frederick's: 'I wish I knew how she manages to dress so beautifully. It's one of the injustices of fate that clothes only hang on a woman really well when she's cast every shred of reputation.' That kind of epigram—Wilde and water at its best—had them rolling in the aisles around 1908, and indeed for some time to come. Lonsdale did very well with it as late as 1925. A laugh for its own sake is always popular in the commercial theatre; the trouble with it is that it is likely sooner or later to go out of fashion, with the result that what once caused merriment comes to cause embarrassment, if not bewilderment. In time it finds its author out, exposing him for what he is, which too often is far from what he appeared once to be. This has been Maugham's experience. He knows it. And the fact leaves him unmoved, since it has always been a conviction of his that in any case the stage play is merely a reflection of the fashion prevailing at the time it is written, and therefore of small account once that fashion has changed. Into the validity of this opinion we will look more closely in a moment.

Few managers ever made a mistake in backing Maugham's plays. They dealt with him for years, like customers faithful to the firm whose goods never lose their quality. It was possible even to order a particular brand of play from this most accommodating dramatist who wasted no time seeking inspiration, but executed the commission with promptitude. Charles Frohman once suggested to him a modern version of *The Taming of the Shrew*, and thinking the idea a good one, he wrote it. For this play he embroidered a theme that had come to him when a companion of his aunt decided to give up her post and go to live on her brother's farm in Canada. While on the farm the ex-companion married the hired man, and what the two made of their married life became, by the time Maugham had finished with them, a play called *The Land of Promise*. This play, like so many of his others, was a success. And nobody will blame him for that. No, one's quarrel with Maugham—if one quarrels with him at all—is not on account of the thirty plays he has contributed to the theatre; we can take these or leave them, according to our taste; but on account of his oft repeated assertion that the theatre is not a medium in which an artist can expect to attain perfection, or anything like perfection. He persists in looking on it, quite objectively, as a box of tricks that nobody who aims at anything higher than the creation of an amusing charade need bother about. Can the theatre as an institution be dismissed as lightly as this? Or must Maugham, for holding such an opinion, be dismissed himself—as a critic of no consequence whatever? The question is not too easily answered; and before investigating it, it will be helpful to look once more at the curious career of this theatrical conjuror with whom we have to reckon.

The kind of comedy that Maugham kept alive for so many years, with the dexterity of a juggler keeping a number of balls in the air at once, was finally driven from the stage by the arrival in England of what can best be described as the 'domestic drama'. Dodie Smith, and her many followers, were largely responsible for this type of harmless entertainment whose characters, unlike Maugham's svelte and witty creatures from Mayfair, resembled in detail the very housewives who themselves made up an audience; and who, tired out after a day's shopping, found delight in watching people like themselves wrestling with problems that might easily have been their own. It was only to be expected that when Miss Smith's suburban housewives walked on the stage, Mr Maugham's elegant ladies would walk off. The fashion had changed so definitely that any return to the old *milieu* would have spelled financial disaster. It is true that Maugham had from time to time varied his steady output by attempting to write plays with a more serious theme, such plays as *For Services Rendered* and *Sheppey*; but these were out of his usual *genre* and added nothing to his reputation. The fashionable comedy was his line of goods; he was quick to note a drastic change in its style, and being by that time weary of it anyway, he shut down that department of his business and continued with the novels and short stories that had all along kept pace with the plays. He had forgotten the theatre almost as soon as the theatre might have forgotten him—had he not written two comedies that somehow managed to get the better of his well-worn tricks, and insisted on coming to life in spite of them. *The Circle* was produced in 1921, revived with great success in 1931, and in 1944 found a place in John Gielgud's repertory, beside *Love for Love* and *Hamlet*. The other comedy, *Our Betters*, first presented in New York, in 1917, and not in London until 1923, is generally, and rightly, considered his masterpiece; and it is likely to make his name known to theatregoers as yet unborn.

It is the belief of some critics—and perhaps of Maugham himself—that the best work of which he is capable has gone into his novels. If this is so, one cannot avoid the conclusion that their creator is capable of achieving little more in literature than he has done in the theatre. Exceedingly well written as a number of the novels are, not a spark of genius is struck on their pages. For the most part, they are feuilletons whose polished style is likely to deceive the average reader into praising them beyond their deserts. And why should not the average reader prove untrustworthy in his estimate, when professional critics are not above making the same mistake? Sir Edmund Gosse was human enough to fall into this trap once—when the trap was set by no less a master of romantic hocus-pocus than Sir Hall Caine. Not that Maugham isn't a vastly superior writer to the author of *The Manxman* whose novels sold by the million; he very decidedly is; what he just fails to do is to take his seat with the giants, just as Arnold Bennett failed before him. Even so, Maugham will not escape the notice of posterity. His undeniable genius for the creation of character in short story form should place him on a pedestal not an inch less in height than one occupied by Maupassant.

What, however, makes Maugham more interesting to students of drama than any of the plays he has published—and the technique of these is not inconsiderable—is his dictum on the theatre: that it is not a medium in which to strive for the attainment of perfection. And, mind you, he adds a rider to this pronouncement of his, which is that he excludes plays written *in verse*. If, he says, a man can express himself in musical prose that lends itself to the actor's powers of declaration, then by all means let him unburden his soul in terms of theatrical art; but lacking that rare gift, he can expect no more than transitory fame. In short, it is Maugham's contention that the fundamental passions of men can only be expressed in words that soar heavenwards; and one takes it that had this gift of lordly language been his, great tragedy, instead of flippant comedy, might have claimed him. Tragedy, he says, endures; but comedy, being merely a reflection of the manners and customs of a period, becomes meaningless when those manners and customs have changed.

To refute his argument that comedy does not endure, what could be simpler than to confront him with the works of Sheridan, Congreve and Goldsmith? These gay spirits would not, one feels, shake his belief in a theory that it has taken him the experience of a lifetime to develop. Somewhere—it may be in one of the prefaces to the collected editions of his plays, or in his autobiography, *The Summing Up*—he has written that most people enjoy revivals of such plays as *The School for Scandal*, *She Stoops to Conquer* and *Love for Love* only in the sense that they enjoy seeing an object in a museum; and that while to see a popular actor in the revival is entertaining, the play, as a play, is not greatly enjoyed by an audience for its own sake—though an audience, unwilling to admit this stark fact, may unconsciously pretend otherwise.

Remembering the handful of plays that have escaped oblivion, might there be some truth in this credo of Maugham's: shocking though it may at first appear to lovers of the theatre who have never stopped to give it consideration? Each must answer the question for himself. Some will agree with Maugham that the theatre is a box of tricks, and is used as such by most modern playwrights. Others will violently disagree with him. But perhaps, after all, what he means is that our theatre lacks the poets who might make it so much greater than it is, if only they would give their time to it. And none, surely, will contradict him on that point.

144. Unsigned leading article, 'Somerset Maugham', *Times Literary Supplement*

22 January 1954

It is only the least direct of compliments that can hope at this time of day to pass Mr Somerset Maugham's habitual guard. He might be amused, but hardly complimented, if the Anglo-American literary tribute to him on his eightieth birthday went under any superscription less realistic than *The Maugham Enigma*. A tribute implying that the enigma was no longer open would never do. It could hardly fail to suggest to the author of *Cakes and Ale* that there was a conspiracy to treat him as he showed the world treating the octogenarian Edward Driffield, as though longevity in a writer were the one form of genius admitting of no question. It is to be noted that the essays composing this unofficial birthday offering were written at divers dates. Their subject can have no cause to suspect that well-known critics are performing the traditional ceremony of eating their words in his honour.

Mr Maugham is comfortably aware, of course, that the enigma which these essays deviously explore is not what the vast majority of his readers would regard as an enigma. To them he is the least enigmatic of writers, telling a good story with accomplished ease and perfect lucidity. But he has shown plainly that he is also aware that though he has become the most celebrated English story-teller alive he remains a riddle to many serious critics. In its simplest terms it resolves itself into a question why *Of Human Bondage* is different in kind from the rest of his work. Mr Maugham has done what lies in his power to help towards a solution. He has explained that in the midst of his success as a popular playwright he became obsessed by the teeming memories of his past life. He made up his mind that he could only regain peace of mind by distilling these memories into a long novel. 'The book did for me what I wanted, and when it was issued to the world...I found myself for ever free from these pains and unhappy recollections.' This passage of reminiscence explains the extraordinary power of the novel, its candour and human warmth, but not why the artist's mind should never again know experience of like quality. *Of Human Bondage*, for all its implied determinism, is the work of an idealist philosopher dealing with human beings with whose habit of thought he felt at home. After that the realist, the sceptic, the unrelenting, pragmatist takes charge. Again Mr Maugham is helpful. In another passage of reminiscence he remarks that success often separates an author from the circles that gave him his best subjects. Is it that in this one book Mr Maugham rid himself 'for ever' of material vital to his deeper needs as an artist? He has since ranged far and wide in search of subjects, but it is the traveller's lot to enter many societies which he can only view from the outside and can never so penetrate as to become a part of them.

Material gathered in this way lends itself most readily to deft and sophisticated satire in which technical brilliance seeks to conceal the truth that human nature is being presented at a remove. If criticism often appears unjust to such technical brilliance there are good reasons for the inhibition. We cannot but admire art which does with assured accomplishment exactly what it sets out to do. Yet we are conscious all the time that in the greatest art there is always a sense of inadequacy and strain and labour. This we miss often in stories that show Mr Maugham at his most adroit. He has written many stories that pretend by their impeccable workmanship to a perfection which they do not really possess. They amuse, they surprise, they please, but for all their impeccable workmanship they leave us incompletely satisfied. He is instinctively aware of the shortcoming, and in such a brilliant affair as *Cakes and Ale* is careful to try for an effect of studied informality and deliberate casualness. But this is not the same thing as the carelessness in detail of writers who are careless because they are struggling to 'rendre l'irrend-able.' Watching Mr Maugham moving about among the elements of his later works we cannot escape the impression that he is wholly at his ease. He knows what he means to do and nearly always he does it; yet somehow we cannot help comparing the result unfavourably with the results achieved by artists whose less perfect work speaks so hauntingly of a perfection which they suggest yet with all their labour cannot quite reach. *Of Human Bondage* was this kind of work of art, and the puzzle that Mr Maugham has set his critics is simply that he should have turned away from this art and shown such admirable devotion and won such triumphs in a lesser art.

It is a literary, not a theatrical, riddle. In the theatre he set out to be a popular playwright and found the traditional forms of comedy suited to all his purposes, whether he was in the mood to purvey mere entertainment or to attempt to give permanency to a comic idea. At least once his attempt was successful. *Our Betters* would seem now to have wasted its polished craftsmanship and merciless wit on a tiny fragment of society, a group of American expatriates, which has ceased to be recognizable. But contemporary criticism will be confounded if *The Circle* should not keep its place as a classic serious comedy. Here, for once, the philosophy is integrated with

the story and the sparkle and wit of the dialogue genuinely enhance
the author's truth—that it is not what we do that matters so much
as what we are. But whatever the final solution of the enigma of Mr
Maugham, his severest critics will freely allow that his writings
have added enormously to the sum of human pleasure.

145. Unsigned leading article, 'Maugham at 80', *New York Times*

25 January 1954

An English author who reaches the age of 80 today, as Somerset
Maugham does, was by obvious calculation a contemporary of
Shaw, Pinero and Jones in the theatre, and of Joseph Conrad, H.G.
Wells, Henry James, Arnold Bennett and John Galsworthy in the
field of the novel. He has survived them all in the flesh, and critical
opinion now ranks him with them in excellence.

'I wanted money and I wanted fame,' he said a long time ago. He
has had both and earned them; in fact, his popularity was what led
to the critical depreciation from which he suffered for so many
years. Best sellers that appeal to the mass reader are seldom good
literature, but there are exceptions. *Of Human Bondage* is certainly
one; *Cakes and Ale* probably; *The Moon and Sixpence* possibly. Some
of the short stories will undoubtedly prove immortal. Of the plays
one can be less sure, but the endurance of *Rain* is proved by the
latest screen distortion in which Rita Hayworth is a Sadie
Thompson in name if not in character.

Our debt to Mr Maugham is all the greater for some of the screen
adaptations of his short stories. He could always tell a good story
with mordant, sharply etched characters, and he could rarely be
accused of subtlety. His gifts suited the screen, which has treated
him no worse than it did Hemingway.

Having, in his own phrase, given up 'creative writing' a few
years ago, he has nevertheless provided much pleasure and profit
with his essays and his introductions to classical works. The creator

has turned critic and judge, and few men of our time are better qualified or more articulate for the purpose. His brain was always clear and logical; it has become less tart and more mellowed.

Now, at 80, the fame he sought is securely his in a better sense than he intended it to be in his ambitious youth. He does not qualify for greatness and would not claim such a superlative for himself, but he has given millions of readers much pleasure for all the years of this century and he will doubtless bring some pleasure to future generations. This is a good deal to say, and it justifies the tributes that Somerset Maugham will be receiving today on his birthday.

146. John Raymond, review of *The Maugham Enigma*★ and *The Vagrant Mood, New Statesman and Nation*

n.s. XLVII, 23 January 1954, 101–2

John Raymond (1923–77) was a literary critic and journalist. He was literary editor of the *New Statesman* for a while; some of his 'Books in General' articles for that paper were published in *The Doyen of Dover* (1960). He also published a study of Simenon, *Simenon in Court* (1960), and wrote reviews regularly for the *Sunday Times*.

Evening, so the Lesbian poet tells us, brings home all things. It even sets the Muses' crown on the brow of great craftsmen. In his eighty-first year Time is still proving a good servant to Mr Somerset Maugham. It has carried him far out on the rollers of fame, leagues beyond the contemporaries whom he once sailed alongside. He has survived the Walpoles and Galsworthys of his middle years and

★ *An Anthology of Criticism*, ed. K.W. Jonas (London, 1954).

such survival, in a writer's lifetime at least, is sufficient to engender reputation. *'J'ai vécu'* is no more idle a boast in literature than in revolutionary politics. There is always an imperceptible moment at which the 'little deadly question' becomes, by common consent, the 'madness of art.' The English appreciate such metamorphoses more than any other people. We like our great writers, our great actresses, our great artists of every kind, to be as old as possible. No one knows this better than Mr Maugham himself, who made delicious mockery of the national weakness long ago in *Cakes and Ale*. The creator of Edward Driffield and the whole *machine à la gloire* revolving round him has become the Grand Old Man of English Letters.

But Mr Maugham's sheer wealth of output—it could almost be called 'productivity'—has done more than time to increase his stature. Ever since the Diamond Jubilee he has been pouring forth a profusion of novels, plays, travel books and short stories. Each work bears the mint stamp of its period. *The Razor's Edge* is as perfectly of 1944 as *Lady Frederick* is 1911, for Mr Maugham's fountain-pen ('I have never found a typewriter through which the subconscious seems to penetrate') is the only unfashionable thing about him. He has written almost every day of his life for the last sixty years, seldom for less than four hours a day. He blocked up the window of his writing-room because he found the view of the Mediterranean too distracting. Behind his desk at the Villa Mauresque, so he told a *New York Times* critic, stands a large radiator: 'When I go up to write in the morning I feel bright and warm, but as I write my hands and feet grow colder and colder. The blood—if I may venture a medical opinion—all goes to my head.' When at seventy-five he retired from the writing profession and announced his amateur status, he declared that in future he would confine himself to essay writing. Since then he has published his first volume of essays [*The Vagrant Mood*]—it includes a brilliant analysis of Burke's prose style—and no doubt is even now writing some more. Such Jamesian devotion, unallied to James's genius or portentousness, is a shade stupefying. As we read the long muster-roll of his books, Mr Maugham becomes elongated in our imaginations, like Proust's Duc de Guermantes, who 'had aged so little although he had so many more years under him than I.' Like Guermantes, Maugham stands erect on the stilts of his years—and the years, in this case, have turned to achievements.

This anthology of Anglo-American homage [*The Maugham Enigma*] will be something of a puzzle to English readers. As a race, we are inclined to take our literary pleasures ungraciously. We respect, even if we do not always take on, the tough assignments—*Finnegans Wake*, *Nightwood*, *The Anathemata*. But for those writers who pack the most readable punches (Trollope, Kipling, Waugh) we too often have high-spirited contempt. Since Mr Maugham, like Maupassant his master, is among the world's supremely readable storytellers, he wins from us only our time and our delight and seldom our vocal appreciation. We read a tale like 'The Outstation' breathlessly, and, having read it, damn the plot—'that object of scorn to quite a few writers of our time'—as factitious. Mr Maugham is too explicit, too obvious about his aims and intentions. And it is by no means certain that he appreciates Henry James ('Oh, I knew the old fellow, you know. It is hard to judge his work because one liked him so much'). Even the fact that Maugham's criticism of *A Passage of India*—'I cannot bring myself to believe that a young woman, such a sensible well-balanced woman, would make that charge of rape after that business of the caves saying "Boom" '—tallies so well with the Leavisite strictures, fails to conciliate the English intellectual. He is all the more surprised, therefore, on opening Mr Jonas's anthology, to hear (for the first time, perhaps) of the Center of Maugham Studies, of Mme Suzanne Guéry's *La Philosophie de Somerset Maugham*, Professor Dottin's lectures at the University of Toulouse, of the doctoral theses at Graz and Würzburg, of Papajewski's surely formidable *Die Welt-, Lebens- und Kunstanschauung William Somerset Maughams*. Such exegesis must be equally astonishing to Mr Pritchett, Mr Waugh and Mr Graham Greene, whose appreciative but sharp comments alternate so oddly in this book with the intelligent bowing and scraping of Mr Jonas's college professors.

One has only to note the deep respect accorded Miss Lehmann and Mr Morgan in Paris to see that a popular writer is not without honour save among his own country's reviewers. 'In my twenties,' Mr Maugham wrote in *The Summing Up*,

the critics said I was brutal, in my thirties they said I was flippant, in my forties they said I was cynical, and in my fifties they said I was competent, and then in my sixties they said I was superficial. I have gone my own way, with a shrug of my shoulders, following the path I have traced, trying with my work to fill out the pattern of life that I have made for myself.

In fact, Maugham has always been his own best critic. No one has diagnosed his shortcomings better than the writer himself. In his autobiography he admits that his native gifts were not remarkable, but he goes on:

> I have a certain force of character which has enabled me in a measure to supplement my own deficiencies. I have common sense. Most people cannot see anything, but I can see what is in front of my nose with extreme clearness; the greatest writers can see through a brick-wall. My vision is not so penetrating...

Maugham's estimate of his niche in 'Eng. Lit.' is equally dispassionate. *Of Human Bondage* is, he thinks, perhaps his best book, yet 'posterity is little inclined to occupy itself with works of great length,' and it will probably be forgotten within a generation. One or two of his plays may 'retain for some time a kind of pale life,' for they are written in the central tradition of English comedy. A few of the best short stories will continue to figure in the anthologies, 'if only because some of them deal with circumstances and places to which the passage of time and the growth of civilisation will give a romantic glamour.' Say two or three plays and a dozen short stories. 'This,' he concludes, 'is slender baggage with which to set out on a journey to the future.'

This is a modest but probably a fair estimate of Maugham's eventual place in literary history. To the critics of tomorrow he will never be an interesting writer. He is already so much *there* in his work, explicit, lucid, unmysterious. He leaves the literary journalists little or nothing to say, and in the past many of them have eked out the obvious perceptions with tributes to his diamond-hard prose. This vulgar error has been exploded by Mr Connolly. 'Mr Maugham,' he wrote, reviewing *The Razor's Edge*, 'has never been a master of words; he has always preferred the *mot moyen* to the *mot juste*.' (And not always even the *mot moyen*. One remembers the 'exquisitely gowned' lady in the same book; 'her delicate features, the aristocratic shortness of her upper lip and her wealth of fair hair suggested the marquise again, and it must have been obvious, even if it were not notorious, that in her bones flowed the best blood in Chicago.' We remember the wearisome repetition of the word 'malaise' in *Christmas Holiday*, of 'notion' in all his books.)

Despite his great gifts, Maugham seems at first sight to lack one quality that is vitally important if he is to survive in the mind of the

next generation. His work displays no wound. Thanks to Mr
Edmund Wilson's penetration, it is now recognised that in the
make-up of a creative writer a good sized wound is essential. The
contemporary common reader has eagerly caught on to the idea
that 'genius and disease, like strength and mutilation, may be
inextricably bound up together.' Dickens had his father-, Zola his
mother-complex, Proust had his asthma (caused, the psychologists
tell us, by his hunger for affection), Kafka had his T.B. Mr
Maugham has long enjoyed fame, riches, excellent health and a
swimming-pool on the Riviera. Unlike most writers, he is a master
of life. He drives a farm-truck, has served his country as a secret
agent, speaks perfect French, 'mixes a potent Martini' (Asst. Prof
Karl G. Pfeiffer) and, as a medical student, delivered 62 babies in
the slums of South London. The contrast speaks for itself.

In fact, as Mr Jonas's book shows, Maugham did receive his
wound early in life. The shy small boy with the stammer was left
an orphan at ten. He was bullied and miserable at his public school,
ill and lonely as a young man. The later Maugham turned into
Ashenden, the worldly cynical sentimentalist. But before
Maugham became Ashenden he was Philip Carey. The hero in *Of
Human Bondage* is a raw, unhappy youth, Somerset Maugham
before self-protective success touched him; in place of a stammer he
had a club-foot. In one of those delightful digressions that occur in
Cakes and Ale, the author remarks that the great advantage of being a
writer is that you can rid yourself of painful experience by
projecting it on paper. Desmond MacCarthy, Maugham's next-
best critic, comments that the aside 'suggests a core of sensibility'
beneath Maugham's 'wary and aloof attitude as an observer.'
Maugham put the whole of his wound into *Of Human Bondage*.
'The book,' he has said,

did for me what I wanted, and when it was issued to the world... I found
myself free for ever from those pains and unhappy recollections. I put into
it everything I then knew and, having at last finished it, prepared to make a
new start.

The therapy succeeded all too well. Ashenden took over control
of Mr Maugham's imagination, and though in novels like *The
Razor's Edge*, in plays like *Sheppey* and *For Services Rendered*, he has
occasionally suffered a setback, he has remained virtually in control
ever since. The easy, super-efficient style, the smooth, dexterous

craftsmanship, the mellow bachelor philosophy—Mr Maugham can thank Ashenden for all these. Yet it is Ashenden who pulls him up short of the brick wall, Ashenden who keeps him apart from the men and women of whom he writes. One of Maugham's greatest drawbacks as a writer is that, except in rare instances (Driffield, Elliott Templeton), he remains outside his own characters. Writers only begin to see through the brick wall when, like the dying Balzac, they can exclaim 'Only Bianchon can save me now!'

This refusal to be involved, this decision to write *off* life rather than from it, is the price Ashenden has forced Maugham to pay for his efficiency. It is part of the devil's bargain, the *gran rifiuto* made after the author has exorcised his unhappiness in *Of Human Bondage*. Ashenden has brought Mr Maugham fame and success. He has given him material affluence beyond most artists's dreams and ourselves a vast amount of pleasure. Yet he remains an evil genie. Writers will continue to find a powerful literary parable lurking in this tale of the Slave of the Lamp who turned into Mephistopheles.

147. J.D. Scott, 'The Maugham Effect', *Spectator*

CXCII, 29 January 1954, 129

John Dick Scott (b. 1917) is a novelist and critic. He did administrative work for the Government as a civil servant during World War II, then became literary editor of the *Spectator* 1953–56. His novels include *The Way to Glory* (1952); his wartime career is reflected in *The Administration of War Production* (1956).

The following is a review of *The Selected Novels* (3 vols, London, 1953).

'I have no illusions,' Mr Somerset Maugham has written, 'about my literary position. There are but two important writers in my own country who have troubled to take me seriously, and when clever young men write essays about contemporary fiction they never think of considering me.' Mr Maugham's eightieth birthday, however, has ensured that, for this month at least, clever young men writing essays about contemporary fiction have written about no one else. The occasion, and the selection of Mr Maugham's novels, re-issued by his publishers to mark it, makes a return to these works irresistible. And when you return to them—and to Mr Maugham's snide remarks about them, and to Mr Maugham's fabulous success, and to the memories of a thousand issues of *Nash's Magazine*—the old questions begin, so gently, like sneezing powder, to insert themselves once again. One had thought, perhaps, of a birthday party, of the making of a few suitable remarks, of a murmur of 'many happy returns'; but contact with that monumental worldly wisdom, that elegant yet searching irony, that felicitous power, recalls one to seriousness and to a sense of the *métier*. And the questions pose themselves again.

How good *is* he? Is he an artist, or a clever fictioneer whose successes are, according to Mr Robert Liddell, 'no more than technical triumphs'? Does he write well or is he, as Mr Edmund Wilson has suggested, 'not really a writer at all'? One thing is clear. If Mr Maugham really writes English badly, he must be astonishingly lacking in talent, for he has certainly not been lacking in application. In *The Summing Up* he describes how, as a young man, he went to the British Museum, and there 'noted down the names of curious jewels, the Byzantine hues of old enamels, the sensual feel of textiles, and made elaborate sentences to bring them in.' It is a curious picture, the young Willie Ashenden at the feet of Pater and Wilde, curious because he so quickly and so completely removed himself. But he continued his studies; the Augustans claimed his attention. 'The prose of Dryden,' he writes, 'is delicious. It has not the perfection of Swift nor the easy elegance of Addison, but it has a springtime gaiety, a conversational ease, a blithe spontaneousness that are enchanting. Dryden was a very good poet, but it is not the general opinion that he had a lyrical quality; it is strange that it is just this that sings in his softly sparkling prose.' These are not the opinions, nor in my view is this the style, of a man indifferent to English prose.

Nevertheless, of the qualities he admires in Dryden's prose only one, conversational ease, could be said to be characteristic of his own. The qualities which he himself aims at, Mr Maugham has told us, are 'lucidity, simplicity and euphony,' and lucidity and simplicity above all are in fact the virtues of his prose. They are to be found in his first book, *Liza of Lambeth*. The first paragraph of this, a description of heat wave weather in the slums, has almost exactly the same note of simple directness as *Of Human Bondage*. There is, however, one difference; the opening paragraph of the early book consists of a single sentence which requires two semi-colons and four commas to punctuate it. It could be made simpler, although it could not be made more lucid, by splitting into separate sentences; and I believe the later Mr Maugham would have done this. For Mr Maugham's lucidity and simplicity are based upon the short sentence. He makes a great use of the simple sentence strictly so-called, the sentence without subordinate clauses, and even his compound sentences could without violence be broken up into simple sentences, often by the mere substitution of a period for a colon. These simple sentences are the vehicle for the quality which peculiarly distinguishes the best of Mr Maugham's writing.

This quality is one of force, of swiftness, of the dramatic leap. We might call it the Maugham Effect. It is to be seen at its most ruthless in the opening of *The Painted Veil*, where Kitty and her lover are discovered by her husband, Walter. This is one of the most extraordinarily sudden and tense openings to a novel ever written; to read it is like realising that there are burglars in the house. The whole book has a kind of quiet, tense speed like ski-ing. It is made up of short sentences, short paragraphs, short chapters—eighty of them. In its concision it seems to me the most Maugham-like of Mr Maugham's books, and in my opinion it is the best of his books.

Yet its limitations are very sharp. The short sentence, which is Mr Maugham's instrument, is an instrument for stating things. For this purpose it is admirable. But it is not an instrument of suggestion, of implication. It does not echo; it has no reverberations. It can define; it cannot readily explore. So Kitty and Charlie Townsend and Walter are sharply delineated but not deeply comprehended. Nor, in his ripple of short sentences, does Mr Maugham often permit himself the arresting image—presumably because it *is* arresting, and would hold up that flow of narrative which Mr Maugham values above all else. In *The Painted Veil* there are very few images, and most of them are so familiar that they do not engage the mind at all:

> She was as white as the sheet....
> Her night was tortured with strange dreams.
> He gazed at her reflectively, that malicious ironical look in his bright eyes, but mingled with it, a shadow, like a tree standing at a river's edge and its reflection in the water, was an expression of singular kindliness.

Re-examined in their context these images are less common-place than they appear. In the first, the sheet is not any sheet; it is the particular adulterous sheet from which Kitty has just risen. It directs the eye again, like a panning film-shot, upon the bed, with all its significance. Nor, in the second quotation, is 'tortured' a random image. Her husband, in showing up the worthlessness of her lover and then taking her into the epidemic, is in truth deliberately torturing Kitty, and the word 'torture' comes out, not as a dead image, but bringing a glimpse of the rack, the boot, and the pincers. But it is the third image which is the most complex and meaningful. It refers to Waddington, the sympathetic Deputy Commissioner at Mei-tan-fu, but may in fact be taken as a description of the author's own attitude to Kitty; and it communicates his compassion. At the same time the image of the wavering evanescent reflection in the water throws the mind back to, and enriches, the title of the book: 'The painted veil that those who live call Life.'

The Painted Veil is certainly a technical triumph. Is it 'no more than a technical triumph'? It seems to me that it is a good deal more, and especially the later part of it, the story of Kitty's belated growing-up; of her husband's death, her growing understanding, her sharpening perceptions, her lost illusions, her final reconciliation with the father she had exploited and neglected. This, with its sadness, its moral tension, its irony and compassion, its biting evocations of lust and terror and remorse, is a work of art.

In creating Edward Driffield, that dubious and engaging writer who lived on into a deified old age, Mr Maugham has, characteristically and ironically, got in ahead of the clever young men who, on his eightieth birthday, are writing about his work. In Driffield, Mr Maugham relished the unregenerate humanity which lived inside the whited sepulchre which other people had built. What we on this occasion relish—and salute—is something different: it is the artist who lives on in the skyscraper of success, which he himself has built.

148. Christopher Isherwood on the Eastern stories

1957

Christopher William Bradshaw-Isherwood (1904–86) was an English novelist, autobiographer and (in collaboration with W.H. Auden) dramatist; he settled in America in 1939, receiving American citizenship in 1946. In 1938 Maugham made the claim that Isherwood 'holds the future of the English novel in his hands'. He was not, as is sometimes supposed, the original of Larry Darrell in *The Razor's Edge*, although he was for many years a student of Indian philosophy as promulgated by the Vedanta Society in Hollywood.

The following is the Introduction to 'The Book-Bag' included in *Great English Short Stories* selected by Isherwood (New York: Dell Publishing Co., 1957, 294–6).

There must be many thousands of readers who have wished themselves, as I often have, at Maugham's side on board some small slow freighter, as it steams up a tropical river or into the harbor of a Pacific island. On the jetty, the Maugham characters are waiting: the cynical District Commissioner with the secret sorrow, the prim adulterous Married Lady, the handsome curly-haired callow Secretary, the drunken Doctor. They invite you to stay with them, they offer you honorary membership of their club, they are delighted to welcome you—for, now that you have arrived, their drama can begin.

There is a passage in Flaubert's novel *Sentimental Education:* 'He traveled. He knew the melancholy of the steamboat; the cold awakening in the tent; the tedium of scenery and ruins; the bitterness of interrupted friendship.' These words might well have been written about Maugham; for, oddly enough, his great charm as a travelling-companion is his boredom—or perhaps I should say his *air* of boredom, since, if he were really so bored, he would hardly make the effort of telling us his stories. Exotic place-names drop from his lips with the weariness of utter familiarity. About one character he says, 'he was glad to settle down quietly in Apia for twelve months at least'; and you would think, from Maugham's tone, that he was speaking of some particularly dreary London suburb. Like Kipling, Maugham is an 'old hand.' He knows the ropes. He can tell you what to expect from any given situation. His information is pessimistic enough and yet, unlike Kipling's, it is strangely reassuring.

I have chosen 'The Book-Bag' for several reasons other than the fact that it is less well known than it deserves to be. I like its leisurely, autobiographical opening which introduces us to Maugham himself and thereby greatly strengthens the credibility of the whole story. I admire it for its extraordinary narrative tact. I don't mean that I think reticence is *necessarily* a virtue; but you cannot help admiring such a classic demonstration of how to handle a 'shocking' subject—incest—in an absolutely inoffensive manner, yet without sacrificing any of the shock. Notice how the nature of the situation is conveyed entirely by the violence of the reaction to it, not by any description of the situation itself. In other words—*because* Olive cares sufficiently to commit suicide when her brother Tim gets married, we know that she and her brother must have been lovers. Maugham does not need to elaborate; there is no other possible explanation.

I find the end of the story deeply moving in its quietness. It beautifully illustrates a quality in Maugham's writing which I have already mentioned—the quality of giving reassurance. When we are introduced to Mark Featherstone and Tim, the woman they have both loved has been dead for many years. Tim's wife has long since left him and gone back to England. (Ironically enough, she—the injured party—is the only unsympathetic character in this story.) The two men meet occasionally at the club and play cards, never speaking of the past. And that is how Life is, Maugham seems to say—one survives somehow, and it is, after all, not quite as bad as one might have expected. To borrow one of those double negatives of which the Master is so fond—I am not disinclined to agree with him.

149. Walter Allen, 'Summing up Somerset Maugham at 90', *New York Times*

19 January 1964, 1, 24

Walter Ernest Allen (b. 1911) is a novelist, critic and literary journalist, many of whose reviews appeared in the *New Statesman*, of which he was literary editor 1960–61. His novels include *Rogue Elephant* (1946) and *All in a Lifetime* (1959); he is also author of such critical books as *The English Novel* (1954) and *The Novel Today* (1955). His memoirs *As I Was Walking Down Grub Street* appeared in 1981.

Somerset Maugham is 90 this week. His career as a writer, which began 67 years ago with *Liza of Lambeth*, has been longer than that of any other British author. To anyone reading *Liza of Lambeth* when it first came out it must have seemed certain that the book heralded the appearance of a new Naturalistic novelist. Maugham never followed up this novel of slum life in London, the fruit of his observation as a medical student. He presented himself, instead, as the author of smart comedies for the West End stage. He wrote nothing of the order of his first novel until *Of Human Bondage* appeared in 1915. And nothing comparable to that novel followed. He continued his course as a fashionable playwright and became, too, an indefatigable traveler whose stories chronicled the lives and amours of generally faintly seedy Empire-builders in the British colonies of the Far East.

Books have been written about his work, but his place in literary history is still uncertain. During the thirties he was largely dismissed as 'commercial.' Indeed, the very enormity of his success, and its extent, have seemed to rule him out of the consideration of highbrow critics. His reputation has always been higher abroad than in his own country; and he, in turn, when writing about his own work, has tended to be on the defensive—has, in a way, even if ironically, tended to write himself down. He has been content to put himself forward as an entertainer and made no larger claims.

He writes in *The Summing Up* (1938): 'I am almost inclined to say that I could not spend an hour in anyone's company without getting the material to write at least a readable story about him.' A happy position for any author; but here is the paragraph that follows:

But though I have had variety of invention, and this is not strange since it is the outcome of the variety of mankind, I have had small power of imagination. I have taken living people and put them into the situations, tragic or comic, that their characters suggested. I might well say that they invented their own stories. I have been incapable of those great, sustained flights that carry the author on broad pinions into a celestial sphere. My fancy, never very strong, has been hampered by my sense of probability. I have painted easel pictures, not frescoes.

On the face of it, the passage may seem to demonstrate the modesty that comes from self-knowledge; and the utter inadequacy of his account of the nature of imagination, one might feel, proves his own lack of knowledge of it. Yet, when one looks at the whole range of his work, it is impossible not to dissent from what the paragraph implies about its author. Variety of invention is not so small a thing or one so easily come by as is suggested here. In self-defense, it seems, Maugham does himself down. Over the years, he has obstinately asserted that the story is the thing and that he is satisfied to be taken as an entertainer. All this has been part of his private war on critics who have given him, at best, only grudging recognition.

That he is a brillant entertainer there can be no question. His stories still stand up as stories, no matter into what medium they are translated. They are frequently slight and some times trivial, but they are never botched: the signature of the craftsman is on them all. There are times when one thinks that British television and radio would have to shut up shop if there were not an apparently inexhaustible supply of stories by Maugham to turn into 30-minute plays. One recalls, too, the long list of movies that have been made from his novels—*Of Human Bondage, The Moon and Sixpence, The Painted Veil, The Razor's Edge* and the rest.

Yet, at his best, he is much more than a 'mere' teller of stories, a 'mere' entertainer. The truth is, as the date of *Liza of Lambeth*—1897—indicates, Maugham is the last survivor of a vanished age, an age which had not divorced, as ours has largely done, the idea of entertainment from the idea of art. It was an age in which Henry James could turn aside from the novel to attempt comedies for the West End theater without thinking, or anyone else thinking, that he was demeaning himself, an age when the fiction of serious writers—George Eliot, Hardy, Wells and James himself—could appear in magazines of general interest catering to ordinary, educated, middle-class readers who did not have to wonder whether they were high-, low-, or middle-brow because the words, and the cultural situation they stand for, did not exist.

To remember this is to realize that objections to Maugham's works as 'commercial' are irrelevant. The real problem is why, in England at any rate, he has never quite received the recognition as a serious writer that is surely his due.

Part of the answer lies, I believe, in the English attitude toward Naturalism. Naturalism, the pure thing, never caught on in England; and Maugham began as a Naturalist and has remained one in some essential respects. Consider *Of Human Bondage*, a flawed novel certainly—the last chapters strike one as fantasy—but still a very considerable achievement by any standard, and accepted as a classic work everywhere except in England. It is a novel of a kind very common in English, the record of a young man's discovery of himself and his sentimental education. Arnold Bennett's *Clayhanger* and D. H. Lawrence's *Sons and Lovers* belong to the same category, and to place *Clayhanger* and *Of Human Bondage* side by side is illuminating.

Bennett, too, set out to be a Naturalist and apprenticed himself to Maupassant; and his interpretation of life had its roots in the same 19th-century science as Maugham's. But Bennett's incurable Englishness defeated the Naturalist in him, and *Clayhanger* is warmer, much warmer, than *Of Human Bondage*. Affection and human sympathy have crept in; whereas *Of Human Bondage* is cold, detached, clinical and, as a study of human isolation, the more impressive because of that.

Maugham's attitude toward life and toward his fellows has not changed over the years. It is that of an aloof, sardonic clinician who expects little from existence, is surprised at nothing, is skeptical of aspirations and amused by the spectacle of the follies of mankind. Often the attitude has degenerated into a formula, and then one is aware of an irritating note of superiority in Maugham, a note of condescension to frailer mortals. In many of the short stories he appears as altogether too knowing, too unsurprised, too worldly. And one becomes aware, too, of something else: what might be called an unduly limited sense of curiosity.

Maugham then appears as the collector, the connoisseur, of specimens of human folly and oddity. He mounts and displays the specimens with formidable skill, but as specimens they differ greatly in intrinsic interest and somehow do not throw much light on the species to which they belong. There is in Maugham, one sometimes thinks, a lack of interest in the motives of behavior.

Yet it is from this prevailing attitude that his greatest triumphs also spring: *Of Human Bondage* apart, these are, in my view, *Liza of Lambeth, Cakes and Ale* (1930), and what might be called the worldly half, the Elliott Templeton half, of *The Razor's Edge* (1943).

The more outrageous the specimen confronting him, the greater Maugham's success. Then one finds him responding to the incalculability, the absurdity, of human behavior with a fascinated admiration—admiration in both the original and the current sense of the world—that is in no way lessened by the sardonic irony with which it is expressed. His response to absurdity, to the particularly gorgeous specimen, such as Alroy Kear in *Cakes and Ale* has the effect not of diminishing but of enhancing the specimen. The response, indeed, is the response of the imagination Maugham denies he has.

Along with these three and a half novels and a handful of short stories, I would put, as the peaks of Maugham triumphs, three of his plays—*The Circle* (1921), *The Constant Wife* (1927) and *The Breadwinner* (1930). These plays are of a kind madly unfashionable today, instances of conspicuously well-made artificial comedy in the line of descent from the Restoration through Oscar Wilde. To say this is not to imply that they are in any way derivative. The wit is their own, and so is the point of view from which character and action are seen.

With Maugham, one comes back always to the point of view. It is not the most agreeable in the world, and its limitations are obvious; what it catches in its sights it often trivializes. Yet every now and then, in three or four novels, some short stories and three plays, it has provided a vision that is compelling and lingering. And in the end, one is forced to conclude that the man who could face up to and create the bleakly pessimistic world of *Of Human Bondage*, and also create the comic version of English literary life that is *Cakes and Ale*, is not a small writer—nor, for that matter, a so very limited one.

150. Cyril Connolly, 'Maugham: Compassionate Cynic', *Sunday Times*

19 December 1965

William Somerset Maugham was the last of that group of professional men of letters with more than fifty books to their credit, whose mark or totem is as familiar to us as their signature, whose name is a household word in every country.

In the last few years he had become a kind of up-to-date version of the grand old man of literature through his conquest of the cinema and television with his stories and of the audience through his personality, which appears on the screen in all its Edwardian warmth and courtesy. He did not easily come by this fame.

His career falls into four overlapping sections: the sentimental-realist, the man of the world (and the theatre), the oriental traveller, and the Western sage.

The sentimental-realist was brought up in Whitstable, after childhood in Paris, and like Marlowe before him, and Hugh Walpole after, went to King's School, Canterbury. He then became a medical student and studied at Heidelberg and St Thomas's Hospital: he always wanted to write, but was conscious of possessing very little talent, and he vacillated between imitations of French realism, like *Liza of Lambeth*, 1897, and the Flaubertian *Mrs Craddock*, 1902 (novels which appeared in the heyday of Gissing, James and Hardy, even as his last were contemporary with John Osborne and Angus Wilson), and travel books of Paterian preciousness like *The Land of the Blessed Virgin*, 1905.

He began at the same time to write for the theatre, and set out to scale those twin peaks, with such a drop in between, that loom so close together for a poor and unknown young man of small stature with an embarrassing stammer: literary fame and social success. In his career one may watch the formation of two personalities—one outward and social, at first aggressive and cynical, afterwards wary, attentive and charming, and the other introverted and speculative, at first diffident and over-sensitive, slowly becoming more confident and ultimately serene and Faustian.

The medical student who turned serious novelist became in the late Edwardian age the serious novelist who turned fashionable playwright, but the two selves remained quite separate: the man of the world (whom we see in the famous portrait by Sir Gerald Kelly) raked in the takings from his brilliant comedies, from *Lady Frederick* in 1907 to *The Circle* and *Our Betters* in 1921 and 1923, while the artist groaned at the shallowness of his reputation and went on with *Of Human Bondage*, which appeared in 1915 as the final expression of the autobiographical novel of sentimental realism.

After the war the man of the world continued to turn out the plays which were purchasing his freedom, but in *The Moon and Sixpence*, 1919, he undertook a different kind of novel (about Gauguin) and one which revealed a deep dissatisfaction. A fortunate voyage coincided with the flowering of his talent. He discovered the East and came under the astringent anti-romantic influence of Maupassant.

From this moment he set about, unconsciously perhaps, creating his own world, using Maupassant's naturalistic methods of brevity, clarity and intuition, to describe the dramas of ordinary people in tragic situations; making use of the exotic background of the Far East to set off his humdrum expatriates and his own rather colourless style. Six novels and books of short stories, including 'Rain,' explored these oriental themes, and one delightful travel book, *The Gentleman in the Parlour*; while the man of the world continued to evolve through *Ashenden, Cakes and Ale* and *First Person Singular*.

In *The Summing Up*, 1938, Maugham set down his conclusions on life, literature, the theatre and philosophy in the first of his many farewells. He had settled on Cap Ferrat and now seemed to have all the advantages that fame could bring. The second world war took him from his yacht to propaganda work in France and finally to America, where he produced his novel of the religious quest, *The Razor's Edge*, which sold several million copies. His life since the war became a leisurely process of winding up—renewed visits to Spain, publication of his notebooks, endowment of travelling scholarships for young writers, and further examination of oriental religion and philosophy, broken into by excursions into the limelight: making films, sitting for busts and portraits, being lionised in America, as if the man of the world had said to the aged magician deep in study, 'I want my kind of old age as well.'

It is difficult to foresee what posterity will think of his work. His commentaries were sometimes petty, and much will fall away through the mediocrity of his diction, which would out in spite of the immense care he took to be clear and readable. But, if all else perish, there will remain a story-teller's world from Singapore to the Marquesas that is exclusively and for ever Maugham, a world of verandah and prahu which we enter, as we do that of Conan Doyle's Baker Street, with a sense of happy and eternal homecoming.

For the last thirty years of his life Maugham moved between hotel sitting-rooms in London, New York, or wherever he happened to set up his bridge table, and his villa on Cap Ferrat, into which he gradually withdrew. He had the most beautiful manners and a capacity for sympathy which was felt in his voice, redolent of the Pax Britannica; yet his gaze, though warm, was extremely penetrating and could give people a look, especially if they were being unkind or pretentious, like that of a gila monster. Like many people with unhappy childhoods and small physical disabilities, he built up a great wall of wealth and luxury and courteous shyness against the world, but if you were admitted behind all this you would have found not a bored millionaire or even a bland old humanist counting his Impressionists, but the endlessly inquiring mind of the speculative philosopher. 'He had so little love when he was small that later it embarrassed him to be loved.'

Wherever he was, he would gather some younger writers round him, listen to their opinions and give them oysters and advice and especially warning. But to have seen him surrounded by all that had gone into the shaping of his personality for half a century one must have visited Cap Ferrat in the good years when, after the morning's work (for he rose at eight), he would climb up to his freshwater pool, where the blue dragonfly endlessly patrolled the surface like a flying boat. Here he would swim or dive or sit explaining Spinoza to his guests, his sarong round his small body, on his face the fastidious expression, as in Graham Sutherland's portrait, of one who understands humanity and both pities and forgives, finding much to enjoy and very little to hope for.

Being deprived at an early age of his beloved mother, and thrown on unfeeling relations, marked him for life. As a doctor and the brother of a great lawyer he saw deep into the human heart and his cynicism masked both a compassion of which he was almost ashamed and a bitter rage against the terrible tragedies, disablements and stupidities thrust, by its own limitations, upon the human condition. His excessively rare gift of story-telling, now so unfashionable, is almost the equal of imagination itself; his lapses are into the florid rather than the banal.

At the end of his life he most unexpectedly released his autobiography to the popular Press and accused his wife of having married him for worldly motives when with child by a former lover. Pent-up rage over this deception (never authenticated) of many years ago broke out in the Lear-like denunciations of what still remains a most remarkable document, which must be taken into account as showing the fire smouldering under that urbane exterior. But urbanity triumphed, and I think that one of the best things about him was the way that, for over fifty years, he graced the social scene. He gave the Riviera point, so that it became more than just a rest-camp for rich Philistines; he made it seem an occasion to run across him in Salzburg or Bad Gastein or Soho or Edgartown. One always left his company refreshed and feeling that the literary life was worthwhile.

He was too much impressed by money, and by being able to associate with millionaires as a millionaire, but it never interfered with his habit of writing, his interest in philosophy, his affectionate sympathy for the young, young writers especially. He lived long enough to see his reputation dwindle in home circles while reaching astronomic proportions in Russia and Japan; he lived so long that he did not want to go on living or to look for signs of the revival of interest in him which will infallibly come. His death is our loss rather than his. A magician has vanished.

Select Bibliography

A. BIBLIOGRAPHIES

BASON, FREDERICK T., *A Bibliography of the Writings of William Somerset Maugham*, London, 1931.

HENRY, WILLIAM H., JR. *A French Bibliography of W. Somerset Maugham* Charlottesville, Virginia, 1967.

SANDERS, CHARLES, *W. Somerset Maugham: An Annotated Bibliography of Writings About Him*, De Kalb, Illinois, 1970.

STOTT, RAYMOND TOOLE, *A Bibliography of the Works of W. Somerset Maugham*, revised and extended edition, London, 1973.

B. BIOGRAPHIES

BROWN, IVOR, *International Profiles: W. Somerset Maugham*, London, 1970.

CURTIS, ANTHONY, *Somerset Maugham*, London, n.d.

KANIN, GARSON, *Remembering Mr Maugham*, New York, 1966.

MAUGHAM, ROBIN, *Somerset and All the Maughams*, London, 1966.

MAUGHAM, ROBIN, *Conversations with Willie*, London, 1978.

MENARD, WILMON, *The Two Worlds of Somerset Maugham*, Los Angeles, 1965.

MORGAN, TED, *Somerset Maugham*, London, 1980.

NICHOLS, BEVERLEY, *A Case of Human Bondage*, London, 1966.

PFEIFFER, KARL G., *Somerset Maugham: A Candid Portrait*, London, 1959.

RAPHAEL, FREDERIC, *Somerset Maugham and His World*, London, 1976.

C. CRITICISM

ALDINGTON, RICHARD, *W. Somerset Maugham: An Appreciation*, New York, 1939.

SELECT BIBLIOGRAPHY

BRANDER, LAWRENCE, *Somerset Maugham: A Guide*. Edinburgh and London, 1963.

BROPHY, JOHN, *Writers and their Work: Somerset Maugham*, revised edition, London 1958.

CALDER, ROBERT LORIN, *W. Somerset Maugham and the Quest for Freedom*, London, 1972.

CORDELL, RICHARD, *Somerset Maugham: A Biographical and Critical Study*, London, 1961.

CURTIS, ANTHONY, *The Pattern of Maugham*, London, 1974.

CURTIS, ANTHONY, *Writers and their Work: Somerset Maugham*, London, 1982.

DOBRINSKY, J. (ed.), *Studies in Somerset Maugham* (by various hands), in *Cahiers Victoriens et Edouardiens*, No. 22, Montpellier, 1985.

DOUBLEDAY ,ELLEN, and others, *W. Somerset Maugham: An Appreciation*, New York, 1965. (Not seen.)

JONAS, KLAUS W. (ed.), *The Maugham Enigma*, London, 1954.

JONAS, KLAUS W. (ed.), *The World of Somerset Maugham*, London, 1959.

MACCARTHY, DESMOND, *William Somerset Maugham: 'The English Maupassant'*, London, 1934.

MANDER, RAYMOND, and MITCHENSON, JOE, *Theatrical Companion to Maugham*, London, 1955.

NAIK, M.K., *W. Somerset Maugham*, Norman, Oklahoma, 1966.

TOWNE, CHARLES HANSON, and others, *W. Somerset Maugham: Novelist, Essayist, Dramatist*, New York [1925].

WARD, RICHARD HERON, *William Somerset Maugham*, London, 1937.

Index

The index is divided into three parts: I Works by Maugham; II Themes and characteristics; III General index

457

II THEMES AND CHARACTERISTICS

adroitness, 254, 278, 433
adultery, 5, 241, 246, 247–8, 251, 252, 290, 337, 415, 423, 443
agnosticism, 317, 336, 388
anecdote in Maugham's short stories, 287, 371, 423
art for art's sake, 339
art which conceals art, 160
Ashenden, Maugham as, 439–40, 441
autobiographic strain in Maugham's fiction, 189–91

beauty, 388, 406
belles lettres, 412
British Empire, 86, 184, 337, 446, 452

censorship, 217–18, 384–5
Champs Elysées décor, 357
characters: drawn from life, 6, 14, 147, 185, 187–8, 190, 265–7, 320, 354; as exposures, 262; inhuman, 248
cheapness, Maugham's, 153, 345, 423
China, 12, 155–9, 238–44, 290
class, 340, 414
clergymen in Maugham's work, 43, 108–10, 112, 227
clichés, 284, 287, 316, 361, 366, 368, 424, 438, 443
clinician, Maugham as, 449
commerciality, 447, 448
common sense, 395, 398, 438
compassion, 443, 450, 453; lack of, 423

competence, 14, 157, 188, 192, 194, 255, 284, 301, 305, 336, 341, 437
condescension, note of, 449
contempt for human nature, 274, 318
contrived illusion, 281
Cool Hand, Maugham as, 343
craftsmanship, 315, 322, 324, 342, 348, 403, 413, 422, 433, 440, 447
criticism of life, 170
cynicism, 14, 94, 97–100, 106, 110, 153, 154, 169, 182, 187, 190, 194, 214, 231, 233–4, 237, 243, 264, 281, 285, 291, 293, 302, 306, 336–7, 344, 348, 353, 367, 375, 376, 386, 387, 396, 405, 423, 437, 439, 450, 451, 453

detachment, 206, 215, 296, 339, 342, 357, 372, 387, 389, 422, 439, 449
domestic drama, 429
domestic servants, 97–8, 409–10

enigma, Maugham as, 17, 293, 324, 398, 432, 433
entertainer, Maugham as, 8, 9, 94–6, 303, 353, 368, 370, 378, 382, 412, 433, 447–8

faking of stories, 177
Far East, 12, 18, 139, 168–9, 171–2, 180–4, 191, 200, 203–6, 252, 284–5, 290, 423, 444–6, 451–2

INDEX

III GENERAL INDEX

(A figure in *italics* indicates the first page of an article reprinted in this collection)

THE CRITICAL HERITAGE SERIES

GENERAL EDITOR: B. C. SOUTHAM

Volumes published and forthcoming